Loneliness and Longing

We all experience loneliness at some time in our lives and it often motivates people, consciously or otherwise, to enter treatment. Yet it is rarely explicitly addressed in psychoanalytic literature. *Loneliness and Longing* rectifies this oversight by thoroughly exploring this painful psychological state.

In this book contributors address the inner sense of loneliness—that is feeling alone even in the company of others—by drawing on different aspects of loneliness and longing. Topics covered include:

- loneliness in the consulting room
- the relationship between loneliness and love
- the effects of social networking and the internet
- how loneliness changes throughout the life-cycle
- healing the analyst's loneliness.

Loneliness and Longing draws on both theory and practice to discuss ways to help people to understand and cope with this important emotional state, encouraging them to make loneliness and longing less pervasive in their lives. This will be ideal reading for analysts, psychotherapists, and related practitioners facing the challenges of loneliness in their consulting rooms.

Brent Willock is President of the Toronto Institute for Contemporary Psychoanalysis, a Board member of the Toronto Child Psychoanalytic Program, and a faculty member of the Institute for the Advancement of Self Psychology.

Lori C. Bohm is a Supervising Analyst, faculty member, and Director at the Center for Applied Psychoanalysis and Intensive Psychoanalytic Psychotherapy Program at the William Alanson White Institute.

Rebecca Coleman Curtis is a member of the faculty and Supervisor at William Alanson White Institute, Supervisor at the National Institute for the Psychotherapies, and Professor of Psychology at Adelphi University.

Loneliness and Longing

Conscious and Unconscious Aspects

Edited by Brent Willock,
Lori C. Bohm and
Rebecca Coleman Curtis

Routledge
Taylor & Francis Group

LONDON AND NEW YORK

First published 2012
by Routledge
27 Church Road, Hove, East Sussex BN3 2FA

Simultaneously published in the USA and Canada
by Routledge
711 Third Avenue, New York NY 10017

Routledge is an imprint of the Taylor & Francis Group, an Informa business

British Library Cataloguing in Publication Data
A catalogue record for this book is available from the British Library

Library of Congress Cataloging in Publication Data
Loneliness and longing : conscious and unconscious aspects / edited by Brent
Willock, Lori C. Bohm, and Rebecca C. Curtis.
    p. cm.
    Includes bibliographical references and index.
    ISBN 978-0-415-61097-1 (hardback) – ISBN 978-0-415-61098-8 (pbk.) –
ISBN (invalid) 978-0-203-00000-0 (ebk.) 1. Loneliness. 2. Interpersonal
relations. I. Willock, Brent. II. Bohm, Lori C. III. Curtis, Rebecca C.
    BF575.L7L664 2011
    155.9'2–dc22

                                                             2011012299

ISBN: 978-0-415-61097-1 (hbk)
ISBN: 978-0-415-61098-8 (pbk)

Typeset in Times by Garfield Morgan, Swansea, West Glamorgan
Paperback cover design by Chris Prewett
Printed and bound in Great Britain by TJ International, Padstow, Cornwall

Contents

List of contributors

Elizabeth Allured is a faculty member in the Postgraduate Program in Psychoanalysis and Psychotherapy at Adelphi University; the Postgraduate Program in Psychodynamic School Psychology, Adelphi University; and the Suffolk Institute for Psychoanalysis and Psychotherapy. She is a co-chair of the Port Washington Parks Conservancy. Elizabeth works in private practice.

Lori C. Bohm is a Supervising Analyst, faculty member, and Director at the Center for Applied Psychoanalysis and Intensive Psychoanalytic Psychotherapy Program at the William Alanson White Institute.

Sandra Buechler is a Training and Supervising Analyst at the William Alanson White Institute. She is a Supervisor at the New York State Psychiatric Institute, internship and postdoctoral programs, Columbia Presbyterian Medical Center, New York; and the Institute for Contemporary Psychotherapy, New York. Sandra is the author of *Clinical Values: Emotions that Guide Psychoanalytic Treatment* (Analytic Press, 2004); and *Making a Difference in Patients' Lives: Emotional Experience in the Therapeutic Setting* (Routledge, 2008).

Art C. Caspary is a faculty member at the Toronto Institute for Contemporary Psychoanalysis; the Toronto Child Psychoanalytic Program; the Institute for the Advancement of Self Psychology; the departments of Psychology, Psychiatry and Social Work, University of Toronto; and the Hincks-Dellcrest Centre. Art works in private practice.

Philip Classen is a Guest at the Toronto Society for Contemporary Psychoanalysis. Philip works in private practice.

Mary Beth M. Cresci is Director of Postgraduate Programs in Psychoanalysis and Psychotherapy at the Derner institute of Advanced Psychological Studies, Adelphi University, and a faculty member in both the Psychoanalytic Program and the Psychoanalytic Supervision Program. She is a former President of the Division of Psychoanalysis of the American Psychological Association. She has a private practice in Brooklyn Heights, New York.

Rebecca Coleman Curtis is Professor of Psychology and Director of Research at Adelphi University; Supervisor of Psychotherapy (formerly Director of Research) at the W. A. White Institute; Supervisor at the National Institute for the Psychotherapies; faculty member and N.G.O. Committees advisory to the United Nations on Mental Health, and Status of Women. She is the author of *Desire, Self, Mind, and the Psychotherapies: Unifying Psychological Science and Psychoanalysis* (Jason Aronson, 2009).

Barbara Eisold is a faculty member at the Institute of Contemporary Psychoanalysis, New York, and adjunct faculty member at Yeshiva University.

Kenneth Eisold is a faculty member at the William Alanson White Institute and the author of *What You Don't Know You Know* (Other Press, 2010).

Roger Frie is Associate Professor of Education at Simon Fraser University, Vancouver; Affiliate Associate Professor of Psychiatry at the University of British Columbia; and Supervisor and faculty member at the William Alanson White Institute.

Evelyn T. Hartman is Supervising Analyst, Director of Outreach, and faculty member at the William Alanson White Institute; faculty member of the Manhattan Institute of Psychoanalysis and Supervising Analyst at the Institute of Contemporary Psychotherapy. Evelyn works in private practice.

Bruce Herzog is a faculty member at the Toronto Institute for Contemporary Psychoanalysis and the Institute for the Advancement of Self Psychology. He is a council member of the International Association for Psychoanalytic Self Psychology. Bruce works as a psychoanalyst in private practice in Toronto.

Jenny Kaufmann is a faculty member and Supervising Analyst at the William Alanson White Institute.

Joan Lavender is a faculty member and supervisor for the Focusing Oriented Relational Psychotherapy Program, a learning center based on the work of Eugene Gendlin, and for the Institute for contemporary Psychotherapy: Center for the Study of Anorexia and Bulimia. She has a private practice in New York City.

Karen L. Lombardi is Professor of the doctoral program in clinical psychology at the Derner Institute for Advanced Psychological Studies, Adelphi University, Garden City, New York. She is a faculty member of the Postdoctoral Programs for Psychoanalysis and Psychotherapy at Adelphi University; and the Northwest Center for Psychoanalysis, Portland, Oregon. She is the co-author, with Naomi Rucker, of *Subject Relations: Unconscious Experience and Relational Psychoanalysis* (Routledge, 1997). Karen works in private practice in Glen Cove, New York.

John V. O'Leary is a faculty member and supervisor of psychotherapy at the William Alanson White Institute and a Supervisor at the Teacher's College of Columbia University. John works in private practice in Manhattan.

Michael O'Loughlin is Professor at the Derner Institute of Advanced Psychological Studies and the School of Education, Adelphi University. He is a training analyst for the Postgraduate Programs in Psychoanalysis and Psychotherapy at Adelphi University. He is author of *The Subject of Childhood* (Peter Lang Publishing, 2010) and of *Psychodynamic Psychotherapy in Contemporary South Africa: Theory, Practice, and Policy Perspectives* (University of Witwatersrand Press, forthcoming). He works in private practice in New Hyde Park, New York.

Arlene Kramer Richards is a training and supervising analyst at the New York Freudian Society, the Institute for Psychoanalytic Training and Research, and the International Psychoanalytical Association.

Ionas Sapountzis is Associate Professor and Director of the School Psychology program at the Derner Institute, Adelphi University. He is a faculty member and supervisor of the Psychoanalytic Psychotherapy, and Child, Adolescent and Family Psychotherapy programs, at the Derner Institute. Ionas works in private practice in Garden City, New York.

Henry M. Seiden is an adjunct faculty member and clinical supervisor at Pace University and Yeshiva University; and Clinical Instructor in the Mount Sinai Psychiatry Department at Queens Hospital Center, Jamaica, New York. He is Chair of the Publications Committee of Division 39 (Psychoanalysis) of the American Psychological Association. He is the co-author of *Silent Grief: Living in the Wake of Suicide* (Jason Aronson, 1997) and is a published poet. Henry works in private practice in Forest Hills, New York.

Amira Simha-Alpern is an adjunct professor and supervisor at the Derner Institute of Advanced Psychological Studies in Adelphi University and a faculty member at the Suffolk Institute for Psychotherapy and Psychoanalysis. She is a founding director and faculty member of The Potential Space for Continuing Education in Psychology and Psychotherapy. Amira works in private practice in Smithtown, New York.

John A. Sloane is Assistant Professor in the Department of Psychiatry at the University of Toronto. He is a faculty member of the Institute for the Advancement of Self Psychology and the Toronto Institute for Contemporary Psychoanalysis. He also works in private practice.

Lucille Spira is a Board Member and Facilitator of the Psychoanalytic Literary Group of the New York Society for Psychoanalytic Psychotherapy and Psychoanalysis. Lucille works in private practice.

Graeme J. Taylor is Professor of Psychiatry at the University of Toronto and Mount Sinai Hospital and faculty member of the Toronto Institute for Contemporary Psychoanalysis. He is the author of *Psychosomatic Medicine and Contemporary Psychoanalysis* (International Universities Press, 1987) and senior author of *Disorders of Affect Regulation: Alexithymia in Medical and Psychiatric Illness* (Cambridge University Press, 1997). He is the recipient of a Sigourney Award in recognition of distinguished contributions to psychoanalysis.

Matthew J. Tedeschi is a graduate of the Postgraduate Programs in Psychoanalysis and Psychotherapy and Child, Adolescent, and Family Psychotherapy at Adelphi University; staff psychologist at the Western Suffolk Board of Cooperative Educational Services, Long Island, New York; and faculty member and supervisor at the Postgraduate Psychodynamic School Psychology Program, Adelphi University. Matthew works in private practice in Northport, New York.

Susan Weisser is Professor of English at Adelphi University. She is co-editor of *Feminist Nightmares: Women at Odds* (New York University Press, 1994), author of *A Craving Vacancy: Women and Sexual Love in the British Novel* (New York University Press, 1997) and editor of *Women and Romance: A Reader* (New York University Press, 2001).

Brent Willock is President of the Toronto Institute for Contemporary Psychoanalysis; Board member of the Toronto Child Psychoanalytic Program; faculty member of the Institute for the Advancement of Self Psychology; and on the Advisory Board of the International Association for Relational Psychoanalysis and Psychotherapy. He is the author of *Comparative-Integrative Psychoanalysis* (The Analytic Press, 2007).

Acknowledgments

The ideas in this book began to take shape at a symposium held in 2008 on the spectacular campus of the University of British Columbia in Vancouver, Canada. This event was sponsored by the Western Canada Psychoanalytic Psychotherapy Association, the Psychoanalytic Society of the New York University Postdoctoral Program, the William Alanson White Psychoanalytic Society, the Adelphi Society for Psychoanalysis and Psychotherapy, and the Toronto Institute for Contemporary Psycho-analysis. As Chair of the organizing committee for the conference, Dr. Lori Bohm first proposed the topic of Loneliness. Other individuals who helped develop the theme and shape the symposium were Dr. Michael Stern, Professor Rebecca Coleman Curtis, Dr. Mary Ann Geskie, Dr. Joan Pinkus, Professor Ionas Sapountzis, Professor Michael O'Loughlin, and Dr. Brent Willock. The more we immersed ourselves in the theme of loneliness and yearning, the more we felt it required a book length treat-ment to begin to do it justice. At Routledge, Kate Hawes and her associates (such as Jane Harris) provided invaluable encouragement and facilitated the creation of this volume. It has been a pleasure to work with such a professional team. Needless to say, our authors have also been highly dedicated to this collective effort. Working with them has been delightful. As usual, our families provided important emotional support, enabling us to commit ourselves to this challenging endeavor.

Acknowledgments

Introduction

Lori C. Bohm

> The greatest disease in the West today is not TB or leprosy; it is being unwanted, unloved, and uncared for. We can cure physical diseases with medicine, but the only cure for loneliness, despair, and hopelessness is love.
>
> (Mother Teresa, *A Simple Path*, 1995)

Loneliness and longing. The mere mention of these emotional states evokes a painful emptiness. As Mother Teresa observed, loneliness, and the despair and hopelessness that often accompany it, are pandemic afflictions that have not been adequately addressed. We all experience loneliness at one time or another in our lives; it is a dreaded, though familiar, feeling.

Sullivan (1953) described loneliness as "an exceedingly unpleasant and driving experience connected with inadequate discharge of the need for human intimacy, for interpersonal intimacy" (p.290). Beyond having to endure extreme discomfort, the lonely person is also more prone to falling ill. Contemporary multidisciplinary research has demonstrated that chronic loneliness is a "serious risk factor for illness and early death, right alongside smoking, obesity and lack of exercise" (Cacioppo and Patrick, 2008, p.108).

Despite the familiarity and grave impact of loneliness, it is rarely explicitly addressed in the psychoanalytic literature. Two of the few psychoanalytic papers concerned with loneliness, one by Frieda Fromm-Reichmann and one by Melanie Klein, were the last papers each author produced before her death, and were published posthumously. We can only speculate about what motivated Fromm-Reichmann and Klein to muse about loneliness at that particular moment in their lives, and not before. Fromm-Reichmann (1959) wrote, "Loneliness seems to be such a painful, frightening experience that people will do practically everything to avoid it. This avoidance seems to include a strange reluctance on the part of psychiatrists to seek scientific clarification of the subject . . . Thus, loneliness is one of the least satisfactorily conceptualized psychological phenomena . . ." (p.1). This book makes a significant step towards addressing that gap.

I find that loneliness is a painfully ubiquitous emotion for many of my patients. They may seek to camouflage it through electronic connections, but in quiet moments it returns. A young woman confided that whenever she is walking from place to place she must be talking on her cell phone so as not to feel unbearably lonely. Another patient, well into her teens, still slept with her neglectful, profoundly self-absorbed mother—a vain attempt to quell her perennial feeling of missing her mother, feeling lonely for her mother, even as she shared her bed. It is this experience of loneliness and longing described by Melanie Klein (1963) in Khan (1975) as "the inner sense of loneliness—the sense of being alone, regardless of external circumstances, of feeling lonely even when among friends and receiving love" (p.300)—that is addressed in many of the chapters of this book.

Indeed, one seminal psychoanalytic paper by Winnicott (1958), "The capacity to be alone," approaches the topic of loneliness and longing by theorizing about what the child must have as she develops to enable her to escape that inner sense of loneliness. He emphasizes that the capacity to be alone is achieved first in childhood by being able to "be alone in the presence of mother" (p.417). Such an achievement requires the non-intrusive but constant availability of the "good-enough" mother. Adler and Buie (1979) propose that the failure of this "holding environment" (Winnicott, 1958) may culminate in the powerful, central experience of aloneness that characterizes borderline pathology.

Perspectives on loneliness

Our foray into the topic of loneliness and longings begins with a poetic examination by Dr. Sandra Buechler of what makes loneliness so painful, and what may befall a psychoanalytic treatment when the loneliness of patient and/or analyst remains unformulated. Buechler posits that the loneliness of the analyst is often a result of losing touch with ourselves as we work. "Who we are with when we are alone," i.e., the qualities of our internal objects, may modulate or exacerbate the analyst's loneliness. She focuses on ways of reducing unnecessary loneliness as well as on ways of learning to bear the inevitable lonely feelings that arise both in our patients and in ourselves.

Dr. Roger Frie follows Dr. Buechler in a complementary piece that also sees loneliness as a "basic, inescapable facet of human experience" (p.30), not as an indication of psychopathology. Drawing on the work of Binswanger and Buber, and their writings on the I-Thou dialogue, Frie understands loneliness and love to be inextricably linked, each experience serving to elucidate the other. This existential-phenomenological approach to loneliness has implications for contemporary psychoanalysis and its emphasis on the relational matrix as the locus of therapeutic action (Abend, 2003).

Loneliness in cyberspace

The book turns next to the technological context that we now live in, asking whether the proliferation of cyber-connections provides ways for people to feel less lonely or, instead, new venues for feeling loneliness even more strongly. Dr. Barbara Eisold discusses on-line "love-making" and "text-sex" as ways that people might seek to treat loneliness/emptiness following failed, unsatisfying relationships. She suggests that those engaged in "cybersex" may learn about aspects of their sexuality via this medium, and that the listening clinician may be able to understand her patient's "sexual excess" more vividly and immediately than would occur without this venue for sexual expression. Whether this type of relationship is fully satisfying is quite individual, dependent upon what the participants are longing for in their lives.

Likewise, the experience of living "on the grid" through one's Second Life avatar may quell loneliness or may promote it. Dr. John O'Leary created an avatar and spent time in Second Life to try to understand its appeal and its psychological impact on participants. He conveys the compelling quality of this experience, while acknowledging that he often felt quite lonely wandering around the open spaces, shopping malls, and parks of Second Life. There may be a balance, difficult to achieve, between using Second Life to explore certain dormant parts of oneself and getting lost in the fantasy world of this alternative reality.

And do the wildly popular social networking sites provide antidotes to loneliness? Dr. Karen Lombardi asks what it means to have 650 "friends." She wonders whether children and adolescents of this generation have the opportunity for the "solitude that leads to personal discovery and creativity," given the ever-presence of the internet and on-screen (superficial) connections. Her chapter is perhaps the most pessimistic of this section of the book, in terms of what the author sees as the damaging effects of the pseudo-intimacy promulgated by online relationships and the culture of "hooking-up." Unlike Dr. O'Leary, who proposes that people may explore hidden parts of themselves through their Second Life avatars, Dr. Lombardi sees the potential for people to hide, presenting a self on social networking sites that is fictive. She worries that these sites may serve to maintain a schizoid adaptation for some, as opposed to opening up their social worlds.

On yearning, love, and loneliness

We move next into the realm of longing. Dr. Amira Simha-Alpern offers a brief history of the psychoanalytic theories that "place the desire for human connection at the center of the motivational system." She begins with Fairbairn's object relations theory and continues with a discussion of contemporary Intersubjective and Relational approaches, noting Mitchell's

(1988) assertion that desire is always shaped and defined by the relational context in which it occurs. She then provides a clinical illustration of her points. She suggests that her patient's desire and longing became a "not-me" state in order to protect herself from the disappointment of not being affirmed and supported by her self-absorbed parents.

Drs. Arlene Richards and Lucille Spira use Marcel Proust's masterpiece, *In Search of Lost Time*, to explore the dynamics underlying a person's preference for living a lonely life, filled with longing, rather than getting involved in an intimate relationship. Through this lens, longing is seen as innocent, "a state where closure has not yet occurred." Unfulfilled love is desirable; indeed, Proust seems to believe that "satisfaction destroys love." Some of the points in this scholarly, thorough exegesis of Proust's work echo those made by Dr. Stephen Mitchell in his posthumously published last work, *Can Love Last? The Fate of Romance Over Time*. Mitchell (2002) believes that in order to maintain erotic attraction in a long-term relationship, there must be an element of mystery and insecurity for the lovers. In Proust and in Mitchell, longing is partially desirable, never to be fully extinguished.

The final chapter in this section further explores love and its connection to loneliness and longing. Using Plato's *Symposium*, the work of Freud, and two clinical cases, Dr. Evelyn Hartman demonstrates how falling in love involves the re-finding of the infant's original relationship with the mother. There is an element of fantasy in falling in love, the delicious experience that the loved one and being in love provides an indescribable soothing. But Hartman also observes that being in an unrequited love relationship confronts the lover with love's "twin," loneliness and longing.

Loneliness through the life cycle

Although loneliness is ubiquitous through all of life's epochs, there are particular moments and life circumstances that make it more prevalent and poignant. Three of the authors in this section describe such circumstances. Dr. Matthew Tedeschi gives detailed clinical process of his work with an adolescent with Asperger's Syndrome who is frequently locked in his solipsistic and lonely world. Only when he is able to get in touch with his longing for real contact with his father does the boy's suffering truly touch the therapist, and the boy and his therapy come alive.

The next chapter in this section of the book was written not by a mental health professional but rather by an English professor, Dr. Susan Ostrov Weisser. She chronicles her life-long love/hate relationship with her own loneliness and solitude, using a poem of Wordsworth as a beacon and a symbol. This open, self-searching piece helps the reader understand the trajectory loneliness may take in the life cycle, as one is subject to the vicissitudes of life.

Dr. Joan Lavender describes the "relational void" (Rucker, 1993), the experience of women who find themselves without a life partner well past the time when their peers have married and had children. She uses clinical process to take the reader into the feelings and thoughts of the therapist working with this thorny issue, as well as to give a vivid sense of the painfulness of this form of loneliness. Lavender demonstrates how psychoanalytic psychotherapy can be immensely helpful to women suffering a relational void.

Late life is another time when people often feel lonely. Dr. Mary Beth Cresci notes that while loneliness is not a given in older adults, the many losses that often accompany this time in life make the aging person particularly vulnerable to loneliness and longing. Cresci offers vignettes from three long-term cases, to guide the reader in grasping the variables that distinguish those who become chronically lonely in old age from those who do not.

The difficult, lonely patient

Working with a patient's intense loneliness is always challenging. But working with the loneliness of an alexithymic patient, a person who does not have the words to describe their internal states, presents profound problems for a treatment. Dr. Graeme Taylor's scholarly theoretical explanation of alexithymia and his moving clinical description of his work with a lonely alexithymic man provide a window into what can be done to reach and help these difficult patients.

Likewise, people who have suffered severe trauma in childhood and are later diagnosed "borderline" can be among the most difficult patients to treat. In his thoughtful, often poetic chapter, Dr. Ionas Sapountzis presents such a case. We are drawn into this treatment with its many challenges, and into the emotions evoked in Sapountzis as he struggles to understand what can be mutative for this deeply troubled and lonely woman.

Healing the analyst's loneliness

In this section of the book, three analysts courageously share tales of their own personal traumas that left them with nagging feelings of loneliness and longing. Dr. Jenny Kaufmann survived her mother's suicide, which took place when she was 26 months old. Kaufmann's lifelong struggle to make sense of this terrible tragedy, its impact on her development as a person, as well as her work with others who have suffered the same fate is sobering and inspirational.

Dr. Bruce Herzog describes the trauma of experiencing his wife's sudden death, including finding her body and later having to call over 30 of her patients to tell them of his loss. Although afflicted with post-traumatic symptoms himself, Herzog decided to carry on with his own practice, rather than to suspend it in the wake of this terrible event. He describes the soothing "self-righting" effect of being able to continue his work and his work-role, and the various ways that patients learned about and responded to his grief.

What is needed to survive and to make sense of traumatic loss and the ensuing lonely and often conflicted void it leaves differs for each individual. In the case of Dr. John Sloane, healing the childhood void left by the early death of his rough, demanding father occurred via the combination of psychoanalysis and re-connecting with his religious faith. Through both, Sloane emerged from his deep hurt, feeling that "we are not alone."

Loneliness and yearnings in the sociocultural surround

This portion of the book considers factors that make a crucial impact upon the experience of yearning and loneliness, beyond the intrapsychic and intersubjective ones implicated above. Human beings are all embedded in a sociocultural milieu, a multifaceted environment with diverse effects and implications. Dr. Art Caspary uses the alienation and sociopathy of a central character, Anton Chigurh, in Cormac McCarthy's *No Country for Old Men* to launch an argument about the alienation-promoting priorities of the corporate culture. Caspary, quoting Noam Chomsky in Bakan (2004), notes that the ideal for the corporation is "to have individuals who are totally dissociated from one another, who don't feel concern for anyone" (p.135). The corporation's only priority is to increase shareholders' profits. Caspary argues that the corporate culture that dictates cultural imperatives in developed countries is one in which "anything goes" as long as it adds to the bottom line. Chigurh is a "new" kind of character, one who is totally unconcerned with the other, disconnected from people and from his own humanity—a product of this corporate climate.

Another sociocultural institution with tremendous historical and contemporary impact is religion. Dr. Phil Classen, a psychologist who grew up in a Christian missionary family, suggests that both religion and psychoanalysis have much to offer the lonely, longing individual. In this chapter, Classen offers clinical vignettes and biographical examples of ways that both religion and psychoanalytic psychotherapy may come together to help people in their darkest, loneliest hours to recover.

Dr. Michael O'Loughlin takes the reader into the world of people with "unformulated yearnings," people who have suffered unspeakable traumas due to genocide and war. Indeed, O'Loughlin argues that by not literally speaking about these traumas, by not passing down the truth about what happened during, for example, Ireland's Great Hunger, the trauma is transmitted, unknowingly and surreptitiously, to subsequent generations. O'Loughlin's powerful piece places the cultural milieu in its rightful central position in our psychoanalytic understanding of the yearnings of a traumatized population.

Yearning for nonhuman connections

Psychoanalysts tend to privilege connections with other human beings as our object of study, as the locus of intervention, and as a prime indicator of emotional well-being. Two authors in this volume wisely point out that longing and loneliness can take place with and be affected by nonhuman factors. Dr. Elizabeth Allured's chapter focuses on "the other mother," nature, and the importance of our environmental surround in "holding" us. At a time when most have become acutely aware of the fragility of our environment, Dr. Allured suggests that being in solitude in nature may yield awareness of vivid, important feelings and relational patterns. She offers a case example of a patient on the brink of a terrible loss for whom managing the environmental surround provides soothing and containment.

Dr. Henry Seiden uses case vignettes, literary references, folk tales, and biographical material to evocatively illuminate a universal yearning: the "longing for home." In this scholarly, wide-ranging chapter, Seiden convincingly places the childhood home as the centerpiece of humankind's experience of longing. As they contemplate Seiden's contribution, readers will find themselves daydreaming about their own experiences of home and what feels missing still. Seiden ends by asserting, "Odysseus—not Oedipus—[is] the figure from antiquity most representative of the universal psychological experience of our species," and it is likely that the reader will agree.

Healing psychoanalysis, healing loneliness and yearnings

This section of the book scrutinizes the psychoanalytic profession itself, asking in what ways does it need to change in order for its institutions to minimize the alienation of its practitioners? In what ways do its theories need to change in order to maximize the possibility that patients will suffer less from loneliness? Dr. Kenneth Eisold takes a hard look at the early history of psychoanalysis, reviewing the myriad instances of isolation and extrusion of theorists who did not adhere to the current orthodoxy of their respective institutions. He uses the history of Dr. John Bowlby as a case in point, illustrating the way that such exclusionary practices damage the field. Eisold then turns to the current state of psychoanalysis, arguing that the need to survive as a profession should be the primary focus. Fighting about the wisdom of offering psychoanalytic training possibilities to differently qualified individuals and to those interested in a less intensive but still psychoanalytically based practice is seen as potentially calamitous for the future of the field.

In the erudite and comprehensive next chapter, Dr. Brent Willock demonstrates that conceptualization of loneliness and longing lies at the heart of much of the psychoanalytic literature. First, Willock reviews the key theoretical approaches in psychoanalysis, demonstrating that the affects each grapples with often involve loneliness. He then turns to potential failures of psychoanalytic theory in meaningfully reaching some patients. His solution is to adopt a "comparative-integrative" approach to theory, rejecting orthodoxy and urging the embrace of a multifaceted understanding of human motivation and human suffering. Like Eisold who argues for inclusiveness amongst those interested in learning psychoanalysis, Willock believes that inclusiveness in the theoretical realm is the key for psychoanalysis to thrive.

Summary

This volume makes an important first step toward psychoanalytically conceptualizing and grappling with loneliness and longing. These core human experiences have been neglected in the psychoanalytic literature to date. The rendering offered is contemporary and historical, theoretical and practical, personal and impersonal. This chapter began with a quote by Mother Teresa (1995) who asserted that love is the only cure for the greatest ills that afflict mankind, "loneliness, despair, and hopelessness." Indeed, love comes up as a mirror image of loneliness and longing in much of the work in this book. Some have argued that psychoanalysis is a cure by love, a controversial proposal (Hirsch, 2000; Loewald, 1960; Schafer, 1991). Whether or not one agrees with this idea, it is clear that loneliness is a painful psychological state that often motivates a person to enter treatment. It behooves psychoanalysts to think about loneliness and longing, both in their patients and in themselves, to help people cope with inevitable loneliness and to change their lives to make loneliness and longing less pervasive.

References

Abend, S. (2003). Relational influences on modern conflict theory. *Contemporary Psychoanalysis*, 39(3):367–377.

Adler, G. and Buie, D. H. (1979). Aloneness and borderline pathology: The possible relevance of child development issues. *International Journal of Psycho-Analysis*, 60:83–96.

Bakan, J. (2004). *The Corporation: The Pathological Pursuit of Profit and Power*. New York: Free Press.

Cacioppo, J. T. and Patrick, W. (2008). *Loneliness*. New York: W.W. Norton, and Co.

Fromm-Reichmann, F. (1959). Loneliness. *Psychiatry*, 22:1–15.

Hirsch, I. (2000). Alone yet connected: Response to discussion. *Contemporary Psychoanalysis*, 36(2):289–300.

Klein, M. (1963). On the sense of loneliness. In: *Envy and Gratitude and Other Works 1946–1963*, M. R. Khan (Ed.), 1975, The International Psycho-Analytic Library, 104:1–346.

Loewald, H. (1960). On the therapeutic action of psychoanalysis. In: *The Work of Hans Loewald*, G. I. Fogel (Ed.), 1991, Northvale, NJ: Jason Aronson, Inc., 13–59.

Mitchell, S. (1988). *Relational Concepts in Psychoanalysis: An Integration*. Cambridge, MA: Harvard University Press.

—— (2002). *Can Love Last? The Fate of Romance Over Time*. New York: W.W. Norton.

Mother Teresa (1995). *A Simple Path*. New York: Random House.

Rucker, N. (1993). Cupid's misses: Relational vicissitudes in the analyses of single women. *Psychoanalytic Psychology*, 10(3):377–391.

Schafer, R. (1991). Chapter 4: Internalizing Loewald. In: *The Work of Hans Loewald*, G. I. Fogel (Ed.), Northvale, NJ: Jason Aronson, Inc., 77–89.

Sullivan, H. S. (1953). *The Interpersonal Theory of Psychiatry*, H. S. Perry and M. L. Gawel (Eds.), New York: W.W. Norton and Co.

Winnicott, D. W. (1958). The capacity to be alone. *International Journal of Psycho-Analysis*, 39:416–420.

Part I

Loneliness in life and in treatment: Psychoanalytic and existential perspectives

Chapter 1

Someone to watch over me

Sandra Buechler

I don't usually attend the weddings, graduations, birthdays of my patients, but I made an exception when a long-term patient of mine died. I went to the funeral. As I walked in, I realized I had not allowed myself to think about what it would be like to be there. I knew no one, in one sense, and I knew everyone, in another sense. That is, I had heard about her parents, siblings, colleagues, and friends, for over a decade, yet I had never met any of them. With a jolt, I asked myself what I would say if someone came over to me. Does my patient still deserve some measure of confidentiality? Would it make her father uncomfortable to know I am here, given what I know about his abuse of her when she was a child? Should I be worrying about what he feels?

I reflect on how young she was, only 35. She never really had a chance. She suffered from physical disabilities, poverty, sexual and other kinds of abuse. We had had a stormy beginning, replete with her suicidal threats and rages at me. But that was so many years ago, so far away. Lately, she had let me know how much our work meant, how much I meant to her. In the subtlest of ways, by quoting me, using my words as her words, she let me know how much she had heard me, and taken me into her mind and heart. She still had too much pride to say it, but she could show it.

We had made a good deal of progress lately, I thought. She so desperately wanted to be wanted by a man. To be loved, desired, despite everything. From my point of view, the extreme injuries to her self esteem, repeated over and over, had left her unable to choose someone who had the capacity to partner her. Instead, she had affairs that only confirmed her sense of worthlessness. But all that was changing and, recently, I saw her choosing more carefully, more wisely. Finally. And not too late to have a child, if she wanted to. Then, with a suddenness that will never be completely understood, she died. Yes, we can explain it to some degree as a consequence of a disability she had. But there had been no indication this would happen now.

The pain of "almost," we almost made it, and the pain of "never," she and I will never have another moment, another chance. Assailed by "almost" and "never," I cry, as I realize that I am at the funeral, partly, to give myself a chance to think these thoughts. I look around at all the sad faces of the strangers I know and do not know. Are any of them thinking the same things I am thinking? Did anyone know her as I knew her? Is everyone here angry, along with me, that she didn't finally get a break, after thirty-five uphill years of fighting for her life?

Along with my grief, words can't convey the loneliness I felt that day. Why was my loneliness so painful, so different from the aloneness I often seek? My approach to our topic starts with some thoughts about what, in general, can make loneliness hurt so much. I then take up the analyst's position, to reflect on some contributions to our loneliness. I mention some dangers when loneliness remains unformulated and, finally, some suggestions for reducing unnecessary loneliness and bearing the part that is inevitable.

Its quintessential force

> For at bottom, and just in the deepest and most important things, we are unutterably alone, and for one person to be able to advise, or even help another, a lot must happen, a lot must go well, a whole constellation of things must come right in order once to succeed.
>
> (Rilke, 1934, pp.23–24)

Life has taught me that it is never wise to ignore Rilke's insights. I approach our aloneness as human beings from a different vantage point, but I still come to Rilke's conclusion. My understanding stems from the emotion theory that has captivated me for decades now. Without getting sidetracked into its details, I will just mention that its central premise is that emotions are among the most powerful human motivators, and each of a number of fundamental emotions is a discernibly different state with its own subjective and expressive characteristics. An angry face can be discriminated from a terrified face. Another premise, originally contributed by Silvan Tomkins (1963), is that we each have gone through a socialization process that taught us how to feel about our emotions.

I have taken all this to mean, clinically, that each human being has a personal history of experience with each of the fundamental emotions. Part of how we know ourselves is that we know what we are like when we are ashamed, anxious, or frightened. The adult who threw tantrums as a child has a relationship to being angry that is valuable to explore in treatment. Part of my sense of self, then, is built on my lifetime of experience of Sandra Buechler when she is anxious, Sandra Buechler when she feels guilty, and so on. Extending this conception can help us understand one aspect of loneliness. Perhaps part of human loneliness results from our inability to fully communicate our emotional experience. No one will ever know exactly what I feel when I am frightened, or overjoyed, or ashamed. Each of us has a rich, complex, experiential history of each of the fundamental emotions. When someone feels angry today, a lifetime of angry experiences shade and shape this anger. To some extent s/he will always be alone with the fullness of this experience, unable to get all of it across to someone else. Even the most painstaking effort to acquaint the analyst with this history will not fully express it in all its particularity. I do, nonetheless, make an attempt to get a sense of the patient's life-long relationship with each of the fundamental emotions early in treatment.

We are, as Rilke says, unutterably alone in the deepest and most important things, that is, the things that evoke our strongest feelings. For the most part, we can't even describe our loneliness, as Sullivan (1953) admitted. "I, in common apparently with all denizens of the English-speaking world, feel inadequate to communicate a really clear impression of loneliness in its quintessential force" (pp.260–261). Given Sullivan's abiding interest in interpersonal life, his statement is especially interesting. Although he saw relating as at the core of human survival, Sullivan still felt unable to understand and express the power of loneliness. It is so difficult to describe its pain, and what differentiates it from benign, or even satisfying experiences of solitude. Loneliness is an experience human beings cannot escape, yet it can be difficult to describe why it hurts so deeply. As analysts, I suggest, we are in an excellent position to observe its effect, in ourselves and our patients.

Turning to Winnicott's paper on the capacity to be alone (1965) we get a picture of the fortunate person's situation. "The relationship of the individual to his or her internal objects, along with confidence in regard to internal relationships, provides of itself a sufficiency of living, so that temporarily he or she is able to rest contented even in the absence of external objects and stimuli" (p.32).

But what, exactly, can give us the "sufficiency of living" that enables us to "rest contented"? Extrapolating from Winnicott, I believe who we are with, when we are alone, tremendously affects the quality of the experience. As I shall elaborate later, if we can tap into fundamentally good internal objects, if we have access to curious play, if the aloneness is, in some sense, willed, and if it does not feel permanent, aloneness can be a backdrop for intensely positive self-experience.

Anthony Storr (1988), a psychiatrist, ardently describes the virtues of being alone. Writing about creative individuals, like Beethoven, Henry James, Goya, and Wittgenstein, he says: "The creative person is constantly seeking to discover himself, to remodel his own identity, and to find meaning in the universe through what he creates. He finds this a valuable integrating process which, like meditation or prayer, has little to do with other people, but which has its own separate validity. His most significant moments are those in which he attains some new insight, or makes some new discovery; and these moments are chiefly, if not invariably, those in which he is alone" (p.xiv). In Storr's examples, creative individuals choose aloneness, taking advantage of its silence to connect more deeply with internal life. He suggests that psychoanalysis in particular, and Western culture in general, over-value relationship, at the expense of the equally valid need for solitude.

This aloneness contrasts so completely with the gnawing loneliness we so often meet in our patients and ourselves. A patient, desperate for attention from her husband, would rather engage him in an unpleasant argument than endure his silence. This makes them both deeply unhappy. Another wisecracks and flirts with other men, using sexual provocation to disturb stillness. There is the nearly unbearable loneliness of some adolescents, who feel themselves inferior to their socially more competent peers. "No one will ever like me," they cry. Nothing reassures them, for they feel their loneliness is deserved, and their only truthful state.

The quality of our internal object relationships determines what it is like to be alone with them. A patient whose inner life is ruled by a tyrannical, sadistic despot (modeled after her cruel father) suffers merciless loneliness when alone. Nothing comforts. Efforts to turn toward the cultural or spiritual worlds for support are met with mocking derision. Her inner objects rule at night, when daytime distractions are unavailable. Dreams, filled with extreme dangers and surreal monsters, frequently shake her back to an exhausted wakefulness. This patient understood immediately when I said that how aloneness feels depends on who you are with when you are alone.

Since another premise of emotion theory is that emotions exist in a system, with each affecting the intensity of all the rest, it would follow that how curious we feel would impact on the experience of aloneness. Access to curious play can mitigate the potential sting in loneliness. We see evidence of this in attachment research (Goldberg et al., 1995). Some children, left alone by their mothers, turn toward involvement with the non-human environment, presumably using their curiosity to create a kind of alternate form of companionship. In a paper on loneliness in psychoanalysis (Buechler, 1998), I suggested that the loneliness of both patient and analyst can be modulated by curiosity.

The experience of aloneness is therefore shaped, partially, by who we are with when we are alone, and by whether or not other emotions, such as curiosity, are prominent. A third factor is whether or not the aloneness was chosen. Once again Rilke is my guide. He (1934) emphasizes the importance of using the experience of solitude as a consciously willed tool. "You should not let yourself be confused in your solitude by the fact that there is something in you that wants to break out of it. That very wish will help you, if you use it quietly, and deliberately and like a tool, to spread your solitude over wide country" (p.53).

Fromm-Reichmann's (1959) poetic, posthumously published paper on loneliness eloquently attests to the importance of whether solitude is felt as having purpose and is therefore, at least to some degree, willed. Describing the experience of a prisoner kept in solitary confinement during World War Two, she suggests that what mitigated his suffering was his belief in the spiritual validity of the political convictions that were the cause of his imprisonment.

Storr (1988, p.42) also differentiates willed, potentially useful aloneness from enforced solitude, although he mentions a few, highly determined people who have been able to make creative use of their horrendous imprisonment. For the most part, solitude that has been chosen is more easily embraced. Perhaps when we will it, we have to contend only with loneliness, and not, also, with rage and the terror of helplessness. In chosen solitude, our sense of purpose and even our loneliness itself may become a tool that expands our reach to the widest possible country.

We have briefly considered how internal objects, other intense affects, and the feeling of choice affect the experience of aloneness. The last factor is the dimension of time. Painful loneliness is often experienced as a permanent condition, rather than as a temporary hardship. Teenagers frequently see themselves as forever unacceptable and, therefore, alone for life. Fromm-Reichmann (1959) emphasized the lack of hope of human connectedness in the profoundly lonely person. She focused on the importance of hope of future interactions, and the subjective meaning of the loneliness, as determinants of its impact. A patient who felt she would never attract a man who would want her, was unconsolable. She turned to spiteful envy of any woman who had a seemingly satisfying relationship with a man. The envy became obsessive—a constant, hurtful companion. Another patient despairs of anyone, least of all her analyst, understanding her depression. Someone who understood could not endure, so the analyst must be either uncomprehending or as lost in pain as she. This conundrum had no solution, making her loneliness unending.

Most of us can bear temporary hardships. One of the biggest developmental advances is the ability to modulate pain with an awareness that time often heals. Even severe depressions sometimes respond to this reassurance. But when we feel locked in pain forever, when an illness or an emotion seems without end, we may not feel we have the strength to go on. Intractable physical pain can easily elicit suicidal wishes. Writing of his own depression, William Styron (2001, p.121) notes that it is of great importance that those suffering a depressive episode be convinced that it will run its course and, eventually, they will feel differently.

To some, permanent pain elicits a very primitive, claustrophobic anxiety. The thought of it evokes the same terror of being trapped that science fiction and other writers exploit. Aching loneliness can stretch endlessly, like a measureless sea.

Another way to understand the "quintessential force" of loneliness is to consider it as a reaction to loss. But what, exactly, has been lost by the lonely? In a previous paper (Buechler, 1998), I summarized various approaches to this question. Briefly, for writers who see interpersonal connection as core to the sense of self, our own psychic center is threatened by loneliness. For others, for whom anxiety is a key determinant of pathology, security is undermined. Still others see the pain of loneliness as mainly resulting from impoverished hope. These authors emphasize that the meaning we give our experience colors its emotional impact.

Like the proverbial elephant described differently by the various blind men, each of us focuses on the losses in loneliness that fit our theories of what counts most. Ultimately there can be no final answers. Loneliness is too vast and too often fogged over to make entirely clear. But the human spirit will always rail against it. Poets will always complain about loneliness, and portraitists will attempt to capture it in poignant expressions. Biblical scholars will study Job's abandonment by God. Fiction writers, like Dostoevsky, will give a voice to an embittered, alienated Underground Man, enabling him to cry out against the society that spurned him. We will never end our dialogue about human loneliness, hoping to understand better why some of us can "spread it over wide country," and others can only succumb to its pain.

The lonely analyst

We were alerted to our own difficulties recognizing our loneliness by Fromm-Reichmann (1959).

> The psychiatrist's specific problem in treating lonely patients seems to be that he has to be alert for and recognize traces of his own loneliness or fear of loneliness, lest it interfere with his fearless acceptance of manifestations of the patient's loneliness. This holds true, for example, when the psychiatrist, hard as he may try, cannot understand the meaning of a psychotic communication. He may then feel excluded from a "we experience" with his patient; and this exclusion may evoke a sense of loneliness or fear of loneliness in the doctor, which makes him anxious.
>
> (p.329)

I don't remember anyone in my analytic training warning me about the profession's potential for loneliness. Perhaps partially because we are never alone, the pain of loneliness is not emphasized as a hazard of analytic practice. Yet I have come to regard it as one of the greatest dangers we face, and probably the single greatest cause of burnout. While I have never subscribed to the notion of our work as "impossible," I do think of it as the lonely profession.

One reason for this loneliness is that we frequently feel trapped in some, or all, of the following feelings:

1   This patient will never understand what I am really trying to do for him. He will never recognize my good intentions. I will always be alone with my own knowledge of what I am attempting on his behalf.

2   This patient will always want me to be someone I can't become, and I will always feel the same way toward him. We will go through time endlessly disappointed in each other, forever trying to get the blood the stone can't give.

3   I will always dread this patient's sessions because as I enter the room my head buzzes with all my old supervisors telling me I am doing a bad job with this patient. They say my countertransference is too intense, my interpretations are incorrect, my timing is unempathic, and I am violating the principles of analytic technique.

4   I am bored. I feel sleepy with this patient. I am perfectly awake before and after his session, but with him my mind goes blank. As he waits for a response, I scramble to think of something. No theory, nothing coherent occurs to me, and the 45 minutes stretch on endlessly.

5   I am a fraud. What I do has no meaning to me, no purpose, but I have to continue to go through the motions. I can never be fully known to this patient because I will always have to hide these feelings, lest the patient become aware of them and quit the treatment.

6   In my effort to retain analytic neutrality, I have lost touch with my passions. I feel empty and dead.

7   In selectively attending to the patient, and away from my own concerns, I have often paid a heavy price for my effort to be selfless. Personal worries, physical discomforts, unrecognized feelings still occur but they are suppressed, sometimes making them powerfully evident to me. Fearing being swept up by their intensity, I feel I have no choice but to hide, waiting, hoping for the storm to pass. In hiding, I will always be alone.

8   Sharing the patient's life story has meant knowing painful stories. Analysts hear all of life's sorrows and must keep much of what we know within the four walls of the consulting room. The partner, friends, or family who most could help us with our feelings might not be someone with whom we can share the details. Patients pour out the heartache of losing a child, the sorrow of broken promises, the terror of life threatening disease. We listen. We take it in. Much has been made of the trauma clinicians feel vicariously, but what of the sorrow? Some of our experience may be shared with the patient, but some of it may emerge in our own lives in delayed, disguised, displaced forms, perhaps only partially understood even by ourselves.

Our profession often places us in a uniquely lonely, although rarely alone, position. We are frequently the only one who knows what we know. We can share our perspective with no one, sometimes for reasons of confidentiality, sometimes out of our own self-protection. This isolation can often feel permanent. Our focus is on someone else, so we have lost the centeredness that can provide some comforting ballast. At times, we don't even have ourselves to turn to, since, with certain patients, we don't feel like ourselves. Vicariously we may be experiencing trauma, but we may not be able to give ourselves any decent interval to recover, as the buzzer sounds for the next appointment and, like a good Pavlovian subject, we do what is expected of us, and go on.

As clearly as I can, I will now describe my own thoughts one Monday morning, just before my first patient arrived. You will, no doubt, hear many sources for my loneliness. "What was disturbing to me about our last session? Let me look at my notes before she comes in. Oh, yes, the drinking. And the outbursts with the kids. What if she loses control and really hits them? I should be saying something more, doing something more. But if I do, she'll find a way to leave treatment, as she has ended almost every relationship she ever had. What good would that do? I would feel the self-satisfaction of having done my duty, but nothing would really change. She and her husband have all the resources they would need to make sure their children stayed right where they are. But am I just rationalizing now because I do not have the guts to really confront her? I know how enraged she would get. Sure, I could tell myself I have no real evidence, but is that because I am not asking the right questions? Without consciously deciding to, I stop short of getting the evidence. Well, I won't do that today! If she tells me anything that sounds suspicious, I'll keep asking questions until I am sure whether those kids are being hurt . . . But, who am I fooling? Of course they are being hurt! God, I'm a psychoanalyst, and I am discounting the meaning of psychological pain! She says such terrible things to them when she has had her five o'clock cocktail. Do I hate her? Is that what I am staying away from? Or am I afraid of her? Am I one of her children, cowering, waiting to be hit? What would my analyst have done? What would my supervisors, my supervisees, my analysands think of this treatment? Oh, God, and it's only 8 o'clock Monday morning!"

My own belief is that in this Monday morning moment the person I miss the most is me. I can find no way to be a "me" I recognize and like. This chapter concludes with ideas about finding her. But first, another of my lonely moments as a clinician.

A successful businessman, in his mid-50s, enters a consultation. He would like some help with his wife who seems unhappy but won't consider treatment. He also has trouble lately dealing with a business partner he feels is glad to share their profits, but does not equally share the work. He gets resentful sometimes, but does not want a big blow up. He does not think he really needs "serious therapy." He would just like to manage things better. Is there anything he could read?

As I listen to this man I feel much lonelier than I would if I were alone. It is not that I dislike him. I think he is a perfectly decent person who, under other circumstances, could be my friend. He is a responsible father of grown children, a "pillar of society" who contributes to charities and reaches out to his neighbor when he can. I would really like to help him. And yet I experience us as worlds apart, oceans apart, with no common language, even though we seem to be from the same culture. I feel unalterably alone with my own thoughts.

Part of my mind is engaged in shaping a picture of this man as having schizoid aspects. In his speech I hear some schizoid accents. Guntrip (1969) might remark on his over-functioning "false self." Making light of his "true self" wishes for help, minimizing dependency needs, focusing on "managing" life rather than living it fully, this man seems to me to fit the schizoid profile in many ways although, of course, no human being neatly occupies a pigeon-hole.

I sit at the cross-roads. On one side is this stranger, asking for a few tips on how to arrange things better interpersonally. He wants therapy-light. He is not interested in dismembering his psychic structure. But sitting on my shoulder are many former supervisors, teachers, analysts of my own. They tell me it would be hypocritical to seem to go along with his agenda. They ask if I am that hard up for cash that I have to sell out this way.

Another voice joins the babble. I start to wonder what would happen to this man if I did persuade him, somehow, to engage in a treatment that confronted his schizoid character structure. What if he got in touch with tremendous unmet needs and stopped functioning so smoothly? How many lives would that disrupt, perhaps permanently, if we could not get "Humpty Dumpty" back together again? What right have I to make that kind of choice for another human being? Yet how can I enlist his collaboration at this point, when his thinking about the problem and mine are so far apart?

No wonder I am lonely. I am alone, possibly permanently, with what I feel I know, and with a sense that my intentions are honorable, even though I am confused about what to do. I don't even have myself with me, since I don't feel my usual (somewhat clearer-headed) self. Critical internal objects are attacking me, and I feel defenseless. I am tempted to just get through the consultation, saying meaningless but reasonable things. Then I realize this would be succumbing to my own schizoid aspects. I would be acting like an interpersonal manager, rather than exploring his compulsive coping style.

I am lonely because I don't have my usual sense of purpose and conviction, so I don't feel like me. I have lost part of me, as well as any hope of engaging this man as a patient. I don't have the good opinion of my (internal) supervisors, and I can't engage in an interesting (inner) dialogue with Guntrip. My isolation feels permanent, since I see no way out of it. I cannot justify rejecting the patient, who is only asking for help according to terms he can understand. Yet I agree with the findings of the (internal) case conference. I cannot offer him "suggestions" that skirt the issue of his schizoid character structure. What if I postpone the whole issue, and work to "engage" him in treatment? Perhaps I can convince myself this is appropriate therapeutically. But in my heart of hearts, I will still feel like I am seducing him, seeming to go along with his agenda, but planning to try to inveigle him into signing up for "real" treatment. Now I feel like I am betraying everyone, including the patient, my training, and myself. There is no greater loneliness than having a bad opinion of oneself.

Because of space limitations, I will only mention some other sources of the analyst's loneliness. Eventually we lose every treatment partner we ever had. Do we acknowledge the effect this has on us over the course of our careers? Not sufficiently, I believe.

In a more subtle sense, I feel a loneliness that stems from the unavailability of time for me to process what happened in the last session before I go on to the next. Again, this loneliness grows from a feeling of missing myself. I don't have all of me with me, for the rest of the day.

The most acute feelings of loneliness I can remember are associated with the few serious illnesses I have had. Feeling unclear about how much of the details to share, I have felt profoundly alone, making myriad decisions every moment, while coping with being unwell. The impact of illness on the analyst's loneliness is a topic worthy of discussion.

The lonely analyst acts out

One of the reasons we are able to remain ignorant of our own loneliness is how clever it is at disguise. Sometimes it takes the shape of an unusually high level of activity. We feel as though this patient "needs" more from us, so we interpret frequently. Or we may project our own loneliness onto the patient, seeing her as isolated and in need of connection. We see ourselves as helping the patient become more comfortable interpersonally. We rationalize behavior we don't realize stems, at least in part, from our own lonely bids for attention.

Other signs of analytic loneliness can include the over-use of jargon with the patient. The lonely analyst may unconsciously want to relate to the patient as a professional colleague. Sometimes loneliness drives us to over-emphasize the patient's likenesses to ourselves. We selectively inattend to differences, so the patient does not feel like a stranger.

Perhaps even more commonly, the analyst suffering from loneliness may be impatient toward the patient's pathology, as though it were an obstacle, keeping them apart. Thus the schizoidness of the schizoid, the obsessiveness of the obsessional, the paranoia of the paranoid, the narcissism of the narcissist, becomes a personal enemy, preventing closer collaboration. In this situation we may be driven to attack the patient's defenses, needing to rid the patient of them. Our efforts are over-determined, in more than one sense. We are too determined to make the patient give up his defenses and move closer to us. It can be all too easy, in this emotional climate, to treat the patient's defenses contemptuously, or take them personally, as resistances to us.

An example is a supervisee who found himself unusually active in working with a depressed patient's dream. Interpretation followed interpretation, all barely getting the muted attention of the patient. I ask who the interpretations were for, a bit playfully suggesting that when we give a gift we usually think of what the recipient wants, rather than what we want to give. Perhaps playfulness was my attempt to assuage loneliness in both the supervisee and myself. The impoverished, depressed patient may have evoked the potential for loneliness each of us carries with us, even when we go to work.

Lacking empathic engagement for whatever reason, the analyst may then try to "get through" the session. This can be particularly disheartening for both participants. There is nothing more deadening than going through the motions in any relationship that is supposed to be intimate. Such hours can sound a death knell for the treatment. The resulting dispirited disillusion can be extremely hard, or even impossible to repair. Avidity is, I suggest, impossible to fake. If the analyst does not manifest some passion for the work and tries to slide through the forty-five minutes mechanically, both people know it, and the "expectation of benefit" Sullivan (1954) considered essential to treatment will be insufficient. In this situation, with no heartfelt connection, both participants are probably painfully lonely.

Antidotes to the analyst's loneliness

Analytic collaboration

Analysis can be a truly alive encounter between two emotionally present and responsive people. Moments can be thrilling. Other moments can unsettle us, terrify us, enrage us, touch us with sorrow. I think of the relationship possible in treatment as similar to poetry in its distilled fullness. Every feeling potential in human beings can be intensely present. Our human condition is manifested in pure form in this absurdly limited and gloriously limitless embrace.

Elsewhere (Buechler, 2004) I have addressed how the analyst's values shape the treatment she provides. Who we each are as curious, hopeful, kind, courageous, purposeful, emotional, sorrowful, integrated human beings reveals itself in how we work. What we focus on, remember, fight for, cry about, disagree with, laugh at, tire from, and ignore speaks volumes about who we are.

Together, I feel the analyst and the patient create a collaborative relationship by being willing to contribute whatever of value they can give, in the service of their work. If I have a thought, if I can make the hour more convenient when the patient is pressed for time, if I can spend some time studying the patient's history, or a potentially useful theoretical concept, I believe making these efforts can encourage the patient to participate fully. I am communicating that the work is worth pushing ourselves in its interest. I am saying it matters through my actions, rather than in words that may not be very convincing. One way I have understood hopefulness in both participants in treatment (Buechler, 1995, 2002, 2004) is that it is a product of self-knowledge. If I know I will do anything I can to help a patient, I have reason to be hopeful about the treatment.

Two specific aspects of this collaboration are the willingness to expend effort, and the sense of purpose. Each of these plays a crucial role in the process of forging a therapeutic relationship. Dedication to the work should not be an abstract principle but, rather, a value made passionately manifest. The willingness to expend effort reveals itself in how hard we try to understand what the patient is saying. Are we willing to admit we were distracted and ask the patient to repeat what they said? Do we devote time and care to knowing the patient's history, to understanding her cultural background when it differs from our own? Do we work at using dreams? Do we try hard to be aware of the countertransference, and reveal what we feel will further the treatment, whether or not it may make us look competent?

When there is a choice as to whose ego may be bruised, what do we do? For example, if there is a misunderstanding about scheduling, what do we assume? The willingness to be a "fool for love" (Buechler, 2004, pp.58–60) is one of the most essential kindnesses we can extend in therapy. We take a position about what counts in treatment and, more generally, in life, when we willingly expose our own intellectual and emotional limitations. More than anything else, I believe this willingness encourages the patient to be less concerned about how he looks and more invested in knowing himself and being fully known.

I distinguish the sense of purpose from any particular treatment goal. It is a texture that permeates the work (Buechler, 2004, pp.85–101). Through how she focuses, more than any other way, the analyst expresses her expectations about the treatment. A sense of purpose means to me that this work is tremendously important, can change how two lives are led. Improving the quality of a life is worth any amount of work. Life is finite, precious, too potentially rich to be wasted. Treatment can help us savor it. I take a great deal of meaning from the fact that the word "wisdom" is derived from "sapere," Latin for: to taste, have taste, be wise: sage, sapid, sapient, sapor, savant, savor, savvy (American Heritage Dictionary, 1969, p.1537). Like a gourmet's nuanced appreciation of details, the wise savor life. Even pain, if it is keenly felt, tells us we are vividly alive. A treatment that helps people savor life has an inherently valuable purpose.

The internal chorus

Several times, in this chapter, I have come to the conclusion that the analyst's loneliness is, at least in part, most painful when she feels as though she has lost herself. I have also emphasized the differences in the coloring of aloneness depending on the quality of the care we get from our internal objects. Combining these ideas, I will end by describing how I think the people who most nearly touch us can render us less vulnerable to the worst torturing loneliness.

In training we internalize relationships to our analyst, supervisors, teachers, and others. Training often recapitulates some aspects of our own, personal, earlier process of identity formation. If I had been a teenage rebel, I think I would have had a different experience in analytic training. Despite our individual differences, in training we become identified with an analytic family, but also retain our own separate identities. We gradually learn to put our unique stamp on the analytic tradition, developing a particular style and voice.

With a particular patient, if my internal chorus of analysts gives me acceptable feedback, I don't feel too lonely. I am not cut off from them. In this situation, my aloneness feels temporary. Even if the patient completely withdraws from me, I can probably bear it because I still have my good opinion of me. I can think about why the patient is withdrawing, find meaning in the transference and countertransference, and explore it in my mind theoretically. I have plenty to play with, in a Winnicottian sense. But if, with a patient, the chorus cuts me off and, especially if it feels permanent, I am cast out in space, lost forever. This, to me, is true loneliness. It does not end after the 45 minutes are up.

Another way to express this is that the analyst needs a relative absence of persecutory inner objects. This allows her to bear what the patient evokes, most of the time. We each probably differ in our particular Achilles heel, that is, the coping style in patients that evokes undue harshness from our internal chorus. The withdrawn, schizoid patient may leave us feeling like we are sending messages in bottles into an expanse of sea, or trying to play tennis when the ball isn't coming back. Like brides left at the altar, we may feel as though we are the only ones who care enough to make a commitment. Depending on our own character issues, this can be more or less profoundly disorienting, but it always leaves us without the human responsiveness we all use to know, literally and figuratively, where we are with each other. For some of us, our responses to the schizoid withdrawn patient incur great wrath from our internal chorus, evoking a profound, guilty loneliness. Other analysts can maintain a curious, creative aloneness with withdrawn patients, but feel tremendously self-critical about responses to the narcissistically entitled patient. For each of us, there are probably certain patients who most easily drive us into a harshly self-critical state in which we are cut off from the comfort of positive, internalized, professional objects.

For me personally, the worst form of loneliness, the one in which I most profoundly lose myself, is signaled by my effort to coast through a session. I am convinced that the temptation to coast is a dangerous form of burnout. It can be born of many parents, including a marriage of loneliness and fatigue. Unsure whether I will have the stamina for the overly demanding schedule I have created, I feel tempted to look for an hour I can slide through, half-attending. Snapping back after one of these unscheduled mini-vacations, I feel guilty enough to force myself to focus on what is being said to me, hoping to glean what I have missed from what follows. At such moments, just getting through, relatively unscathed, feels like a triumph. To survive undetected can seem ambitious enough. We are scrutinized hour after hour, and we scrutinize ourselves. We hear common and uncommon human misery, as well, of course, as other subjects. It can be tempting to steer clear of pain. Yet coasting has a predictable aftermath, at least for me. It leaves an empty, demoralized, unconnected feeling. Like so many other time killers, such as television and internet addiction, just getting through promises a relief it does not deliver. It does not bring peace or comfort. It does not ease the burden of the work. It is a false hope, a mirage, seeming to offer smooth sailing, but actually depriving me of the meeting that might bring genuine solace.

To conclude, I suggest that some of our most painful loneliness results from losing touch with ourselves. A nurturing internal chorus, a supply of theoretical ideas to play with, and a well developed sense of clinical purpose can certainly help. Also crucial, I feel, is how we feel about the effort that doing treatment entails. It will not surprise you that Rilke (1934) best expressed my feelings about the effort the work requires of us:

> People have (with the help of conventions) oriented all their solutions toward the easiest side of the easy; but it is clear that we must hold to what is difficult; everything alive holds to it, everything in Nature grows and defends itself in its own way and is characteristically and spontaneously itself, seeks at all costs to be so and against all opposition. We know little, but that we must hold to what is difficult is a certainty that will not forsake us.

(p.53)

Recently I have become aware that when I hold to what is difficult I am not alone. Rose Spiegel, who was my training analyst, is with me. I hear the lilt in her voice and the softness it sometimes had. But just as often, it had a fierce, pointed, dogged determination. Rose was probably the most focused, steadfast person I have ever known. Her capacity to concentrate, pursuing the fullest possible understanding of something, was incredible. Her allegiance to discovering the whole truth was absolute. I remember being exasperated sometimes by what I felt to be her stubbornness. I came to realize it was our stubbornness. I came to understand that it was profoundly connected to our strength.

When I don't let go of my point with a patient, I feel Rose is with me, watching, perhaps smiling. I, who sometimes balked at her tenaciousness, have made her my model of perseverance. I still ask where strong persistence ends and obstinate recalcitrance begins. On this, perfect clarity will probably always elude me, but one thing is certain. When I need to, I can still see and hear Rose showing me how to hold to what is difficult.

References

Buechler, S. (1995). Emotion. In M. Lionells, J. Fiscalini, C. H. Mann, and D. B. Stern (Eds.), *Handbook of Interpersonal Psychoanalysis*. Hillsdale, NJ: The Analytic Press, pp. 165–188.

—— (1998). The analyst's experience of loneliness. *Contemporary Psychoanalysis*, 34: 91–105.

—— (2002). "Instigating hope in psychoanalysis." Presented at a meeting of the International Forum of Psychoanalysis, Oslo, Norway.

—— (2004). *Clinical Values: Emotions That Guide Psychoanalytic Treatment.* Hillsdale, NJ: The Analytic Press.

Fromm-Reichmann, F. (1959/1990). Loneliness. *Contemporary Psychoanalysis*, 26: 305–330.

Goldberg, S., Muir, R. & Kerr, J. (1995). *Attachment Theory: Social, Developmental, and Clinical Perspectives*. Hillsdale, NJ: The Analytic Press.

Guntrip, H. (1969). *Schizoid Phenomena, Object Relations and the Self*. New York: International Universities Press.

Rilke, R. M. (1934). *Letters to a Young Poet*. New York: Norton.

Storr, A. (1988). *Solitude: A Return to the Self*. New York: Random House.

Styron, W. (2001). From "Darkness Visible." In: N. Casey (Ed.), *Unholy Ghost: Writers on Depression*. New York: HarperCollins.

Sullivan, H. S. (1953). *The Interpersonal Theory of Psychiatry*. New York: Norton.

—— (1954). *The Psychiatric Interview*. New York: Norton.

Tomkins, S. (1963). With the editorial assistance of Bertram P. Karon. *Affect, Imagery, Consciousness*. New York: Springer.

Winnicott, D. (1965). *The Maturational Process and the Facilitating Environment*. Madison, CT: International Universities Press.

Chapter 2

The lived experience of loneliness: An existential-phenomenological perspective

Roger Frie

Loneliness is an enduring fact of human life. Questions about what loneliness is, what causes it, and, in turn, what can be done about it, are central to the work of psychotherapists and psychoanalysts. While descriptive accounts of loneliness are quite common in the clinical literature, the nature and possible meaning of loneliness often go unaddressed. The problem of loneliness is usually subsumed under other topics, such as anxiety or depression and, as a result, not often addressed on its own. When loneliness is identified as a psychological symptom, it is most often portrayed as neurotic or pathological, resulting from problems in infant and childhood development, or from dysfunctions in interpersonal relationships.

Within the interpersonal tradition of psychoanalysis, the development of a theory of loneliness has a tenuous history. The tradition stemming from Harry Stack Sullivan, for example, focuses chiefly on the relational nature of self-experience. For Sullivan, the individualized experience of selfhood is an unnatural state, associated with anxious feelings. By extension, many interpersonal and relational analysts are less interested in conceptualizing the nature of solitude and separateness. An exception to this trend is Frieda Fromm-Reichmann's famous article entitled, rather appropriately, "Loneliness." First published in the Washington School of Psychiatry's journal *Psychiatry* in 1959, it was republished in *Contemporary Psychoanalysis* in 1990.

Fromm-Reichmann's discussion is remarkable because it seeks not to explain the problem of loneliness, but to elucidate the lived experience of the severely lonely person. She uses a phenomenological perspective less concerned with the causes of loneliness than with reaching an understanding of its nature and pervasiveness. She draws extensively on works of poets, writers, and philosophers. This phenomenological approach to understanding lived experience is similarly used in discussions of such human conditions as love and death. It is almost as though empirical and precise definitions fail us when we seek to define such basic experiences as loneliness, love, or mortality.

Rather than viewing loneliness through the lens of psychopathology, this chapter is premised on the notion that loneliness is a basic, inescapable facet of human experience. Using an approach grounded in the philosophical tradition of existential-phenomenology, I will elaborate on the lived experience of loneliness. Drawing on contrasting perspectives within existential-phenomenology, I suggest that loneliness can only be fully appreciated and clinically addressed from the perspective of shared experience and potential for interpersonal love.

For Fromm-Reichmann and the tradition of existential-phenomenology with which she is most affiliated (Burston, 1991), the problem of loneliness is an existential fact. Indeed, one could argue that this philosophical tradition is inconceivable without a conception of what it means to be alone. Existential-phenomenological philosophers and analysts have devoted themselves at length to this topic. Using Fromm-Reichmann's article as a guide, I will focus on the way in which the existential-phenomenological tradition addresses the problem of loneliness.

The work of the existential-phenomenologists allows us to appreciate that a clinical understanding of loneliness can only be achieved from the perspective of love and empathy. I will suggest that loneliness and love are inherently related. For thinkers and analysts in the existential-phenomenological tradition, each person is independent and unique, striving for individually defined meaning and purpose in life, as well as fundamentally relational and social, dependent upon others to become more fully human (Fiscalini, 1994; Carter, 2000). It is precisely this conception of human experience as both personal and interpersonal, or individual and social, which provides the basis for a concept of loneliness that is grounded in the human capacity for love.

For many contemporary observers, the existential-phenomenological tradition may seem oddly dated. Was it not the existentialists who insisted on dressing in nothing but black, wearing their chapeaus at a raked angle, carrying Sartre's *Being and Nothingness* under their arm, and smoking unfiltered Galoises? What can this kind of existentialism add to a smoke-free postmodern world that celebrates difference and otherness? The difficulty when discussing the existential-phenomenological tradition is that one-sided stereotypes abound. More often than not, psychoanalysts (Wolstein, 1971; Hanly, 1979; Mitchell, 1988) associate existential-phenomenology with the isolated Cartesian mind and Sartre's (1943) notion of free will. While I think it is fair to describe some existential-phenomenological thinkers as having a proclivity towards developing theories of human separateness and mortality, others, as we shall see, provide lively accounts of the abiding human need for attachment and the nature of love. Indeed, it is the very combination of, and contrast between, these two approaches that will be of issue here.

I will turn first to the tradition of Soren Kierkegaard, Friedrich Nietzsche, and Martin Heidegger, all of whom emphasize the centrality of human separateness and individuation. Fromm-Reichmann (1959) notes in particular Kierkegaard's account of loneliness. For Kierkegaard, the sense of being cut-off and solitary is both very distressing and painful as well as culturally determined. Indeed, each of these thinkers provides a rich and deep account of loneliness, akin to the approach that Fromm-Reichmann herself develops, namely, a sense of aloneness that can become uncommunicable, private, and severe.

Both Kierkegaard and Nietzsche appear to have suffered greatly from deep depressions in which they felt wholly severed from any sense of relatedness or community (Burston & Frie, 2006). Not surprisingly perhaps, this theme is deeply ingrained in their work. Both thinkers, moreover, share a kind of fervent antipathy toward groups. Kierkegaard tends to lump all forms of society and social action together under the derisive category of "the crowd." Nietzsche presents a different but equally scathing appraisal of groups, altogether rejecting both the possibility of collective experience as well as self-authorship.

For Kierkegaard, a deep-seated loneliness is an inescapable fact of our life, the sole antidote for which is the courage of faith. He suggests that a leap of religious faith provides the means to confront despair through courage; without it, we remain alienated from the ground of our being. Revelation and recovery are achieved through a confrontation with the despair that resides in the loneliness of our being, yet this loneliness is never to be outstripped. Indeed, the pursuit of genuine self-knowledge cements the profound solitude and interiority of the true Christian, as opposed to the tepid, complacent piety of "Christiandom" (Kierkegaard, 1968).

Despite Kierkegaard's noted proclivity toward isolated individualism, it is Nietzsche who most often conveys the image of the brooding, pessimistic philosopher. Indeed, his negative worldview was perhaps only outdone by the unadulterated pessimism of his mentor, Arthur Schopenhauer. Nietzsche's life is both fascinating and tragic. He ultimately succumbed to illness and insanity by way of syphilis. He believed that creative originality is central to life. Such creativity is only achieved in states of constructive aloneness that separate us from the anonymity of everyday society. Indeed, genuine self-knowledge can only be acheived through the overthrow of mass religion and its slave morality. Ultimately, Nietzsche's concept of the authentic individual—the so-called *Uebermensch*—overcomes the need for sociality precisely because he or she is above the chattering masses. Yet we also know from his biography that Nietzsche felt deeply alone, especially in the latter stages of his intensely creative and productive life. After his death in 1900, his legacy was for many years besmirched by the political opportunism of his sister who selectively published her brother's writings in order to further her own right wing agenda.

For Kierkegaard and Nietzsche alike, loneliness is an unavoidable condition of our humanity that must be endured, lest we be reduced to the masses that seek solace in the banality of everyday existence. For Kierkegaard (1968), a crowd is in its very concept an "untruth," by reason of the fact that it renders the individual completely impenitent and irresponsible. Nietzsche presents an equally scathing perspective when he declares: "The masses deserve notice in three respects only: first as faded copies of great men produced on paper with worn out instruments, then as a force of resistance to great men, finally as instruments in the hands of great men" (Nietzsche, 1983, p.113). For Kierkegaard and Nietzsche, loneliness is implicit in the very notion of separateness they so idealize. It is almost as though loneliness defines the life that is lived fully and authentically.

The theme of a separate, authentic existence is more fully developed by Heidegger (1927) in his famous work, *Being and Time*. In his existential-ontology, the state of authenticity is an utterly individualized experience (*Jemeinigkeit*) that cannot be shared. Aloneness becomes an ontological necessity that exists in the moment of confrontation with our mortality. If this state of aloneness and anxiety can be endured, it provides an opportunity for greater self-understanding and authenticity. When persons are confronted with the anxiety of their own mortality—"being-towards-death"—they are faced with a choice of whether to act on this awareness. A person can choose to live more fully with an awareness of life's finitude, or flee a sense of being alone and surrender to an inauthentic and potentially anguished life in the masses (*das Man*). Although Heidegger emphasizes that human beings are fundamentally social and contextualized beings, defined by their "being-with" in a world of others, the process of achieving authenticity is curiously, if not severely, detached from others.

Lest the existential-phenomenological tradition be seen as exclusively devoted to such themes as separateness, loneliness, and impending death, it is important to recognize an alternative perspective that views human existence through the lens of relatedness (Frie, 1997, 2000). This perspective is equally a part of the existential-phenomenological tradition, but often overlooked by English-speaking observers. Fromm-Reichmann is personally and philosophically connected with this alternative, intersubjective perspective which provides a philosophical grounding for her article. She is especially appreciative of the Swiss psychoanalyst and philosopher, Ludwig Binswanger, and, by extension, Martin Buber, whom she knew personally. This pairing of Binswanger and Buber is fortuitous.

An erstwhile student of Freud and Heidegger, Binswanger seeks to provide a phenomenological account of human experience that avoids privileging separation over relatedness. Binswanger's clinical interest in the nature of relatedness and the interpersonal realm led him to develop trenchant critiques of both Freud and Heidegger. In Binswanger's (1942) view, Freud's theory of libido fails to account for the phenomenological reality of interpersonal love, which he sees as central to the field of psycho-analysis. Similarly, he suggests that Heidegger's approach to authentic existence overlooks the importance of love and thus fails to account for the role of other human beings in the achievement of self-understanding and authenticity.

According to Binswanger, psychoanalytic practice and theory are premised on the potential for achieving a type of loving I-Thou relationship. This form of interpersonal love is grounded in the possibility of empathic attunement and based on the immediacy and shared presence of the other person. In order to develop this perspective on human relating, Binswanger turned to the work of the philosopher, Martin Buber, and his concept of I and Thou (Buber, 1923). Binswanger wrote in a letter to Buber: "I not only follow in your every step, but see in you an ally, not only against Kierkegaard, but also against Heidegger. Although I am methodologically deeply indebted to Heidegger, I take exception to his conception of Dasein (as mine). . . . It is very important that you want to achieve a conceptualization of human interaction" (Buber, 1973, p.621). Not by chance perhaps, Binswanger's clinical interest in the work of Buber is shared by a number of contemporary interpersonal and relational analysts, all of whom have discussed the clinical relevance of Buber's ideas (Ehrenberg, 1992; Aron, 1996; Frederickson, 2000).

Buber argues that human beings can never be fully understood apart from relationships. The problem of relation, or dialogical life, is central to his entire philosophy. He maintains that each component of a relation "considered by itself is a mighty abstraction. The individual is a fact of existence insofar as he steps into a living relation with other individuals. . . . The fundamental fact of human existence is human being with human being" (1965, p.203). The character of a relationship is always determined by which of the basic words is spoken: when I-Thou is said, the I is different from the I that speaks the primary word I-It. "I-Thou can only be spoken with the whole being. The primary word I-It can never be spoken with the whole being" (1923, p.54). Dialogue, in this sense, is not only a mode of linguistic communication, but denotes the interhuman dimension generally.

Like Buber, Binswanger emphasizes the dialogical nature of human existence. Human beings develop and exist through interaction with others. In *Basic Forms and Knowledge of Human Existence*, Binswanger (1942) delineates different forms of social existence—dual, plural, and singular modes—oriented toward the achievement of authenticity or self-understanding in loving dialogue with another person. Binswanger's aim is to elaborate the structure or character of a loving I-Thou relationship that permits that achievement of self-understanding. This objective also has clinical significance because it is precisely in and through an I-Thou relationship that growth and change become possible.

According to Binswanger, the I-Thou relationship is based on interpersonal love and is characterized by mutuality, openness, and immediacy. Sullivan makes a surprisingly closely related point: "When love occurs, another person matters as much to you as do you yourself." Under such conditions, "It is quite possible to talk to this person as you have never talked to anyone before." For Sullivan, "the relatively uncomplicated experience of love is entirely ennobling. Sympathy flows from it. Tolerance as a respect for people—not as an intellectual detachment from prejudice—follows it like a bright shadow" (Sullivan, 1953a, p.43).

The problem of dialogical life, and the possibility of love, become central to practice and theory alike. The potential for love is not simply a means to an end. Rather, the other person is a participant in the process of self-understanding. On this basis, Binswanger suggests the I-Thou relation forms a basic facet of human experience, alongside loneliness. Indeed, he suggests the opposite of an I-Thou relation is the frozen isolation of schizoid detachment or psychotic delusion.

Binswanger relates his discussion of utterly individualized existence to the experience of severe loneliness, which can be characterized by a state of utter hopelessness. As Fromm-Reichman (1959) states in her essay on loneliness: "I think that Binswanger has come nearest to a philosophical and psychiatric definition of loneliness when he speaks of it as 'naked existence,' 'mere existence,' and 'naked horror,' and when he characterizes lonely people as being 'devoid of any interest in any goal'" (1959, p.12). This type of loneliness renders people who suffer from it emotionally paralyzed and helpless because it carries the threat of being entirely incommunicable. Sullivan (1953b) likewise states that abject loneliness is "the exceedingly unpleasant and driving experience connected with an inadequate discharge of the need for human intimacy, for interpersonal intimacy" (p.290).

In seeking to define loneliness, the existential-phenomenological tradition can help us make an important distinction between the loss of a sense of relatedness and the loss of relatedness (Stolorow, 2007). The loss of a sense of relatedness is akin to a form of loneliness that is often described by depressed persons who feel isolated and shut off from others. The loss of relatedness, by contrast, is akin to delusional or psychotic states of mind in which the psychotic person quite literally exists in a private world of their own making. It is precisely this loss of relatedness that spurred Fromm-Reichman's interest. "The kind of loneliness I am discussing is nonconstructive if not disintegrative, and it shows in, or leads ultimately to, the development of psychotic states" (1959, p.2).

For Binswanger, who worked with many schizophrenics, the loss of relatedness is central to understanding the range of human experience. In the development of delusional and psychotic states, contact with others becomes meaningless, determined neither by desire nor will, as evidenced by the psychotic person who believes she is communicating with extraterrestial beings, or who exists within a private language and syntax. The utter loss of relatedness described by Binswanger is closely associated with Lacan's conception of "the Real" in which psychotic experience is characterized by the loss of meaningful speech (Lacan, 1977). In a similar sense, Sullivan (1953a) considers the loss of relatedness which, as he says, "actually menaces one's survival" (p.48) the core of psychotic symptom formation. For Binswanger and Sullivan alike, the psychotic is able to return from a state of delusion only through the repair of his or her relations with other people and the world. Similarly for Lacan, the psychotic is only able to gain a sense of relatedness through his or her reemergence in the symbolic order of language.

On this basis then, Binswanger and the existential-phenomenological tradition show us the way in which relatedness and loneliness are each facets of human experience. Like Kierkegaard, Nietzsche, and Heidegger, Binswanger recognizes that self-understanding can be achieved in states of introverted self-reflection and creativity, but he sees such experiences as separate from, and secondary to, the shared nature of most human experience. He specifically cautions that the celebration of separateness is at odds with the relational nature of therapeutic work which is based on the interaction of its participants. For Binswanger (1955), the analyst is not simply treating the patient, but sharing in his or her existence. What is crucial when working with patients, according to Binswanger, is the relationship itself, which always involves both participants. The aim of psychoanalysis, for Binswanger and Sullivan alike, is to provide the patient with the opportunity to glimpse the possibility of change through a process of mutuality.

To be sure, the relational nature of the analytic setting cannot simply ameliorate severe loneliness. The dreadful sense of isolation that follows emotional trauma, or the loss of relatedness associated with temporary psychosis, creates enormous clinical challenges. By providing the potential for shared experience of a range of emotional states, the therapeutic relationship allows for the reemergence of a sense of relatedness. In the process, the patient may experience a concomitant lessening of the sense of singularity, loneliness, and emotional estrangement. This therapeutic process is dependent upon a careful and caring attunement to the other, one that, for Binswanger, Buber, and others, is necessarily grounded in the possibility of interpersonal love.

Psychoanalysis, on this view, is a means of engaging, and even expanding, the potential to relate. The therapeutic relationship helps the other to experience a form of emotional intimacy. Through such intimacy one becomes sensitive to the needs, possibilities, and limitations that characterize human existence, be they states of loneliness or love.

Drawing on the different existential-phenomenological perspectives, I have suggested that loneliness be seen not as secondary to the potential for loving, but a state of being that is equally relevant and present in human experience. At the same time, loneliness should not be valued above connection or sociality. While self-experience can never take place outside of social contexts, it may seem alternatively separate from and connected to others. On this view, human experience can be characterized as a continuous movement between the two possible modes of being which are indelibly connected. The challenge is that when selfhood is conceptualized as relational or social in nature, it becomes difficult to account for our basic sense of aloneness and states of loneliness. Similarly, when selfhood is viewed as separate and isolated, it becomes hard to account for the relational nature of human experience.

Psychoanalysis is at heart a relational endeavor that values the nature of human attachment and potential for relating to oneself and others in ways that are new or different. As such, psychoanalysis provides a means of addressing the separateness and concomitant sense of loneliness from the perspective of a loving attunement to the other. Recognition of the potential for love and relatedness can only be achieved, however, if the human potential for separateness and loneliness is acknowledged as a basic and abiding fact of human experience. As the different perspectives within the existential-phenomenological tradition suggest, neither loneliness nor love can be defined through exclusion of the other. Indeed, loneliness and love are not only inherently related, they can only be truly understood from the perspective on one another. Only thus can we appreciate the range of human experience that necessarily includes the abiding nature of loneliness along with the longing for love.

References

Aron, L. (1996). *Meeting of Minds*. Hillsdale, NJ: The Analytic Press.
Binswanger, L. (1942). *Ausgewählte Werke Band 2: Grundformen und Erkenntnis menschlichen Daseins*. M. Herzog & H. J. Braun (Eds.). Heidelberg: Asanger, 1993.
—— (1955). *Ausgewählte Vorträge und Aufsätze, bd. II: Zur Problematik der psychiatrischen Forschung und zum Problem der Psychiatrie*. Bern: Francke.
Buber, M. (1923). *I and Thou*. Trans. Walter Kaufmann. New York: Charles Scribner's Sons, 1970.
—— (1965). *Between Man and Man*. Trans. R. G. Smith. New York: MacMillan.
—— (1973). *Martin Buber Briefwechsel aus sieben Jahrzehnten, bd II: 1918–1938*. Grete Schaeder (Ed.). Heidelberg: Lambert Schneider.
Burston, D. (1991). *The Legacy of Erich Fromm*. Cambridge, MA: Harvard University Press.
—— & Frie, R. (2006). *Psychotherapy as a Human Science*. Pittsburgh: Duquesne University Press.
Carter, M. (2000). Abiding loneliness: an existential perspective on loneliness. *Second Opinion*, 3:37–54.
Ehrenberg, D. (1992). *The Intimate Edge*. New York: Norton.
Fiscalini, J. (1994). *Coparticipant Psychoanalysis: Toward a New Theory of Clinical Inquiry*. New York: Columbia University Press.

Frederickson, J. (2000). There's something youey about you: The polyphonic unity of personhood. *Contemporary Psychoanalysis*, 36:587–617.

Frie, R. (1997). *Subjectivity and Intersubjectivity in Modern Philosophy and Psychoanalysis*. Lanham, MD: Rowman and Littlefield.

—— (2000). The existential and the interpersonal: Ludwig Binswanger and Harry Stack Sullivan. *Journal of Humanistic Psychology*, 40:108–130.

Fromm-Reichmann, F. (1959). Loneliness. *Psychiatry*, 22:1–15.

Hanly, C. (1979). *Existentialism and Psychoanalysis*. New York: International Universities Press.

Heidegger, M. (1927). *Being and Time*. Oxford: Basil Blackwell, 1996.

Kierkegaard, S. (1968). *Attack upon "Christiandom."* Princeton, NJ: Princeton University Press.

Lacan, J. (1977). *Ecrits, a Selection*. A. Sheridon (Trans.). New York: Norton.

Mitchell, S. A. (1988). *Relational Concepts in Psychoanalysis*. Cambridge: Harvard University Press.

Nietzsche, F. (1983). *Untimely Meditations*. Cambridge, UK: Cambridge University Press.

Sartre, J.-P. (1943). *Being and Nothingness*. New York: Philosophical Library, 1956.

Stolorow, R. (2007). *Trauma and Human Existence: Autobiographical, Psychoanalytic, and Philosophical Reflections*. New York: Taylor and Francis.

Sullivan, H. S. (1953a). *Conceptions of Modern Psychiatry*. New York: Norton.

—— (1953b). *The Interpersonal Theory of Psychiatry*. New York: Norton.

Wolstein, B. (1971). Interpersonal relations without individuality. *Contemporary Psychoanalysis*, 7:75–80.

Part II

New forms of loneliness in cyberspace

Chapter 3

Loneliness and love-making on-line

Barbara Eisold

Recently in my practice there have been a few people—solid citizens all—
who used the internet for sexually related encounters. They seem to be
searching for a relationship which they hope will assuage a kind of
loneliness, a sense of injury, or incompleteness, sometimes after failed relationships have left them scarred. For them, the internet seems to encourage
the presentation of a pressing, often shameful aspect of themselves, a certain kind of sexual "excess," to quote Ruth Stein (1998a, b; 2008).

In a series of compelling articles, Stein painted a picture of sexual
"excess" as driven originally by the "enigmatic," over-the-top nature of the
message the nursing infant receives from the mother as she herself enjoys
the wholeness of her own sensual/sexual pleasure while nursing. Because of
the confusing nature of this communication, the infant, and later the adult,
is driven to comprehend it in sexual excess of its own. It is this passion to
comprehend, Stein hypothesizes, which explains the excessive nature of
sexuality.[1] For my patients, the goal in using the internet seems to be to
have this part of themselves met in some way, and condoned.

In thinking about sexual "excess" and its on-line display, a recent article
by Peter Fonagy (2008) on the development of sexuality comes to mind.[2]
His hypothesis is a bit different from Stein's, but may, in fact, have been
inspired by hers.[3] Based on research (a questionnaire sent to mothers and a
series of infant–mother observations), Fonagy and his co-workers found
that, in general, mothers do not feel comfortable with the sexual tension
(erection or vaginal play) of their infants. Instead, such behavior is largely
ignored. Thus it remains un-"mirrored" and does not become part of a
"congruent metabolized representation" (p.23) for the infant of his or her
emotional experience. Later in life, Fonagy hypothesizes, it is this aspect of
sexuality which contributes to both its intensity and its externalization. Un-
metabolized sexuality thus tends to become an "imposed burden" unless, or
until, it is met and shared by a partner. Pleasurable as it may be, sexual
intensity tends to exist beyond the ordinary, acceptable boundaries of the
self, according to Fonagy.

Leaving behind its origins for the moment, the internet, it seems, is an almost perfect tool for those who need to have their sexual "excess" seen, if not actually "mirrored." On the net, the presentation of a single aspect of self is assisted by the aborted communication that the technology encourages. Text messaging, because it takes place in short-hand, may be the best way to begin to stake out and exaggerate such a single aspect of self. Email messaging and the telephone may also be used. In my experience, if it does not start with pictures and/or video-texting, sex on-line eventually ends with these because seeing is the most efficient way to show one's sexual "excess" en route to having it condoned.

As a clinician listening to descriptions of these net exchanges, I have a speeded-up opportunity to learn which aspect of their sexual selves seems to be most pressing and which the least compatible with the way they otherwise view themselves. In addition, I learn if they are interested in moving on into a relationship which will include other aspects of themselves in "mutual" interaction (Urist, 1977)[4] or whether they are stuck in a less inclusive, more specifically part-focused, parallel sexuality, endlessly driven by "excess." Let me present an illustrative case.

Ms. Y

I have been seeing Ms. Y, a highly intelligent, very attractive young woman, in a once a week treatment, on and off, for a few years. In our sessions, she is often quite constrained in describing what she feels. Her speech does not always flow easily; it often seems like sound bites to me. She is an artist and has recently won considerable recognition for her work.

Ms.Y is the youngest, most successful child from a large Southern family. Both her parents had a difficult time being adults and wanted to be included as equals in their children's lives. They divorced when she was thirteen when it became known that her father had had sexual relations with an older girl, a close relative and good friend of Ms. Y's. Following the divorce, Ms. Y's relationship with her father was compli- cated, to say the least. She badly wanted attention from him, but feared that if she let down her guard, he might take sexual advantage of her, too. Thus she visited him infrequently. When she did, they spent much of the time outside, going to galleries or driving around in his convertible so he could show her off. On the telephone between visits, they related through shared ideas. Himself an artist, he introduced her to painting. He taught her about perspective, letting her practice with his materials at her mother's home.

Ms. Y always loved learning. She also enjoys the sensations of sex and the undivided male attention she experiences when engaged in it. She says, however, that because her father chose her best friend over her, she has never really believed in her own sexual appeal.

When she was barely out of adolescence, Ms. Y traveled alone to Paris. She let herself be picked up by a student, a young man, who took her to a "party" in the unfamiliar outskirts of town. At the party, all four of the participants got drunk. The men decided that each of them, in succession, should have sex with Ms. Y. Fearing that if she did not comply, they might rape her, she agreed. Although the sex was a chore, it was also physically painful. Once it was over, the men took her home. None of them ever contacted her again.

In retrospect, uncertain about what she should or could have done to protect herself in Paris, she worried that, under the influence of alcohol, she had complied much too easily. She felt terrible about herself—cheap, dirty, like a prostitute, as if her sexual parts were ugly and dispensable. With her shame came increased confusion about her attractiveness. What was she good enough for exactly, she wondered, sexually and otherwise?

With age, as an outcome of her earlier experiences, Ms. Y has passionately wanted to prove to herself that she has "the power" to be sexually attractive to men. To her, "power" is about being seen, first as beautiful enough to entice men to her, and then as being good enough to give sexual pleasure in a loving, long-term relationship, in which needs are reciprocally met. Along with these intense sexual wishes, however, Ms. Y has never wanted to be perceived as "good only for that" (to quote her). She has wanted men to appreciate her mind and artistic abilities as well.

Ms. Y has had two unsatisfying, long-term, live-in, love relationships. Sex and pleasure in both had diminished over time because it became boringly routine. She "cheated" in both relationships because, she says, she felt "driven" to have her "looks" reaffirmed by outsiders.

Otherwise, until recently, Ms. Y's relationships with men were short-lived. As in Paris, they included a considerable amount of both alcohol and sex. In addition, she tried in each case to serve the man sexually (believing that this was the thing to do) and got no satisfaction (or appreciation) in return. After a number of these encounters and the discussions between us that followed, Ms. Y. was able to cut her alcohol consumption considerably. As a consequence, her willingness to give her self profligately decreased.

For nine months when she had no steady boyfriend, Ms Y carried on an on-line sexual relationship, initiated by a married man, Mr. D, whom she met at her gallery. Text and email messaging led to video texting. For the first few months following these discussions, this pair shared little about their lives and rarely referred to one another by name. But they did expose one portion of their respective anatomies at a time to one another. She teased slowly while he showed how "big" he was. Soon he was masturbating, his genitals taking up the entire screen. They experimented a great deal. This allowed Ms. Y to see his sexual "excess" which he focused on having her see his penis while he "got hard" (her words) by seeing her body parts and reached orgasm. Gradually she began to believe she had enough sexual power to "get him off" just by having him look at her. In this way, she was able to overcome some of her feelings of uncertainty and shame about her body. Feeling stronger as a result, she began to want much more personal interaction and in-the-flesh sexual satisfaction with him. In fact, Ms. Y gradually became possessed with the wish to have him "relate," as she put it. She wanted him to take in her "whole" self, her intelligence, as well as her body. In our sessions, she became passionate about this, connecting it to her inability ever to have a "whole" relationship with her father. On-line with Mr. D, meanwhile, she began to hold sex back and to talk about art and other interests. He ignored these maneuvers at first. It became clear that she was much better informed about their mutual field than he. Eventually, wanting to continue his relationship with her, he began to let her educate him. They talked on the telephone a bit about intellectual things. After some months, she enticed him into her office at the gallery where she kissed and pleasured him orally. It still made her feel "powerful" to please him this way she said, but his lack of reciprocity, especially to her kisses, and his unwillingness to look her in the eye, upset her. She began to think that pleasuring him orally was more demeaning than power-annointing because she was doing all the giving. With this realization, her interest in Mr. D waned.

Meanwhile, Ms. Y met Mr. R. He condoned and admired her intelligence, good looks, and sexuality. He wanted mutuality, to give as well as get. He could "relate," she said, and knew from past experience how to contend when "relating" got difficult. Eventually, she ended her relationship with Mr. D as her in-the-flesh relationship with Mr. R grew. A year after she said goodbye to Mr. D, she and Mr. R discussed marriage. When things with R have seemed particularly routine, she has been tempted by a new on-line encounter. Her feints in this direction have been brief however. Rapidly she has become bored by what she calls their one-dimensional quality.

Discussion

Sexual "excess"

There are, Ruth Stein (2008) tells us, various sorts of "excessive" sexual feelings and/or behaviors "such as an excess of physical sensations beyond regular containment . . . of desire over sensible judgment . . . of meaning beyond symbolization, and the other's ungraspable excess over me" (p.44). Variable as it may be, shame is implicit always in sexual "excess," according to Stein.

"Excess" well describes Ms. Y's driven need for sex, largely determined by a desire to overcome shame and inadequacy about her body. If these originated in her infancy (the hypothesis of both Stein and Fonagy), they were infinitely exaggerated by events that occurred later. Her father's rejection, in addition to the date-rape in Paris, left her feeling most cheapened and ashamed. She wanted to counteract these experiences through showing her body to her partner.

In the course of nine or ten months of doing just that, Ms. Y did begin to feel he valued her sexual "power" because he wanted to be exposed to it again and again. As she consistently experienced her value in this way, she was able to "metabolize" or integrate this more positive sense of herself which, in turn, led her to feel a pressing desire for greater intimacy. When she tried to get Mr. D more involved, she learned he had severe limitations. He was not interested in "seeing" more of her or in satisfying her sexually. As an outcome of the off-line, in-the-flesh contact that she contrived, she concluded that servicing his needs felt demeaning when equivalent sexual pleasuring was not returned. Ms. Y finally able to experience her sexuality as "congruent" (Fonagy, 2008) with the rest of her self, then moved on to an off-line relationship which contained greater affection, respect, and mutuality (sexually and otherwise) than any she had ever had before.

I can only speculate about Mr. D. His sexual "excess" seemed related to a pressing (shameful?) desire to have Ms. Y see how erect his penis could become and then to see it climax. He wanted to do this specifically with her, again and again. In their face to face encounters, however, he seemed to make an effort not to get to know Ms. Y in greater depth and to keep their relationship in as pornographic a mode as possible, perhaps hoping to save his marriage.[5] Whatever he gained from his relationship with Ms. Y, he never felt comfortable establishing eye contact with her. Indeed, he appeared only to want to continue things as they were.

Seeing the sexuality of the other: "Mirroring"

The effects of "mirroring," per se, are debatable, in part because the term is often used as a naive metaphor for the "the complexity actually occurring when one is seeing oneself being seen" (Reis, 2004, p.349).[6] Winnicott (1967) among others (Benjamin 1988) well described the complexity that can take place in a relationship through eye contact, as one partner returns to the other a vision of him or herself which alters the original image. Those who believe eye contact (called "mirroring" by them) is important to growth (Balsam, 2008; Elise, 2008) understand that its effect continues beyond infancy. In my own work (Eisold, 2005), in some situations, eye contact has at times seemed crucially important to the preservation of a positive self-image and can partially contradict otherwise negative, extremely self-destructive intentions.

Seeing another on-line is different entirely from ordinary, face-to-face contact. A most important aspect of on-line contact is the distance it establishes. In addition, it breaks communication down into frame-by-frame steps, the content of which is under each person's control. While subject A is filling the screen with a chosen part of his body, he observes only the response that subject B chooses to show. Because A's face is generally out of view, he is not called upon to give back anything beyond the image he has already presented. Mr. D was able to look at Ms. Y's eyes or (more likely) imagine her gaze while he showed her his erect penis. She, in turn, could (and did) watch, not his eyes, but his erection (because that is what he chose to show her) as it grew, in response to the pictures he was shown of her body parts, manipulated and otherwise, as she chose. She interpreted his response as a measure of her power to affect him. Although this reassured her about the allure of her body, it was, in the end, precisely the absence of in-the-flesh eye contact which frustrated her and drove her to want more. For Ms. Y (and apparently not for Mr. D) the distance and control allowed by the video exchange hastened the speed with which she was able to overcome shame and "metabolize" a more positive sense of her body. At the same time, it helped her to crystallize her need for a relationship less pornographic (less for the sake of sexual excitement alone) and more inclusive of both herself and her partner, in mutual gaze and satisfaction.

Clearly, we need more information about the ways in which on-line sexual contact may (or may not) assist people in learning about their sexuality. In addition, we need to know more about the origins of sexual feelings, as they relate to other aspects of self development. Meanwhile, descriptions of on-line sex continue to be useful to me, as a clinician.

Notes

1 Stein's work is based on the work of, among others, Freud (1905, 1908), Laplanche (1995), and Bataille (1957).
2 Fonagy describes his theory as relevant to the sexual development of men. I see no reason why it might not also apply to women.
3 In a recent, on-line discussion (JAPA netcast, 2/2009), Fonagy gives Stein credit for having contributed to his thinking about sexual development.
4 In 1977 Jeffrey Urist developed a scale to measure the degree to which responses to Rorschach ink blots were perceived in terms of "Mutuality of Autonomy" (p.1). Other possibilities, presumably less articulated than relating to the other as mutually autonomous, included a relationship enjoyed in parallel activity, or leaning on another, or imitating another absolutely, or controlling another, etc. Although the internet is not a Rorschach and thus his scale is not absolutely applicable, I have found Urist's concepts useful in many ways for many years.
5 A year or so after his on-line relationship with Ms. Y that had served to assuage a kind of loneliness, a sense of incompleteness, Mr. D's marriage ended in divorce, according to Ms. Y.
6 For example, in a recent JAPA netcast (2009), an on-line discussion of Fonagy (2008), Richard Friedman remarked that he has doubts that much will be made of the power of "mirroring" when and if it is ever studied in a rigorous way.

References

Balsam, R. H. (2008). Women showing off: notes on female exhibitionism. *Journal of the American Psychoanalytic Association*, 56:99–121.

Bataille, G. (1957). *Eroticism, Death and Sensuality*. Trans. L. Dalwood. San Francisco: City Lights Books, 1986.

Benjamin, J. (1988). *The Bonds of Love*. New York: Pantheon.

Eisold, B. K. (2005). Notes on life-long resilience: perceptual and personality factors implicit in the creation of a particular adaptive style. *Psychoanalytic Psychology*, 22:411–425.

Elise, D. (2008). Sex and shame: the inhibition of sexual desire. *Journal of the American Psychoanalytic Association*, 56:73–98.

Fonagy, P (2008). A genuinely developmental theory of sexual enjoyment and its implications for psychoanalytical technique. *Journal of the American Psychoanalytic Association*, 56:11–36.

Freud, S. (1905). Three Essays on the Theory of Sexuality. *S.E.*, 7.

—— (1908). On the sexual theories of children. *S.E.*, 9.

JAPA Netcast: APA Psa-NETCAST: February, 2009. Topic: "A Genuinely Developmental Theory of Sexual Enjoyment and its Implications for Psychoanalytic Technique" by Peter Fonagy. Moderator: Robert White. At JPN@LS.Psychoanalysis.net.

Laplanche, J. (1995). Seduction, persecution, revelation. *International Journal of Psycho-Analysis*, 76:663–682.

Reis, B. E. (2004). You are requested to close the eyes. *Psychoanalytic Dialogues*, 14:349–371.

Stein, R. (1998a). The enigmatic dimension of sexual experience: the "otherness" of sexuality. *Psychoanalytic Quarterly*, 67:594–625.

—— (1998b). The poignant, the excessive and the enigmatic in sexuality. *International Journal of Psycho-Analysis*, 79:253–268.

—— (2008). The otherness of sexuality. *Journal of the American Psychoanalytic Association*, 56:43–71.

Urist, J. (1977). The Rorschach test and the assessment of object relations. *Journal of Personality Assessment*, 41:3–4.

Winnicott, D. W. (1967). Mirror role of mother and family in child development. In: *Playing and Reality*. New York: Basic Books, 1971.

Chapter 4

Less lonely in second life? A psychologist goes under cover in virtual reality

John O'Leary

The prospect of a new generation hooked on video games is alarming enough. Now the technology that got us there is voyaging to increasingly bizarre destinations. The on-line parallel universe of Second Life has become, arguably, first home to millions of adults and youngsters who sit long hours at their computers engaged in simulation of daily life. Second Life is a virtual reality platform in which participants invent a physical and social persona, called an avatar. They live through this computer-animated image and navigate the host environment with the click of a mouse. It is estimated (Boellstorff, 2008) that during one month in 2008, Second Lifers spent nearly 30 million hours inworld.

Does this technological novelty provide, for better or worse, some means of dealing with feelings of loneliness and alienation? Does computer-enhanced fantasy life in Second Life (SL) presage an evolutionary leap or a dead end in the human capacity for relatedness? What is the compelling attraction of SL that has driven its enormous success? This writer became interested when a colleague called attention to SL's possibilities for my studies into increasing rates of depression in a technological society. It seemed that SL might provide a conveniently structured environment in which to glean insight and frame new questions. In this spirit, I embarked on a personal experiment with SL, the major focus of this article. My brief odyssey in SL is framed here in the context of selected literature to illuminate both sides of the argument posed above.

Launched in 2004 by Linden Labs, the Internet-based, 3-D world of SL grew to an adult population of 15 million by 2008. A similarly successful teen spin-off prepares the next generation for life in the metaverse, also called the grid. While about half of SL residents are from the U.S., thirty-seven other countries are represented. Membership among Asians, especially South Koreans, is very high. The Swedish Government has established an embassy within SL, and Harvard, Stanford, and New York University provide educational opportunities for its residents. Large corporations such as IBM, Chrysler, Sony, Nike, and Adidas have purchased "space" for development within its cyber-boundaries equivalent to twenty times the size of Manhattan. These commercial activities are supported by SL's internal economy, based on Linden dollars that can be converted into real money (Meadows, 2008).

Far more than a video game, I soon discovered, SL's cutting-edge software allows residents to interact in a fully elaborated, computer-generated social context. Not only do they converse, they buy homes, start businesses and careers, travel (in the blink of an eye), attend cultural events, enjoy wild parties, make friends, and find romantic partners. The virtual community attempts to simulate the complexity of real life. Within its programmed limitations and minimal rules of conduct, it offers an unthreatening avenue for exploring identities, fantasies, and yearnings. For many, on-line existence in SL appears to provide a successful means to dissipate feelings of loneliness and isolation.

As an outsider prowling the website, I became increasingly curious as to whether SL might be viewed as part of a problem, part of the solution, or possibly both. It was immediately clear that pure scientific detachment would hamper observation. The only way to grasp the phenomenon would be to join it, and experience it first-hand. So, I signed on and became a resident to study SL from within.

Inworld

The first step of this undercover adventure was the construction of my personal avatar, complete with costume and all moving parts. It expresses how you want to be seen in this other world. Age, sex, race, and all other individual and demographic characteristics are within one's power to choose. The graphics software that permits this invention has limitations. There is a visual sameness to avatars and the SL environment, both natural and architectural. Mine, a somewhat heroic-looking SL everyman, was dubbed Nine Borin.

Most daunting for me was the steep learning curve in building and manipulating Nine Borin in his virtual world—especially since I had little experience in video gaming. Gradually, I became adept at directing my alter ego to explore a dazzling array of shops, malls, beaches, parks, and public venues of every kind. I encountered other residents, introduced myself, and was invited to visit their homes. The experience was immediately social, interactive, and noncompetitive.

What distinguishes SL from all other video platforms is that it is not a game; there are no dragons to slay, no points to be earned, and no prevailing myth or narrative such as rescuing a Queen, or getting safely back to earth. Instead, you create a self and life narrative, just as you want it to be. It is all about you. There is headiness in this, a definite feeling of being in control.

During my time on the grid, I met many apparently warm and interesting people. SL has a large representation of artists and, unsurprisingly, a significant number of computer literati. Most avatars I got to know seemed young and well-educated. Of course, it was impossible to peer behind their SL personae, any more than they could determine how closely I matched the one I had generated. Despite this dissociation, I had a sense of interactive connection, a startling contradiction since the actual senses are in no way involved. There is no sound, touch, taste, or smell. What you see is disembodied, displaced from reality, but powerfully convincing in its own way. Acceptance of this develops as you associate with the other residents. It happens quickly, incrementally, and seductively. At times, it is actually fun.

Just as quickly, however, come startling moments of rejection. Residents are free to associate with whomever they want and under no obligation to observe simple courtesies. They vanish abruptly. You wonder what you've done or said, and the onus suddenly rests on your shoulders, not your avatar's.

Early on, I strolled Nine Borin through a vast shopping mall where I encountered a group chatting (this means instant messaging) about purchasing a home. Why would one need a home, I cautiously intruded in their conversation, when you don't sleep or eat there? One avatar, a real estate agent on a mission, eagerly explained that a home is where you invite your friends and enjoy social gatherings. If you start a club, you can have meetings there. You could bring a date home, or share it with an online spouse or partner. Online spouse? I had not even considered such an extraordinary possibility!

My new acquaintance decided the best way to introduce me to the system would be to transport both of us to his home, and—*swoosh!*—we were teleported to the front door of a large, modern house complete with lush garden. My host graciously insisted that I step into a little stream running through the property, his pride, where I could see the water ripple gently around my virtual foot. The effect was surreal. Next, he rang the bell and his fiancée answered the door. This young, beautiful Barbie-like avatar was welcoming and eager to show me around her elegantly furnished home. In the middle of this experience, a living, breathing patient of mine arrived for a Real Life (RL) session. I was obliged to leave my desk to buzz her into the office waiting room.

Back in SL, I was now presented with a social dilemma. My host's interior decorator happened by in my brief absence. The fellow wanted to show off a magnificent fireplace he had installed on the third floor. I thought of my patient. I thought of my status as a guest in another avatar's home. It felt difficult to dislodge myself from the virtual situation to attend to the real one. I lost my way on the ground floor as I hastened to exit the house, the program, and the alternate universe.

Ten minutes late for my appointment with the patient, I apologized for tardiness but was unwilling to engage in full self-disclosure. I see this brief episode as a measure of the powerful pull the virtual experience can exert upon participants, even those who are not fully dedicated to it. I can attest to the fact that alternate reality is alluring and that the edge between SL and RL is easily blurred.

More questions than answers

Why do people become so deeply involved in SL? Many say it staves off loneliness. Second Lifers tell you they sign on to make friends. These relationships supposedly serve the same function as RL friendships, but are often perceived by residents as closer or more varied, even though physical closeness is impossible, and any emotional connection must leap a technological divide. Self-disclosure in SL is fiction; honesty is whatever you say. Nevertheless, Second Lifers appear to derive some measure of satisfaction from synthetic intimacy.

The graphics software severely limits true individuality. One sees ubiquitous macho muscle and feminine curve. Most avatars have a stereotyped appearance of sexuality and behave accordingly. They generally express enthusiasm for romance, party hard, hook up, and never have to worry about safe sex. Some claim to enjoy a kind of virtual polygamy where a long-term SL relationship parallels a real-world marriage. Second Lifers do not age.

It is noteworthy that I experienced loneliness, unmistakable and full-blown, wandering around empty lots, unoccupied buildings, beaches, and theme parks. There is a great deal of empty space in virtual reality. The people you meet may disappear in a second. They're just going offline and don't mean to insult you, but it takes some getting used to. This might engender abandonment anxiety in individuals so disposed.

As psychoanalysts, how are we to understand all this? On one hand, SL would seem to characterize a schizoid and decidedly lonely adaptation. At the very least it would appear to foster the very detachment that we professionals work so hard with our patients to repair. The hours spent in virtual reality substitute a false sense of connection for the real thing. Hunching over a computer all day, in actual solitude, takes away time that might be devoted to real relationships and the learning this entails.

Ellen Toronto (2009) underscores the need for ebb and flow between fantasy and reality, the imaginative and the concrete, to develop and maintain normal individuation. She warns that Internet over-involvement can create an imbalance difficult to deal with in the analytic setting. Virtual activity "may become sequestered, outside of time, intensely private, couched in shame, and usually underreported. It can thus remain a personal space, the repository of dissociated thoughts and emotions" (p.121). Of dissociation in the virtual world, she writes: "When the world of fantasy in any form becomes a seductive alternative that breaks with ongoing experience, it disrupts the biographical narrative that is critical to the development of agency and the functioning of the relational self" (p.121).

Second Lifers counter criticism that they lose themselves in fantasy by saying the time spent inworld is far less passive and isolating than watching TV. They believe RL is enhanced rather than diminished by SL participation. The fascinating Stanford Study (Nie & Lutz, 2000), short and somewhat controversial, argues both sides of this question and supports my own unwillingness to assume the negative position unconditionally.

Certainly, from the moment you enter SL, you are challenged to learn something new, from operating your avatar to negotiating within the terms and norms of the community. Formal learning opportunities exist as well. Residents may actually develop social skills by trying on a fantasized self. A strong argument might be made for the practice a socially inexperienced, insecure individual might get as a contributing member of this safe, unthreatening society. Could this help develop a baseline of confidence and savvy in the same way that flight simulators are used to train pilots before they take to the skies? In SL, you can experiment with being bold, sexual, nasty (griefers), political, creative—almost anything you are afraid to try in real life, including tolerance, one of the few virtues encoded in Linden Labs guidelines for SL.

It is equally arguable that the illusion of human interaction obviates the need to risk seeking the real thing. And what about the issues of deception and secrecy, authenticity, and owning who one is? Your personal avatar might resemble you slightly, or not at all, and can be altered, drastically, in seconds. Some create multiple personae. These possibilities suggest certain personality disorders with which we are all familiar. A resident's choice to invest time this way might further entrench self-destructive behavior or aggravate pathology while keeping these problems "under the radar."

Some Second Lifers create an avatar of a different gender, and may never reveal their own. Is this inherently deceitful, or does it create an opportunity to "try it on for size," or to develop through experience some genuinely new perceptions of the opposite sex? Perhaps. On the other hand, it might just confirm already stereotyped and "objectified" notions of relationships, as has shown to be the case with pornography (Carnes, 2001).

It is as easy to add to these questions and arguments, pro or con, as it is to be critical or dismissive of them. My own hands-on exposure to virtual living did not produce a clear-cut answer, nor did it satisfy curiosity. A course of interest and objectivity seems prudent because any rush to judgment may be moot, and Second Life is not likely to go away any time soon.

The popularity of the product, its global and rapidly growing usage, suggests there will be more of this kind of thing in the future. It behooves our professional community to study the effects of technologically simulated social environments on their participants, especially in regard to the issues of loneliness and alienation. Such research should not be difficult to design. One avenue of particular interest to me is the role of neuroplasticity, the capacity of brain neuron clusters to re-colonize, to service or replace a diminished function. Recovery from a stroke often involves such an alteration. The brain is able to allocate different areas to handle disabled functions where only clumps of destroyed neurons remain. The brain determines other regions that can, at least partially, compensate for a functional loss. One might say the brain is not hardwired, that it is "neuroplastic" with respect to many functions.

Considerable evidence (Doidge, 2007) supports the idea that communication processes benefit from neuroplasticity. For example, when people learn to write, large sections of their brains are colonized to enable intricate eye-hand coordination, and to increase the individual's capacity to mature in this skill. Whenever there is a massive shift to a new communication channel, this kind of restructuring takes place. Studies show that television, and especially the Internet with its incredible processing speeds, place a premium on what is termed "scanning surfaces." Neural redistribution to accommodate this need tends to make deep attention to content, such as in reading a book, more difficult. This is because fewer neurons are being maintained at the older, "reading" sites.

Teachers have been reporting on these phenomena for quite some time. Nicholas Carr (2008), in *Harper's Magazine*, writes convincingly about this tradeoff. He suggests we risk turning into pancake people as we connect with the vast network of information accessed by the Internet. The kind of deep reading that a sequence of printed pages demands is valuable not just for the knowledge we acquire from words, but also for the intellectual vibrations those words set off within our minds. As the neuroplasticians say: use it or lose it.

What does the concept of neuroplasticity harbinger in a world where increasing amounts of brain activity are handed over to a virtual life of limitless simulations of friendship, love, cooperation, competition, and to skills that are reduced to manipulation by a computer mouse? Will spending so much time in simulated living disable or re-wire neural capacities for genuine intimacy and relatedness? Will there be shrinkage in RL capacities as SL capacities are strengthened and expanded? Will real-life skill sets and their respective neural pathways become endangered—like the polar bear? This is scary stuff, Matrix-like in its possibilities and, at the very least, worrisome. Perhaps it is our responsibility as psychologists and psychoanalysts to warn society of these dangers, locating and describing the pathologies new technology, novelties like SL, may engender.

We might, however, better fulfill our responsibility by becoming more familiar with the inevitably evolving technologies. Our task might be to de-mystify the virtual world, explore its possibilities, and find out how to derive benefit from what people are actually doing and will inevitably continue to do—no matter what we say.

A postmodernist view—and additional thoughts

Some in our field propose new possibilities for psychoanalytic theory with the advent of the Internet, chat rooms, and virtual realities. Sherry Turkle (1997) argued years ago that the boundary between people and technology is arbitrary and becoming harder to maintain. Today, millions spend hours at a time attached to portable visual and auditory devices, talking, living, and breathing in essentially a different place. This illustrates the moving boundary to which she refers, as do highly adapted artificial limbs and writing devices animated by the brain (like Stephen Hawking's) with which the user merges, identifies, and becomes one.

Turkle's basic position is that our notion of a unitary self is illusionary to begin with. In her view, we constantly move between various self states, various aspects of being. The experience of playing at different selves in alternate cyber contexts, perhaps even at the same time on multiple windows, reifies another way of thinking about the self, not as unitary, but as multiple. For her, this mobility is a good thing. It enables us to function; it reflects how things actually are.

To support this notion, Turkle cites Phillip Bromberg's (2001) view that dissociative experience comes not only from severe trauma but also from nontraumatic early interpersonal experiences that may be reactivated in the therapeutic relationship. He offered that such states are far more common than we think. He was not the first to suggest the mind does not function in a unitary fashion, with a single self state prevailing. Turkle (2005) exemplifies the postmodern assault against the notion of "one human nature" with a bounded, singular self. "Psychological health is not tanta-mount to achieving a state of oneness, but the ability to make fluid transitions among the many and to reflect on our-selves by standing in a space between states" (p.72).

These tantalizing insights might cast cyber-living in a very rosy light. SL might be viewed as a kind of fitness venue where the individual can work out, develop strength and flexibility for transitions and to avoid emotional cramp. Perhaps loneliness and alienation could be eased by learning to maintain better balance in the space between states. Virtual reality has been accepted in some professional circles as a useful adjunct to therapy in treatment for phobias and PTSD.

A CBS/AP report (2007), however, suggests the possibly addictive nature of video games. Debate heats up in the blogosphere. One side likens the games to hard drugs. Parents agonize over the reclusive, self-destructive behavior of their teenagers. Solid citizens recount the dissolution of their careers as a result of getting hooked. Online Gamers Anonymous, a non-profit self-help program, was formed in 2002 to support sufferers of computer game addiction. It is said that the American Psychiatric Association may include it as a category in their new Diagnostic and Statistical Manual of Mental Disorders (DSM-5).

On the other side, some "experts," and of course software marketers, dismiss the idea of negative effects from video game preoccupation. They propose that almost any habitual behavior, such as text messaging, might qualify as addictive, if gaming does. A hopeful view is held by Mychilo S. Cline (2005) whose webpage describes him as "a leading thinker and pioneer in the field of Virtual Ethics and Design." He sees the eventual integration of SL type worlds into the social fabric. He feels that media coverage of the nascent technology has built up false and premature expectations. It obscures possibilities he sees that virtual environments might ultimately be used to "extend basic human rights into virtual space, to promote human freedom and well-being, and to promote social stability as we move from one stage in socio-political development to the next." Pretty grand!

Call it harmless diversion. Call it indulgence, dependence, or full-blown addiction. Internet fantasy worlds, such as Second Life, are at the center of a serious controversy over Massively Multiplayer Online Role Playing Games. The satisfaction derived from MMORPGs depends on the feelings of success and self-esteem experienced in alternate reality, and on the amount of time engaged in play. In this familiar dynamic, the more you play, the better you feel; and the better you feel, the more you want to play. Thus, virtual worlds like Second Life encourage increased involvement in an activity that is self-perpetuating and perpetual.

Whether the reader is inclined to view Second Life as wave of the future, the embodiment of alienation, or simply an acceptable and possibly thera-peutic way to expand the sense of self and address the pain of loneliness, there is clearly much more to be learned. As for me, I am still more interested in the questions than I am certain of the answers. The jury is still out.

References

Boellstorff, T. (2008). *Coming of Age in Second Life*. New Jersey: Princeton University Press.

Bromberg, P. (2001). *Standing In the Spaces: Essays on Clinical Process*. New York: The Analytic Press.

Carnes, P. (2001). *Out of the Shadows: Understanding Sexual Addictions*. Minneapolis, MN: Hazelden.

Carr, N. (2008). Is Google making us stupid? *Atlantic*, July/August.

CBS report. (2007). *Ovecoming Internet Addiction*. CBS News Technology Correspondent Daniel Sieberg, June 22.

Cline, M. S. (2005). *Power, Madness, and Immortality: The Future of Virtual Reality*. Universityvillagepress.com

Doidge, N. (2007). *The Brain that Changes Itself*. New York: Penguin.

Meadows, M. (2008). *I, Avatar: The Culture and Consequences of Having a Second Life*. Berkeley, CA: Pearson/Peachpit.

Nie, N. & Lutz, E. (2000). *Study of the Social Consequences of the Internet*. Stanford, CA: Stanford Institute for the Quantitative Study of Society (SIQSS).

Toronto, E. (2009). Time out of mind: Dissociation in the virtual world. *Psychoanalytic Psychology*, 26(2):117–133.

Turkle, S. (1997). *Life on the Screen: Identity in the Age of the Internet*. New York. Simon & Schuster.

——— (1999). An Interview with Sherry Turkle, by Mike Featherstone. *The Hedgehog Review: Critical Reflections on Contemporary Culture*. Fall, vol. 1, no. 1, pp.71–84.

——— (2005). *The Second Self: Computers and the Human Spirit*, Twentieth Anniversary Edition. Cambridge, MA: MIT Press.

Chapter 5

Internal space and (dis)connection in cyberspace: Adolescent longings in a pseudo-connected society

Karen L. Lombardi

"My daughter is so popular. She has 650 names on her buddy list," a mother told me. Her pride contrasted dramatically with my horror—how is it possible to have the psychic space for 650 "buddies?" Soon after, she experienced her own horror when she received a cell phone bill for $1200 in overcalls. Her daughter had been compulsively speaking on the telephone all over the country to buddies she had never met.

With the advent of buddy lists, Myspace, and other mechanisms that promote increasingly disembodied interpersonal experiences, adolescents are increasingly connected to others they "know" only on the screen. The sense of internal loneliness can be erased in the space of a second with hundreds of buddies or, worse, with fictive personalities, criminal and otherwise, seeking to exploit the loneliness of others.

Lasch's (1978) social critique in *The Culture of Narcissism* seems to have "progressed," in our increasingly technological cybernetic culture, to a personally and culturally disembodied subjectivity that seems more schizoid than narcissistic. The long-term effects on our children have yet to reveal themselves, but what seems increasingly clear is that academic, extracurricular, and social over-scheduling, modern alterations in the structure and functioning of family life, and various forms of cybernetic communications, both in the United States and globally, have altered the ways our children live. Data on the "achievement chase" indicate increased academic pressures, including more competition for spaces in the best colleges and universities, increased and prolonged private tutoring for standardized tests, pressure to take Advanced Placement courses, and the oxymoron of required volunteer hours for high school graduation, all coexisting with steep declines in reading and studying time. Self-motivated reading has decreased most precipitously, leading some (e.g., Bauerlein, 2007) to call this a generation of bibliophobes. For many, close reading has been replaced by internet searches, which often yield superficial or inaccurate "facts." Some (e.g., Kelsey, 2007) find the phenomenon of friending on the Internet accompanied by a decrease in personal intimacy, as measured by the number of close friends teenagers report having. Real-time, real-life, face-to-face dialogue, replaced to some extent by life on the screen, mirrors a complementary decrease of face-to-face time in the family, as more and more parents (including both adults in two parent families) work, while discussions at sit-down family dinners are no longer common. Twenge's (2008) much quoted study of narcissism in undergraduates shows a 30% increase in narcissism from 1982 to 2006, as measured by the Narcissistic Personality Index. Although aspects of her methodology have been criticized (Trzesniewski et al., 2008), her research suggests that current technology, especially YouTube and MySpace, fuels narcissism. Postman (1985), in *Amusing Ourselves to Death*, describes the effect of life on the screen thus: "The screen atomizes individuals, isolating and pacifying them while purveying illusions of worldly contact" (p.124). My concern is whether these present circumstances tend to deprive children and adolescents of the solitude that, at its best, leads to personal discovery and creativity, a productive subjectivity grounded in the body and the imagination.

Denizet-Lewis' (2004) essay, "Whatever Happened to Teen Romance? (And What Is a Friend with Benefits, Anyway?)," portrays a major shift in the ways contemporary teenagers conduct relationships, which further suggests alterations in contemporary subjectivity. Writing on middle and high school culture in the U.S., he describes "an underage sexual revolution . . . where casual sex is common, online ratings are scrutinized, everybody wants to be so detached—and boys still get what they want on Saturday night" (p.30). He portrays boys and girls hanging out together as friends, occasionally hooking up with each other, or with casual acquaintances from outside the group. "Hooking up" has replaced dating. The vague term refers to any sexual encounter, from kissing to oral sex to intercourse. What marks hooking up is the absence of romantic involvement. Speaking to nearly 100 high school students, mostly white and middle class, mostly suburban and exurban from the Northeast and Midwest, Denizet-Lewis heard a common refrain: hooking up is more common than dating. Friends with benefits has replaced romance. "To a generation raised on MTV, AIDS, Britney Spears, Internet porn, Monica Lewinsky and 'Sex and the City,' oral sex is definitely not sex (it's just 'oral'), and hooking up is definitely not a big deal" (p.33). Interestingly, these teenagers believe they will somehow seamlessly move into monogamy and marriage in their mid twenties to early thirties, when they are "no longer hot."

Whereas Denizet-Lewis refers to friends with benefits as an underage sexual revolution, it seems to me more like a sexual devolution, to a place where sexuality exists as a defense, not something sought as part of a larger desire for love and intimacy. While psychoanalytic object relational theories tie eros to love, not simply to sexual drives, the current generation of young people seems to make conscious efforts to uncouple sex from emotion.

Irene, interviewed by Denizet-Lewis, had a friend with benefits whom she began to desire. When he never asked her out, she was devastated. "Since then, I've become really good at keeping my emotions in check. I can hook up with a guy and not fall for him." Melissa, who said she never had a good relationship, says, "Dating causes pain. It's easier not to get attached. And I realized that if it's O.K. for guys to play the field and have sex with 28,000 people, I should be able to, also" (p.35).

Denizet-Lewis' article mirrors my own personal and clinical experience. Many of my teenaged daughter's friends do not have boyfriends, nor do they speak about boys in tones of longing or romance. It doesn't seem they lack interest in boys, but they do lack the desire or motivation to get involved romantically or sexually. Another group of her friends do "hook up" and have reputations for doing so in all sorts of places, including the back of the school bus and semi-secluded places on campus, as well as at week-end parties. These girls are not especially stigmatized by others, nor criticized; at most, their parties are avoided. While we can see such behavior as an acting out of psychic conflicts that originate in personal relationships in the home, it also seems to be a broader cultural phenomenon with more general implications.

I first learned about hooking up from a teenaged patient who, while too reticent to provide details, wanted me to know she had casual sexual encounters with boys in her group who remained friends but never achieved "boyfriend" status. A second teenaged patient also has no boyfriends, but does hook up. Her hooking up with boys seems more to do with her relationships with her girlfriends than to any real interest in boys. She feels much more involved with her girlfriends, and is motivated to compete with and impress them. She speaks of boys in more objectifying, less personal terms. The old "possessiveness" that marked being "pinned" (wearing one's boyfriend's fraternity pin as a public statement of exclusivity) in my generation seems to be more oriented today toward girls' worries about close friends and loyalty, about being recognized by their girlfriends more than being recognized or desired by the boys they hook up with.

This apparent cultural shift does not appear in a vacuum, but is central to the families of these girls as well, with parental relationships contributing to the deployment of the body in a defensive absence of feeling. These two girls from intact families have parents in problematic relationships with each other and with their children. The mothers, both unusually narcissistic, are regarded by their daughters as "losers" who are over-invested in their daughters rather than in the meaningfulness of their own lives.

The mother of the first patient idealized her early relationship with her daughter, saying her daughter had been shy, very sweet, obedient, talented, and hardworking. The mother used to finish sentences for her daughter, which underscored for the mother not only the daughter's sweet shyness, but also their close intimacy. She used to read her daughter's mind, and now couldn't comprehend how totally lost her daughter seemed to her. My patient was desperate to create some space between herself and her mother, but failed to sustain that space outside her family, as her goodness and talents were based on mimicry of her mother's desires. In opposition, she became the disobedient, recalcitrant daughter who neglected her talents to pursue a shallow relational existence. Her deeper personal desires remained hidden to her.

The second mother treated her daughter like a possession, simultaneously over-involved in a tyrannically controlling way and emotionally detached. This artistically talented child managed to cling to those talents, but attempted to use them as an equally tyrannical defense, painting her room black to horrify her very particular, designer-oriented mother. Both mother and daughter had serious difficulties with body image. The mother's was acted out in extreme overweight, at the same time that she was dissociated from her body, unconcerned with her personal appearance but very much concerned with social appearances, showing off her privilege at every opportunity. The daughter was quite a beautiful girl who felt damaged and ugly, paying undue attention to a birth mark that she spent hours each day obsessively covering up. This mutual body dissociation contributed to my patient's hooking up as a way of projecting and controlling her self-contempt.

Driving to Vermont, I had an unexpected passenger, a friend of my daughter who is also a family friend. She asked to go with us because her parents were leaving too early—25 minutes before us. I wondered what was up, as this was a lame excuse. It turned out she wanted advice. She was upset that a close friend of hers had "hooked up" with a boy whom she wanted. What was worse was that her friend had lied to her, and she heard the truth from another girl who was considered an inveterate liar. This was all very confusing and distressing—she could not believe the person she had put her trust in, and had to believe the sexually active liar because this time the liar was telling the truth and the trustworthy friend was lying. In this complex conversation, I found the courage to ask what "hooking up" meant. She said it was not friendly kissing or kisses on the cheek, but real deep kissing that lasts more than a few seconds.

Literature on hooking up (any sexual contact, from deep kissing to intercourse) is sparse, with no reported studies before 2000 (Bogle, 2008). The studies Bogle reports, and her own research, strongly suggest that hooking up has replaced traditional dating in the current college generation. Hooking up is defined variously as a single sexual encounter with strangers or brief acquaintances, and as sexual relationships with no expectations and no strings attached. The latter definition is closer to friends with benefits, as researched by Denizet-Lewis.

Why is this term so nonspecific? We used to talk about kissing, petting, heavy petting, and "going all the way." Although they were euphemisms, we knew what they meant in a way "hooking up" does not convey. What is conveyed by that term which goes beyond the more specific past euphemisms? I now think of "hooking up" as an appetitive term. When people have boyfriends and girlfriends, they do not hook up; they have relationships. Hooking up is absent the relational ingredient; it defines what is missing. It is literally the hook by which people exploit each other's bodies, without the element of personal feeling that we felt so necessary (or hid our appetites behind). Does this constitute an increase in freedom—that we no longer need to pretend we are cherished or beloved in our pursuit of pleasure? Or is this an increase in exploitative relating, a disembodied experience of connection that focuses only on the body? I am beginning to think it is more the latter. I am reminded of the patient of a supervisee who describes her sexual activity as a two-minute foray, a sexual sound bite transferred to an anesthetized body. It seems we are speaking of psychic deadness rather than newfound or revolutionary sexual freedom. My concern is that what women and men seem to have gained from the struggles of the 1960s are in fact losses. These losses of deeply personal, embodied relationships are symptomatized in the form of 650 on-line buddies—more connections than ever before, but of a disembodied, almost fetishistic nature that masks and distorts our sense of subjectivity. The significant increase in anorexia and bulimia points in this direction too, as a form of part-object relating, not just with others, but also with ourselves and our internal constitution of our subjectivity.

The computer screen serves as metaphor (as well as mechanism) for this sort of object-relating. We project images and words onto the screen, throwing them into cyberspace, a place simultaneously fictive and real. We create identities whose truths or falsehoods are indeterminate; then deploy them to an unknown international audience. Others have written about the narcissism in such activity. I am more concerned about the schizoid qualities. What was once private is now impersonal and there for anyone to view. There is a danger that, in some instances, meaningful links between self and other are all but abolished, as the other becomes too impersonal to conceptualize. This lack of private space, that seems cloistered (as if it's just you and your keyboard), is complex and often hard to grasp.

In terms of our children, I have many examples of the dangers of exposure that cyberspace presents. For instance, while a teenaged girl was at a party, her brother, living hundreds of miles away, found a nearly instantaneous photo of her on an internet site drinking alcohol at that party. Before she got home, her mother had been informed of her behavior. In another instance, a patient of mine came into a session in tears after she was emailed by another family member some bitter words her daughter had used to describe her relationship with her mother on Facebook. What we may think is private is all too public. I have repeatedly counseled my own daughter to never put into cyberspace anything she doesn't wish the entire world to know about her.

The paradox of computer communications is the simultaneity of exposure and secrecy. A "truth" we thought reserved for 650 buddies is all too
easily exposed to the world; at the same time, we may create fictive personalities, masking parts of ourselves. Our increasingly mechanistic culture
affords us instruments that can be used for as-if, projective object relating,
assisting in disobjectualizing others and de-subjectifying ourselves. The
blank screen presents the possibility of disembodied relating where we may
impose our words, even our most tortured and passionate thoughts, onto
an eternally blue and infinite sky. What is reflected back is that eternal
background, not the gaze of the beholder.

A teenaged boy whom I will call Derek came to treatment suffering from
dark moods and symptoms of schizoid retreat. Very tall, with a very large
frame and problems with overweight, he was brilliant, verbally creative, and
artistically talented. He had great dreams—of becoming an important
filmmaker, producing great art, writing meaningful music—but felt others'
demands as criticisms, and increasingly retreated into positions of failure. It
was difficult for him to fail; his brilliance saw him through all but the most
demanding situations. He showed me an exceptionally fine paper he had
written as a high school assignment on *The Color of Water*. The surprising
element was that I had read the book, but he had not. Ultimately, his
failure consisted of total retreat. He not only failed to do assignments, but
also failed to show up for class, keeping himself ignorant of what assignments were due. At the same time, he was paid nominal fees to write
papers—which he tossed off the top of his head—for less talented, but
wealthier friends, and they would get A grades. He went from one college
to the next, starting with resolve, ending in retreat, eventually closing
himself off in his room.

In treatment, Derek began to speak about being trapped in his body. As
soon as he began to feel he might lose weight and have a beautiful body to
match his mind, he would attack himself, collapsing into paranoid anxieties
that took the form of cultural fears—of anthrax contamination, HIV, and
of being regarded as racist or a pedophile. Loving feelings would with
terrible suddenness turn to hate, and his interest in the welfare of children
or his concern for the state of the world would become projected persecutory fears of his own perverse nature. Previously riddled with terrible
anxiety and repressed rage if I dared mention his relationship to his body (I
believe we both treated his body as a foreign object), he became able to
approach this topic, warily but decisively. He spoke of not being able to
tolerate his physical presence in the world, of not fitting into those horrible
little desk-chairs in college classrooms, of being viewed as a monster, a
threat, because of his size. He shrank into his large frame, his upper back
curved into a half-moon shape in an attempt to take up less space, refusing
to stand tall and gain his true stature, instead looking alternately like a
slinking criminal and a version of Quasimodo. He researched diets that

required unusual purity of purpose—raw food diets, for example—then feared he was making himself deathly sick when he tried them. Having whittled his relationships down to one, a longstanding childhood friend, he and a few others hung out at this friend's house into the early morning hours, smoking pot, talking, and watching movie after movie.

His most compelling relationships were conducted on the computer screen. His desire for women was tainted by the very fact of his desire. He refused to seek out their actual company not only because he was certain of rejection, but also because desire seemed monstrous to him. On the screen, however, where he could compose himself through words without the imposition of flesh, his desire could become manifest. For some time he had two relationships, one with a younger woman faraway, the other with a woman his age from his neighborhood. The younger woman spoke of her sexual and physical abuse, and he protected and counseled her from afar. The local woman, much closer to him in many ways, became his soul-mate, someone with whom he identified as well as counseled. This relationship took hold in him. He once saw her in the flesh, having met through friends, and thought her beautiful. She also insisted she had seen him, but he believed that impossible. There were fleeting moments when he talked of love for her and desire for marriage, and others when he spoke of her deep psychic disturbance and the insanity of it all. From time to time, she would insist on meeting him, and pressure him with her feelings of rejection at his refusal. At these times he would say he might as well agree to her demands, that it was time to get it over with. I believed him to be saying simultaneously that he couldn't put her off any longer, and that their internet intimacies would be over once they met in the flesh. Interestingly, every time they would agree to meet, one or the other would cancel at the last moment.

The psychic deadness that surrounded full-bodied relationships for this brilliant and talented boy brings to mind Green's (1980) description of the Dead Mother introject, a place of malignant narcissism with significant schizoid overtones. Green spoke of a form of depression that is closer to deadness, a blank place of mourning, a psychically dead maternal introject who has, in catastrophic bereavement, transformed vitality into a distant, toneless, inanimate figuration. There is a precipitous loss of once-held pleasure in a breast that has catastrophically collapsed. Green speaks of entering the crypt of the psychically dead mother introject, shrouded in an inanimate place of grays and whites, absent the red (passion, feeling) of bloody castration depression, to unite with her.

Derek is caught in the eye of his depressed, brilliant mother, who sees him as her golden boy as well as her evacuated, broken self. His escape from her shroud of failed ambition and deadness takes him only so far as the wild blue horizon of the screen, where his brilliant mind is free to roam without the encumbrance of his own reflection in the other's eye. Here, for moments, he can be beautiful, vital, desirous, and desired. His struggle, both on screen and in the consulting room, is to exist simultaneously in union and dissolution, outside the reflecting eye of the beholder, without having to destroy or fetishize himself in the process.

While Derek's clinical problems are rooted in his psychic life, cyberspace presents him with a way of living through his desires without necessarily leading to a bridge to actualization. It facilitates a form of schizoid connectedness that exists imaginally, often split off from real relationships and from his corporeal existence. Many have argued for the positive aspects of internet connectedness and would see Derek's case as an isolated one, dependent on his pathology and not related to cybernetic culture. While I can speak in detail about the psychic origins of Derek's suffering, I also question the effect of cybernetic and mass media culture on the current generation's sense of subjectivity and interpersonal relatedness. Although there is value to the many forms of instant communication that have multiplied in the last twenty years, it is also important to raise the problematics of new media on relationships and sense of self. I see more teens picking up computers or iPhones than novels. I wonder about the effects of instantaneous public communication versus the letters that we used to write to faraway friends and family. We once pondered over those letters, rewrote them, sent them off in sealed envelopes meant for one set of eyes only, and waited for a response. What is the effect of not waiting? Does the erasure of time and space bring us closer to intimacy, or closer to a paranoid-schizoid form of relating? It seems more and more difficult to achieve solitude, a depressive position form of being alone with oneself, when loneliness, a paranoid-schizoid form of aloneness, seemingly can be erased with the click of a screen. When disembodied forms of connection replace the internal space of solitude, we stand in danger of creating a culture of schizoid detachment that goes unrecognized, masked by a screen of 650 buddies.

References

Bauerlein, Mark (2007). *The Dumbest Generation: How the Digital Age Stupifies Young Americans and Jeopardizes Our Future/ or, Don't Trust Anyone under Thirty*. New York: Penguin Books.

Bogle, Kathleen A. (2008). *Hooking Up: Sex, Dating, and Relationships on Campus*. New York: New York University Press.

Denizet-Lewis, Benoit (2004). Whatever Happened to Teen Romance (And What Is a Friend with Benefits Anyway)? *New York Times Magazine*, May 30, section 6, p.30.

Green, Andre (1980). The Dead Mother. In *Life Narcissism, Death Narcissism*. London: Free Association Books, 2001.

Kelsey, C. (2007). *Generation MySpace: Helping Your Teen Survive Online Adolescence*. New York: Marlowe and Company.

Lasch, Christopher (1978). *The Culture of Narcissism*. New York: W.W. Norton and Company.

Postman, N. (1985). *Amusing Ourselves to Death*. New York: Penguin.

Trzesniewski, K. H., Donnellan, M. B., & Robins, R. W. (2008). Is "Generation Me" really more narcissistic than previous generations? *Journal of Personality*, 76:903–918.

Twenge, Jean (2008). Egos Inflating over Time. *Journal of Personality*, 76:875–902.

Part III

Yearning and its vicissitudes

Chapter 6

"I hate to choose . . . you choose": On inhibition of longing and desire

Amira Simha-Alpern

This chapter title was inspired by my patient Sara, a divorced woman in her early 40s who often uses these words when dining with her boyfriend, negotiating what to order. This phrase became our motto whenever we referred to her tendency to disown wanting, needing, desiring, or longing. "Wanting" was dangerous for Sara. It risked not attaining her object of desire, or burdening and alienating others, leaving her with perpetual longing. Disowning the need for connection, the wish to be taken care of, loved, desired, or seen for who she is, was Sara's way of both avoiding the pain of longing and securing the attachment. Sara's manner of coping with painful, unfulfilled yearnings is not unusual. "The world is not a problem for a person with no preference" (Epstein, 2005, p.5) reflects the Buddhist belief that the cause of suffering and discontent is desire itself. To achieve happiness, one should curb desire.

Fairbairn (1956) was the first to position desire for human connection at the center of the motivational system. Struck by how abused children remain attached to their abusive parents, he concluded that, "man is by nature object-seeking rather than pleasure seeking" (p.132), thereby challenging a basic principle of classical drive theory. Consequently, "the earliest and original form of anxiety, as experienced by the child is separation-anxiety" (p.155). As development progresses, the dread of social isolation becomes a major factor in personality formation and psychopathology.

Maintaining the human bond in the absence of secure, satisfying care-giving does not come without a price. The individual develops self-preservative mechanisms to both avoid the pain and disappointment of rejection and keep the attachment figure close, involved, and invested. This process profoundly affects personality organization and the configuration of the unconscious. Fairbairn (1963) suggested that as a defensive measure, when the real relationship with the original object is unsatisfying, the individual internalizes the object. The exciting (i.e., libidinal) aspects and the rejecting (i.e., antilibidinal) aspects are split off from the main core of the object and are repressed by the ego. This process has a long-lasting effect on ego structure, preventing optimal integration.

Although Fairbairn's concepts grew out of an object relations viewpoint, a model of mind in which personality is organized around the development of the drive and through internalization of object representations, his ideas are consistent with relational and intersubjective views (Sullivan, 1953, 1956; Mitchell, 1988; Stolorow & Atwood, 1992; Aron, 1996; Bromberg, 1998). Relational writers support the idea that "the human infant is programmed to be social . . . [and that] the very nature of the infant draws him into relationship" (Mitchell, 1988, p.24). Like Fairbairn, Sullivan believed that the personality develops out of the need to maintain a relationship with an object and that the self is organized around interpersonal experience. Furthermore, the self system designs itself for the purpose of maintaining significant relationships. "The self system . . . is invented for facilitating the acquisition of a feeling of security, for success in dealing with others" (1956, p.50). Parts of self that threaten attachment become "bad me" or, when the threat is more intense, "not me," a dissociated part of the self (1953, p.162).

Sullivan (1956) challenged the classical view of the unconscious as containing repressed infantile drives. He "discarded the concept of suppression and repression from . . . [his] thinking" (p.63), replaced it with "dissociation" and normalized it, suggesting that dissociation is "universal" (p.45). Individuals restrict their awareness via "selective inattention" to keep awareness off "events that impinge upon [the self]" (p.38), and "maintain self respect and security with others" (p.62). Sullivan and more contemporary writers suggest that what becomes unconscious (or dissociated) is "affect states that have been defensively walled off because they failed to evoke attuned responsiveness from the early surroundings" (Stolorow & Atwood, 1992, p.31). For "the child's conscious experience to become progressively articulated it needs to be validated and responded to by the early surround" (p.31). In contrast, if aspects of experience are felt as "unwelcome or damaging to the caregiver" (p.32) and the latter is not responding or is rejecting, "whole sectors of the child's experiential world must then be sacrificed (repressed) in order to safeguard the needed tie" (p.32). In that case, conscious articulated memory of the experience never develops. Instead, its traces are pushed to the unconscious and remain unformulated. Boundaries between conscious and unconscious remain "fluid" and "ever shifting," influenced by environmental responsiveness.

Contemporary theoreticians (Mitchell, 1988; Stolorow & Atwood, 1992; Aron, 1996) went further than Fairbairn in challenging the concept of an isolated, individual mind. In their view, the mind is not an autonomous entity with defined boundaries. Rather, it is a "unit" with permeable boundaries embedded in and interconnected with other minds. In this "intersubjective system" (Stolorow & Atwood, 1992, p.22) the intrapsychic and interpersonal are interrelated, and the mind develops its sense of subjectivity and meaning through interaction with other subjectivities. Mitchell (1988) argues similarly that the intrapsychic is "composed of relational configurations . . . [that are] fundamentally dyadic and *interactive* . . . [and] psychic organization and structures are built from the patterns which shape those interactions" (pp.3–4). He adds that "like Escher's *Drawing Hands* . . . [the] interpersonal and the intrapsychic realms create, interpenetrate, and transform each other in subtle and complex manner" (p.9). Although core relational configurations are shaped in early formative years, these constantly reconfigure to assimilate new interactive patterns. "Inner experience *and* its embeddedness with other such worlds [are] in a continual flow of reciprocal mutual influence." In other words, the mind is not fixed in a certain formation, but evolving (Stolorow & Atwood, 1992, p.18).

Sullivan's formulations evolved and inspired a redefinition of the self. Relational psychoanalysis accepted and celebrated the notion of multiple self-states (Mitchell, 1998; Davies, 1996; Bromberg, 2006a), embracing the idea that self is an amalgamation of different self-states, each organized around a central theme, conflict, self/other representations, levels of organization or, in Bromberg's (2006a) term, "realities" (p.3). This model relies on dissociation rather than repression as the main organizing process. Experiences validated by the environment are integrated into self-states that are more organized, articulated, and available for reflection. Experiences not validated remain un-symbolized, stored primarily in somatic form, not readily available for reflection, i.e., dissociated. These less developed self-states tend to manifest themselves through disorganized enactments (Bromberg, 1998, 2006a).

Specific to our discussion on loneliness and its concomitants—longing and desire—the relational perspective proposes that "*desire* is experienced always *in the context of relatedness*, and it is that context which defines its meaning" (Mitchell, 1988, p.3). Longing for an object becomes unconscious or dissociated not only as a defense against the pain of frustration and deprivation for not having what one desires, but also because one's need is ignored, ridiculed, or burdensome to the other. Longing and loneliness are dissociated in order to maintain whatever object tie is possible without the "noise" of negative affective states. When longing is stimulated, it often manifests in a disorganized form inconsistent with what the individual "knows" about him/herself. Embarrassment and questions such as, "Why did I do it?" often follow these behavioral manifestations.

Bromberg (2006b) believes that corruption of longing and desire occurs when:

> the child's healthy desire to communicate her subjective experience to a needed other is infused with shame because the needed other cannot or will not acknowledge the child's experience as something legitimately "thinkable" . . . She feels, not that she did something wrong, but that there is something wrong with her "self"—Something wrong with her

as a person. To survive this destabilization to selfhood, she expels the now 'illegitimate' part of her subjective experience by dissociating the part of herself that knows it to be legitimate. Once dissociated, that part of herself becomes "not me", and she is thereafter in doubt both as to her own legitimacy as a person and the reality of her internal experience . . . [Her experience of longing is] not organized as a cognition; she is left not with the memory that is felt as belonging to "me" . . . but with its affective ghost—an uncommunicated state of longing that shrouds an implicit memory. The longing is a "not me" ghost that haunts her . . . because her own desire to communicate it . . . becomes a source of shame in itself. Thus, a double shame develops: the first source of shame comes from her belief that what she feels will not be "real" to the other. Second: her fear that she loses the other's attachment (and thus her core sense of self) makes her even more desperate for evidence that the other has not withdrawn his attachment, and the more evidence she seeks the greater is the shame she feels . . . She cannot mentally experience the longing as "desire" without being shamed by other parts of herself, leaving her feeling undeserving of consolation or solace.

(pp.19–20)

Similarly, in thwarted longing, "mentalized affectivity," i.e., the capacity to feel feelings, identify them, and reflect upon their meaning, is compromised. In general, research has shown suppressed activity in brain regions associated with mentalization during experiences of maternal and romantic love. In addition, "attachment stress" (e.g., fear of rejection or abandonment) seemed more disruptive to mentalization than "normal stress" (e.g., studying for a final). It is, therefore, not unreasonable to assume that the individual obliterates mentalization of longing and desire in reaction to depriving and rejecting object relations (Bartels & Zeki, 2004; Fonagy, Gergely, Jurist, & Target, 2002; Nolte, Hudac, Mayes, Fonagy, Blatt, & Pelphrey, 2010).

Following is an illustration of an intelligent, capable woman Fonagy would conceptualize as inhibiting mentalization regarding her desire and longing, and Bromberg (1998) would describe as dissociative personality organization.

Clinical illustration

Sara, an intelligent, witty woman in her early 40s, presented with relentlessly obsessive thoughts that caused severe sleep disorders. Diagnosed with anxiety disorder earlier in her life, she was prescribed Paxil and sleeping pills. She did not have many childhood memories; the few that she shared were either fragmented or made no sense to her as she relied heavily on dissociation and disownership of feelings and thoughts to avoid emotional discomfort. With no abuse or gross neglect in her childhood, it was hard for her to locate the origin of her profound sense of not being cared for and loneliness. Both parents appeared relatively benign, but each in his/her own way was self-absorbed and fragile. Sara's pleas for soothing and affirmation were ignored, trivialized, or harbored the danger of overburdening her parents, turning them away from her. To survive this confusing household, Sara dissociated her affective states—her loneliness and yearning for affection and caring. She adopted a perpetual state of somatic "alertness," experiencing only an unarticulated, diffuse sense of doom that had no identifiable explanation. Perhaps not surprisingly, she developed two serious autoimmune diseases.

For many years, "longing Sara" was a "not-me" self-state. When longing Sara "accidentally" manifested, it was in a disorganized form consistent with insecure attachment style. Although I was perplexed about the intensity of her disorganization during those times, I was less worried about how intact she was. As a relational analyst holding the notion of multiple self-states, I believed what looked like unregulated reaction was activated by a need state that had been disowned rather than a more pervasive deficit.

One episode in Sara's history was particularly significant. After Sara was bullied, causing her great despair in middle school, she consulted the school psychologist. He was kind, affirming, helpful, and, most importantly, protected her from the bullies. She yearned for her weekly contacts with him and became "obsessed" with him. She knew his schedule, the different cars he drove, or his parking spot, and followed him around school to get glimpses of him. Sara kept this activity hidden from him, terrified of being discovered, and being "totally embarrassed." Although the memories of her secretive pursuits were coherent, they did not make sense to her. Why couldn't she just say a hello to him in the hallway? Only after we understood her way of negotiating her longing did it occur to us that Sara was ashamed of longing for adult attention, of needing the soothing, affirmation, protection, and safety she felt in the psychologist's office. She felt something was wrong with her if she needed these so badly.

When she began analysis, Sara had been married for 19 years to her high school sweetheart, her first and only sexual partner. He was distant, cold, and critical, and she was constantly demeaned, expected to do more than possible. When she failed to "perform," she was further demeaned. When she expressed her yearning for love, it was met with callous criticism of her infantile dependency. She was called "selfish," "self-centered," or "lazy" when she pursued any self-generated activity rather than housecleaning. She was ridiculed for being "out of control" and "impulsive" when she expressed delight and excitement or was playful and humorous. Her bids for affection and sensual exchanges were never reciprocated. Sara felt lonely in her marriage, and the outside world was beyond reach.

The reasons behind Sara's inability to reach for support outside her marriage were complex. Her immediate family members, the nesting ground for her internal working models, were dismissive, aligning themselves with those parts of her which shared her husband's version of who she was. She was also afraid to face the validation of the outside world. If indeed she was deprived and treated unfairly, she might be forced to sever her attachment to her husband. She could not "not see" her husband's unkind attitude, but to survive, she disowned the parts of herself that were yearning for support and caring and disavowed the "needy" parts which caused her to cling to him in spite of his abuse.

For years, Sara avoided psychotherapy, fearing insight would compel her to face the truth about her marriage. She felt ashamed to disclose the emotional abuse and, at the same time, embarrassed to ask for something better. Because of shame, and the threat of disconnection, she sustained not knowing, not feeling, not seeing. Her "obsessions" with mundane, trivial worries were her way of emptying her mind from the pain of unsatisfied longing for an unattainable object.

Our initial engagements were colored by Sara's profound fear of rejection. After scheduling her first appointment and before meeting me, she wrote her close friends the following e-mail (forwarded to me three years into treatment): "If I don't meet her [i.e., analyst's] needs, in terms of the type of client she would like to treat, or if she feels we are not a good fit . . . then I will again be on the reject pile of mental health professionals . . . I only hyperventilated a little bit this afternoon, so I am sure I will be just fine by the time I obsess for the next 36 hours until I see her. Oh yeah. I am going to make a great impression. I am going to have to go into a dissociative state and act like a normal person in the vain hope she will accept me. I will trick her into accepting me as a client. That is my plan for now. Then I will be her analysand until I piss her off and she refuses to see me anymore . . . I wanted to be sure I did not come off as 'difficult.'"

It was not easy for Sara to be open and honest in sessions. Parts of her were unarticulated, hard to put into words; other parts were shameful. Even more so, she was terrified of saying the "wrong thing," something that would chase me away. In the first year, she was consumed by fear I would find her unfit for analysis and would terminate treatment. At times she would stop in mid-sentence and say, "Never mind." When I inquired, Sara admitted being concerned that if she exposed her mind, I would find her intolerable.

Paradoxically, Sara also bombarded me with intrusive questions about my life: Where did I live? How old were my children? Which car did I drive? Where did I buy my shoes? These investigations felt more aggressive than inquisitive. Although generally I self-disclose when I deem it appropriate, I found myself withholding information. Sara, however, was persistent, seeming both embarrassed and delighted by this push-pull dance. She "googled" me several times and found who my husband was, where I lived, and which conference I attended when I rescheduled her session. I felt attacked and invaded not by what she found but by how she discovered it. Sara refused my invitations to reflect on what transpired and it seemed like the potential space between us collapsed. She did not want to find out why she needs to know about me. "What's the big deal? Just answer me!" she protested. Nothing short of concrete responses satisfied her. I imagined that her preoccupation with details of my life served to fill her otherwise empty spaces and preclude mentalization of her affective states.

Sara pulled me into her internal drama, alternating roles of "doer" and "done to." We were both protective of our agentic selves, the driving force of our desires, dreading its confiscation by pressures from the other. I did not mind disclosing, but could not tolerate being forced to. I feared hijacking of the part of me that thinks through appropriate interventions, weighing suitable responses. Sara, on the other hand, became disorganized by her longing to be cared for by a therapist. She feared that by needing me she surrendered to my influence and gave me power to abandon, reject, or take possession of her soul. This became clear later in treatment when we revisited this enactment.

As I reflected on this experience, I understood it as Sara's attempts to test my resilience and commitment. Would I collapse under her pressure to reveal? Would I reject and humiliate her? Will I demean and humiliate her? I felt constrained between Scylla and Charybdis, as I considered my possible responses: If I surrender to her pressure, I am fragile like her parents, not to be trusted as a secure support, not competent enough to hold her. If I stand my ground, I am withholding and dismissive of her need to know. If I admit to her that I am disturbed by her demands, it will confirm her view of herself as toxic. If I do not acknowledge the tension between us, I am colluding with her dissociative mechanisms.

Surviving this enactment without rupturing our relationship felt more important than knowing what it was about and interpreting it. Being with each other through this was more important than knowing about each other or ourselves. We would have time to reflect on it when Sara felt more securely attached to me. I surmised it was important to avoid shaming her by premature exposure or criticism, yet I knew I should not ignore the tug of war between her desire to know and my desire to hide. I told Sara it makes sense that she would not trust that I'd be there for her unless she knew everything about me. Not knowing anything about a needed object leaves her with no compass to orient and guide her in how to adapt to the other's expectations. Lacking this comforting compass, she is flooded with free-floating panic, overwhelmed by terror of abandonment. Sara seemed relieved that her disorganized "childish" behavior was not ridiculed and made sense.

A year and a half into analysis, Sara recognized that her emotional needs were not met in her marriage and that she deserved to be loved and respected. She no longer dismissed her yearnings as "infantile" or "weak," and owned these parts of herself that longed for a warm, nurturing relationship. When she asked for a divorce, she and her husband separated in an amicable, civilized manner.

Sara began exploring other relationships immediately. She soon met someone whom she nicknamed "Niceguy," her longed for, good object. He stood in stark contrast to her ex-husband. Niceguy expressed pleasure in being with her. Not judgmental, he was interested in her mind, curious about her thoughts and feelings, respectful of her wishes, and "took things slowly" in an attempt not to exploit her yearnings and desires. Although they acknowledged their sexual desire, they refrained from a full sexual relationship. Sara enjoyed his company and devoured his affection and affirmation. Repeatedly surprised by how "nice he was," she shared their encounters with me with delight.

I wanted to celebrate Sara's finding a nurturing relationship. However, I had a nagging discomfort listening to how she would make sexual advances, openly expressing her desires to spend more time with him, to which he responded cautiously, saying they should "take it slow" in order to guarantee it would work. It was impossible to ignore that she found herself in a familiar position of being the pursuer with a withholder. Once again, her desires were denied and she remained with her longing, only this time it was for the "right reasons" and the denying object was a Niceguy.

What was interesting was not whether Sara and Niceguy actualized their desire, but how Sara went about negotiating this relationship. Characterologically, Sara was intellectually curious and inquisitive. When she wanted to learn about something, she exhausted the information on the Internet. This is how she initially approached dating. However, once in a relationship, this exploration stopped. To better understand the meaning of this relationship, I attempted to explore Niceguy's reactions to her from his own biographical context. Surprisingly, Sara knew very little about his past. I was bewildered. Why wouldn't she want to know about his past relationships? Why wouldn't she want to know the circumstances of his divorce? Why wouldn't she question the fact that he was twice divorced? Why wouldn't she want to hear more about his family? When I posed these questions, she rationalized, "This is private information. He does not have to tell me."

I knew how much comfort Sara derived from this relationship. She did not want to discover what was intolerable to "know." Instead, she wanted to feel happy and nurtured, and not know she was still deprived and lonely. She did not want to find information about Niceguy that would make her doubt his ability to meet her needs. How could I burden her by spotlighting what she did not want to see? I felt like a "party pooper."

Sara is in the midst of negotiating her relationship with Niceguy, therapy being a dance between knowing and not knowing. Many times she cannot recall what we have talked about. My frequent dilemma is whether to "remind" her or let her negotiate what she knows and doesn't know her way. The metaphor of me being a "memory stick" which temporarily holds information, waiting to be downloaded into her hard drive, often comes to mind as I struggle with this quandary.

Summary

This chapter discusses thwarted longing from a relational view which suggests that forbidden desires are dissociated and remain unformulated, leading to an underdeveloped, "not me" self-state, not fully recognized by the individual, but powerfully affecting his/her behavior and affect. The case of Sara illustrates the transformation of longing when one's needs are ignored, deprived, and experienced as burdensome to caretakers. As most often is the case, Sara chose romantic partners with whom she relived her internal working models. In relationship to parents and romantic partners, Sara had to dissociate her longing for affirmation and caring. She pushed out of her awareness any sign that would make her realize her unsatisfied longing and sense of loneliness, in order to tolerate and preserve the attachments she had.

The author wishes to thank Drs. Veronica Fiske, Julie Lehane, Kate Szymanski, Jani Klebenow, Karen McKinnon, Elizabeth Allured, Susanne Cooperman, and Gerry Andrews for their valuable comments. Special thanks to Ms. Lisa Lempel-Sander for editorial remarks. Deep gratitude is also owed to Drs. Estelle Rapoport and Suzanne Phillips for stimulating supervision, and to the patient Sara whose dedication and commitment to treatment inspired this paper.

References

Aron, L. (1996). *A Meeting of Minds: Mutuality in Psychoanalysis*. Hillsdale, NJ: The Analytic Press.

Bartels, A. & Zeki, S. (2004). The neural correlates of maternal and romantic love. *NeuroImage*, 21(3): 1155–1166.

Bromberg, P. M. (1998) *Standing in the Spaces: Essays on Clinical Process, Trauma and Dissociation*. Hillsdale, NJ: The Analytic Press.

—— (2006a). *Awakening the Dreamer: Clinical Journeys*. Mahwah, NJ: The Analytic Press.

—— (2006b). "It never entered my mind": Some reflections on desire, dissociation and disclosure. In J. Petrucelli (Ed.), *Longing: Psychoanalytic Musing on Desire* (pp.3–24). New York: Karnac.

Davies, J. M. (1996). Linking the 'pre-analytic' with the postclassical: Integration, dissociation, and the multiplicity of unconscious process. *Contemporary Psychoanalysis*, 32: 553–576.

Epstein, M. (2005). *Open to Desire: Embracing a Lust for Life: Insights from Buddhism and Psychotherapy*. New York: Gotham Books.

Fairbairn, W. R. D. (1956). Reevaluating some basic concepts. In E. Fairbairn Birtle & E. D. Scharff (Eds.), *From Instinct to Self: Selected Papers of W. R. D. Fairbairn: Vol. I. Clinical and Theoretical Papers* (pp.129–138). Northvale, NJ: Jason Aronson, 1994.

—— (1963). An object relations theory of the personality. In E. Fairbairn Birtle & E. D. Scharff (Eds.), ibid., 155–156. Northvale, NJ: Jason Aronson.

Fonagy, P., Gergely, G., Jurist, E., & Target M. (2002). *Affect Regulation, Mentalization, and the Development of the Self*. New York: Other Press.

Mitchell, S. A. (1988). *Relational Concepts in Psychoanalysis: An Integration*. Cambridge, MA: Harvard University Press.

Nolte, T., Hudac, C. M., Mayes, L. C., Fonagy, P., Blatt, S. J. & Pelphrey, K. A. (2010). The effect of attachment-related stress on the capacity to mentalize: An Fmri investigation of the biobehavioral switch model. *Journal of the American Psychoanalytic Association*, 58: 566–573.

Stolorow, R. D. & Atwood, G. E. (1992). *Contexts of Being: The Intersubjective Foundations of Psychological Life*. Hillsdale, NJ: The Analytic Press.

Sullivan, H. S. (1953). *The Interpersonal Theory of Psychiatry*. New York: W. W. Norton.

—— (1956). *Clinical Studies in Psychiatry*. New York: W. W. Norton.

Chapter 7

Proust and the lonely pleasure of longing

Arlene Kramer Richards and Lucille Spira

> My Love is forever longing still / For that which nurseth the disease / Feeding on that which doth preserve the ill, / Th' uncertain sickly appetite to please.
>
> (William Shakespeare, *Sonnet 147*)

How can we understand loneliness? We think of it as an unpleasurable affect. It is often a complaint, sometimes accompanied by a loss of mental functioning. How can we figure out why a patient says she wants a relationship, but refuses to go out and find one? When so many people are available on the internet, when so many of her colleagues and relatives and neighbors want to "fix her up," why does she refuse? Why do so many patients complain they cannot find "Mr. or Ms. Right" while not out looking for a serious connection? Why are people going to the kind of bars where they can only find one night stands instead of trying to get acquainted with people who can be their friends and among whom they can find a best friend and/or lover? Can it be they prefer to be alone, that they are not lonely when alone? Is it possible some people prefer the state of longing to the fulfillment of connection?

Marcel Proust in *In Search of Lost Time* shows us a hero who wrestles with such questions. Proust saw and delineated in exquisitely fine detail the parallels between the psychological and the social, uniting in the form of fiction what has been divided, to the mutual loss of the sciences of psychology and sociology. He understood society as organized pleasure attained by inflicting pain. A party, a club, a fraternity, even a night club gives pleasure only as the participants are aware that they might have been excluded, that they are privileged to be invited. Part of the pleasure in belonging to a social circle is the pleasure of excluding others or knowing that others have been excluded. This view is supported by the experience of an elderly gay man who remarked to his therapist that he missed the thrill he had felt by patronizing secret gay clubs. He felt pleasure in knowing that as a gay man he would be welcome at such clubs when others would not.

With the increasing acceptance of homosexuality and gay clubs and the loss of secrecy, he believed the thrill had gone out of the clubs because anyone could go to them now.

Proust saw this social truth as emanating from the personal. His great novel can be read as a history of how a person develops a love of exclusion; how one comes to prefer being lonely over intimacy. In an ironic turn worthy of Proust himself, it is only now, over half a century after he finished his great psychological novel, that psychoanalysts have attained a view of loneliness that can intersect with his.

Brenner (1974) characterized loneliness as a longing for a specific unattainable object of desire. Using this definition, how can being lonely, longing for an unattainable other ever be a state a person chooses? How can it be prized over the fulfillment of satisfaction? By way of answer, if the oedipal drama determines who one loves and how, then Proust's story shows how oedipal wishes can lead to renunciation of sexual fulfillment in love. When the child, like Oedipus, wins his mother's love and banishes his father from the picture, the child is humiliated rather than satisfied. In the novel the grown man banishes everyone from his life. Only at the end of his story, when he has secluded himself from social life, does he reach the fulfillment of his fantasy. Then he is free to write his great novel, free of the fantasy of winning the love of a woman, or man, free to devote himself to the fantasy life that is his art. Being lonely guarantees that he will not be the best beloved of either a woman or a man; he will neither win the parent nor give up the fantasy of winning the parent's exclusive love. How did he come to this? The rest of this chapter will attempt to answer this question.

Proust and Freud

Like Freud, Proust discovered that love is transference. We love those who rekindle earlier loves. Also like Freud, Proust viewed the state between waking and sleep as the dream state and as the access to the unconscious, as well as to the thoughts and feelings of childhood. Proust and Freud show how dreams connect us to the past and can show us what we have lost. For example, in Proust's novel, an older hero of the narrator is Swann. When Swann can no longer remember the Odette he fell in love with, suddenly that Odette appears to him in a dream, making the connection between the woman he has and the one he lost. A parallel can be drawn between Proust's "involuntary memory" and Freud's "primary process." Both are timeless; both use condensation, displacement, and imagery. Similarly, Proust's "voluntary memory" is like Freud's "secondary process." Both use the laws of time, logic, and reality. Both believed that jealousy is a necessary condition of love. But what Proust called love, Freud considered perversion. For Freud, normal development entails giving up the intensity and exclusivity of the attachment to one's original love object and the transformation of jealousy into a wish to be like the rival, to identify with him. What Proust idealized was the jealousy that creates passion. Freud thought that normal sexual love attains satisfaction through release of tension; Proust believed that satisfaction destroys love.

Proust's novel

In Search of Lost Time portrays characters yearning for love to be requited. Proust shows us the complexity of object choice as he takes his characters through life. As we get to know them, we are struck by how much they are driven by the same passions that influence the patients in our offices. Just as our patients recount their experience, so Proust used his experience, but he created a narrative that illuminates the personal and social dimensions of experience. The story in both cases is that of lovers' wishes and longings. Proust takes us to a French aristocrat's drawing room in the late nineteenth century, to seaside resorts on the North Atlantic coast of France, to exotic Venice, celebrated for its courtesans, and to a house of sado-masochistic male prostitution. In these settings the affects, wishes, fears, and social mores his characters present are all too familiar.

Proust makes dramatic use of free association in a long monologue at the beginning of the novel in which we hear thoughts engendered by suffering from insomnia. He uses the concept of time to illuminate the transitoriness of human relationships. Proust shows the power of sensory experience to awaken repressed affect and the connection to memory that is, in turn, awakened by that affect. He tantalizes us with the idea that the experiences of earlier time could thus be regained and life could be continuous. Thus memory makes it possible to gain some control over the ephemeral nature of life. As memory preserves time, it also makes us aware that time has passed. The tragic nature of life with its inevitable losses is balanced by the recreation through memory. Love and hate, and the many affective tones in between, are the glue that binds the themes of our repressed memories.

Memory has to do with the preservation of connection. Lack of connection is what makes loneliness. Proust illustrates the tenuousness of human connections with a poignant scene between M (the protagonist) and his grandmother. While vacationing away from his grandmother, he talks to her by telephone, but talking makes him feel lonely. M's longing on hearing his grandmother's voice is an interesting twist on a charming anecdote Freud (1916/1917) tells about a child who fears the dark except when his aunt speaks to him. The child says, "If someone speaks, it gets lighter" (p.407). For Freud's little boy, his aunt's voice comforts because it signifies the presence of a protector. By contrast, Proust's character experiences hearing the grandmother's voice and not seeing her as evidence of her absence. Paradoxically, speaking to her stirs longing rather than providing comfort.

The disparity of experience in each of these episodes is partly explained by Cacioppo and Patrick (2008) in their comprehensive study of loneliness. They believe that mind set contributes to whether or not a person feels lonely even in the presence of others. This sense of being lonely can occur where a person imagines or anticipates an unpleasant scenario that impels her to turn away from others. Rather than experience anger or rejecting others, she experiences herself as the object of anger and rejection. Such ideas are called projection or projective identification in analytic discussions. We believe a person's cognitive picture of the world and other people is highly dependent on the interplay between psychic structure and reality. One way, therefore, of understanding the preceding paradox is that Freud's little boy anticipated being comforted and heard his aunt's voice as the comfort he wanted; Proust's character anticipated loss and heard the grandmother's voice as confirmation of his expectation.

Proust on love

Proust's multi-dimensioned characters, seen mostly through the eyes of his narrator, provide variations of love that expand the boundaries of Freud's ideas. Freud thought one chooses a beloved based on memories of the earliest beloved—parents and early caretakers—or by wishes to be loved in terms of images of oneself at early ages, or what one dreamed of being in those early years, or an image of what one is now. Proust shows how these images of the beloved are transformed as later experience shapes and distorts them.

Love gives rise to jealousy. The child loves his mother, but suffers jealousy because she belongs to his father. He loves his father and suffers jealousy because he belongs to his mother. Originally oedipal love caused jealousy, but what makes later love exciting is the jealousy that keeps the lover in a state of anxiety. The pain caused by jealousy penetrates and permeates the victim. This pain is the experience of falling in love in Proust. Cupid's arrow hurts, but is cherished because it recalls the painful jealousy of infantile love. For Proust, erotic love is always sadomasochistic; longing is both pleasurable and painful.

Because of space limits, we cannot use Proust's cast of characters to flesh out our ideas about the dynamics that drive not only the choices made by some of his exciting lovers, but some patients as well. We will limit our discussion of the vicissitudes of love and loneliness as they are sketched out in the story of the main character, M.

Toward the ill-fated kiss

At first, Proust's anonymous narrator tells us about a young boy. The drama begins at bedtime. It is dark. The young boy is in bed, a time and place for regressions. The young boy struggles with love, passion, fragile self-esteem, and, most importantly for us, longing. He sees his parents' marriage as comfortable, convenient, never passionate. They are always depicted in the company of other family members and friends. They dine; they walk; they converse. Their bedroom is never described. There is no hint of romance or sexuality between them.

In contrast, the narrator describes the young boy's passion for his mother. She sends him to bed accompanied by the maid while she remains downstairs with adult family members and a dinner guest. All the little boy could think about was getting a good night kiss from her. He advocates with the maid to tell his mother about his wish for her to come give him the kiss he longs for. His pleadings do not move her to come. He does not give up. Waiting for her after the end of the dinner, he catches her on the staircase as she is going to her room. She looks annoyed that he is still awake. She encourages him to go back to bed. His father enters the scene. Seeing his son's suffering, he becomes alarmed the boy will become sick. He urges his wife to stay with him.

M suffers conflict about his having enjoyed his mother's tender kisses and her staying all night in his room, reading to him and, presumably, sleeping with him. It is important to him that she reads to him. As we will see later, it may be the last moment of happiness before the great tragedy of his life. She reads a story about a woman named Madeline who, early on, acts as a surrogate mother to a boy, and later loses track of him only to be reunited with him much later. Eventually they fall in love and marry. M's suffering, his father's compassion, and his shame set the stage for his life as a person who values longing because he cannot tolerate satisfaction in love. M recognizes that his father's indulgence would ultimately cost him dearly. He believes that his father gave his mother to him because he saw him as a pitiful child rather than a rival. The father's willingness to step aside for his son appears like a screen memory that organizes his experience of himself as weak, passive, and uncertain of his role with women.

The feeling in the last moment before the shame was his longing for his mother. What could match the anticipation he felt as a boy awaiting his mother's kiss? Would he come to believe that he was entitled to have other men's women? Would winning love be equated with weakness? Or would tender love be equated with the suffering prototype of the sadomasochist (Halberstadt-Freud, 1991)? Is M an oedipal victor doomed to suffer in love?

Life after the bitter satisfaction

Young M is always hungry for love, admiration, or sexual excitement. His romantic interests are fleeting; jealousy attracts him to many different women. The idea that a woman would love other women attracts him the most. We see him imagine how it would be if one of the women or girls he thought he wanted desired him. M is excited by the fantasy of being loved by Gilberte, the Duchess de Guermantes, Madame Swann, a milkmaid, a fisher girl and, in turn, various members of what he describes as a band of girls whom he meets at the seashore, and on and on. These love affairs exist mainly in fantasy; there is little interaction and limited sex.

Later he falls in love with Albertine, a strong, tough, athletic, young woman cyclist. If opposites really attract, M's sense of himself as sickly and weak makes her physical strength and toughness appealing. In the Freudian sense she is what he wishes himself to be. He becomes obsessed with her comings and goings. While he admires her, he is also ambivalent because she is not as educated or sophisticated as he is. Despite his ambivalence, he persuades her to move in with him. Once Albertine appears to love him, he spoils the relationship by hounding her about whether or not she is betraying him by having sex with one of a number of women. Possessive of Albertine, he has her spied on. She feeds his suspiciousness by behaving secretively and allowing him to catch her in a number of lies. Albertine had shown signs early on that she was sexually excited by women, yet he believes he can win the sexual loyalty he wants from her with gifts and careful watching to make sure that she has no contact with the women with whom he suspects her of having sex. Once he promises marriage, Albertine accepts a life of virtual prisoner. When he succeeds in keeping her to himself, his interest in her fades.

Eventually, Albertine leaves M because he is not making good on his promise of marriage. In this act, she wrests control from him, and rekindles his fading interest; once more he falls under the thrall of longing. Recognizing his ambivalence, he attempts to comfort himself and regain control by having an affair with one of her friends and telling Albertine about it. If he can make her jealous she might beg him to take her back. If she is jealously longing for him, he will not have to be longing for her.

Desperately angry at the narcissistic injury she has inflicted on him by walking out on him, he calls a very young peddler girl into his room. The text hints at his having sex with this child. Is he moving from sado-masochistic perversity to child abuse? If his loneliness left him feeling powerless, that feeling may have incited him to exert power.

The instrumental nature of his affair with Albertine's friend is clear. When Albertine dies, M's affair with her friend dissolves. Ironically, he has attained the love of his life; the dead Albertine can only be longed for, never again possessed. Longing itself is what he has been longing for all along.

Following Albertine's death, M consoles himself by going on a trip to Venice with his mother. There he visits prostitutes, but leaves Venice with his mother at her urging. She is the Madonna, they are the whores. By giving them up, he establishes his mother as the love of his life and never has sex with someone he can love and respect again. The longing for the perfect nurturer lasts even after he has forgotten the story of Madeline, but the image of a mother who can marry her son after he has grown up never leaves him again.

By the end of *Search*, M realizes that what he has learned about himself and others is worth preserving in a novel. He sees that for him the sweetest pleasure is the anticipation of what might be—the sensation of longing. The excitement of unrequited love is what he believes will provide the juice that would allow him to succeed in his goal of becoming a writer. At this moment M, the hero of the book, becomes the narrator who has been telling M's story from the beginning.

Marcel needed to create his novel more than he needed to possess a lover or a family. He thereby becomes the novelist, Proust. He also achieves what his mother and grandmother valued most; he becomes the writer, the person who provides the reader with a novel. His story is a more adult version of the kind of stories his mother read to him. These stories were the connection she made to the lonely, frightened little boy in bed. Being read to was having his mother with him. When she was reading, he could enjoy her closeness in a way that made him more grown up, not a helpless, sick child any more, but an audience to her performance, a part of the community of those who read these stories.

Discussion

Proust shows us a life in which love is only sustainable when unfulfilled, thus only pleasurable insofar as one is able to enjoy pain. He believed satisfaction produces dullness and boredom. Envy and jealousy prevent the dullness and boredom of satiety. Thus he understands pleasure in inflicting and suffering pain as the inescapable dynamic of human existence. Sadomasochistic reversals of social status in which humiliation accompanies physical pain are the consequence of this prototype of erotic excitement for Proust.

Thinking about love and its vicissitudes according to Proust, the question becomes: Why is longing idealized and requited love equated with boredom? Longing engenders excitement by allowing the fantasy of perfect gratification or satisfaction in the future. By having his wish gratified, the child M missed the chance to master his conflict by finding his own solution to temper his frustration.

Leavy (1990) examined longing as a wish for an idealized desexualized object. In his view, the object does not have to be desexualized, but is always idealized. Phillips (2001) builds on Leavy's idea. For Phillips, longing is the repudiation of unavailability of what is desired. Longing allows the "no" to be magically undone in fantasy even as it is accepted in dull reality. Klein (1963) believed that turning to fantasy was a defense against loneliness. By concretizing his fantasy in his writing, Proust managed to achieve through his art what he could not achieve in social life: an end to the pain of loneliness and a beginning of the pleasure of it.

Longing is a state where closure has not yet occurred so a person in longing has the experience of being in motion, going toward the desired object rather than stasis. The fantasizer has control. While little M was in the state of longing, he had not paid the humiliating price of becoming the object of his father's pity. No rival in his father's eyes, he was an invalid, an identity that would plague him for the rest of his life. So, longing is also safety.

Longing can be associated with innocence, a time before the superego is fully formed and prohibitions solidify, a time where anything might be possible—no limits, barriers, or taboos. This kind of longing represents a fantasy of a return to paradise or state of omnipotence. Here wishes are more powerful than judgment. In Freudian terms, it reflects the Oedipal conflict, when one is in the thrall of love and allowed any person, even an incestuous one. The rules do not apply. No act will be punished. No one will frustrate desires or wishes. Fulfilling the wish will not draw aggression from others. All this is endangered by the intrusions of reality. Once the father allows the mother to spend the night with her son, reality shatters the illusions of longing.

Longing allows one the fantasy of control of one's own impulses as well. If you have no contact with another person, you never have to experience aggression toward or from that person when the other wants something different from what you want. Proust shows this in the scene where Albertine leaves M because she wanted something that he did not give: marriage. This leaves him alone and longing for her. By averting the pain of aggressive conflict, choosing longing over fulfillment causes pain as it also provides safety.

In Proust's novel, when the lover does not get what he wants, he abandons the beloved and eventually returns to longing. Cacioppo and Patrick (2008), like Zilboorg (1938) before them, believe aggressive behavior leads to social rejection, isolation, and loneliness. When the beloved changes and her needs and wishes change, she provokes the aggression that ends up causing her to reject him, isolating the lover and returning him to his lonely longing. Thus even when love is gained for a moment, it changes with time as the beloved changes and the lover's needs and wishes change also (Beckett, 1931/1999).

For Albertine, the difference between her wish for marriage and M's failure to provide it would have seemed a failure of empathy on the part of M. The capacity for empathy is the crucial feature for providing a feeling of being loved. Her leaving him without warning can be seen as a flight from the loneliness of being a prisoner with a jailer who has no empathy for her feelings.

Cacioppo and Patrick (2008) use the neuroscientist Decety's definition of empathy as consisting of "shared affect, awareness that the other is separate from the self, the mental flexibility nonetheless to 'put yourself in the other's shoes,' and the emotional self regulation necessary to produce an appropriate response" (p.166). This suggests empathy is an antidote to loneliness for both the person in pain and the therapist. Only the shared affect is an autonomic brain function. The other three ego functions Decety posited are: awareness of separateness, putting oneself in the other's place, and producing an appropriate response. These ego functions are impaired by the affect of loneliness, so the lonely person is less able to be empathic.

An important corollary of the need for empathic nurturance is the observation that even in the presence of a spouse or group of other people, when the other is not experienced as being emotionally resonant, a person feels lonely. The lack of empathy causes loneliness. This view leaves out the analytic understanding that if one is angry at or envious of another person, that person can seem to be angry or indifferent. Pointing this out to patients can be therapeutic. Kauffman (2009) has shown the value of such confrontation from the perspective of self psychology. Patients can benefit from knowing that it is their own anger that makes them believe the therapist does not care for them. The same thing can happen outside the therapeutic relationship. It is this understanding that allows the psychotherapeutic process that frees the person from loneliness.

In contrast to the view that empathy is the hallmark of love and the antidote to loneliness, Proust's understanding of human relationships is that longing for love comes out of oneself and one's own experiences; the only one who can know what to do to fulfill one's desire is oneself. The other is irredeemably different, irredeemably alien, altogether motivated by different wishes and needs. This view is embodied in the incident in which M abuses a very young peddler girl in the aftermath of Albertine's flight. M does not get the girl to abuse him. Not even viciousness can reliably call out the same feeling in another person. The other will always be doing things for her own reasons.

Romantic love, the great ideal of the nineteenth century, stands denuded of its major illusion: the key importance of possessing the object of love. In this Proust extends Freud's idea that the object is the least fixed part of the wish. For Freud (1905), the aim and source of the wish are more fixed and stable than the choice of an object. What distinguishes love from the sexual perversions or simple lust is the longing for the object and the fixity of that longing. The person who comes to stand in the real world for the ideal becomes the unattainable object. The crucial difference between sex and love is the ability to choose, maintain, and be satisfied with that relationship. For Proust, as for some patients who have been oedipal winners, the beloved gained is love destroyed; longing is everything.

Almost at the end of the novel, M attends a party. He is stunned by the way in which the years gone by have altered the faces, shapes, and even in one instance the personality of former friends and acquaintances. Some have undergone a change in status that he would never have believed possible; a grand noblewoman who always commanded full attention was off center-stage, while a woman previously shunned by haute society was elevated to the wife of an esteemed nobleman. Just before this episode, M had uncovered memories and experiences of the time when he knew these people and they were everything to him, a time he thought was lost to him. With this awareness, of seeing into the past, he recognized that he could regain lost time and that what he remembered and uncovered was worth preserving in a novel. What might have been gratifying to M about his discovery is the sense of being filled rather than empty.

Psychoanalysts are familiar with lonely patients who fantasize they are empty. Here once again, Proust and Freud come together in the importance of connecting with that which is deep inside ourselves; it reinforces awareness that we are not alone or empty. Through helping patients recover apparently lost memories, psychoanalysts help them feel more filled, powerful, less lonely and alone. The presence of an analyst is particularly comforting when the memories are painful. Knowing someone is there to see them through the pain might make possible mourning where necessary and, in turn, reduce the need for only longing.

And what of Proust the novelist? He ends the narrative by writing the novel. His solution to the loneliness is to create a book treasuring the very loneliness he is writing about. In an obituary for another author, Eric Konigsberg (2008) reports: "Mr. Franzen said he and Mr. Wallace, over years of letters and conversations about the ethical role of the novelist, had come to the joint conclusion that the purpose of writing fiction was 'a way out of loneliness'" (p.A29). Proust came to the conclusion that remembrance, and writing the memories, was more satisfying than spending time in society. Longing and memory of longing create the paradox of filling one's inner emptiness. Rather than exacerbate loneliness, the memory of having longed and having been frustrated in that longing gave the novelist an utterly reliable and reliably empathic companion. Unlike a person, the page takes no contrary positions. The novel, by speaking inner truth, frees the author from the contrary demands of quotidian reality.

For patients, as for ourselves, reading novels requires giving up everyday reality and becoming immersed in the world the novelist has created. It does that same thing for the lonely reader that it did for the lonely writer. It gives us a world of characters who interest us enough to fill our reading time with what may be alternate selves or alternate beloveds, friends, groups, and even nations.

The novel challenges Phillips' (2001) vision of longing as a refusal to accept and mourn the reality of loss. Proust celebrates the function of memory in finding the affective connection to the other. As he uncovers what he thought were lost memories, his loves live in him and on his pages of fantasy. It goes further than individual fantasy in that it provides connection with a world of others by touching readers' lives. Proust managed to publish at least part of his work during his lifetime. He knew that he had readers. When he could not find a publisher, he self-published. He believed enough in his vision of the social world to send it out to find readers. No longer alone in his cork-lined bedroom, dependent on others to visit and tell him about what was going on in the world, he became the creator of a world that resonated to his needs, mirrored his feelings, and connected him to a wider world.

Proust did all this through his art. We can aspire to assist patients to use memory and fantasy to fill their internal worlds with affect, thereby helping them to enjoy the creative potential of the state of loneliness.

References

Beckett, S. (1931/1999). *Proust and Three Dialogues with Georges Duthuit*. London: John Calder.

Brenner, C. (1974). On the nature and development of affects: a unified theory. *Psychoanal. Q.*, 43:635–654.

Cacioppo, J. T. & Patrick, W. (2008). *Loneliness: Human Nature and the Need for Social Connection*. New York: W.W. Norton & Company.

Freud, S. (1905) Three essays on the theory of sexuality. *S.E.*, 7:125–244.

—— (1916–1917). Anxiety. *Standard Edition*, 16:392–411.

Halberstadt-Freud, H. C. (1991). *Freud, Proust, Perversion and Love*. Berwyn, PA.: Swets and Zeitlinger.

Kaufmann, P. (unpublished manuscript, 2009). The Reparative Quest and the Integration of the Traumatic Past.

Klein, M. (1963). On the sense of loneliness. In: *Envy and Gratitude & Other Works 1946–1963*, pp.300–313. London: The Hogarth Press, 1975.

Koningsberg, E. (10/24/2008). Remembering the Writer of "Infinite Jest". *The New York Times*, p.A29.

Leavy, S. A. (1990). Alain Fournier: Memory, youth and longing. *Psychoanal. Study Child*, 45:495–532.

Phillips S. (2001). The overstimulation of everyday life: New aspects of male homosexuality. *J. Amer Psychoanal A*, 49:1235–1267.

Proust, M. (2003). *In Search of Lost Time (vol.1–6)*. Translated by C. K. Scott Moncrieff and Terence Kilmartin. Revised by D. J. Enright. New York: The Modern Library.

Shakespeare, W. (2002). Sonnet #147. In: Stephen Orgel and A. R. Braunmuller (General Editors), *The Complete Pelican Shakespeare*. New York: Penguin Books.

Zilboorg, G. (1938). Loneliness. *Atlantic Monthly*, 161:45–54.

Chapter 8

Twins in fantasy: Love and loneliness

Evelyn T. Hartman

Introduction

When we fall in love, one particular person becomes unlike anyone else. In often an instant, we prioritize someone in a particular way. Our imagination transforms that someone into an object of desire. Similarly, our imagination transforms us into a special object of desire for them. This happens whatever the outcome or actualized relationship is. Fantasy brings this person alive for us, spicing up our experiences in a vibrant and very personal way. Falling in love becomes a preoccupation, like an exciting companion we keep closely with us.

What gives a particular moment in our lives this kind of awe, this kind of specialness that we hold on to? Why do we infuse a particular moment, a particular person with our most precious feelings? Why do these images become, in some way, our most special companion?

Like an infant and a mother, being first in someone's life is the defining premise of passionate love. Loneliness, writes Helene Deutsch (1973), is the result of not being first for someone like we were in infancy, never having returned to that special place.

A sustained fantasy of love may bridge a gap between loneliness and real love and become a solution, though a compromised one, for people too afraid to stand in either position: passionate love or intense loneliness. In this chapter, I will focus on the experience of falling in love during which our minds are filled with images that evoke awe. I'll examine the origins of this experience, its hold on us, our hold on it, and the intrapersonal power of romantic fantasy to enhance as well as impede an engaged experience with others and in living life.

Emma and Eric: Two cases related to the literature on love

Freud's (1912) writings on the impact of fantasy on erotic and romantic love refer to the following Biblical decree: "A man shall leave his father and mother and cleave to his wife." We have to separate before we can attach to another.

In Plato's *Symposium*, Aristophanes elaborates on the source of our desire to love each other. Love, he says, is born into every human being. He cites a myth that originally there were two-bodied people. Some had two sets of female sexual organs, some had two sets of male organs, and some had one of each. As they got rambunctious, they were cut in half. In agony, they sought their other half. The oneness they experienced when they found him or her is, according to Aristophanes, love. Love, he says, calls back the halves of our original nature. It tries to make one out of two to heal the wound of human nature. We must win the favors of a lover so as to recover our original nature.

Also in Plato's *Symposium*, Phaedrus pointed out how love reduces shame. One never does anything shameful the lover might see as it would create too much pain. Love helps man gain virtue. It also inspires courage, to defend the loved one.

When a love relationship is at its height, there is no room left for any interest in the environment, Freud (1912) wrote. A pair of lovers is sufficient unto themselves. A loveless person is left insufficient. Is this loneliness? In the same paper, Freud described the damaging impact a loveless life, a sexually abstinent one, has on creativity. The artist, he says, finds artistic achievement powerfully stimulated by romance. Does the inability to access creativity present, for the artist, an experience of loneliness?

Emma came to see me as she was turning 45. She had been feeling bouts of extreme anxiety. She felt her life was over: her children were on their way to college; in her marriage she struggled with intimacy issues; her elderly parents were infirm; her friendships seemed distant; her professional life was not where she wanted it to be; she worried about getting academic tenure.

After some months, Emma's anxiety lessened and she focused on one issue that had been absorbing her for several years. She had been asked to work on an interdisciplinary project with Peter, a colleague from another department. After weekly project meetings, they had lunch. Emma started to have a crush on him. She found herself daydreaming about their conversations and imagining romantic involvement. She loved the feeling. She felt attractive for the first time in her life, more confident, more creative in her work. It was as if she were alive for the first time, she said. She had more fun with her family. As she and her husband struggled with intimacy, her fantasized romance assuaged troubling feelings about her marriage. Externally, she continued her friendship with Peter, but supplied it with imaginative romance in which he reciprocated feelings of love for her. She was certain that in reality these feelings were not mutual. Time absorbed in this fantasy increased.

After a year, the project ended. Emma frantically tried to come up with other reasons to meet regularly. Peter nastily thwarted her efforts. Their contact ended. Emma's experiences lost their vitality. She no longer felt she had that attractive spark. She withdrew from active involvement at work. She felt ashamed that she had these feelings outside of her loving marriage and humiliated that these feelings were not reciprocated. Three years later, shame and humiliation continued to cloud her everyday experiences. She did not miss Peter's company nearly as much as she missed imagining that he loved her. Without that, she could not imagine regaining the feeling of how good it felt to be her. In these ways, the fantasy of love, now of unrequited love, continued to grip her.

Freud derived his discoveries about love, as he did most of his findings, from his ongoing process of psychoanalytic discovery. His idea of transference, as rooted in infantile experience, allowed him to understand love, also rooted in infancy. According to Freud (1905), infantile sexuality reaches its peak during the oedipal phase. Following the repression (infantile amnesia) that occurs during latency, the libido makes a fresh start during adolescence, looking for a new, nonincestuous object that, nonetheless, is reminiscent of the original love. The beginnings of the search for later love occur during the early experiences of sucking at the mother's breast.

> At a time at which the first beginnings of sexual satisfaction are still linked with the taking of nourishment, the sexual instinct has a sexual object outside the infant's own body in the shape of his mother's breast. It is only later that the instinct loses that object, just at the time perhaps, when the child is able to form a total idea of the person to whom the organ that is giving him satisfaction belongs. As a rule the sexual instinct then becomes auto-erotic, and not until the period of latency has been passed through is the original relation restored. There are thus good reasons why a child sucking at his mother's breast has become the prototype of every relation of love. The finding of an object is in fact a refinding of it.
>
> (p.222)

The infant begins to learn about the challenge that will confront him years later. Freud describes that what is left over from the sexual relation to the first object "helps to prepare for the choice of an object and thus to restore the happiness that has been lost" (p.222). Is this early state of lost happiness a prelude to loneliness? Is the infant getting a glimpse of this pain? Is it this pain that compels her to later try to refind her early happiness?

Adam Phillips (1994) also describes the experience of falling in love as an act of remembering childhood love. "If sex is the way out of the family, falling in love is the route back . . . What is being evoked, what makes these transforming experiences possible, is the knowledge and desire of childhood . . . When we fall in love, we're remembering how to fall in love" (p.39).

"Childhood love," according to Freud (1931), is "boundless . . . It demands exclusive possession . . . but . . . is incapable of obtaining complete satisfaction . . . and . . . it is doomed to end in disappointment" (p.231). The memory of this boundlessness returns when we fall in love. "We are now bewitched by . . . [its] insatiability" (Phillips, 1994, p.39).

As we examined Emma's relationship to her fantasy, she described its profound soothing capacity. I asked what it soothed? "It could be anything," she replied. "It could soothe me of some worry I had about someone in my family. It could soothe me from some of the competitiveness I felt with colleagues if I felt that they were succeeding quicker than me. I could also daydream when I was bored with someone." Later she added, "A lot of the times the fantasy that he loved me soothed me from the anxiety I felt thinking that he didn't love me."

Emma remembered the fantasy had two parts. After the lunches, she found herself reviewing what she said, what he said, how she looked at him, how he looked at her. If she remembered an ambiguous glance or a word that might indicate Peter disapproved of her, she became anxious, kind of panicky. It would be hard to hold on to her uncertainty of his feelings, the possibility that he was indifferent or disapproving, until their next meeting. Often she came up with reasons to contact him, perhaps a project related question, then waited anxiously until she'd hear back from him. If the tone of his voice and what he said sounded gentle, at least not disapproving, she'd experience that awesome feeling all over again. She was instantly soothed.

The centrality of idealization in romantic love is a projection of primary narcissism, Freud (1912) wrote. Idealization originates in infantile non-differentiation of self from other. In this narcissistic state, the baby feels the world and I are one, and that is pure pleasure. Slowly the infant's narcissism gets dispersed onto those around him, those upon whom he depends. Inevitably this is disappointing, for no one can love the infant as well as he loves himself.

In romance, the beloved is perfect and complete, just as the baby loves himself. The highest degree of idealization occurs in this state of being in love. When love is reciprocated, when the other idealizes the person in the same way and is equally willing to sacrifice him/herself for the other, we feel at our most ideal self. We feel richer and freer and love who we are.

In unrequited love, idealization is not reciprocated. The self feels impoverished, depleted, suffering lowered self-esteem and an onslaught of self-degrading, self-loathing fantasies. Emma's romantic fantasy had the power to awaken repressed expressions of herself. Love unrequited took it all away.

Describing why we fall in love when we do, Ethel Person (2005) attributes this phenomenon to intense loneliness, perhaps triggered by a major loss, being away from familiar surroundings, or longing to escape a lonely marriage. She also writes about the experiential qualities to falling in love. We cannot will ourselves to fall in love. We cannot will the time we fall in love, nor the person. The fantasy of being the object of someone's passion can feel like, or lead to, falling in love with that person. Feeling oneself to be the object of someone's idealization can open new possibilities.

"Actually," Emma remembered, "it was even before the crush began that things began to go well at work." She was less reserved at meetings, had two close female friends, liked the classes she was teaching, and felt excited about the interdisciplinary project. Once the crush began, this well-being increased exponentially.

Idealization poses threats. Because the fantasy forms from an infantile state of mind, it can be dangerous to incorporate it into an adult relationship. Stephen Mitchell (2002) considered that we do not simply give up idealizing fantasies as we get to know mates better. He suggested the feeling of safety and familiarity that sets in contains a different fantasy component. Safety may also be a fantasy. The breakup of a long-standing relationship often comes with the shock of how undependable the so very dependable mate "really" is.

Eric entered treatment with me in pain and shock after his wife announced she was leaving. During their five-year marriage, he understood their lives to be permanently connected. His wife's career preoccupation would subside once her goal was reached. Surely then he would have more time for his. Surely then they'd have more time for each other, for sex, and for children. If they had problems, they'd work on them. As the reality of separation set in, Eric recognized the important role this "surely they would in the future" fantasy of permanence played in his experience of their relationship. His actual in-the-present marriage and spouse were not as wonderful as the fantasy of permanence that sustained him. We came to understand that his fantasy of forever love originated out of feelings of hopelessness in response to his parents' permanently despairing, tumultuous marriage.

Mitchell argued that a safety fantasy is critical to a long-lasting relationship. Collusion in an illusion of predictability is the most common way lovers reduce the threat that aggression can have on relational stability. As safety builds, however, passion tends to leave. As feelings of dependency set in, passion becomes more risky. To desire someone, to want something from someone who is important, puts us at risk of disappointment. Perhaps that dependable, safe person is not so dependable. Perhaps I'll lose her. To combat insecurity, we develop fantasies of permanence. This fantasy replaces idealization. The challenge is to be able to move from one fantasy to another within one relationship rather than staying in the fantasy of permanence with the passionate idealization cut off, or splitting the two experiences between two separate relationships.

As our work continued, Eric came to understand the power his future oriented fantasy had over him. It prevented him from recognizing thorns in his marriage. Later he entered a new relationship, felt thorns, and learned how to move into a patch that had some roses.

Several analysts have discussed conflicting characteristics of love objects, with the search for mature love being seen as a struggle to unite exciting and gratifying early maternal imagoes. Differentiating libido from lust, Dimen (2003) defines libido as the straight and narrow of one's biology. Lust marks the contradictions, the twinned joy and suffering of the psyche. Frustration is a necessary dimension of sexual excitement, Davies (2006) believes. Pleasure depends on enjoyment of frustration and being able to tolerate arousal without any guarantee of immediate satisfaction. She identifies "pleasurable anticipation" as the early, erotic experience that holds intensifying arousal and excitement, making it tolerable and enjoyable because of a belief in ultimate satisfaction. This developmental achievement bridges one's relationship to an exciting good object to that of an exciting bad object. Coexistence of these two self-other configurations allows sexuality to unfold and elaborate. Davies describes endless cycles of need oriented toward resolution by a caring, empathic other marking the child's beginning capacity to believe in ultimate satisfaction. This achievement can develop into a later ability within intimacy, emotional and sexual, to hold frustration and even get pleasure from the frustration and arousal while anticipating resolution. Within romance, this object relational domain becomes the site of mutual adoration and oedipal idealization.

The early state of infantile bliss, the safety we yearn to return to when we fall in love is, Mitchell (2002) suggested, itself a fantasy. In the infant's overly stimulating, overly frustrating life, a state of safety and security may be, even for the infant, a fantasy. Perhaps what we remember when we remember how to fall in love is the infantile struggle to negotiate frustrations and gratifications.

Entering treatment, Emma felt she was losing herself as who she knew herself to be. She had daily bouts of panic. Although she had not been actively thinking of having another child, now perimenopausal, she had lost the possibility. With her twin daughters leaving for college, they would never be a family living together in quite the same way. Already they did not need her. Her parents, at various states of dementia, were lost to her as well.

When I asked Emma to describe her relationships with her parents, she said they had always been like pillars for her. She described very strong mutual dependence, mostly with her mother. Emma struggled to make decisions without consulting her mother and described the difficulty she had when her daughters were younger to resist her mother's overwhelming eagerness to impose her presence in their lives. Though Emma lived far from her mother, her mother's hold on her persisted. Her mother disapproved of Emma's attempts at independence throughout her life and Emma found this intolerably anxiety provoking. Often she would relent (her mother never would) and change a decision or plan. Things then returned to normal in her relationship with her mother and her anxiety would subside. Work presented a respite from this pressure. It was Emma's own domain.

We examined ways in which the crush resembled this dynamic with her mother. It entered her life when she had begun to feel freer, more expressive and more independent at work. The crush enabled her to hold an idealized image of herself. Feeling more attractive and outgoing was, in her mind, approved and idealized. If she imagined disapproval from Peter, she felt abandonment and, like with her mother, would have to do something (change a plan, find a reason to call him to hear something reassuring in his voice) so that things would go back to normal, to the idealized, exciting state of the crush. "The only other time I felt as overwhelmed as I do now by this anxiety was with that crush," she exclaimed. "There were times when I was so absorbed by it that I'd have to stop on the street to see where I was walking!"

Emma and I continued to examine her anxiety, the crush, and the losses, some imagined and some real. We wondered if the anxiety as well as the crush served to distract her from other feelings the losses threatened to generate and from feelings in her loving marriage. Despite the security of its 20-year duration, and also because of its duration and safety, this subject felt dangerous.

As our work progressed, Emma became less absorbed by her fantasy. She focused more on everyday life, family, and work. Anxiety emerged when life pushed her to confront independence, separateness, and aloneness. Without the fantasies of love that she came to depend on throughout her life for feelings of competence in various spheres, she learned to accept, with some anxiety, living life on her own.

Coda

Falling in love is, in part, refinding an earlier love. This rediscovery brings with it hopes and fantasies that initially arose out of the frustrating and gratifying negotiations within the parent–infant relationship. Falling in love sometimes brings more fantasy about the special person than reality; at other times, it brings more reality about one's loneliness than one can bear.

References

Davies, J. M. (2006). The times we sizzle, and the times we sigh: the multiple erotics of arousal, anticipation, and release. *Psychoanalytic Dialogues*, 16:665–687.
Deutsch, H. (1973). *Confrontations with Myself*. New York: W.W. Norton.
Dimen, M. (2003). *Sexuality Intimacy Power*. Hillsdale, NJ: The Analytic Press.

Freud, S. (1905). Three essays on the theory of sexuality. *Standard Edition*, 7:207–230.
—— (1912). On the universal tendency to debasement in the sphere of love. *Standard Edition*, 11:177–190.
—— (1912). Papers on technique: The dynamics of transference. *Standard Edition*, 12:99–108.
—— (1931). Female sexuality. *Standard Edition*, 21:221–244.
Mitchell, S. A. (2002). *Can Love Last? The Fate of Romance over Time*. New York: Norton.
Person, E. (2005). Love, forgiveness and betrayal. Plenary address, *National Association for the Advancement of Psychoanalysis* Annual Conference, October.
Phillips, A. (1994). *On Flirtation: Psychoanalytic Essays on the Uncommitted Life*. Cambridge, MA: Harvard University Press.
Plato. (1989). *Symposium*. Trans. A. Nehamas and P. Woodruff. Indianapolis, IN: Hackett.

Part IV

Loneliness through the life cycle

Chapter 9

Silence the grinch: The loneliness of a boy who yearned to hear his father's voice

Matthew J. Tedeschi

"While I was in the next room, I heard a child who was afraid of the dark call out: 'Do speak to me, Auntie! I'm frightened!' 'Why, what good would that do? You can't see me.' To this the child replied: 'If someone speaks, it gets lighter'" (Freud, 1917, p.407). For Freud, the first situational phobias of childhood are related to darkness and solitude. He believed this anxiety was related to "when a child feels the absence of some loved person who looks after it" (p.407).

Later, Freud (1926) spoke to the anxieties inherent in longing for someone who is missed: "Only a few of the manifestations of anxiety in children are comprehensible to us, and we must confine our attention to them. They occur, for instance, when a child is alone, or in the dark, or when it finds itself with an unknown person instead of one to whom it is used—such as its mother. These three instances can be reduced to a single condition—namely, that of missing someone who is loved and longed for" (p.136).

Melanie Klein (1963) addresses the topic of loneliness in a paper published posthumously, entitled "On the Sense of Loneliness." She argues that loneliness is part of the human condition, an internal experience everyone encounters at various times. It is the result of "a ubiquitous yearning for an unattainable perfect internal state. Such loneliness . . . springs from paranoid and depressive anxieties which are derivatives of the infant's psychotic anxieties" (p.300). Loneliness is experienced in exaggerated form in mental illness, particularly in psychotic disorders and primitive states. In an earlier paper, she argued that healthy personalities are less lonely (Klein, 1960).

Loneliness is one of the characteristics of the schizoid personality: "Loneliness is an inescapable result of schizoid introversion and abolition of external relationships. It reveals itself in the intense longing for friendships and love which repeatedly break through. Loneliness in the midst of a crowd is the experience of the schizoid cut off from affective rapport" (Guntrip, 1969, p.44).

A supervisee who trained as both a clinical and school psychologist once told me he was having difficulty working clinically/analytically in a school because he was told periodically by mental health colleagues and school administrators, "We do not do that here." He described how so much of the treatment emphasis was on reaching goals from an Individual Educational Plan. Attention to maladaptive behaviors seemed the priority, not understanding the child as a whole.

Another supervisee who trained as a social worker described how in being taught how to conduct behavioral social skills groups with children and adolescents, she was instructed not to let the clients "go on and on about their experiences." She was taught to keep clients focused on goals that were developed for them. The other material, she was told, was irrelevant and, at best, a waste of time.

Each of these practitioners believed there was much to be gained from allowing and encouraging patients to share their life stories without restriction. They experienced the associations and fantasies of their patients as rich, though at times disturbing, road maps of a struggle toward wellness. There was a loneliness these practitioners experienced as they longed to bring their psychoanalytic knowledge into their work, in settings where it was not encouraged or welcomed. I understood their dilemma, having had similar experiences. I've often been comforted and encouraged at similar times by the kind, firm words of a former supervisor, "If you are to be an analyst you will remember to always think like an analyst—always."

In this chapter I will describe a portion of my analytic work with a patient I will call Teddy. Teddy sought to hear a voice he had never heard from someone whom he missed and longed for. When it came to relating to others, particularly peers, Teddy was in the dark. Around peers, he behaved in ways that would risk, if not result in, abolishing any potential for friendships. As a young adolescent, much of his day was spent alone and in schizoid fantasy and pursuits—attempts at attaining a perfect internal state. His was a poignant experience of loneliness and of the agonizing struggle with associated longings that at times were manifest in primitive mental states, both in as well as outside of treatment.

Central to this chapter is my struggle to help Teddy with his struggle by thinking like an analyst in a clinical setting where such thinking was not often encouraged. The work necessitated that I be open to encountering primitive mental states within myself upon entering into "an identity between the states of mind of patient and analyst" (Jacobs, 1992, p.238). This phenomenon was described by Otto Isakower as the analytic instrument. For Isakower, "Without regression on both sides of the couch there can be no analytic process and without attaining a state of matched regression the analyst is not in the position to receive the bits and pieces of fantasy memory, and imagery that arise as he listens and that give him access to the unconscious of his patient" (Jacobs, 1992, p.238). In the clinical material that follows, this process is exemplified in the "dream" that I describe having had in my office, while Teddy was speaking.

One of the staff at the day hospital where I practice asked me if I could see Teddy right away. They said he was agitated and distraught. They had never seen him so upset. I agreed to see Teddy immediately.

Teddy entered my consultation room and began to pace. "Dr. T, I don't think I want to live anymore." Teddy spoke with his characteristic flat affect and monotonous voice. I had never heard him express suicidal ideation in the six months I had been treating him three times per week. He continued, "They all laughed at me at lunch." I asked Teddy to describe what had happened. He told me he was sitting at his table, minding his business, drawing a picture of the "top secret" submarine he was hoping to create for the U.S. Navy. All of a sudden, one of the boys at Teddy's table yelled, "Look, he's drawing dicks. He's gay." Teddy ran out of the cafeteria after everyone began to laugh. He bolted down the hall and sat in a corner, huddled in a ball. He was brought to his empty classroom by the staff member who asked if I would see Teddy.

Teddy was 15 years old, chronologically. He acquired the nickname, Teddy, when he was four. Fond of teddy bears, his family affectionately called him Teddy. Teddy had been diagnosed with Asperger's Syndrome years before entering treatment with me. The name Teddy seemed to fit him well. There were times when he spoke, particularly when standing, that I could picture him as one of the mechanical bears I had seen as a child at Disney World, in the Country Bear Jamboree show.

"You know," I said, "submarines, torpedoes, rockets and all of that; they can look a bit like penises at times." Teddy agreed, but how could Billy think he was drawing a penis when he was drawing a top-secret submarine? "You were drawing a top-secret submarine in such a public place?" I asked. "Uuuuuhhhhh," Teddy replied, and took a seat.

Teddy was one of those patients who frequently bored me to tears. He would speak about obscure topics that were an admixture of television programs and his embellishments of what he believed he had learned from them. For hours, I listened to Teddy drone on about this indestructible submarine he was going to create. It would make Teddy famous, as it would end all wars. I will spare you the boredom of listing other areas that I was introduced to throughout treatment but, I must confess, there were times he captured me. Periodically, in the midst of an apparently dead session, he could bring the analyst in me to life. I recall one session when Teddy was lecturing me about how his submarine might save us from Armageddon, a time when rockets would rain from the sky to destroy us. All the while, his hand was in his pant pocket, pulling on an obviously erect penis. Completing the story, he took his hand out of his pocket and sat down, like nothing had happened. I thought of this as a type of parapraxis. But I couldn't help but wonder, how Teddy could do this so obviously, obliviously when, in group sessions, he would cover his ears and squeal if any group member ever said "dick," "pussy," or "fuck," let alone attempt to discuss anything sexual, as adolescents at times do.

Another time, Teddy spoke about how our world could be saved if a threatening asteroid could be exploded. A split second after having said "exploded," Teddy looked startled, and became rosy-cheeked, following the sound of intestinal gas seeping out of his anus. Another parapraxis? Perhaps. But something struck me as primitive about this. I found myself thinking about the time when Angel, my family dog when I was a teen, farted in the family room. Angel's ears flattened as she startled and looked at her tail with an expression as if to say, "That came out of me?!"

Thinking about parapraxis, I became curious about the pictures that Teddy had been drawing in the cafeteria. "You have described the submarine to me so many times. I'd like to see the pictures." "Uuuuurrrrr. They're gone," Teddy replied. "I ripped them to shreds and threw them away." Teddy's characteristically affectless expression conveyed a hint of sadness. I offered an interpretation. "When you were invaded by the loud laughter that entered your ears, you experienced the terror of your insides, and the world around you, exploding and being ripped to shreds; a terror that attacked you from both within and without. You found yourself in a state of nothingness. Billy's confusing your drawing of a secret submarine with a penis confirmed to you that no one could ever understand those secret parts of yourself that you keep away from others and, at times, from therapy, as you try to make sense of them on your own. By destroying the pictures of the submarine, an invention that could become dangerous in the wrong hands, or save life when in the right ones, you managed to destroy that part of yourself that could attack and harm others, while at the same time you were left unprotected." "Uuuuurrrrr, Dr. T. Maybe it could have looked like a penis," Teddy said, referring to his drawing. "Too bad we don't have the picture to look at and think about together," I replied. Teddy continued, "I'll never do that again. Next time if something like that happens I'll bring the picture to you so you can see." "Yeh I want to see the picture Teddy, the whole picture." "I'm feeling better now, Dr. T. Can I go back to class? I'll see you on Thursday." "Sure," I replied. "And remember I'm here if you need me."

Teddy enters my consultation room for another session. "Uuuuurrrrr Dr. T. You're cold." "No, I'm just fine," I replied. Teddy continued, "Uuuurrrrr Dr. T. I'm cold. Can you make it warmer in here?" "Unfortunately I don't have the ability to make more heat than what is already coming out of this vent," I replied. I continued, "I guess we'll both just have to find a way to raise the temperature in the room on our own."

As I sit down, Teddy stands in front of me and begins a narration that sounds worthy of a cable documentary. "Dr. T, do you know about that symbol that goes back to ancient times? It's been around almost since the beginning of history. It's an ancient symbol that is with us even today.

Many people follow it and worship it. They celebrate it. So important a symbol it is that they keep it in their homes, and their places of worship. It's a symbol known as the manure." "The what?" I ask. "You know, Dr. T, that great ancient symbol, the manure." "Oh Teddy. Do you know what you have just done?" I ask. "Uuuuurrrrr," he replies, cheeks beginning to flush. "You've shit on that ancient symbol." "Uuuurrrrr," Teddy moans. "You've turned the great ancient symbol, the Menorah, into shit, manure," I interpret.

Teddy wondered aloud what he had done, how this had happened. What would the people who reverenced the Menorah think of him if they had heard him say such a thing, even if by accident? Perhaps he would be punished in some way. Perhaps he deserved to be. Teddy noticed he was feeling somewhat like he did in the cafeteria earlier that week, when Billy suggested the secret submarine Teddy had been drawing looked like a penis. But it was different this time. No one was laughing.

Teddy changed the subject. "Dr. T, I wish my family could celebrate Christmas again. A long time ago we used to build hills of snow and sled down them. We would have a Christmas tree and get gifts. It's been such a long time since we've had a Christmas tree, but we can't anymore because of that damned contract my father signed. That damned contract! All I want is to have Christmas again, and a tree. Those Jehovah's Witnesses made my father sign that shit contract so that we can't celebrate holidays any more. That shit contract. I wish my father never signed it." "There's the shit," I said. "You meant to attack the Jehovah's Witnesses who made your father sign that damned contract, but the Jewish people had to suffer your rage instead. Who should suffer?" I asked. "Dr. T," Teddy changes the subject again. "My best friend just died, and I went to his funeral." Listening, I give myself over to reverie. In a meditative, dream-like state, eyes closed, I experience the following:

My dream: I'm in the funeral home where one of my best friends was waked—my grandfather, affectionately called FuFu. He passed away, all too prematurely and, for me, tragically, when I was 15. I find myself there as Teddy describes, as I asked him to, what the funeral of his friend was like. I close my eyes trying to visualize what Teddy experienced, to gain some understanding about who this best friend was that he lost, and how the loss was affecting him.

Teddy: "There was a big grandfather clock in the funeral home."

My dream: I experience myself walking through FuFu's funeral home. I can vividly see the grandfather clock that was there. Tall, polished brown wood, shiny gold pendulum. Just as Teddy was describing, but as I had seen decades earlier.

Teddy: "I'm going into the room where the coffin is. The coffin is in the front, down a long aisle. The coffin is brown, polished wood. It has big shiny brass handles. My friend is in the coffin. I see him lying in there."

My dream: I'm trying to visualize Teddy's best friend whom I assume to be an age peer, an adolescent. But I can't. All I can visualize is my 15-year-old self walking down the long aisle to see FuFu lying in his polished brown wood coffin. Decades earlier it had been surreal to see FuFu lying there like that. In the session, it was just as surreal to be having this dream as my patient was speaking to me about the funeral of his best friend, a best friend he had never spoken of before.

Teddy: "I go up to the coffin and I can see him clearly. His curly brown hair and moustache, lying there."

My dream: I'm startled. Who was this man, I wondered, this best friend? I'm kneeling at the coffin but FuFu is no longer in it. It's me! (I had a moustache at the time I was treating Teddy.) My patient is describing my death, my funeral!

In this dream/session, emotion floods me as I attend my own wake, as narrated by Teddy. Paranoid anxiety grips me as I wonder what my patient unconsciously knows about me that I have yet to discover. Am I destined to die an early death due to some undiagnosed illness of which Teddy has some primitive awareness? Why is Teddy putting me through this agony? As Teddy drones on in his mechanical voice, taking me on this journey, I wonder if he is a danger to others or himself. Does he want to kill me, have me dead? Is he going to kill himself and, by proxy, annihilate my career? Who is this mechanical bear that is trying to destroy me and my mind? That's it. I'm losing my mind. I'm in a heightened state of arousal, in the grips of psychotic anxiety, at the edge of my seat, all set to leap out of my therapist's chair/role and strangle, destroy, this machine-person and save my life. I open my eyes.

During the dream, and a split second before my eyes opened, I expected to see a monster in front of me. Instead, upon opening my eyes I discovered tears pouring out of Teddy's eyes, running down his face. I'd never known Teddy to cry, nor up to that point did I hear anything to suggest he had been. These were silent tears—tears to be discovered only when I opened my eyes to encounter that which up to that point could not be spoken or heard, only seen.

Reminiscent of the second, more violent meteorologic event that typically follows the calm serenity of the passing of the hurricane's eye, Teddy suddenly began to cry hysterically. I sat, watched, waited, wondering what I might hear when this turbulence passed, and Teddy could once again speak. "All I want is for Santa Claus to give my father his voice back," Teddy struggled to say, gasping for air. "But we're not allowed to celebrate Christmas so I can't ask Santa for this gift. I think my father could speak when he was a boy, but something happened to him so that he can't speak anymore. And he can't hear either. He's deaf. He hasn't heard or spoken for years." Teddy's crying intensified. He struggled and gasped for air so he could continue. "I've never heard my father's voice. All I want from Santa is to hear my father's voice, and maybe for him to hear mine. Just one time. But it'll never happen because of that damned contract my father signed. Why did he have to sign it? Why?" Teddy asked, sobbing uncontrollably.

As Teddy once again began to cry, a second emotional storm entered me. I was on the verge of tears, of losing control. What would happen if my eyes welled up and Teddy noticed? Worse yet, what if I were to lose it and cry hysterically, gasping for air, unable to speak? In the psychoanalytic situation I believe I am responsible for the emotional safety of my patients first, then my own safety. I struggled to preserve the composure I was on the verge of losing. I sprung out of my chair and stood facing the large windows in my office that look onto a courtyard. I needed a few seconds facing away from Teddy, so I could regain a feeling of safety within myself, then be able to sit facing him once again.

As I began to feel I was standing with my back to Teddy for far too long, I lifted one of the slats of the lowered venetian blinds as if to peek out, giving me a reason to continue standing there. While not yet confident I would be able to hold back my tears, I heard Teddy approach from behind and call my name. "Dr. T." I found myself unable to speak. My voice was gone. "Teddy, go away," I wanted to say. Teddy called again, "Dr. T." Upon hearing this, my inner terror returned. I couldn't speak. And all I could see in front of me were the blinds that obscured the view of the courtyard, while protecting me from having to face Teddy and risk falling to pieces. I reached for the cord and yanked the blinds open. Teddy stood next to me. "Dr. T, do you believe in Santa?" "What?" I asked, giving myself brief pause to consider how I might answer.

Santa is one of those creations many of us believed in as children, fostered by parents and culture. An ageless, timeless old chap who has something to do with childhood wishes and yearnings. He's all knowing, all-powerful, and provides what we need or deserve, perhaps even what we've wished for. He arrives when we are asleep and dreaming. As children, we never got to see him at work, but encountered his work, when we awoke and looked under the tree. Santa, a metaphor for the unconscious, I thought.

"Dr. T, do you believe in Santa?" Teddy asked again. I was captured. "Yes," I replied. "You do?" Teddy inquired. "Absolutely," I said with conviction.

Teddy and I looked out the window and entered into a verbal squiggle game. It was winter and the sky was gray. "I really wish it would snow so that we could build a sledding hill," Teddy began. Noticing a grass covered hill in the courtyard, I replied, "Look Teddy, there's the sledding hill. All it needs is snow to cover it." "Where?" he asked. "There," I pointed. "Oh wow!" Teddy replied with childish enthusiasm. "Oh Dr. T, there's scary trees out there. You know the haunted kind with faces," Teddy continued in a somber voice. "Where?" I asked. "There," he pointed.

I looked out the window and saw the tree Teddy was referring to. It had black circles where limbs had been, giving the appearance of a face, the sort of thing you see in fairy tale pictures when trees become personified. I continued, "Yeh Teddy, I see. They're real scary. But look. There's a Christmas tree out there," I said, as I noticed a tall pine tree in the back of the courtyard, beyond the other barren oaks we had been speaking about. "Where?" he asked. "There," I replied. "I don't see it Dr. T." "Teddy, beyond the scary trees. It's there. Look beyond the scary trees," I said. "Oh it's a Christmas tree!" Teddy exclaimed. "Do you think we can decorate it?" he asked.

In response to this question, I found myself thinking about a family tradition my mom created near the end of her life. After years of decorating the family tree with ornaments purchased at Christmas shops, she began to collect pine-cones from the property of my parents' home. She would paint some pine-cones, leaving others natural, placing them on my parents' Christmas tree, along with the purchased ornaments. I noticed pine-cones on the tree in the courtyard. "Look Teddy, the tree is already being decorated." "Where, Dr. T?" "There, Teddy. See the pine-cone ornaments," I replied. "Oh wow, Dr. T! But the tree needs one more ornament. Do you think we could put a big gold star on top?" "What do you think, Teddy?" I asked. "I don't know Dr. T. I think Mr. Jenkins (the principal) would get mad. Maybe we shouldn't talk about this anymore." "I don't think Mr. Jenkins would mind, Teddy. Oh, but what about your father? What would he say if he heard us talking this way?" Teddy said he didn't think his father would mind; his father would understand.

"Look Dr. T, it's beginning to snow!" "Where?" I asked, not seeing any snow. "There," Teddy replied. I looked out the window and saw a faint hint of what could have been a few snowflakes blowing around the courtyard. "Oh I see, Teddy." As soon as those words came out of my mouth, the sky opened and a snow squall began. Huge white snowflakes began to fill the courtyard, blowing in the air, covering the ground. "Look Dr. T. It's snowing. Look at the snow hill!" The green-brown grass on the hill began to be coated in white. Teddy looked to the sky. "Do you think he heard?" Teddy asked. "Absolutely. I know he did, Teddy." I continued, "I imagine that our tears evaporated up into the sky and were transformed into the snowflakes that are falling." Teddy replied, "This is going to be a good Christmas. I know it's going to be a good Christmas this year." I interjected, "We have to stop for today, Teddy."

References

Freud, S. (1917). Introductory lectures on psychoanalysis. In J. Strachey (Ed. and Trans.). *The Standard Edition of the Complete Works of Sigmund Freud*, 16:243–496. London: Hogarth Press.

—— (1926). Inhibitions, symptoms, and anxiety. Op. cit. 20:77–175.

Guntrip, H. (1969). *Schizoid Phenomena, Object-relations and the Self*. Madison, CT: International Universities Press.

Jacobs, T. (1992). Contemporary reflections on the analyzing instrument. *Journal of Clinical Psychoanalysis*, 1:237–241.

Klein, M. (1960). On mental health. In *Envy and Gratitude and Other Works*, 1946–1963, New York: The Free Press, pp.268–274.

—— (1963). On the sense of loneliness. Op. cit., pp.300–313.

Chapter 10

Loneliness, emptiness, and Wordsworth's "Bliss of Solitude" in life and literature

Susan Ostrov Weisser

Sometimes I think I was born lonely. I first remember loneliness when I was very young, as an emptiness that could be filled up from outside me, a scared shivery awareness of something missing. As psychologist Eric Ostrov and Daniel Offer have written, "Loneliness is a feeling of deprivation that painfully, *but hopefully*, turns outward for fulfillment" (Ostrov & Offer, 1980, p.184).

The earliest I remember, my mother was like a pilot light whose warmth felt necessary for anything to happen at all. I knew I was alive most when I was physically connected to her, her arms around me or my head in her lap, but my dominant memories are of the *absence* of this sensation, being cut off from it and helpless. When I was growing up, she was always in the kitchen slogging away at the meat, potatoes, and vegetables that had to be served every evening and cleaned up afterward, when she wasn't away working at her succession of menial jobs. Most often, I recall her exhausted from both. When she was at work, I came home from school to a dog that didn't like me because I'd pulled his tail when I was a toddler and a big brother who babysat for me by ignoring me, unless he could entertain my second brother by making me cry for my mother. Then I felt the loneliness of the human condition in the way that an 8-year-old feels it.

Yet paradoxically, I also enjoyed being alone more than almost anything else. The need for affection was a sharp hunger, but fraught with the anxiety of loss; playing alone was pure peace. Loneliness cuts; solitude soothes and cradles. You might say I protected myself from the miseries of childhood by what Wordsworth called "the inward eye/which is the bliss of solitude." That inward eye was the imagination, and I remember sinking into my world of play with relief and deep, unspeakable pleasure, the kind that needs no justification and for which one pays no price. This was literally a world, constructed by me, in which I experienced a wonderfully stimulating community of feeling and connection. My favorite (and pretty much only) toys were a blackboard on which I drew maps of imaginary countries, naming the rivers, mountains, and cities as my made-up colonists explored the new land and settled there, and some marbles, tiny plastic soldiers, and chess pieces, all of which I pretended were communities of assorted people also exploring and settling into new homes in some dangerous and unknown landscape. Is there a theme there? It was a dream of a life both risky and yet controlled by me, daringly free yet secure, an adventure requiring individual courage, strength, and stamina, undertaken with a group of others who were there for mutual comfort and aid. I have never found anything quite like it in adult life, and I wish I could.

I was also a great reader as soon as I could manage it on my own, not surprising in someone who became an English professor. The imaginary landscapes of the books I read were extensions of and sources for my own play: they never failed me, the happy groups of friends having adventures together, the families with parents who never argued as mine did and who guided their children with wisdom and warmth, the neighborhoods where everyone knew and helped each other, the schools where groups of children laughed, played, and learned under the eyes of strict but caring teachers. In children's fiction, no one is ever lonely for long. Loneliness isn't a condition of life; it's a temporary problem to be solved, the path to a secret garden one learns to share, or the trial of a Little Princess who gets her reward of parental love in the end.

It was about this time that I began to read poetry because my mother, though like my father not educated past the eighth grade, loved and recited it often. The first poem I memorized was Wordsworth's "Daffodils," my mother's favorite, and therefore a connection to her. It begins, "I wandered lonely as a cloud/That floats on high o'er vales and hills/When all at once I saw a crowd,/A host, of golden daffodils." I had no idea what vales or hosts were, but then I listened to the music of it rather than tried to make sense of it. It seemed a simple nature poem with a happy ending: after a worrisome moment in which the poet lies on a couch in "vacant and pensive mood," he remembers the daffodils, and then his heart dances and fills with pleasure.

My idea of literature in general, and especially poetry, was that it was unrelated to actual experience, certainly any like mine. The whole point of it was that you escaped into another world where beauty lifted you into a different realm with rules of its own.

A pivotal point came when I read *Little Women* at barely age ten, my first real introduction to romantic love, such as it was in the novel. I blame Louisa May Alcott for much of my life since then.

The idea of romantic love in *Little Women* is recognition; one's virtues and attractions are recognized and valued by a worthy observer, and the reward is what the Sixties' song "Going to the Chapel" calls "And I'll never be lonely anymo-o-re" ("Chapel of Love" by Jeff Barry, Ellie Greenwich and Phil Spector, 1964). You, the lonely half-formed individual, metamorphose into part of a well-formed couple, who fit perfectly, like two Legos or jigsaw puzzle pieces interlocking. Where Jo is rebellious, Prof.

Baer is serious and wise; where Jo's sister Amy is flighty and a little greedy, her future husband Laurie represents benevolent indulgence; where the oldest sister, Meg, is sweetly and ditzily domestic, i.e., feminine, her husband John is upright, sturdy, and protective, the very definition of Victorian masculinity. In finding this complementary half of your lost self, I saw you also become securely bound to the social world.

In junior high a new front against loneliness opened up: friendship. I had almost no friends before this, oddly enough, something I can't quite explain. Actually, I don't remember missing being with other children; in fact, I remember resisting parental urging to go outside and play. The neighborhood kids seemed brutish and unnecessary. I preferred Jo March, Emily of New Moon Farm, and Black Beauty. These were superior beings. I felt that if they were to magically materialize, I would have instant friends, plus a horse I would be really nice to.

In seventh grade I became one of a trio of girlfriends; my mother was relieved, and I saw with wonder that while Sue Dworkin and Rona Halperin were no Jo or Emily, there were pleasures in friendship with real human beings that had advantages over the imaginary. For one thing, they could *laugh with* me, as the literary friends could not. This was followed by another bare period when Sue moved away and I went to a high school where I knew no one. What I remember most from this period is the feeling that, as Heidi Klum says as host of Bravo TV's *Project Runway*, "You're in or you're out." I was lonely and depressed, slinking like a ghost through the halls of the huge drab building. By this time I was terribly aware that other girls were dating, and though I had loved one boy passionately since age eleven, he had never so much as lifted an eyebrow at me. My virtues were distinctly *not* being recognized and appreciated, as Elizabeth Bennet's were in *Pride and Prejudice*. It left me feeling that my own high estimation of myself as possibly superior, or at least *normal*, was probably a complete mistake.

Then one of those turnarounds happens that takes you to a different place from where you thought you were going. One day a nondescript girl whom I knew vaguely and inattentively as Alice Gilbert came up to me and asked me to join the high school literary magazine that she helped edit. Since I wrote poems on occasion, I don't know why that thought had never occurred to me. My loneliness had formed a protective coating, sealing me in so I had avoided considering what might be possible. When I submitted and went with her to a meeting of this group, I saw that the girls and one or two boys were all friends already, joking and easy with one another, and I hesitated. I felt awkward and different. But Alice wanted me to be there, and everyone loved brilliant, shy, laughing Alice, for the same reasons that I would grow to love, admire, and bitterly envy her. Soon I found myself for the first and only time in my life in a tightly-knit circle of companions. Though I never quite felt a full-fledged member of this group, never as valued as Alice, the exhilaration of having those multiple connections, the joyful, stimulating play of different personalities, ideas, and activities, lasted for a long time . . . past Alice's death at age seventeen.

It was around this time that I first read the novels of the Brontë sisters. Literature both models life for us and is interpreted through the lens of selfhood. Looking back I see how my reading of *Jane Eyre* in particular exemplifies how literature can inform one's perception and experience of loneliness. The novel opens with Jane as a 10-year-old who doesn't fit in the family she lives with. Jane's account of her emotional isolation is the story of an unhappy child who is gifted but unappreciated, given harsh limits, held back from what she needs, and abused in some ways. When Jane is grown, she feels what Charlotte Brontë called in her real-life adolescent journal a "craving vacancy." Hearing the wind, the young Brontë wrote: "Glorious! That blast . . . has awakened a feeling I cannot satisfy . . . now I should be agonized if I had not the dream to repose on . . . its scenes to fill a little of the craving vacancy" (Gerin, 1967, p.103). In Brontë's journal, the "dream" refers to her early fictional writing, but in the novel, Jane Eyre satisfied the "craving vacancy" with romance, the dream of love with Rochester. As an adolescent I began to read love stories and look to the same dream. The problem of loneliness seemed a question, as it had been in the novel, of finding the right person, the one who merged with you into joyful wholeness.

Having a group of friends gave me confidence to try to attract men, and my amorphous yearnings focused with a vengeance. From there it was shockingly quick and only too easy to go down the path of one or two unsatisfying romances, and then early marriage. My mother once again seemed relieved. My new husband had the ambition to be a professor— maybe I was thinking of Professor Baer. I clung to him as I had clung to my mother in childhood, yearning and expecting to inhabit him and for him to live in me, just as I had longed for this with her. Though dedicated to the idea of having a wife and family, he was just as elusive as my mother, probably not coincidentally. Nevertheless I did not think of loneliness as an issue any longer; it was taken care of. My husband liked to spend time with me and keep in touch frequently by phone when he wasn't there. That attention made me happier than I had been, or at least more secure. It was double-edged, though: it kept me from noticing that when he was physically there, he wasn't always really there, and when he was calling me seven times a day, I did not necessarily know what he was thinking and feeling.

I am now at the stage of life people refer to as "older" rather than "old," as in "the older woman," which to me implies that I am somehow older than I should be, older than the normal woman, who is in her 20s or 30s. I arrived here by an unforeseen and circuitous path, through love and dating, then marriage, children, and divorce, more dating and love, and then—once more but more than ever—being alone. That is, I am single; of course I am not alone in one sense, as I purposely live in a crowded city, near two of my grown children, and very importantly, near my three grandchildren, who provide a lot of connection and stimulation, emotional and physical. I have good friends as well, though not quite the circle I had in my last year or so of high school and college.

Though I am surrounded by more people than I ever was in my childhood, I spend a great deal of time by myself, certainly compared to when I had a husband or children at home. I almost always come home to an empty apartment, go to bed by myself, wake up, eat breakfast and dinner alone. I have cats, two of them, which surely marks me off as the stereotypical lonely, failed creature who was not able to bag a lasting relationship and who will wither from older woman to *Old Woman*. People say, "You're living *alone* with *cats*." It doesn't help when I explain that I got them twelve years ago as kittens for my young son who'd always wanted a pet, not as a substitute for love and maternity, or a bulwark against isolation in my old age. "*Anything* but an older woman with cats," insisted a man on an online dating site.

That brings me to how I feel about loneliness and solitude now. I used to think of being alone as a kind of enemy that had to be guarded against and fought with any weapon I could find. Being alone meant being abandoned; my worst nightmare, literally, was a dream I had, in which I visited the house I grew up in and found my aged mother dead on the floor, having died of starvation and neglect, forgotten and unable to reach me or anyone. I didn't need my shrink to tell me the dream was partly about my fears for myself.

I now think of loneliness as a kind of challenge, and of being alone as a great privilege and pleasure. When I come home, it is to peace, to a place that is in perfect harmony with my wishes and moods, where I control the little world I've made just as I did in childhood play, but without the magic. It's only too easy for me to adapt myself to what someone else wants me to do and be; I've done it all my life, as a price paid for affection and companionship. I may need the physical space apart from others to be able to make the choices, especially the small daily choices of taste and pleasure, that define who I am. As someone dependent by nature, who yearns to lean on someone, it also brings me special pleasure to take care of myself, to show the world I can do this. Elizabeth Cady Stanton once said, "No matter how much women prefer to lean, to be protected and supported, they must make the voyage of life alone, and for safety in an emergency, they must know something of the laws of navigation . . . The solitude which each and every one of us has always carried with him . . . [is] . . . the solitude of self. Our inner being . . . no eye nor touch of man or angel has ever pierced . . . Such is individual life" (quoted in Gornick, 2005, pp.7–8).

I feel like a being neither as superior as I hoped nor as normal as I appear, but someone I am quite comfortable with, at least most of the time.

After years of responding to the needs of others, it gratifies me to serve myself, not to ask for "More, please," like Oliver Twist, from someone else. I am brave, as when I led an imaginary colony into the uncharted lands I drew on my childhood blackboard. To be brave yet at ease, I need what Virginia Woolf called "a room of one's own," which is exactly what I have, since I live in a studio apartment.

Nevertheless, I am lonely a lot, and I suspect that won't ever go away entirely. It's true that proximity is not intimacy (and conversely, there is no necessary relationship between being physically alone and loneliness . . . but it can feel that way.

What I'm left with is that "inward eye" of Wordsworth's with which I started. When I studied the Romantic poets in graduate school, I saw finally what "Daffodils" is about. The loneliness with which the poem begins, Wordsworth's metaphor of self as the wandering lonely cloud that "floats on high o'er vales and hills," is a kind of alienation from humanity and the world, an inability to enter into it fully. The experience of the sublime beauty of the daffodils he comes upon allows the poet to recall his connection to a kind of community, the community of nature. This apprehension is what I could not appreciate when I memorized the poem at age ten; the aesthetic imagination is not an *escape* from the world, but a certain kind of engagement with it.

As the poet May Sarton (1973) says in her *Journal of a Solitude*, "I have time to think. That is the great, the greatest, luxury. I have time to be. Therefore my responsibility is huge. To use time well and to be all that I can in whatever years are left to me. This does not dismay. The dismay comes when I lose the sense of my life as connected . . . to many, many other lives whom I do not even know and cannot ever know" (p.40).

I am now more in the world and more in tune with the rest of humanity than I ever was when I was a child. My own humanity implies to me an interest in and involvement with the rest of humanity, including those I don't know and will never meet. I am not lonely when I am with people I love; I am not lonely when I am doing what gives me pleasure; I am not lonely when I am in the zone of work, teaching and writing. These are my equivalents to the world of imagination that Wordsworth's poem extols, where literature, art, and beauty occupy what he calls the "vacant and pensive mood."

The struggle with the meanings of being alone goes on, the love and hate relationship I have with it continues, and we will see how it feels to move on to the next stage, where I really am an old woman, with or without cats.

References

Gerin, W. (1967). *Charlotte Bronte: Evolution of a Genius*. Oxford: Clarendon Press.
Gornick, V. (2005). *The Solitude of Self: Thinking about Elizabeth Cady*. Stanton, NY: Farrar, Straus and Giroux.

Ostrov, E. & Offer, D. (1980). Loneliness and the adolescent. In J. Hartog, J. R. Audy & Y. A. Cohen (Eds.), *Anatomy of Loneliness*. New York: International Universities Press.

Sarton, M. (1973). *Journal of a Solitude*. New York: Norton.

Chapter 11

The phenomenology of the relational void: Probabilities and possibilities

Joan Lavender

In 1986 The New York Times reported the results of a study (Bennett & Bloom, 1986) indicating that women over 35 had only a 5% chance of finding an appropriate mate. This news created an outcry in women of this demographic. The achievement of a marriage—the relational gold standard of the times—could no longer be assumed. Fifteen years later a Newsweek article (McGinn, 2006) revisited the issue with both revised data from the original study as well as retrospective data. Both refuted the original dire predictions. By 2006, the study observed, 90% of baby-boomer women (and men) either had married or would marry.

Between 1986 and 2006, the predicament of the woman in a state of unremitting, unchosen singlehood underwent an apparent transformation. The popular press emphasized women's ability to live well without a partner and implied that it was passé to need a man. A familiar saying from this time period, "A woman without a man is like a fish without a bicycle" epitomizes this sentiment. The upper middle class imperative encouraged women to feel they could be whole without being in a relationship with a man. Women created new options for themselves including professional advancement, single motherhood, homosexual partnerships, and the newly socially sanctioned preference to defer or reject marriage. The zeitgeist now proclaimed a woman's ability and choice to adapt effortlessly to life without a partner. The gold standard—a heterosexual marriage partner—was out.

Even as the media exploits one or the other side of the marriage/relationship dilemma, and psychoanalysts study with increasing refinement the nature of attachment and relationality, a large number of our patients are women experiencing relational voids (Rucker, 1993).

A touchy topic

My initial interest in this topic developed as I overcame the pain and shame I felt as I grew older while still yearning for a partner. I was not alone in this. I wished to document our lives to counteract the invisibility we felt and to give dignity to our circumstances. I wanted these women—friends, colleagues, and patients—to know that someone was thinking about them. Yet how many of these women wish to be recognized as a member of this club? The status of a failed search for a significant partner is the unenviable psychic "hot potato" (Harris, 2000). No one wants to be the last one caught holding it.

During the eleven years I was alone, I saw many women in psychoanalysis dealing with the same circumstance. My personal discomfort with the issue affected the way I sat with them. I squirmed when patients leaned forward to confirm that I was, indeed, married. The intensity of my need to disidentify stifled our developing spontaneity. I considered purchasing a wedding band for relief. With the benefit of hindsight, I now identify dilemmas, raise questions, and make suggestions about how to proceed when one or both participants in the therapeutic partnership is living with a relational void.

The first dilemma deals with the private awareness therapists must maintain, yet hold lightly, as we listen to patients. What do we do when we sense discrepancy between our patient's stated wish for a partner and her levels of avoidance of same? How do we hover in this gap suspended amidst validation, hope, uncertainty, and sober wisdom? What happens to the therapeutic partnership when the woman's stated need for a relationship transforms as she allows herself to notice that things are not what they seemed at first glance? As one wise woman now in her 80s told me recently, "We can think we know what we want, but . . . we don't!"

The second issue raises questions about our method. My psychoanalytic heritage, even revised, still makes me listen more for the tragic than the resilient side of things. Yet I know that our capacity to make meaning, often in small steps, is inherently optimistic. How do I create an experiential environment that manifests this process?

Finally, I will make observations regarding the vagaries of life in an attempt to contextualize our deeply held notions of attachment and intimacy.

I used the word touchy in describing the shame that women can feel if they have found themselves in this situation, regardless of the reason. But the risk of my hitting a psychic nerve goes beyond that. It's one thing if the woman classifies herself as suffering from a relational void; it is quite another if someone else classifies her.

Let me say who I am writing about. I no longer use marriage as the variable distinguishing whether or not a woman is experiencing a relational void. A woman in a long-term intimate relationship without the formality of marriage is not in a relational void. She does not have to be in partnership with a man; homosexual women in relationships with primary intimacy are not in relational voids. I am not including widows, recently divorced women, or those with partners whose work demands long distance relationships. With some hesitation, I exclude women with children, including single mothers, although this will raise objections. I arrive at this decision based upon the all-encompassing bond most mothers have with their children regardless of the quality of that bond. The unique nature of this kind of bonding makes for an inner life different from that of the woman who has no one "coming up behind."

Men have relational voids. They may have not found a suitable partner for all the reasons women haven't, although demographics suggest their chances for success are better. Not having sufficient experience working with such men to include them in this chapter, I look forward to hearing from analysts who do.

Also very touchy is making generalizations. A large segment of our population lives alone (Alternatives to Marriage Project). We are each unique and the way we have arrived at our aloneness has much private and personal meaning. I do not wish to engage in bashing of any kind. This paper is not meant to externalize blame (e.g., all guys are screwed up, all women are high maintenance). Doing so ultimately increases despair on both sides.

I am writing about women in midlife who have spent years searching for a partner. They have biological clocks and are feeling pangs of mortality. Their hope is waning. In Rucker's view their situation is currently irresolvable.

Primary intimacy and the relational void

Rucker's original paper spoke out against the fish without a bicycle ideology:

> I posit the continuing importance of a primary intimate bond throughout one's lifespan for maximally integrated identity and for maximally stable sense of psychological well-being. This attachment is characterized by exclusivity, loving mutuality and continuity over time . . . Although individuals in difficult marriages may experience ruptures in primary attachment or some degree of relational deprivation, they seldom present the same psychological residue of lengthy deprivation of a primary bond that is felt by single women living alone. It is virtually impossible for the qualities of primary relatedness to be experienced in isolation from a mutually desired, continuous, physically intimate relationship with another. The need for primary intimacy is either met by the presence of a suitable other or left unfulfilled; it cannot be resolved, and its gratification cannot be self-generated. The absence of primary intimacy forms a primary relational void.
>
> (p.379)

Rucker's deepest sentiments about primary intimacy strike me as having a timeless quality in most ways. Yet the value of such relatedness is something we may take for granted without articulating just what an intimate relationship provides. It is often a ticket to participate in the social milestones of life. Many solitary women describe a loss of status and identity. The presence of a viable partner amplifies the resources brought to bear in any given life situation. From a psychological perspective, a working intimate bond captures aspects of childhood while challenging mature capacities. It provides opportunities for humor and passion—alternate psychic domains that may be essential for providing relief from life's harshness. Such relatedness, affording novelty and familiarity, can be thought of as rejuvenating our capacities for communication and communion. On the other hand, like the Vietnam Memorial, unremitting singlehood makes an eloquent statement through the painful presence of an absence. The fact remains that while there are women who have chosen to remain single, women in unhappy marriages, etc., we all know women who enter treatment because they are on a search for a partner. They may even make up the majority of our patients.

While their dream of an enduring partner is the first thing they tell us, their life histories or temperament may have made them less than poised for one. We might be their initiation into the experience of an intimate relationship. Other women, capable of primary intimacy, may have had limited choices and may simply never find that one special relationship.

The phenomenology of the relational void

What if something happens to me?

The initial stage of the relational void may be ushered in by a single dramatic circumstance. Alone at night and suddenly very dizzy, Renee, a single woman, faces, in a new way, that she is alone. Family and friends love her, but the realization of aloneness persists and elaborates. The thought is fixed in her mind: no one thinks of her first.

Ann described her entry into the relational void with the following metaphor: "I was walking down the streets with my friends, and all of a sudden I fell into a crack in the sidewalk. I started to scream, but no one heard me. They just kept walking." She had many coupled friends and was invited to their gatherings but was shocked by the intensity of her envy.

A nagging internal dissonance plagued one woman who watched herself pursue an ill-fated relationship with an unavailable man despite knowing it would have an unpleasant ending. Caught between her "normal middle-class values" and a compelling need to survive her loneliness, she asked, "How could this have happened to me?"

Whom should I leave my album to?

Rucker compared deep immersion in the relational void to phantom limb—"nothing is there, but it always hurts." When a woman begins to face that this is happening to her, there is shock and outrage. No longer desperately seeking any partners, she avoids them to preserve precious energy for inner sustenance. One woman used the image of a camel in the desert storing up her memories of special relationships. Another woman wondered about the meaning of a gap in her photo album between the ending of one significant relationship and, many years later, the start of a new one. She had been professionally productive during the years between the relationships, but she had felt too uncomfortable traveling alone to ask anyone to take her picture. She was also less interested in retaining memory of events during this time. She wondered to whom she would leave her photo album after her death.

My fantasy has run out!

As women enter their forties and fifties still alone, it is clear "this is indeed happening to me." Menopause, aging, aging parents, etc., co-exist with advances in professional life and the inclusion, as a valued friend, in friends' and family milestones. Life goes on, with the relational void asserting itself with greater or lesser salience.

Socially, missing the first milestones of adult life (marriage, children, divorce even) is well past. Only rarely do friends or family inquire about prospects of partners due to tact, awkwardness with the situation, or even relief that the problem is not expressing itself with outward urgency. By now, most have had firsthand contact with one or more forms of misfortune, and unremitting singlehood cannot lay claim to special sympathy.

While many women are invested in meaningful pursuits, they still describe "dead" time in which the voice of the void is deafening. Winnicott's (1989) "think not of trauma, but of nothing happening when something profitable might have happened" (p.93) applies here. Such prolonged deprivation might make a woman prone to attacks from internal bad objects, precipitating bitterness, envy, and despair. Years of loneliness could affect the stability of the representational world itself, creating a kind of involuntary de facto meditation process. Women who have experienced this void report a terror which resembles that of the advanced meditation student (Engler, 1994). This may bring them to the brink of a dimension claimed both by psychology and spirituality, i.e., an encounter with emptiness itself. But this emptiness does not feel like a spiritual phenomenon achievement; it is a psychic specter.

One woman's story

A good friend was willing, though not eager, to recount with me her encounter with the relational void. She was in treatment during most of this period. Ellen grew up in the sixties in a family that friends described as friendly and "colorful." Her father and sister had substantial untreated psychiatric problems camouflaged by the freewheeling atmosphere of the sixties. Her mother seemed unaware of the impact the family's extreme, disturbing behaviors had on Ellen. Ellen took on the role of observer, warding off the mad hatter's tea party quality with a deadened demeanor. They loved her, yet no one seemed able to hold her in mind for very long. This was the context of her earliest loneliness.

A child of the sixties (and of this family), Ellen had many romantic adventures. In her 20s and early 30s she had long monogamous relationships with nontraditional, creative men drawn to her intensity and tolerant of her unrealistic expectations for excitement. During this period, there was no void but a different kind of loneliness resulting from the gap between realistic expectations of a relationship and Ellen's overblown fantasy—her psychological inheritance. She was in relationships, but not in relation.

Ellen was 34 when depression, loneliness, and confused longings brought her to a gentle, yet formal, male analyst. In the first meeting, his deep voice and gentle handshake responded to the lonely child needing security. The sultrier aspect of her personality masked the underlying depression that she attempted to medicate through sex. As their therapeutic bond took hold, she had her first experiences of steady boundaries and containment. Over time she began to feel the inevitable loneliness of individuating from her family and entered her relational void.

There was another side to this treatment experience. Sensitive to shame, Ellen felt her analyst was uncomfortable with her. She had been told he was single. In fact she had seen him with different women. She wondered why a man of his professional stature and kindness was still alone, but could not bring herself to ask him.

Feeling both protective and critical, she asked herself, "Were they both losers?" Something crucial to acceptability and self-esteem was being exiled from their relationship. Where was the discomfort coming from? Was it her projection? Was he warding her off? Did he find her capable of hurting him? As her relational void continued in her "outside" life, her shame and loneliness increased. Was she too much for him? Was she too much for any man?

Most of what we do operates in the realm of the implicit. If Ellen could have felt safe enough to ask him about himself and to sense that he felt okay enough with himself to respond, she might have begun the process of accepting herself. Maybe "the two of them against the world" could have developed. With that bond, it would have been easier to do the hard work of articulating why she was having a hard time settling down.

Entering the third year of her void, Ellen remembers feeling a "different playing field" (men were few and far between) as well as "an internal sea change." Now she was drawn to steadier men, none was available. This was the era of the "fish without a bicycle," but for Ellen, capacity for a realistic relationship was an achievement, and now she was supposed to not need it! Too late! Envy, with its intrinsic relational nihilism, became her companion. She had the financial means to support herself, fine friends, mentors, and a great place to live. She was terrified at the thought of spending the rest of her life alone.

Further inner clarity was needed. Terror of infinite loneliness is not the same thing as genuine motivation to find and sustain an enduring intimate relationship. Neither is the urgent need to fit in, nor the need for status and social identity. Ellen struggled with these dilemmas and arrived at the conviction that "fish without a bicycle" was a load of bull.

Now in her mid-40s, Ellen tried to keep her inner life alive. She found masturbation to be a source (albeit a sad one) of autonomy and psychic sustenance, but worried about potential for compulsion. She was tormented by vivid memories of intimate moments with one special man from her past. As she continued, she could barely connect with this source as "my fantasy life has run out." This prospect was more terrifying than being alone socially; it meant loss of self! This detachment must be the end of the line. The treatment process itself had narrowed. Was this an emotional hunger strike, depression, or simply a winding down of her inner life? Was this a determined attempt at renunciation? If so, could renunciation be considered adaptive?

Now in a different city for graduate education, Ellen found a new, older, pithier therapist. Her therapist "leaned in" as she challenged her with polemics on hopelessness. She wanted to tear down the walls of her middle-class office and (she assumed) marriage. This therapist seemed passionately invested in Ellen and proud of her courage to keep searching. She was impressed with Ellen's homemade desensitization method for recovering from a failed encounter with a man. (She tape recorded the final phone messages and listened to it until it became absurd. She played them in sessions.) This analyst vigorously supported Ellen's overdue decision to try antidepressants, resulting in alleviation of lifelong depression. She studied her envy and it morphed over time into sadness, longing, admiration, and a commitment to stay close to those whose happy relationships included her. She was readying herself for immersion into wherever life would take her, making the distinction between submission and surrender.

Silent confessions

When one lonely patient cries out, "I am alone!" it is monolithic and unnerving. Am I going to be The One who can make a partner appear. I recall hearing that Otto Kernberg gave a disclaimer to female patients in yearning, stating he could not guarantee that after treatment they would find suitable partners.

Shame stops her from showing me her depth of despair. I feel my presence makes it worse. She doesn't feel our implicit solidarity. She is rushing through sessions with no allowance for emotional breathing or even a moment to receive a supportive nuance from me. Her best friend is getting married; she should be over all this by now. Is it awful of me to indicate that a struggle with envy is something I can understand? Do I wear a ring? Am I afraid of her envy? Self-conscious, I hear cultural biases I didn't think I had leaking through my comments.

Can we open a space where intimacy emerges? I may be praying for this, but my patient dismisses my bait and switch with a wave of her hand! Her mission, cast in concrete terms, is unwavering. I think this work is beautiful, perilous, expensive, and of great practical value. It is worth the time, money, and effort. But build a relationship with yourself first because, regardless of the future, you're going to need it! When does her biological clock become our time bomb?

Finely attuned listening and validation are the essentials of a therapeutic relationship. But don't go out there expecting to find this! You will be searching for a unicorn in the garden.

Our engagement takes us into her history and how loneliness became the better of two sad choices: choosing loneliness over intensely conflicted feelings about relatedness. I listen more for what was needed that was missing and what was welcome but endured than for the resilience that is equally a part of our human heritage. This type of listening, still in my psychoanalytic bloodstream, can, paradoxically, increase her despair.

I appear cloaked in the words and worlds of the psychoanalytically tragic but I am a actually a closet optimist. The strongest influence in my work, based on the intrinsic hopefulness inherent in our capacity to make meaning, is the philosophy and method of Eugene Gendlin (1962). I know that psychotherapy, in its most meaningful moments, is not talking about your self; it is speaking from your insides, your vivid, highly specific sense of things forming inside you. It is speaking poised at the point where the complex bodily-sensed meets the poetic possibilities of language (Lavender, 2007). My patients need to sense this aliveness in me, then within themselves, or else we are done for. A specific image—of my own analyst—comes to mind. Her quiet involvement in her experiential process as she sat with me had the natural effect of bringing me into my own, and coming into myself enriched the evolution of our relationship. She trusted herself and me enough to have a "process intimacy" (Lavender, 2009) with me. She listened to herself, deeply, while listening to me. My insides knew this immediately, as if we were breathing, emotionally, together. This made us close. No longer hovering above myself, I could ease into my own experiential realm.

I can help people by offering an environment where things are released from how they have been held and fresh constellations can emerge. As life is acknowledged to be uncertain, it may become more interesting. We are unleashed from the grip of language and cultural convention to listen to ourselves, freshly. Can I help her lay down her over-determined, structure-bound burden? Can we float amidst the paradoxical, poetic, chaotic? This experiential "sinking into" is the realm from which new meaning emerges. This is the most sacred part of my work.

New possibilities

Rose came of age in the current era of confusion regarding our theme. She came to me to help her find an enduring, meaningful relationship, uneasy about the fact that she hasn't had one. As she describes her attempts, she can see I can feel how tough it is out there. Although I never say it, she gathers I've been there. I have the impression she wasn't expecting this. She doesn't have to hold back here: we will work on it together.

Rose is a lively, intelligent woman, an only child who learned at a young age how to entertain herself. Her father was irritable, abrasive, and had difficulty relating to his little girl. Her mother was proper and smiling, but Rose sensed her marital unhappiness. Her mother worked hard to protect her from her father's criticism.

Rose continues in her relationship quest like her mother, smiling, but inwardly anxious and stressed. I am struggling, concerned she is trying so hard to present a smiling face while she is suffering. Before long the atmosphere changes as Rose shares disappointment in friends, bosses, and men who don't convey real caring. I can't help but feel I am someone else pushing her out into the world unprepared to face repeated rejection. Rose wants to press on.

I see how painful this search is for Rose. I am doing everything I can to help her form a more compassionate relationship with herself and to take hold of a sustaining relationship with me. Often I want to say forget the guys for a while, come more into our relationship, rest, and find yourself, please! Each encounter with a new man becomes a gauntlet.

A few months into therapy another pattern emerges. Rose is self-supporting and the therapy sessions that her insurance provider underwrites are dwindling. Her job makes travel demands and she cannot come to sessions as steadily. I appreciate all this and wonder if I am making unreasonable demands—not only time, money, etc. Rose has moments when she becomes, in her words, snarky. When I ask her about this, Rose courageously replies she is like her father this way. I tell her I see what she means, as I am feeling kind of brushed off, even though I do appreciate the money, work, and schedule pressures. We have our first explicit relational encounter. I must try to understand that she is busy, not wealthy, and that therapy is no guarantee, yet as a person entering into a relationship with you, I notice myself feeling, well, a bit brushed aside, sitting on the edge of my seat in each session, getting ready for you to leave, just as we were getting into it.

My comment, its vulnerability and directness, touches Rose and she sees the implication. Yes, she is lonely, yet unsure that our time together will be worth the effort. Now I reflect privately, does Rose keep coming because she is afraid to upset me, or is she moved to find her sea legs in the vicissitudes of our relationship? She still wants me to help her assert herself with the cryptic man who calls at all hours to see if he can spend the night. He is friendly but remote. Maybe he will come around.

We talk about loneliness. I find myself sharing some existential stories with her, and we create a language for weathering our relational break-downs. She sees how, when, and sometimes why she backs off . . . with me. She finally confronts that strange guy and it's all over. I am about to take a one-week vacation.

When we meet next, it is clear that Rose has had a very hard time. She has difficulty talking and risks telling me she has had some passing suicidal thoughts. It is my fault. How could I let her pretend she could really work toward a relationship when all along we both knew it was mission impossible? I feel like the mother who pretended everything was okay when it wasn't. This is the subtext of her suicidal cry. Rose and I stick together through this painful scary time. As she starts to feel steadier, I notice she becomes freer to express real feelings. No more Ms. Nice Guy. She is taking a break from her search.

Released from her original agenda, our work can slow down and find its own level, moving from real time to the timeless quality that characterizes experiential processing. How does Rose really want to spend her time alone now? She has always talked about wanting a pet, and I have always taken this seriously. Her new mission is to investigate breeds, temperaments, training, etc. As Rose pursues this goal she questions: am I too self-involved to be a good parent to a dog? How will I handle my anger if my dog chews my new couch? What about that commitment of walking? This is an arranged marriage, with all the effort, time, hopes, and fears. One problem: she cannot afford to come to therapy weekly now. By now we have enough relational heft for me to respond, in a garbled, comical way, when she risks telling me how much she paid for her puppy. My shock worn off, Rose continues with a temporarily lowered fee.

When Brando arrives, his lively, faithful personality surpasses her dreams. I love hearing details of their growing relationship and she likes telling them. Rose's contentment is pervasive. For the first time, her father calls regularly, checking in on them. Her sense of motherhood gives her a better sense of boundaries at work; she has to get home to Brando. She has a home. I listen for signs of relational void and hear none. Rose is content.

Something is clearly shifting in Rose. With Brando stretched out alongside her on my old couch, Rose stays with her process; she is not outside herself. I can see by the rhythm of her speech and tone of voice that she is forming a different relationship with herself as we enjoy a moment of reflection. Her puppy has given her a new role and she has responded with a steadiness she wasn't sure she had to offer. Rose has a presence as she reflects on how she has been living her whole life, with such a distance between how she really feels when she is safely alone, and the smiling face she has cultivated to be acceptable. Now she has a grave expression and tears. She is sad, but "sad" doesn't capture her mood because there is relief in finally being able to see this and to tell it to me. Her tears are a sign she is starting to find herself. She sees more clearly how her need to please overshadowed her anxiety and depression, how her fear of men may have turned her off to men, and how relieved she is to have finally shared this with me.

In the following session Rose has a hard time settling in, uncomfortable like a puppy circling to find the right spot. What is this, we can wonder together? Is she conveying what she talked about last time, that she needs a lot of time to herself, and is missing that this morning? I can see she is trying to want to be here, but is aching to be alone, or with her puppy. I ask, gently, is this what might be happening? She nods and stops fretting. It's okay to be like this, you don't have to perform for me.

She observed that dogs lash out when fearful, reviewing her own history in this light. She leans forward and asks, "Are you expecting me to look for a relationship?" She wonders if she had gotten help sooner, where would she be by now. As Rose takes time to listen to herself, she raises new questions. The wish to choose an occupation that inspires her emerges along with a clearer appreciation of why it didn't happen that way in the first place. Giving herself permission to revisit the issue that brought her to therapy, Rose can now ask, freshly, "Would I have necessarily chosen to get married?" So we continue, the three of us, creating the conditions for new possibilities.

The vagaries of life

Our hope is that we can intervene with what life has given or not given our patients and co-create a deepening relationship that inspires new opportunities. This is the heart of my work. This is the closet optimism I described earlier. Yet there is no bill of rights regarding intimacy. Opportunities for early attachment and adult primary intimacy are not created equal.

A colleague whose expertise is in trauma told me she suffered years of premeditated physical torture at the hands of her father. Her desperation led her to make phone calls to random numbers hoping to find human contact. Thrown into such a life, she created abiding attachments to nature, in particular, blades of grass or the beauty and inspiration of a field of wheat blowing in the wind. I imagine this helped her to have some sense of continuity, alleviation of alienation and loneliness; this was her own version of Camelot. She said, "Let's be serious now, how many on this planet can even come close to the images these attachment guys are selling us. Sure, it's beautiful, but let's get real."

Can we endorse the value of relationship withoug privileging certain types? Our profession has had its share of mythology and I do not want to eliminate any attachment phenomena that help anyone sustain a meaningful life.

Back to Ellen: Who defines intimacy?

In the eleventh year of relational void, Ellen met a guy whose phenotype was opposite to hers but held promise. She didn't bolt. He seemed unique, with many impressive qualities and some mystifying ones. This would be no natural match, but there might be something here. He was loyal, reliable, and handsome enough, with a stimulating mind, but his manner didn't offer her the standard brand of intimacy she had come to assume was universal. No looking into each other's eyes, no private in-jokes, no deepening dialogues, no intimate transparency, no apparent falling in love, no marathon psychological encounters. How could this be happening? Doesn't one size intimacy fit all? She accepted his marriage proposal, took up the offer to learn about another kind of enduring intimacy, and never regretted it.

In closing

I know a fine man, now approaching 70, who recalls his deceased mother with great love and respect. She had been a poor farm girl. (What was she like as a mother?) She took me to the library. We were both voracious readers. She'd talk to my teachers when I got into trouble. She made great pastry. She gave me the box to make the stage for my puppet shows. In the summertime and on weekends, I'd leave the house early, run through the fields all day, and have a great time, a great sense of freedom. I could do whatever I felt like. I made bows out of wood, discovered Osage oranges and disovered things no one else knew about. I'd show up just in time for dinner. (Did you ever share your feelings with her?) I just don't know what you mean by that. Please explain. (Did she touch you, hold you?) No, of course not, parents were taught back then not to do that. (Did you do things together?) Yeah. We sat in the living room and each read a book from the local library. It was great. (Did you feel close to her?) That's another one of those questions . . . I knew she was there for me. (How did you know that she loved you?) What a ridiculous question!

References

Alternatives to Marriage Project. Retrieved from http://www.unmarried.org/statistics/html.

Bennett, M. & Bloom, D. (1986). Why fewer American women marry. *The New York Times*, December 13.

Engler, J. (1994). Paper presented at *The Suffering Self Conference*. New York, April 9.

Gendlin, E. T. (1962). *Experiencing and the Creation of Meaning: A Philosophical and Psychological Approach to the Subjective*. Evanston, Illinois: Northwestern University Press.

Harris, A. (2000). Women's envy: disowned excitements. Paper presented as part of a panel, "To have and have not: Clinical uses of envy," at the annual convention of the *American Psychoanalytic* Association, New York, December.

Lavender, J. (2007). Psychotherapy lite: Spinning gold from straw. Unpublished manuscript.

—— (2009). One therapist's travelogue. Unpublished manuscript.

McGinn, D. (2006). Rethinking marriage after 40. *Newsweek*. Retrieved from http://www.msnbc.msn.com/id/13007828/site/newsweek.

Rucker, N. (1993). Cupid's misses: relational vicissitudes in the analyses of single women. *Psychoanalytic Psychology*, 10 (3): 377–391.

Winnicott, D. (1989). Fear of breakdown. In Winnicott, C., Shepherd, R. & Davis, M. (Eds.), *Psycho-analytic Explorations*, Cambridge, MA: Harvard University Press.

Chapter 12

Challenges of aging: The impact of loneliness

Mary Beth M. Cresci

For many years psychoanalysts accepted Freud's (1905) dictum that people over the age of 50 were not appropriate candidates for the introspective work associated with psychoanalysis. Freud was 49 when he made this statement. Only recently have psychoanalysts begun to write about their work with older adults and to point to the opportunities as well as the limitations they have experienced with these patients. Frank Goldberg (2008) described how both he and his older patients have benefited from the psychoanalytic psychotherapy they have participated in together. He suggests that the relational analytic perspective has given this treatment a wider dimension, enabling him and his patients to find value in the work. On the other hand, Ruth Lax (2008) recently wrote about the sad experience of working with an older woman who was dealing with severe losses. Dr. Lax's patient faced reality issues, such as her dependency on younger family members, health issues, and the loss of loved ones, that limited her opportunity to work through her problems in psychoanalysis.

Although each individual experiences the aging process in a unique way, sociologists have made some observations about different stages of aging. Gerontologists Rapoport and Rapoport (1975) consider people 60 to 75 to be in the "retirement phase," followed by the age range above 75 which they term "old age." Busse (1998) indicated that the distinction between these different age ranges is very important. He states that:

> The health and general physical limitations of the majority of those 65–75 years of age closely resemble the limitations of those between the ages of 55 and 65, but are remarkably different from those 75 and over. Those over 75, particularly those who are 85 or more, are the target population for many of the medical and supportive services provided by public and private programs.
>
> (p.2)

Our experience with patients may be quite different depending on whether they are in the retirement phase or an older age group.

An issue that is sometimes briefly mentioned but not dealt with in depth in the psychoanalytic literature is the impact of loneliness on the problems of aging. Are older people more likely to experience loneliness than younger people? Is the loneliness experienced by older adults the result of difficulties in establishing positive relationships in earlier life? How does loneliness exacerbate other problems that the older adult might be experiencing? What if any help can a psychoanalyst provide when the older adult is dealing with loneliness in the context of myriad challenges to the patient's integrity and well being? Do we need to be more aware of loneliness as a problem for older adults and expand the dimensions of what we do as therapists to be helpful to them, or are our current models of treatment appropriate to this work?

One of the few psychoanalytic authors who wrote about loneliness as a significant psychological experience is Guntrip (1969). Working with Winnicott's (1958) concepts of ego-relatedness and the capacity to be alone, Guntrip describes the opposite side of this phenomenon—ego-unrelatedness and the sense of isolation. Although he does not address loneliness in older adults per se, he does suggest that a person's ability to tolerate being alone in later years is a result of having been securely ego-related to his mother in early infancy.

> The individual who has been securely ego-related from earliest infancy can bear the loss of his external supports, either personal or impersonal. The individual who from earliest infancy has remained ego-unrelated is wide open to the worst and most terrifying fears when his outer supports fail him.
>
> (p.223)

More evocatively, he describes the feeling of isolation and loneliness in this passage:

> *In every human being there is probably, to some extent, a lonely person at heart, but in the very ill, it is an utterly isolated being, too denuded of experience to be able to feel like a person, unable to communicate with others and never reached by others.* So long as that remains, all the rest of the psychopathological phenomena is camouflage, the day-to-day struggle to keep going, to try to deny the isolation, to sustain a secretly despairing effort to maintain physical existence and social activity, always liable to recurring minor or even major breakdowns.
>
> (p.220)

My own experience in working with older adults in psychoanalytic psychotherapy and psychoanalysis is that factors such as loss of job status, loss of loved ones, and loss of health can markedly exacerbate feelings of loneliness and isolation in people who were not securely ego-related from early life. Such losses in later years may be the proximate cause for a given individual to seem much less independent, productive, and content with life than we might expect at a given age. The extent of the resultant depression and loneliness probably depends on the underlying ego-relatedness. Admittedly, even older people who are ego-related and have the capacity to be alone may find it more difficult than they did in previous years to feel worthwhile through the contributions they make to their families and communities, to feel physically fit and healthy, and to be loved and cherished by significant persons in their lives. The following examples illustrate how factors of productivity, health, and strength of interpersonal relations impact the aging process and the resultant feelings of loneliness or connectedness to others.

Rachel

Rachel is a single woman in her early 70s. Although she was a successful business woman who took pride in her responsible position and her power to oversee others at work, she came to me in her mid-40s because she was still living at home with elderly parents and was obsessed with concerns about their declining health and fears of losing them through their eventual death. Rachel appeared to be developmentally delayed in many respects with severe dependency issues and fears of separation that are often confronted in adolescence rather than midlife (Cresci, 2007). We discovered that Rachel had a strong identification with her mother's own fears of separation and loss. Her mother had come to the United States from Eastern Europe as a young bride and found the separation from her family of origin to be quite traumatic. Her mother feared losing her children and clung to them, convincing them on a deep, unconscious level that they too would experience tremendous loss and loneliness if they left her. She also preached fear of sex and men, using as an example Rachel's charming, easygoing father who was devoted to his family but sometimes roused the mother's jealous suspicions.

In our early work, we confronted many of Rachel's fears of leaving her mother and living on her own. She accomplished many milestones, including buying a home, moving out, developing an intimate relationship with a widower from a similar background, and dealing with retirement in her late 50s due to a major down-sizing at her firm. We also dealt with her fears about falling apart when her parents died. She was able to tolerate the first loss, her father's death, but after her mother's death she came back to treatment because she was having severe symptoms of depression.

At this stage, our work focused on Rachel's conviction that the pain of living was not worth the benefits. Severe migraine headaches that had subsided during her 50s resumed, limiting her activity. Her sleep was disturbed by dreams that frightened her. A recurrent theme in many dreams was a feeling of panic as she tried to find her car in a parking lot so that she could get home. A new heart palpitation made her certain she was about to have a heart attack in spite of reassurance from many specialists. Each health problem experienced by a family member convinced her she was about to suffer another loss. She had friends and family, yet she experienced their desire for her company as demands and obligations that wore her out and from which she received no pleasure or satisfaction. She consoled herself that death would free her from the many responsibilities she felt toward others. In treatment, she focused on her inner feelings of isolation in the midst of people who care about her.

Karen

Karen, a divorced woman also in her early 70s, was the youngest in a very large family. Her father was hospitalized with a life-threatening illness while her mother was pregnant with her. He died when Karen was 4 months old and never saw her. Karen's mother was a disturbed, reclusive woman who dominated her family by inducing guilt and requiring the children to take care of her. As the youngest, Karen was designated to stay home with her mother to be her lifelong companion when the older siblings left. She rebelled against this fate in many ways, including making a suicide attempt as a teenager and leaving home to get married in her early 20s. She believed her husband was a hard-working, ambitious man, but she soon found he was overly attached to his domineering mother and did not have the aspirations for education and upward mobility that she had expected. He also made it clear to Karen that he was disappointed because her pregnancies resulted in daughters but no sons. Karen suffered from severe postpartum depression for which she sought psychotherapy and received medication for a brief period. Throughout her marriage, she believed her husband's family saw her as mentally unbalanced and treated her like an outsider.

In her mid-40s Karen decided to go to college to get the education she had always wanted. At the same time, she sought psychotherapy with me. As she completed college and eventually got several master's degrees, her estrangement from her husband continued. Finally, she demanded a divorce. He retaliated for this betrayal by convincing their daughters that Karen was selfishly breaking up their home, thereby permanently alienating her children from her. After the divorce, Karen dated several men, all of whom were limited educationally and unwilling to form a committed relationship. Each time she became obsessed with the man, had a passionate affair, then became jealous, believing she was unlovable and that he was seeing other women or still in love with an old partner. Alternatively, she would denigrate the man for his faults, believing no worthwhile person could love her. When not involved in a romantic relationship, she felt very lonely. Her family of origin has generally been unsupportive. In social contacts with other women, she believes she is often taken advantage of or is the last one to be called for a social event.

In therapy, Karen became aware that she suffers considerable loneliness and has felt empty throughout her life. She traces this loneliness back to basic feelings of being unlovable based on the disregard she received from her mother. She believes that she is only cared about when she is doing something useful for others, comparable to when her mother made her do many errands for her when she was a child. She worries she will have no friends or caring people around her when she is ill or needy.

Karen's frank exposure of her loneliness had a strong impact on me. At one point I was reminded of a song by Otis Redding, "Sittin' on the Dock of the Bay," in which Redding says, "This loneliness won't leave me alone." This picture of loneliness as a shadowing presence conveyed some sense of Karen's experience. No matter where she turned—to a mother, siblings, husband, children, lovers, friends, or even a fantasied father—there has been no feeling of reciprocal love and acceptance. Instead, there have been losses and rejections. However, as she has articulated these feelings in therapy and discussed her fears that I also cannot love her because she is unlovable, she has become more aware that she can change her self-perception and see herself as lovable. As in Otis Redding's song, she finds considerable solace walking by water. She has also turned her advanced degrees into a career that allows her to work with people who have many problems of living similar to her own difficult upbringing. As she has become more accepting of her loneliness, seeing it less as a statement that she is unlovable and more as an expression of her need for the right relationships, she has found more peace within herself and has derived more satisfaction from friendships, work, and leisure activities. She even found that she enjoys time spent alone.

Joanna

Probably the most dramatic resolution of issues of loss and yearnings is my third case, Joanna. Now in her late 70s, Joanna came for help in her late 50s because she was about to lose her job running a department of a large service agency. As a single woman with over 25 years of experience in this agency, she had devoted most of her life to work and felt devastated by criticisms that were being leveled against her. Due to her obsessive demands for perfection, no one wanted to work in her department. She felt completely alone and misunderstood by everyone at her agency. She sought psychoanalysis as a last resort. She had a strong concern about entering therapy because she feared she would discover she was mentally ill like her mother had been.

When Joanna was a young girl her mother suffered a nervous breakdown and was hospitalized. Not allowed to visit her, Joanna feared she would never see her again. She experienced extreme separation anxiety. Joanna also felt great shame that her mother was mentally ill. Her mother had many relapses and continued to act strange and paranoid, sometimes being dangerous to herself and others. While Joanna had been a good student in a local grade school, when she began to attend a high school in another town she felt overwhelmed and began to play hooky. She feared being ridiculed when she did not understand a given subject. She felt very lonely and tended to idealize one or another female classmate to whom she would cling for social support. Too homesick to live away, she obtained a college degree and advanced degree by commuting from home. Sexually molested by a neighbor while a young girl, she feared sexual contact with men. To deal with her fears of being shunned or criticized, she became rigid and obsessional in her approach to life. This had ultimately become too burdensome and intrusive in her job and brought her to therapy.

It took considerable effort for Joanna to trust me. She believed that I, like her mother, would abandon her. She constantly tested the limits of therapy to see if she mattered to me. For instance, she worked very hard to avoid leaving at the end of sessions, finding something else she just had to say or creating a crisis because she felt unsettled about an issue we had been discussing. We had to carefully work through session endings to make sure she felt something had been completed and would not bother her until our next meeting. She prized her fine memory and frequently tested me to see if I remembered some fact or name. She fantasized about being my daughter and found it frustrating when she had to deal with the reality that I was not actually her mommy. As we worked through her many fears of abandonment and demands for proof of my commitment to her, she became more confident that she could count on me and that I did indeed care about her.

In spite of making major efforts to revamp her work habits and provide more thoughtful and kindly supervision, Joanna had been labeled as difficult and continued to be treated as such. She eventually decided to take advantage of a special retirement package even though she would have much preferred to continue to work. Throughout this time we discussed her strong wish to be liked by others, a wish that often collided with her desire to be in charge and get special recognition for her good work. She explored her social isolation and sensitivity to any slight or lack of appreciation she experienced.

During the time she was working and even more so after she retired, Joanna got involved in volunteer activities. Eventually, she was able to sort through the ones that were fulfilling and disengage from the ones in which she felt unappreciated or disliked. She developed a close working relationship with a married woman who was a leader in many of the volunteer activities Joanna valued. Slowly this relationship grew to be mutually appreciative, rather than being a one-sided relationship in which Joanna adored someone who only half-heartedly cared about her. She had finally met a friend she could admire and by whom she felt admired and appreciated. Significantly, during the last few years, Joanna has suffered a severe, life-threatening illness which requires painful, debilitating treatments. She has managed to keep her spirits up and pursue many of her volunteer interests in spite of her weakened condition. She is able to tolerate more separations in our relationship and with friends and family. There has been much positive change in her ability to tolerate loss and to feel appreciated and loved.

Discussion

All three of these women were seeking many of the same things. They wanted to feel self-worth or efficacy. They worried about losing health and vitality. They wanted to feel secure in loving relationships with their families or friends. On the surface, Rachel has achieved many of these things. She was a highly regarded executive and continues to have opportunities to engage in worthwhile volunteer activities. She has a long-standing relationship with a man and has many siblings and friends. Nevertheless, she feels lonely and experiences others' interest in her as demands on her time and attention. Her fears of losing family members through death and her worries about her health have considerably restricted her ability to enjoy life. My second patient, Karen, suffered numerous losses of significant people throughout her life, and is acutely aware of feeling lonely and unlovable. Yet she is able to draw consolation from her relatively solitary existence and feel some satisfaction in her work helping other people with similar problems. Joanna started treatment feeling socially isolated with intractable, angry suspicions and debilitating obsessional traits. She has been able to find considerable satisfaction in her community work and self-worth through her friendship with a woman she admires.

In each of these cases, Guntrip's (1969) suggestion that current social isolation and loneliness is based on ego-unrelatedness in earliest infancy seems relevant. Each of these women had difficulties in her early relationship with her mother that affected her capacity to be alone (Winnicott, 1958). Rachel's mother clung to her and instilled a fear of being abandoned. Karen's father died while she was an infant and could only be fantasized as an idealized, unattainable figure. Her mother, by contrast, was self-involved, neglectful, and did her best to undermine Karen's efforts to reach out to others who would be more supportive of her. Joanna's mother suffered from nervous breakdowns which resulted in hospitalizations that were experienced by Joanna as traumatic abandonments. In addition, Joanna's shame about her mother's oddities contributed to her own social isolation.

I would not necessarily have predicted how each of these women would fare in treatment and in their current lives. I have been saddened and discouraged at times by Rachel's inability to work through her depression and get more satisfaction from relationships with family and friends. I have admired Karen's ability to confront her loneliness and see value in work and life. I have been particularly impressed by Joanna's ability to learn from psychoanalysis and to translate what she learned from our relationship into her life outside. I am hopeful that therapy has played a part in helping these women learn about themselves and confront meaningful yearnings. I am happy to say we are moving forward together to see what other life experiences they may have.

I have learned much from participating in my patients' struggles to find happiness in their later years. I have seen the importance of relationships in their lives and become more aware of my own dependence on support and love from family and friends. I have experienced my patients' needs to feel appreciated and valued for their work and have seen how this can continue to be a satisfying dimension of life even post-retirement. I have admired the courage of my patients in dealing with losses of loved ones and the pain and uncertainty of their own illnesses. I know I will eventually have to experience some version of these losses and illnesses myself. I hope to have the steadfastness they have shown in the face of these difficulties.

I have felt particularly fortunate to have been able to work with these women for a long time. The fact that we committed ourselves to long-term psychoanalysis or psychoanalytic psychotherapy has made the work more rewarding for me and for them. While writing this chapter, I read a novel (See, 2006) that provided a fictional description of enduring friendships between women in traditional Chinese society. Matchmakers would pair up two young girls based on birth dates, astrological signs, and family background. The girls would sign a friendship contract that lasted throughout their lives. As they moved away to join their husband's families, they stayed connected through letters in secret writing known only to women, and they would meet at special feast days several times a year. This relationship proved to be a significant support system for the women as they faced the challenges of living in a society that had little respect for women. They referred to each other as *laotang*, translated as "old same." "Old same" captures some of the special quality of the extended therapy relationships I participated in with my patients. While our relationships do not involve the sort of mutual sharing the Chinese women had, these relationships have been a long-term commitment for both me and my patients. I hope we continue to stay committed to our therapy relationship as we move forward into the next stages of our lives.

References

Busse, E. W. (1998). Old age. In G. H. Pollock & S. I. Greenspan (Eds.), *The Course of Life, Volume VII: Completing the Journey* (pp.1–39). Madison, CT: International Universities Press.

Cresci, M. B. (2007). The case of Regina: Negotiating earlier developmental tasks in later adulthood. *Psychoanalysis and Psychotherapy*, 24: 111–119.

Freud, S. (1949). On psychotherapy. In J. Strachey (Trans. & Ed.), *The Standard Edition of the Complete Works of Sigmund Freud, Vol. 7*, (pp.257–268). London: Hogarth Press. (Originally published 1905).

Goldberg, F. H. (2008). Knowing but not wanting to know: Psychoanalytic therapy with the elderly. Paper presented at the spring meeting of Division 39, April 10, 2008, New York City.

Guntrip, H. (1969). *Schizoid Phenomena, Object Relations and the Self*. New York: IUP.

Lax, R. F. (2008). Becoming really old: The indignities. *The Psychoanalytic Quarterly*, 77: 835–857.

Rapoport, R. & Rapoport, R. N. (1975), *Leisure and the Family Life Cycle*. London: Routledge & Kegan Paul.

Redding, O. & Cropper, S. (1967). (Sittin' on) the dock of the bay. Milwaukee, Wisconsin: Hal Leonard Publishing Corporation.

See, L. (2006). *Snow Flower and the Secret Fan*. New York: Random House.

Winnicott, D. W. (1958). The capacity to be alone. In *Maturational Processes and the Facilitating Environment*. London: Hogarth Press, 1965.

Part V

Treating the difficult lonely patient

Chapter 13

Loneliness in the disaffected (alexithymic) patient

Graeme J. Taylor

Although loneliness is experienced by all human beings at various times in their lives, most people employ defensive strategies in an attempt to escape from or reduce their awareness of this painful emotional state. In the classic psychoanalytic papers on loneliness by Frieda Fromm-Reichmann (1959) and Melanie Klein (1963) which were written toward the end of their lives and published posthumously, and also in later contributions by Satran (1978) and Mendelson (1990), there is an emphasis on how people strenuously avoid or defend against loneliness, sometimes by denial, sometimes by behaviors aimed at lessening its intensity (such as compulsive eating or excessive alcohol consumption), and, often in old age, by a preoccupation with and idealization of the past.

Individuals who have not experienced a secure attachment during infancy and childhood, and were therefore unable to internalize their primary caregiver (usually the mother) as a sufficiently good object, are especially vulnerable to feelings of loneliness, as Fromm-Reichmann and Klein concluded from their work with schizophrenic and depressed patients. While individuals who withdraw from relationships with others may appear less prone to feeling lonely, many of them actually lack the capacity to be alone in the sense that Winnicott (1958) described. As Abram (1996) points out, they have experienced gross traumatic impingements from the beginning of their lives. Their withdrawal is an insulation which protects the core self from further violation but inhibits the development of a rich affective and imaginative life.

In this chapter I discuss loneliness in patients who have difficulty finding words to describe their experience of this emotional state or are so strongly defended that they are unaware of the affect in themselves and of any need for close relationships with others. These patients are often very anxious and may easily express anger, but they are generally out of touch with a broader range of emotional feelings and with other aspects of their inner lives. Joyce McDougall, in an article she published in 1984, and also in her 1989 book *Theaters of the Body*, used the term *disaffected* to depict the affect pathology of such patients. She noted that the Latin prefix "dis-" indicates "separation" or "loss." Hence the adjective disaffected "may suggest, metaphorically, that some people are psychologically separated from their emotions and may indeed have 'lost' the capacity to be in touch with their own psychic reality" (McDougall, 1984, p.386). Rather than feeling their emotions and talking about them, these patients tend to somatize or act out their emotional experiences, discharging them through inappropriate actions. This type of affect pathology corresponds with the construct of *alexithymia*, which has generated considerable interest among clinicians and researchers since it was introduced more than three decades ago (Taylor, 2004; Zackheim, 2007). I shall briefly describe the nature of this construct and discuss how it may be associated with a high vulnerability to loneliness.

Alexithymia

The alexithymia construct was formulated by Nemiah and Sifneos (1970; Nemiah, Freyberger, & Sifneos, 1976) on the basis of several cognitive and affective characteristics they observed initially in many patients with classic psychosomatic diseases. Similar characteristics were later observed among patients with a variety of psychiatric disorders. The salient features of the construct are difficulties identifying and describing one's feelings, an impoverished fantasy life, and an externally orientated mode of thinking (Taylor, Bagby, & Parker, 1997). The latter two features correspond to Marty and de M'Uzan's (1963) concept of *pensée opératoire* (mechanical or operative thinking). Alexithymia is a dimensional construct rather than a categorical phenomenon (Parker, Keefer, Taylor, & Bagby, 2008). Individuals with a high degree of alexithymia sometimes manifest a mechanical mode of living (*vie opératoire*); they rarely experience desire or recall dreams and their ability to think abstractly and use symbols and metaphors is severely limited (Krystal, 1988a, 1988b). They seem especially prone to addictions, eating disorders, and a variety of somatic ailments (Taylor et al., 1997; Taylor, 2004).

Although alexithymic individuals generally have difficulty distinguishing different emotional states, the feelings they are most easily aware of and able to express are anxiety (fear) and anger, which are among the small number of innate, basic, negative affects identified by Tomkins (1963) and other emotion theorists. This awareness is understandable since fear and anger, which are experienced as terror and rage when they become intense, have an old evolutionary history that remains important for the organism as fleeing from harmful or potentially harmful situations and a readiness to fight are in the interest of survival. Alexithymic individuals, however, have difficulty containing these and other affects and using them as signals that can be evaluated and used to guide behavior that might eliminate or change stressful situations (Taylor et al., 1997). And although they may spontaneously use words such as "frightened," "angry," "lonely," or "nervous," alexithymic people manifest considerable difficulty when asked to describe their subjective experience of the specific affects to which the words refer (Nemiah et al., 1976).

Given their limited ability to describe affective states and to create fantasies and work with dreams, alexithymic patients typically make little progress in psychoanalysis and psychoanalytic psychotherapy. They have been described by McDougall (1980) as *anti-analysands*; with these patients, she states, "the unconscious inner theater never reveals itself" (p.335). Nonetheless, several therapists have proposed some techniques for working with these patients, including psycho-educational interventions to make them aware of their alexithymic characteristics, and helping them to develop affect tolerance and a capacity for affect-related fantasy and imagery (Krystal, 1979, 1988a; Taylor et al., 1997; Barth, 1998).

Alexithymia and vulnerability to loneliness

The vulnerability of human beings to loneliness can be attributed to our innate need for attachment which is present at birth and evident throughout life in family relations and adult intimate relationships. The importance of this behavioral system becomes clear when it is disrupted, especially in early life, as Spitz and Wolf (1946) discovered when they observed the development of anaclitic depressions in institutionalized infants, and Robertson and Bowlby (1952) observed in the three phases of protest, despair, and detachment in the young child's behavioral response to separation from the mother. Bowlby's (1977) subsequent elaboration of attachment theory made psychoanalysts and other mental health workers much more aware of the importance of the child's tie to the mother and how the absence or breaking of affectional bonds evokes a sense of abandonment and feelings of emptiness and isolation that are associated with loneliness. Long before Bowlby's pioneering work on attachment and separation, Suttie (1935) declared that separation-anxiety "is really a dread of loneliness which is the *conscious expression of the human form of the instinct of self-preservation* which originally attached the infant to its mother" (p.33).

An important function of the mother in the early attachment relationship is her attunement to and modulation of her infant's emotional states, including pleasurable as well as distressing states. Normal affect development does not occur when the mother is unable to read the emotional cues of the infant and fails to function as a reliable and effective external regulator of the infant's emotional states. This regulatory function is captured in Bion's (1970, 1992) descriptions of the container/contained and alpha function of the mother which influence not only affect development in the infant and young child but also the subsequent nature of the individual's internal object world and capacity to be alone. Krystal (1988a, 1997) has proposed that alexithymia can be a consequence of psychic trauma experienced in infancy before affects have become fully desomatized, differentiated, and represented verbally. What is traumatic for the infant are repeated states of intense, unregulated affects due to a serious failure in the affect attunement and container function of the mother or other primary caregiver. This failure inhibits the development of affect regulating capacities in the infant and also interferes with the emergence of transitional processes which normally make possible the development of symbolization and creativity.

Antedating and anticipating Winnicott's (1953, 1971) ideas about symbol formation, creativity, and play, Suttie (1935) proposed that the capacity for play and the development of interests emerge from the primal attachment to the mother and are substitutes for the mutually caressing relationship of child and mother. He asserted that play and interests form a powerful antidote to loneliness; they generate pleasurable affective experiences that are shared initially with the mother. Tomkins (1962) identifies *interest-excitement* and *enjoyment-joy* as the basic positive affects that human beings can experience. Alexithymic individuals show a limited capacity to experience these feelings; indeed, they usually have few interests and are often anhedonic. Their impaired ability to create fantasies and develop abstract transitional activities limits their capacity to be alone and ability to self-soothe by way of interests in music, books, art, and ideas (Krystal, 1988b). This deficit accounts for their tendency to rely on addictive substances or impulsive behaviors to defend against loneliness and other poorly differentiated and distressing affects.

The vulnerability of alexithymic individuals to loneliness is heightened also by the nature of their interpersonal relationships. Studies with various clinical and nonclinical adult populations have shown that they typically manifest insecure attachment styles, either an avoidant/dismissing style or a preoccupied or fearful/avoidant style (Taylor & Bagby, 2004). These styles inhibit the establishment of intimate relationships that mitigate feelings of loneliness. There is preliminary evidence from a recent study with university students that the association between alexithymia and social loneliness and loneliness in the family (assessed with the Social and Emotional Scale for Adults) is mediated partly by interpersonal distrust, which also interacts with alexithymia in contributing to loneliness (Qualter, Quinton, Wagner, & Brown, 2009). This finding has implications for therapy since it may not be possible for alexithymic patients to tolerate and express loneliness and yearnings until they have developed sufficient trust that the therapist can help contain the affects and not inflict further psychic trauma.

Case example[1]

Mr. J, a 31-year-old single man, sought psychotherapy because he was constantly anxious and felt on the edge of depression. He complained of frequent migraine headaches and reported a past history of duodenal ulceration and one episode of major depression. He had a prior history of abusing alcohol and marijuana, but now relied heavily on caffeine and nicotine to regulate dysphoric affects. Mr. J was anhedonic; he told me that he never experienced pleasurable feelings. "Positive emotion," he said, "is the absence of negative emotion. As black is equivalent to the absence of color, so joy is the absence of anxiety."

In the clinical situation, Mr. J had extreme difficulty identifying and describing specific feelings, including at times an inability to distinguish between anxiety, sadness, loneliness, and depression. He reported an almost total absence of fantasies and that he had never recalled a dream in his entire life. Though he had recently become engaged and was now living with his fiancée, Louise, Mr. J was unable to feel emotionally intimate with her and did not know if he was in love. He had few memories from his childhood, but knew that he had spent little time with his parents, his upbringing having been taken over from age one by his father's two dominating spinster sisters who lived in a nearby apartment.

The only way Mr. J knew if he liked a particular food was if he kept eating it or repeatedly ordered the same dish when he went to a restaurant. He could feel angry quite easily, as when he got a parking ticket or was stuck in a traffic jam, but he said that he generally avoids his emotions and tries to cope by not thinking about his problems. He described himself as a chameleon, adapting his personality to whatever he thinks other people expect him to be. "I don't know who I really am," he said. Mr. J had few interests; he did not cook as he considered it pointless. He said that it was hard to imagine taste sensations. He ate "for sustenance not for pleasure." It "boggled" his mind that Louise and her family were gourmet cooks. He avoided art galleries and movie theaters, but did go to sporting events and frequently watched hockey games on TV. The only time he felt an absence of stress was when swimming or skiing as he found both activities required intense concentration and thereby displaced his negative thoughts. As a college student he often dropped beer bottles from his dormitory window as the sound of breaking glass on the sidewalk below helped him relax and reduced his negative emotions.

Although Mr. J told me that he was a loner, he did not complain of loneliness. He said he preferred to be a nonemotional character like the actor Clint Eastwood. The only times when he was aware of feeling lonely was when his job required him to travel for several days. The loneliness would emerge in the evenings when he would stay in his hotel room and order room service to avoid going alone to a restaurant. He would feel isolated and depressed but was unaware that he was missing Louise.

Because of his extremely busy work schedule, Mr. J could only attend once weekly appointments; my therapeutic goals were therefore quite limited. Employing some of the techniques recommended by Krystal (1979) and Barth (1998), my approach was aimed at increasing the patient's imaginative capacity and ability to tolerate feelings, and helping him develop interests that would generate positive emotions. For example, when he went to restaurants, I encouraged him to pay attention to the surroundings; gradually he began to admire and take aesthetic pleasure from observing unusual lamp fixtures and stylish furniture, which he would later describe in detail to me. Although Louise would usually prepare cocktails and hors d'oeuvres for Mr. J's arrival home from work each evening, he was always surprised—it seemed familiar but he did not anticipate this warm greeting. Following my suggestion, he placed a reminder note on the dashboard of his car and thereafter, on the drive home from work each day, he began to savor the fantasy of drinking a cocktail with Louise. When I explored the loneliness and depression Mr. J experienced when he was traveling on business, I discovered that he was unable to evoke a mental image of Louise. Considering the distinction between recognition memory and evocative memory (Fraiberg, 1969) and the role of the latter in the development of a capacity for imagination (Mayes & Cohen, 1992), I suggested that the patient take a photo of Louise whenever he traveled and place it on the night table in his hotel room. Thinking also of Winnicott's (1953) concept of the transitional object, I reminded him of Linus from the comic strip "Peanuts" who got comfort from a favorite blanket. Some weeks later after Mr. J had returned from a month long business trip to several European and Asian countries, he told me he had been captivated by the photo of Louise and had felt much less depressed when he was alone in the evenings.

In using the term "disaffected" McDougall (1989) stated that "[she] hoped to indicate that such people had in fact experienced overwhelming emotion that threatened to attack their sense of integrity and identity" (p.93). In her view, "they were not suffering from an inability to experience or express emotion, but from an inability to contain and reflect over an *excess* of affective experience" (p.94). Similarly, Krystal (1988a, 1997) concluded that because of infantile psychic trauma patients who are disaffected and anhedonic fear affects themselves—that experiencing them will be unbearable and overwhelming.

McDougall's and Krystal's views are consistent with what Fromm-Reichmann (1959) learned about loneliness from her work with schizophrenic patients. She observed an overwhelmingly painful, disintegrative, and paralyzing loneliness in these patients that virtually defied description. It was a threatening, severe loneliness that patients could not talk about and often kept hidden from themselves. Using Binswanger's term, Fromm-Reichmann referred to this loneliness as a "naked horror" beyond anxiety and tension; when in its grip, patients experience paralyzing hopelessness and unutterable futility. Distinguishing this type of emotional loneliness from social loneliness and from the loneliness of the mourner who has suffered object loss, Fromm-Reichmann proposed that it originates in pathological relations in infancy and early childhood, which is consistent with Bion's (1967) later proposal that the mother's failure to accept and render tolerable traumatic feelings, such as the fear of dying which the infant projects into her, results in a "nameless dread." I had the opportunity to observe and help contain this profound, overwhelming loneliness in Mr. J.

Soon after they first met, Mr. J and Louise got a dog. Over a period of six years, they had both become attached to the dog. During the sixth month of the patient's therapy the dog developed cancer and had to be put down. This loss was very traumatic for Mr. J—he vomited, stopped eating, and could not sleep. He felt very lonely, cried a lot for the first time he could remember, and left the lights and TV on at night as he felt frightened in the dark. Although he feared that Louise would leave him, he sent her to stay with her parents for several days as he could not bear seeing her sad. He saw himself in her sadness and wanted to bury the painful feelings. He told me that he just wanted to be alone and in effect die. Identifying with the dog, Mr. J imagined it being alone and hurt; this made him feel suicidal. Entering into this imaginary scene, I asked him what the dog would want him to do; he replied that it would want him to be with Louise and not alone.

More than a year later, Mr. J got a new puppy but the dog died seven days later from a disease it had apparently contracted a few weeks earlier. Mr. J reported experiencing terrible emotions in his body, but that he was afraid and unwilling to allow them to surface into consciousness as feelings. Yet he felt an extreme desire to let them come out and to cry. But he was fearful of the unpredictability of the feelings and the residual depression that occurs if he experiences emotions as feelings. He said that he knew that sadness, grief, loneliness, hopelessness, and helplessness were all there inside him. He would rather commit suicide or die in a plane crash than have to go on denying the tragedy of losing another dog or of anticipating being overwhelmed by the feelings. He even tried to cope by denying that he was upset by the dog's death. He sensed a "black hole" of despair, but realized that this was an old hole that he feared falling into—a fate worse than death!

Grotstein (1990) has proposed that the experience of a void or "black hole" appears where an internal holding environment and inner container are absent. For Mr. J it strongly suggested psychic trauma in early childhood, presumably at age one when he was placed under the care of his aunts who limited the amount of contact with his mother. Any positive feelings vanish and he fears that the depression and loneliness will never end. He said that the speed at which he could go from wanting to die to how negative he was about to feel was amazing.

With the help of my containing function, Mr. J was able to tolerate and gradually find words to describe the loneliness and other painful affects released by the deaths of his dogs. I chose not to direct the therapy toward a deeper exploration of early childhood trauma. Of relevance to this decision were the infrequency of therapy sessions and Bion's (1962) concepts of K and –K, where K stands for knowing the truth and –K stands for the need not to know, not to learn, not to understand. Although Bion discussed –K in relation to envy and pathology, Schneider (2005) has discussed "not knowing as a means of safeguarding one's very existence" (p.826). "[It is] often motivated," he states, "by an effort to avoid losing one's mind or one's sense of self. As human beings, we cannot tolerate knowing all of what is true to our emotional experience" (p.826). For disaffected patients like Mr. J, –K may be a protection from breakdown as a consequence of being flooded by more affect and knowledge of reality than they are able to psychologically process. As Brown (2005) recently described for other post-traumatic states, we might regard severe alexithymia as a rigid traumatic organization that was developed to maintain a semblance of cohesion but at the cost of the capacity for play, imagination, and symbol formation.

Applying Bion's (1962, 1992) ideas about the transformation of emotional experience, the impaired imagination and symbolic thinking in alexithymic patients can be attributed to a failure of alpha function so that emotions tend to be experienced as sensual impressions, things in themselves (beta elements) that cannot be transformed into alpha elements that can be used in dreams, fantasies, thinking, and learning from experience (Graham, 1988). Grotstein (2004) considers dreams, along with stories and phantasies, the first line of defense against being overwhelmed by emotions. As mentioned earlier, when I first met Mr. J he told me that he had never recalled a dream. Early in the second year of therapy, he was able to recall for the very first time two brief dreams. The first dream was simply a replay of a conversation Mr. J had with his boss the previous day, a man whom he liked. Although he had no further associations to the dream, it suggested increasing trust and the emergence of positive feelings in the transference. In the second dream he was in a locker room either before or after a hockey game. This dream brought back memories of experiencing positive feelings when Mr. J played hockey as a boy, a game at which he excelled; it therefore seemed to involve some unconscious psychological work achieved through linking a past pleasurable experience with the work that he and I were doing together (Ogden, 2003).

Although the patient's capacity to dream did not improve further, over the course of two and a half years of therapy there was a gradual shift in his level of object relating. As he became more aware of his feelings and increasingly secure in his relationship with Louise, he began to experience the feeling of being in love and said it was "like having ice cream for the first time." He felt a sense of disbelief but told me that he now felt the love and warmth he missed as a boy. He was surprised to find himself getting interested in gardening, exploring new places, and socializing with colleagues from work. His business trips to Europe became more interesting to him; he visited such places as the cathedral in Cologne which he could now say took his breath away. During the first two years of therapy Mr. J often declared that he would never have children as they would remove the option of suicide as an escape from his emotional pain. During the last few months of therapy, he was surprised to find himself considering starting a family.

The psychotherapy was interrupted because Mr. J was transferred to work in another country. Although we had not analyzed his internal object relations, the weakening of his alexithymia and strengthening of his capacity to tolerate feeling lonely became a stimulus for seeking deeper interpersonal relationships. In particular, his experience of Louise as a good object in his external world released loving feelings and provided protection from intense loneliness. Mr. J was also now able to experience enjoyment and other positive emotions from his newly found interests, which also reduced his vulnerability to loneliness. He maintained contact with me for several years by sending holiday greeting cards and sometimes photographs of himself with his wife and children.

Epilogue

In reviewing ideas about what makes loneliness painful, Buechler (1998) notes that it always involves some type of painful loss and, in profound cases, the loss of hope of human connectedness; loneliness also affects a person's relationship with his or her self. Although many disaffected and alexithymic individuals have experienced traumatic impingements that have inhibited emotional connectedness in infancy and childhood, like Mr. J, they protect themselves from loneliness and longings for intimacy by evacuating part of their psychic reality rather than feeling it. Without access to an inner world of feelings and fantasies to help know themselves, they develop a pseudo-adjustment to the external world and to other people (McDougall, 1982). This mode of functioning is not based on repression or denial, but on a disruption of or failure to form connections between subsymbolic elements (patterns of bodily sensations generated by emotional arousal) and symbolic elements (images and words) within the individual's emotion schemas (Bucci, 1997). The resulting paralysis of affective liveliness was necessary for psychic survival in childhood; behind the alexithymic insulation, however, is an intense dread of encountering unbearable and overwhelming affect (McDougall, 1982).

The dilemma of alexithymic individuals is well stated by Grotstein (1997): "If feelings cannot be processed, then the feeling, as *signifier* of internal states automatically becomes the *signified* horror that it would normally signal. Thus, becoming aware of one's feelings runs the risk in these cases of unleashing raw proto-affects as avalanches. As a consequence, affect-unprepared individuals (those with alexithymia) must instigate a coarctation of the affect cascade that otherwise would inundate them" (p.xiii).

With this in mind, McDougall (1982) warns that psychoanalysts and psychotherapists must treat the defensive prison of alexithymia with considerable caution. Mr. J's inability to attend sessions more frequently and for a longer period of treatment necessitated caution and prevented me from exploring in depth his early childhood relationships. Nonetheless, he was able to use once weekly psychotherapy and the trust he gradually developed in the relationship with me to become more aware and tolerant of loneliness. The "naked horror" of intense emptiness, loneliness, and hopelessness he experienced following the deaths of his dogs undoubtedly originated in the traumatic disruption of the early attachment to his mother. As Mr. J developed capacities to feel emotionally connected to his wife and to pursue interests that generated some pleasurable feelings, his presenting symptoms of anxiety and feeling on the edge of depression subsided and there was substantial revitalization of his relationship with the world.

Note

1 Brief aspects of this case unrelated to the topic of loneliness have been described in two earlier publications (Taylor, 1995; Taylor et al., 1997).

References

Abram, J. (1996). *The Language of Winnicott: A Dictionary of the Use of Winnicott's Words*. London: Karnac Books.

Barth, F. D. (1998). Speaking of feelings: Affects, language, and psychoanalysis. *Psychoanalytic Dialogues*, 8:685–705.

Bion, W. R. (1962). Learning from experience. In: *Seven Servants: Four Works by Wilfred R. Bion*. New York: Aronson, 1977.

—— (1967). *Second Thoughts*. London: Heinemann.

—— (1970). Attention and interpretation. In: *Seven Servants: Four Works by Wilfred R. Bion*. New York: Aronson, 1977.

—— (1992). *Cogitations*. London: Karnac.

Bowlby, J. (1977). The making and breaking of affectional bonds. I. Aetiology and psychopathology in the light of attachment theory. *British Journal of Psychiatry*, 130:201–210.

Brown, L. J. (2005). The cognitive effects of trauma: reversal of alpha function and the formation of a beta screen. *Psychoanalytic Quarterly*, 74:397–420.

Bucci, W. (1997). *Psychoanalysis and Cognitive Science: A Multiple Code Theory*. New York: Guilford Press.

Buechler, S. (1998). The analyst's experience of loneliness. *Contemporary Psychoanalysis*, 34:91–113.

Fraiberg, S. (1969). Libidinal object constancy and mental representation. *The Psychoanalytic Study of the Child*, 24:9–47.

Fromm-Reichmann, F. (1959). Loneliness. *Psychiatry*, 22:1–15.

Graham, R. (1988). The concept of alexithymia in the light of the work of Bion. *British Journal of Psychotherapy*, 4:364–379.

Grotstein, J. S. (1990). Nothingness, meaninglessness, chaos, and the "black hole": II. The black hole. *Contemporary Psychoanalysis*, 26:377–407.

—— (1997). Foreword. Alexithymia: the exception that proves the rule—of the unusual significance of affects. In: G. J. Taylor, R. M. Bagby, & J. D. A. Parker, *Disorders of Affect Regulation: Alexithymia in Medical and Psychiatric Illness.* Cambridge, UK: Cambridge University Press, pp.xi–xviii.

—— (2004). "The light militia of the lower sky": the deeper nature of dreaming and phantasying. *Psychoanalytic Dialogues*, 14:99–118.

Klein, M. (1963). On the sense of loneliness. In M. Klein, *Envy and Gratitude and Other Works, 1946–1963.* London: Hogarth Press, 1975, pp.300–313.

Krystal, H. (1979). Alexithymia and psychotherapy. *American Journal of Psychotherapy*, 33:17–31.

—— (1988a). *Integration and Self-healing. Affect, Trauma, Alexithymia.* Hillsdale, NJ: Analytic Press.

—— (1988b). On some roots of creativity. *Psychiatric Clinics of North America*, 11:475–491.

—— (1997). Desomatization and the consequences of infantile psychic trauma. *Psychoanalytic Inquiry*, 17:126–150.

Marty, P. & de M'Uzan, M. (1963). La "pensée opératoire." *Revue Francaise de Psychanalyse*, 27:1345–1356.

Mayes, L. C. & Cohen, D. J. (1992). The development of a capacity for imagination in early childhood. *The Psychoanalytic Study of the Child*, 47:23–47.

McDougall, J. (1980). The anti-analysand in analysis. In S. Lebovici and D. Widlocher (Eds.), *Ten Years of Psychoanalysis in France.* New York: International Universities Press.

—— (1982). Alexithymia: A psychoanalytic viewpoint. *Psychotherapy and Psychosomatics*, 28:81–90.

—— (1984). The "dis-affected" patient: Reflections on affect pathology. *Psychoanalytic Quarterly*, 53:386–409.

—— (1989). *Theaters of the Body.* New York: Norton.

Mendelson, M. D. (1990). Reflections on loneliness. *Contemporary Psychoanalysis*, 26:330–355.

Nemiah, J. C., Freyberger, H., & Sifneos, P. E. (1976). Alexithymia: A view of the psychosomatic process. In O. W. Hill (Ed.), *Modern Trends in Psychosomatic Medicine* (vol. 3, pp.430–439). London: Butterworths.

—— & Sifneos, P. E. (1970). Affect and fantasy in patients with psychosomatic disorders. In O. W. Hill (Ed.), *Modern Trends in Psychosomatic Medicine,* vol. 2. London: Butterworths, pp.26–34.

Ogden, T. H. (2003). On not being able to dream. *International Journal of Psycho-Analysis*, 84:17–30.

Parker, J. D. A., Keefer, K., Taylor, G. J., & Bagby, R. M. (2008). Latent structure of the alexithymia construct: a taxometric investigation. *Psychological Assessment*, 20:385–396.

Qualter, P., Quinton, S. J., Wagner, H., & Brown, S. (2009). Loneliness, interpersonal distrust and alexithymia in university students. *Journal of Applied Social Psychology*, 39: 1461–1479.

Robertson, J. & Bowlby, J. (1952). Observations of the sequence of response of children aged 18 to 24 months during the course of separation. *Courrier Centre Internationale Enfance*, 2:131–142.

Satran, G. (1978). Notes on loneliness. *Journal of the American Academy of Psychoanalysis*, 6:281–300.

Schneider, J. A. (2005). Experiences in K and –K. *International Journal of Psycho-Analysis*, 86:825–839.

Spitz, R. A. & Wolf, K. M. (1946). Anaclitic depression. An inquiry into the genesis of psychiatric conditions in early childhood. *The Psychoanalytic Study of the Child*, 2:313–342.

Suttie, I. D. (1935). *The Origins of Love and Hate*. London: Kegan Paul.

Taylor, G. J. (1995). Psychoanalysis and empirical research: The example of patients who lack psychological mindedness. *Journal of the American Academy of Psychoanalysis*, 23:263–281.

Taylor, G. J. (2004). Alexithymia: Twenty-five years of theory and research. In I. Nyklicek, A. J. M. Vingerhoets, & L. R. Temoshok (Eds.), *Emotional Expression and Health: Advances in Theory, Assessment, and Clinical Applications*. London: Brunner-Routledge, pp.137–153.

—— & Bagby, R. M. (2004). New trends in alexithymia research. *Psychotherapy and Psychosomatics*, 73:68–77.

—— Bagby, R. M., & Parker, J. D. A. (1997). *Disorders of Affect Regulation: Alexithymia in Medical and Psychiatric Illness*. Cambridge, UK: Cambridge University Press.

Tomkins, S. S. (1962). *Affect/Imagery/Consciousness. Vol.1: The Positive Affects*. New York: Springer.

—— (1963). *Affect/Imagery/Consciousness. Vol. 2: The Negative Affects*. New York: Springer.

Winnicott, D. W. (1953). Transitional objects and transitional phenomena. *International Journal of Psycho-Analysis*, 34:89–97.

—— (1958). The capacity to be alone. In *The Maturational Processes and the Facilitating Environment*. London: Hogarth Press, 1976.

—— (1971). *Playing and Reality*. New York: Basic Books.

Zackheim, L. (2007). Alexithymia: The expanding realm of research. *Journal of Psychosomatic Research*, 63:345–347.

Chapter 14

"Tell me how to bear myself": On borderline desire, emptiness, and evocative dreaming

Ionas Sapountzis

"Tell me how to bear myself," reads the subtitle for a collection of poems by Jane Kenyon (1993), beautiful poems that evoke the agony individuals in states of turmoil experience as they struggle to make sense of themselves and their lives. This line, actually a verse, from a poem written by Adrienne Rich, always evokes my experience of working with Olga, as if that verse and the collection of Kenyon's poems had been written by Olga, or for Olga.

Olga, of course, could not express herself in such a lyrical, evocative manner. Quite the contrary. A bitter, rather offensive woman with a long history of abuse and neglect, she had never been at peace in her life and did not feel like a woman. She seemed enraged at everyone, dismissive of everything. Sitting erect on the edge of the couch, clutching her handbag tightly by her side as if she anticipated an attack, Olga not only seemed very unsure and distrustful of what was about to transpire in the room, but also conveyed the unmistakable impression that she was a woman who disliked herself, who felt troubled by who she was and how she was perceived by others.

Growing up as the only girl in a chaotic, abusive household where almost every member was a perpetrator and a victim, she was, like Temple—the character in Faulkner's (1931) novel, *The Sanctuary*—doomed. Yet unlike Temple, who knew she was doomed the instant she saw her assailant enter the room, Olga never knew that. What she knew was what had always been present in her life, the abuse she experienced and the violence she witnessed on an ongoing basis that formed the "background presence" (Grotstein, 2000) of her life.

In treatment, she presented as a woman unable to extricate herself from her past. Although she often wondered whether her past actions and reactions contributed to her present predicament, her acknowledgement served more as an attack on herself than as a starting point for exploring that possibility. Her life seemed hopeless, mired in sadistic and abusive relationships from which she felt unable to escape. She was quick to blame herself for what happened to her as a child, what she put up with and did not object to as an adult. She wondered whether she had elicited the abuse, whether somehow she had "asked for it."

It often felt as if she were only interested in expressing bitterness and disgust with everything and everyone. Looking back at the first two to three years of work, I now realize how easy it was to miss her, to feel offended by her offensive acts and dismiss her as the impossible "borderline" she knew she was. It was easy to become affected by the turbulence she created, to feel ineffective in her presence, a victim of her acts, as she herself felt ineffective in life and a victim of others' acts. It was easy to become entangled in the offensiveness of her reactions, to feel put off by her and miss what Bollas (1999) calls the "borderline desire," the desire for a non-offending, facilitating other who would focus less on the manifest and overt and, instead, attend to the unspoken, even unfathomed. It was easy in the wake of her outbursts to miss the fact that her rages were not simply justifiable reactions stemming from an abusive past, but also filled a void inside her, gave her purpose, and momentarily centered her. The literature is full of examples "of the self feeding of rage" (Bollas, 1999, p.131) of traumatized individuals for whom the "catastrophes" they were subjected to form the background of how they experience themselves and respond to others.

Was Olga searching for catastrophes? Did she derive a sense of cohesion and purpose from feeling wronged and enraged? She certainly seemed to feed off her rage, as if being wronged enabled her to feel right. She became furious at the mistakes and inadequacies of others, treating their failures as betrayals and insults. Her husband's shortcomings, an employee's error, the demands of a customer, and even the indifferent attitude of a clerk at a store, were all experienced as personal attacks, unbearable burdens that confirmed her belief that she was alone in the world and could rely on no one.

She was aware that her intense reactions had to do with the traumatic failures and neglect she had experienced growing up, but that insight did not assuage her fury. On the contrary, it fanned it into full blown, prolonged rage that left her feeling utterly empty and more disgusted. Paradoxically and perhaps unavoidably, the more she disclosed, the more enraged and hopeless she felt. The more hopeless she felt, the more paranoid she became and thus the more offensive and dismissive her acts would seem.

Over time, I came to perceive her tirades not as mere projections and acts of evacuation, but as acts that also served to create an edge, a rhythm that gave her a sense of boundedness, akin to the sensory experiences individuals in the autistic-contiguous position (Ogden, 1989) generate for themselves through repetitive sensory experiences. Olga's complaints, outbursts, and the sensations these acts created replicated the harshness of earlier exchanges and served to generate a continuity of being in her experiences with herself and others. Yet these acts left her feeling more deprived and unsettled, as if they reminded her of what she had been subjected to and how empty she felt in her life.

The stillness with which Olga reacted to any statement of mine that touched a chord, the silence that followed any observation she found resonant, the barely audible "yesss" she would slowly utter after a moment or two, as if the impact of what had been articulated was slowly sinking in, conveyed unmistakably that she valued and welcomed the experience of being understood and, with that, the feeling that she was attended to and heard. She wanted to understand her night terrors, her insistence on sleeping with lights on and the radio playing, her inability to fall asleep before midnight, the nauseous feeling she experienced whenever she smelled a whiff of alcohol in someone's breath. She needed to understand the fury she experienced whenever she felt light-headed and unable to control herself. She wanted to understand what triggered these reactions. She wanted to feel that her reactions and her emotional outbursts made sense. She wanted to make sense of herself.

There was considerable progress over the years. Panic attacks ceased, as did fear of flying and night terrors. She enrolled and completed two years of college before dropping out to successfully salvage the family's business. She came to trust and rely on me, and I felt I had come to matter to her. She became respectful of boundaries and did not feel rejected when the time was up. Three to four years into treatment, I realized I had become a companion, a person she counted on not only for answers and advice, but also for neither taking advantage of, nor mistreating her.

What caused these changes? It was not just my insight and understanding, nor my ability to contain and tolerate her. Nor were these changes simply caused by my attention (as Levenson [1994] urges) to the way she elicited reactions and engaged with others, my attunement to her state, and my growing ability to not feel offended or intimidated by her acts. In fact, tolerating her anger and dismissive, destructive acts was not experienced as empathic. Being "tolerated" was intolerable, as if I "put up" with her until the session was over. Our sessions had become the place where she would present mostly the insults of her week, confident that I would listen and give meaning to her experiences. She valued my insight and observations, but my input did not stop her from casting herself as the perennial victim, enraged at others. More important, more mutative than anything else, was the fact that I had come to not just feel sorry for her and empathize with what she had experienced, but to like her and value her honesty and integrity. I had come to respect her strength, to appreciate how discreet and loyal she was, and how caring she could be, despite her bullish demeanor. Most of all, I had come to care for her, not out of a sense that this offered a corrective emotional experience, but out of what I had "found" (Winnicott, 1971a) in her and in our exchanges.

Gone were the earlier paranoid states that had characterized our sessions, the mutual feelings of guardedness, her assaults on the therapeutic frame, her hostility toward me and my objectified stance. Clearly my "maternal pre-occupation" (Winnicott, 1935), my ability to contain her acts and sense the desire underneath the manifest, had a lot to do with how Olga came to experience herself in treatment and to respond to me. She did want the reassurance that despite the rage and hostility others triggered in her, she was still a caring woman and mother who could provide for her family. She would repeat, for instance, how angry and embarrassed she felt at the failures and inadequacies of siblings, or at the inefficacy and self-destructiveness of her husband, and she would feel soothed by my reply that however painful and infuriating their shortcomings were, she was making sure, through financial support and emotional availability, that they had someone to turn to, someone to count on, that she had become a parent to them. I also added that in doing so, she was making sure the chaos of the past would not be replicated and the family would stay together.

Yet even though our sessions seemed comfortable and pleasant, I could not help but notice how repetitive the weekly process felt, listening to her litany of complaints and offering insight every now and then. She would report, week after week, in vivid detail, the assaults and insults she had experienced as if there was nothing else going on in her life, as if she had no inner life other than the rage and bitterness these assaults evoked in her, and my role was that of organizing her, of putting these assaults in context, and enabling her to "go on being" (Winnicott, 1935).

God help me from a treatment that goes well, Sullivan (Levenson, 1991) is reported to have said, a statement that poignantly captures how stagnant our sessions came to feel over time. I felt as if I were participating in an enactment, confirming through explanations and interpretations that she was a victim who still needed to be soothed and contained. There was a risk that in succumbing to her unspoken wish to be explained and my desire and need to explain, I would become the "offending other," the supportive clinician who primarily saw her as weak and lacking. There was a risk of attributing, as I many times did, her emotional turbulence to her internal objects, to her borderline personality, and even to her desire to re-create what she experienced growing up, thereby missing something more elemental—the void inside her, the psychic emptiness she experienced that fed her anxiety and despair.

Something was missing. At times, I would listen to her complaints and feel restless, bored to tears, to paraphrase Bollas (1987a), by their repetitiveness. Listening to her describing offenses, I would notice the same pattern of feeling wounded, searching compulsively for betrayals, for evidence of being wronged. Over time, however, I noticed a shift in her demeanor. She was not offensive any more. She was only a victim if, to use Tustin's (1986a) analogy, she primarily experienced herself not in the "hardness" she generated with her acts, but in the "softness" she felt in being wronged. I had the impression she could only be sympathetic and less dismissive of herself when she experienced herself as an orphan in life. Was that progress?

However successful she was at work, however aware she was that some of her earlier anxieties and fears had subsided, there was always the feeling of being a failure, of a life lived in the margins, devoid of passions and creativity. There was an emptiness in her life, a void underneath the borderline dichotomies and split off reactions, that comes from having been neglected and having no one to turn to, all her life. She was convinced she was utterly unlikable and repulsive (Willock, 1987), a conviction that fostered her isolation and made her envious of others.

She had become less aggressive and offensive, and these changes had reduced the tension in our exchanges. It was, however, always the external, the lives and acts of others, that defined her existence, and never her own acts and initiatives. Olga repeatedly questioned with self-righteous derision others' motives, but her forays into the psychology of others did not provide transformational objects (Bollas, 1987b) that altered her subjective experiences and perceptions of the world. Rather, they served to deflect blame and convince her that it was others who were responsible for her predicament in life.

"It's not my fault," she seemed to be saying, as if this childish denial of agency would absolve her from any wrongdoing. Was this the fear of acknowledging her contribution to the predicament she was in, or was it the state of nothingness she dreaded to face, the emptiness she had experienced her entire life? She was not aware that she brought very little to sessions, never reported a dream, and memories from childhood and adolescence were few and hazy, "fugitive pieces," to use Ann Michaels' (1996) beautiful metaphor, that were scattered all over, as if they were random incidents disconnected from each other and alien to her. She would only "bring" what was done to her, what still haunted and persecuted her, but never what she wanted to do, or what she wished to do. Olga would speak about the future as an impossibility, as the time when the past and present would be simply repeated, and she would experience, yet again, another frustration.

How can one speak about a void, what is not there, what cannot even be dreamt, without triggering the experience of "falling" into an abyss (Tustin, 1986b), into an empty space which cannot be described with words? Even the simplest of daydreams, the daydream of any parent—that his or her child would do well in school and life—would unsettle Olga, triggering a host of paranoid and depressive anxieties, from rage and despair to resignation and utter guilt. Her children, after all, were failing in every area of their lives—school, relationships, and work—and she could not face that. Daring to dream, daring to articulate her wishes and yearnings, risked reminding herself of how much was missing in her life and how much she was afraid she would never have. More important, it risked bringing her face to face with what she could not contemplate, her own limitations, her underlying fear of being damaged and, therefore, of having contributed to the failures she had experienced in life.

The fear of breakdown, notes Winnicott (1963), is not just the fear of a breakdown that has already happened, but also the fear of a breakdown that has never happened. The fear of breakdown, in other words, resides not only in facing what has happened, but also in what one is afraid might happen, what one might find in the future. It is the fear of finding out that what one hopes for and wishes in life would prove unattainable because of external limitations and impingements or, even worse, because of one's own "badness" and inner demons. For Olga, her fear of breakdown was not anymore that of facing the past. She had done that. She had sought answers. She had created links between dissociative states, somatic reactions, and past abuse. The fear she "dreaded" was of finding her own limitations, coming face to face with her own inadequacies, confirming how damaged and bad she was.

The hardest clients to work with, O'Shaughnessy (1981) reminds us, are not the ones who distort and project too much, or the ones who enact too much, but the ones who display no such elements, the ones who do not project and do not introject. Olga did project a lot, but the challenge was not that of containing her projections and pointing to her omissions, but of creating a space to contemplate what was avoided, and, more important, what was just not there.

Alvarez (1992) makes a similar point on how difficult it is to create "a new idea" in individuals who are not just "dismantled" or "unmantled" (p.95) by events in their lives, but who have never been able to associate, individuals for whom experiences and sensations are not just avoided but are simply not there. Olga was a woman whose thoughts were generated by the acts of others and never her own. I could point to her lack of dreaming, fantasizing, and planning, but that felt futile, more like an act to reassure my clinical superego than an act that would enable her to experience and process. I had to find a way to speak not about what left her "dismantled" or "unmantled" (Alvarez, 1992, p.95) but what had never been "mantled," an absence she could not face.

Trains that do not leave the station are not likely to have accidents, remarked Winnicott (1972) to a fearful client who had reported a nightmare about a train that left the station. Like Winnicott's young client, Olga could not leave the station and face the prospect of an accident. The risk of trying and failing, of raising questions about her life and relationships that might have confirmed her abysmal view of herself, was too real and frightening. Olga, of course, had real excuses for not leaving the station, for needing the safety of her psychic retreat (Steiner, 1993), but what was my excuse for being so reluctant to explore and share my associations? Was I reluctant of starting along wrong itineraries, marooning myself inside the safety of the "here and now"? Was I fearful of triggering Olga's anxieties and rage? Or was I fearful of departing and finding myself face to face with what I, like Olga, dreaded the most, the confirmation of my own limitations as a therapist?

Olga's initial story, at least the way I read it several years ago, was that of a difficult woman acting out, externalizing and blaming everything and everyone, unable to process her experiences and think her own thoughts. Her story changed when I started experiencing her as a woman who needed to be tolerated, accepted for who she was and how she was acting. Her story then became the story of a woman who valued my interpretations less for their content and more for their function as "structuring experiences" (Bollas, 1987b, p.21). That understanding, that narrative changed again when I stopped focusing on interpreting her acts or empathizing with her experiences and, instead of limiting my input to what she did or did not do, I left the relative safety of responding to her acts and began to dream her, to imagine her life, following my associations and perceptions of her. I became willing to leave the safety of my "station," not to explore our shared fears, but to contemplate what else might be there "waiting to be found" (Winnicott, 1971a).

There are many ways to create experiences and facilitate journeys. With patients who cannot or do not narrate nor associate, with clients who are tangled up in experiences that frustrate and alienate them from themselves (Kristeva, 1991), the challenge is not to just be the dreamers who interpret the dreamers' dreams (Grotstein, 1981). It is also the challenge to be dreamers who dream the dreams the patients are afraid to have, daring to dream what might be missing in their lives. Focusing on the here and now, pointing out and exploring patterns of engagement, would certainly make patients become more aware of how they present themselves in life and relate to others, but it omits the dream, and runs the risk of rendering patients and therapists orphans of the real (Grotstein, 2000).

Apart from what patients project and enact, there is also the therapists' deeply subjective response to what the patients evoke. Side by side with the interpersonal and/or intersubjective experience there is also the therapist's personal experience, his or her reaction to what the patient evokes. With patients in a state of emptiness, the therapist's subjective and deeply personal response can transform what is projected in the room, and can contribute to an exchange in which each participant feels that he or she can impact the other.

There is, of course, always the risk of avoiding the pressures and pitfalls of the here and now by escaping into fiction, by creating a romantic version of what happened. The psychologist, writes Britton (2003), might, in the course of a session, be tempted to become the preacher who tries to convert the patient, or the poet who seeks to explore his own psychic reality by attributing it to the patient. Doing either of these things, Britton remarks, would result in the therapist forfeiting his role as therapist. The issue, though, is not that of imposing a poetry when none exists, or pursuing a dream or metaphorical image when these do not emerge unexpectedly and unbidden from the flow. Such acts would be tantamount to psychotic or manic folies-à-deux with the patient, as Wilner (1998) noted. On the contrary, it is only when one "does not prescriptively target certain experiences as those to be sought after" (Wilner, 1998, p.621) and, instead, pursues one's experiences as they actually emerge that the risk of creating forced exchanges or imposing one's views becomes a nonissue.

The association to Kenyon's poems, the reference to Anne Michaels and William Faulkner, and so on, are all associations that can romanticize what has happened, that can help one eschew the clinical for the safety and narcissistic pleasures of the fictional. But isn't any therapy that unfolds and renders beta elements into alpha elements, a deeply poetic act in the full sense of the word, that of something being created that had not been there or had been there all along but could not be experienced and played with? Isn't any therapeutic act a poetic, creative act that can transform not only the patient but also the therapist, as Searles (1979) pointed out? Does it matter if the associations one uses are triggered by a verse, a story, a picture, or even a dream? Does it matter if our associations come up when we least expect them, or even when involved in something else?

Several analysts, not necessarily of the same theoretical orientation, remarks Wilner (1998), may balk at the idea of wandering too far from the session's material. They may regard one's readiness to do so as a form of enactment, at the very least or, even worse, as an example of poor technique and discipline. Constricting our focus exclusively to what transpires in the session is, however, tantamount to consciously narrowing our experiences and associations to a certain space and time and, therefore, what we allow to emerge. Experiences and associations not only emerge in juxtaposition to what has happened and what we have noticed. They often just emerge, "unbidden and self moving" (Wilner, 1998, p.621), entering our awareness when we least expect them.

I am not sure whether I thought of Olga when I read Kenyon's poems or whether the particular verse came to me while in session with her. From whichever direction the association came, it captured, in my mind, something intangible about her and the treatment. Other images or associations followed: Temple from Faulkner's book; Winnicott's remark to his young patient; the image of tough, rough, and fast-talking female characters from the movies of the thirties, characters with a loaded past and a hardened exterior but surprising gentleness inside that made them likable to the audience, despite their seeming meanness and ugliness.

The image of Olga came to me when I visited the country from which her parents came. I felt saddened at how unaware she was of the place she is from, how unaware she is of the history, beauty, rhythms, and sensory space that is part of her heritage. Her image came again vividly when I began reading Coetzee's (1976) book, *In the Heart of the Country*, about a middle age woman who lives alone amidst others, somewhere in the world, at some point in history, with an unclear past and a foretold future. The book evoked in me the image of a woman lost in time and space, like Olga, somewhere out there, alone, despite all the coming and going of people around her. Her image came again when I read another book by Coetzee (1983), *Life and Times of Michael K*, in which a lonely, black, destitute young man with deformed lips, somewhere in a South African ghetto, puts his obese and dying mother on a wheelbarrow determined, against all odds, to wheel her with his own hands back to the village of her ancestors, amidst the violence, civil strife, and chaos that erupts all around him.

What does Olga have to do with the story of Michael K? She is neither black nor destitute and her lips are not deformed. Yet, like Michael K, she evokes the same loneliness, the same determination to go on despite the odds, the same decency, and even the same injustice that marks the life of so many. And so it goes, a process where I am not deliberately searching for images and associations to fill a space, but am attuned and attentive to them when they come, from whichever source. It is not an act of escape or imposition. Rather it is an act of suspendedness and finding by being willing to let images and associations come and, when they do, if they do, to let them run their course, wherever they take us. The image of the lonely woman from Coetzee's *In the Heart of the Country* book, and the image of Michael K, enabled me to experience Olga as a woman who perseveres despite all odds, a woman who goes on being and provides for others despite the turmoil around her. These images captured the intersubjective space (Ogden, 1994) between Olga and me, and communicated aspects about Olga of which, until then, I had not been conscious.

What is the difference between a therapist's intuition and willingness to use what may seem like a random association and an "overvalued idea" stemming from a counter-transferential reaction that he or she then imposes on the patient? For Britton (2003), the latter is a defensive act the therapist resorts to when unable to tolerate the sense of impotence and anxiety over the course of the treatment. The former, in contrast, is a creative act that helps organize seemingly random and incoherent associations and experiences. Dreaming Olga, letting my associations about her emerge, was not done to allay my anxiety and impose my views on her. I did not constrict Olga, nor obscure who she was, what she had experienced and what she was enacting with others. Rather, this dreaming created something out of the seemingly nothing, changing the tone of what transpired in the room, enabling us to jointly create (Spence, 1982) a story, her story.

Dreaming, imagining aspects of Olga's life was not a solitary act disconnected from what she created in her sessions. When, for instance, in the latter part of her treatment, Olga walked in the room and began complaining about her business, the stress she felt, and the unreliability of contractors, sales persons, and service managers, I had the strong feeling that inquiring about details of her account only intensified her complaints and strengthened her conviction that she was the victim of others, that she had been failed, yet again, by others. I was also aware that my questions felt "stale," a sure sign that I was annoyed with her and, most likely, that she herself was annoyed at the sadomasochistic exchanges she kept creating. But when I suspended the urge to say something, and thus participate in what she was enacting, and instead let my thoughts wander, the image that emerged was that of a lonely woman who has always been haunted by the failures of others and by her own failures. This thought gave rise to a subsequent one: that however successful she had been in her profession, she derived little satisfaction from it, and more important, felt very ambivalent toward it. A lonely woman who feels destructive, was the next thought, the thought that enabled me to focus on how trapped she felt, how precarious the comfort she derived from her success was, and also, how guilty she felt by her success. When I remarked that complaining about others was a dead-end street for her, one that left her always in doubt of others and also of what she had achieved, Olga's reply surprised me and changed the tone of the session. After a moment of silence, and while shaking her head, she wondered how long would it take for her to not feel as unsure of what she had achieved in life and who she was.

I cannot tell how long it took until I felt that imagining the world Olga did not dare contemplate began to have more of a lasting effect on her. I noticed that, over time, she stopped sounding like the perennial victim and stopped treating others' failures as personal assaults. She started reporting some plans about the future which she slowly began to pursue. She did continue to report unpleasant exchanges, but these incidents served to convey what transpired from one session to the next, not how victimized she felt in her life. The ugliness of others belonged to them. She was less prone to internalize it and feel responsible for it. Although I did find some of the ambitions she reported and some of the initiatives she undertook foreign to my beliefs and stance in life, these dreams and initiatives were her own and, more important, she was not afraid to articulate and claim them.

Making the patient move, writes Levenson (1988), is what distinguishes the novice from the more seasoned analyst. However, this is not simply a matter of the therapist's level of experience for it is not likely to happen in a vacuum, without the analyst being also moved by what he encounters in the room. Regardless of level of experience, the therapist's readiness to wander off through his or her own associations can offset the sense of stagnation in the room, and can create space for the patient's effect to register and generate information that often surprises both participants. Imagining Olga's life as she did not dare to helped dislodge me from my earlier dichotomous, objectified perceptions of her, enabling me to see her differently. It opened up a space, first for me, then for us, to contemplate what was missing in her life, what she hoped for but never dared express. More important, it created space for her to begin making sense of herself, to play with what might have been and could have been, and thus, to begin to imagine her life.

With patients in states of emptiness and retreat, therapists may need to go beyond what is said or enacted in the room. In these cases, one must contemplate the totality of the patients' psychic experience, not only what is there but also what is not there and is unconsciously yearned for, the desire, even longing, to be seen and to feel that they can stir and maintain the therapist's interest. It is exactly because of the patients' states of disengagement and dissociation that therapists have to be willing to associate, to let their thoughts emerge and to pursue them. With such patients, therapists need to associate the most, both for their patients' benefit and also for their own need to feel resonant and creative. This is not so much an issue of technique, nor an act that can be forced. Rather, it is an act that involves suspending one's need to know and, instead, becoming attentive to the thoughts and images the patient's presence evokes. It is an intersubjective act (Ogden, 1994), an act of creative communication (Symington, 2007) that cannot take place without sensitivity and responsiveness to the patient's presence and effect on the therapist.

References

Alvarez, A. (1992). *Live Company: Psychoanalytic Psychotherapy with Autistic, Borderline, Deprived and Abused Children*. London: Routledge.

Bollas, C. (1987a). The psychoanalyst and the hysteric. In: *The Shadow of the Object; Psychoanalysis of the Unthought Known*, pp.189–199. New York: Columbia University Press.

—— (1987b). The transformational object. In: *The Shadow of the Object; Psychoanalysis of the Unthought Known*, pp.13–29. New York: Columbia University Press.

—— (1999). Borderline desire. In: *The Mystery of Things*, pp.127–135. New York: Routledge.

Britton, R. (2003). The preacher, the poet and the psychoanalyst. In: H. Canham and C. Satyamurti (Eds.), *Acquainted with the Night: Psychoanalysis and the Poetic Imagination*. London: Karnac

Coetzee, J. M. (1983). *Life and Times of Michael K*. New York: The Viking Press.

—— (1976). *In the Heart of the Country*. New York: Harper & Row.

Faulkner, W. (1931), *Sanctuary*. New York: Random House

Grotstein, J. S. (1981). Who is the dreamer who dreams the dream and who is the dreamer who understands the dream? In J. S. Grotstein (Ed.), *Do I Dare Disturb the Universe? A Memorial to W. R. Bion*. New York: Karnac.

—— (2000). The ineffable nature of the dreamer. In: *Who is the Dreamer Who Dreams the Dream? A Study of Psychic Presences*, pp.1–36. Hillsdale, NJ: The Analytic Press.

Kenyon, J. (1993). *Constance: Poems by Jane Kenyon*. St. Paul, MN: Graywolf Press.

Kristeva, J. (1991). *Strangers to Ourselves*, trans. Leon Roudiez. New York: Columbia University Press.

Levenson, E. A. (1988). The pursuit of the particular. *Contemporary Psychoanalysis*, 24:1–16.

—— (1991). *The Purloined Self*. New York: Contemporary Psychoanalysis Books.

—— (1994). The uses of disorder: Chaos theory and psychoanalysis. *Contemporary Psychoanalysis*, 30:5–24.

—— (1995). A monopedal presentation of interpersonal psychoanalysis. *The Review of Interpersonal Psychoanalysis*, 1:1–4.

Michaels, A. (1996). *Fugitive Pieces*. New York: Vintage Books, Random House.

Ogden, T. (1989). The autistic-contiguous position. In:, *The Primitive Edge of Experience*, pp. 47–81. Northvale, NJ: Jason Aronson.

—— (1994). The analytic third—working with intersubjective clinical facts. *The International Journal of Psycho-Analysis*, 75:3–20.

O'Shaughnessy, E. (1981). W. R. Bion's theory of thinking and new techniques in child analysis. *Journal of Child Psychotherapy*, 7:181–189.

Searles, H. F. (1979). The patient as a therapist to his analyst. In: *Counter-transference and Related Subjects: Selected Papers*, pp.380–459. Madison, CT: International Universities Press, 1999.

Spence, D. P. (1982). *Narrative Truths and Historical Truths: Meaning and Interpretation in Psychoanalysis*. New York: Norton.

Steiner, J. (1993). *Psychic Retreats: Pathological Organizations in Psychotic*. London: Routledge.

Symington, N. (2007). *Becoming a Person Through Psychoanalysis*. London: Karnac Press.

Tustin, F. (1986a). Autistic objects. In: *Autistic Barriers in Neurotic Patients*, pp. 102–118. New Haven, CT: Yale University Press.

—— (1986b). Falling. In: *Autistic Barriers in Neurotic Patients*, pp. 183–196. New Haven, CT: Yale University Press.

Willock, B. (1987). The devalued, (unlovable, repugnant) self: a second facet of narcissistic vulnerability in the aggressive, conduct-disordered child. *Psychoanalytic Psychology*, 4:219–240.

Wilner, W. (1998). The un-consciousing of awareness in psychoanalytic therapy. *Contemporary Psychoanalysis*, 35:617–628.

Winnicott, D. W. (1935). Primary maternal preoccupation. In: *Through Pediatrics to Psycho-Analysis*. New York: Brunner-Routledge, 1992, pp.300–305.

—— (1963). Fear of breakdown. In: C. Winnicott, R. Shepherd, & M. Davis (Eds.), *D. W. Winnicott: Psychoanalytic Explorations*, Cambridge, MA: Harvard University Press, 1989, pp.87–95.

—— (1971a), Playing: a theoretical statement. In: *Playing and Reality*. New York: Basic Books, pp.38–52.

—— (1972). *Holding and Interpretation: Fragment of an Analysis*. New York: Grove Press.

Part VI

Healing the traumatized analyst's loneliness

Chapter 15

In the shadow of suicide[1]

Jenny Kaufmann

I am concerned with what it means to be a survivor of the suicide by a close friend or family member. My focus is on what it feels like to be left behind, to live in the shadow of the life and death of the person who is gone. My reason for mentioning the person's life as well as death is because it can be difficult to think of the person without fixating on the ending, and the idea that there were telltale signs that should have been seen, but were somehow missed—signs that pointed toward the inevitability of suicide. Some of what I say captures the experiences of many people bereaved by suicide;[2] some reflects my own experience growing up in the shadow of the suicide of my mother, who took her own life when I was 26 months old.

Throughout my childhood, while other people effortlessly breathed in their parents' presence, I imbibed my mother's absence, which was everywhere. Her suicide didn't make sense to me. Somehow I knew she really wanted me to be born. While I had no objective proof,[3] I somehow knew she was smart, funny, attuned, and had really looked forward to being my mother. It just didn't add up. Something had gone very wrong. I couldn't stop thinking about what had gone amiss. Because she died when I was just over two years old, I had not yet achieved verbal proficiency (Stern, 1985; Mitchell, 2000) or object permanence (Piaget & Inhelder, 1973; Mahler, Pine, & Bergman, 1976). While I couldn't access encoded memories, I did have a sense of strength and determination that suggested I had gotten a core sense of self in my first year (Winnicott, 1969; Stern, 1985). I simply could not forget about my mother. I fantasized about the life I should have had throughout my childhood. I could not stop trying to make sense of the circumstances that had exiled me to create a life in the aftermath of her death.

General truths

To be a "survivor of suicide" is stigmatizing, more than most people, including many therapists, appreciate.[4] I cannot state this strongly enough. There is shame. One person who lost his mother when he was two, now in his sixties, put it quite eloquently: "It's like being a member of the most exclusive club in the world: one that nobody would choose to belong to." People agonize about whether or not to tell others that their friend or relative killed themselves. As one person said in our Support Group for Survivors, "People think they know me, but I've never talked about my brother's suicide." Why don't people talk about it? Perhaps one reason is that so many people don't know how to react. Sometimes they get very upset, leaving the bereaved person feeling the need to take care of the person they have turned to for comfort. "Well," you might think, "that person is a lay person. It's not the same as talking with a trained analyst." Yet we have found that many people who have been bereaved by suicide do not experience therapists as being helpful. In my first adult analysis, in my twenties, I spent eight years wondering whether my analyst remembered that my mother had committed suicide. I think it's not so unusual for an analyst to feel uncertain about what to do, and to justify their silence with the thought, "My patient isn't ready to talk about it. If he/she were, they would bring it up. It must still be too early. We'll talk about it when the patient is ready." Perhaps. But they miss the repetitive dimension of the transference (Stolorow, Brandchaft, & Atwood, 1987). Just as it was unsafe for the child to talk with the surviving parent about the parent they lost, the adult patient is scared to broach this taboo with the analyst. Consequently, it is imperative the analyst let the patient know they do not need to protect them (Winnicott, 1969; Epstein, 1979; Russell in Pizer, 2006).

When I was in graduate school I told an older female friend about my mother's suicide. In those days, I told very few people about this central aspect of myself and when I did, I felt bonded to them for life.[5] In this case, I suspect I may have also been looking for some sort of maternal caretaking from my friend. The next day, when I brought it up again, feeling we now possessed a heightened degree of intimacy, my friend had no memory of our conversation, and no idea what I was talking about. Shocked, confused, hurt, dismayed—I reminded her of the secret I had shared. My friend was embarrassed, perhaps even a bit ashamed. She tried to understand how she could have forgotten such a significant fact. As she explored the reasons why she might have dissociated this difficult information, she remembered that her aunt had slit her own throat.[6]

Another frequent way people respond when they hear about a suicide is to ask a barrage of questions about the person who died, steering discussion away from the bereaved person. Questions such as, "What happened? Were they depressed? Were they mentally ill?" leave the bereft person with a host of complex feelings, such as "Yes, no, maybe—but what difference does it make? They may be gone, but I'm here. I'm the one who needs help processing what it feels like to be left behind, haunted by memories and images of their gruesome death." Living in the shadow of someone's suicide is a very lonely place to be.

The specific and the general

Part of my story reflects the experience of many children who have lost parents to suicide in childhood, and has much in common with children who have experienced different types of trauma, including the loss of a parent. Other parts of my experience are more idiosyncratic, and specific to me.

Though my story is one in which I lost my mother and stayed connected to my father, I can relate to people whose mothers have remarried, moved to another city or state, changed their children's names to correspond with their stepfather's, and asked their children to adapt to a new reality as though the past had not happened. In some cases there may be stepsiblings to contend with, in other cases, new half-siblings may be born. These parents are frequently driven by anger and disillusionment toward the parent who fathered their child, as well as by hope and idealization around the qualities of their new mate who, they fantasize, will bring about their redemption and transformation. In these cases, a common denominator is the parents' sense of shame about the past. The parents may minimize their children's need to hang on to the past, or act as if the past never happened, or acknowledge the past occurred but fail to appreciate its impact and significance. Children may have trouble adapting to stepparents, and parents may be angry with them for "not trying hard enough." The child may become dissociated, while their parents are angry with them for being "out of it." These parents may associate their children with the discarded, defective parent. Their narcissism can interfere with their ability to differentiate between themselves and their children, further contributing to the child's difficulty making sense of his/her own, internal experience. To make matters worse, these children cannot be honest with their surviving parent, yet are dependent on them, further complicating and sometimes impairing the separation process.

The scenario just described fits my own experience, though it is not specific to me or to losses due to suicide. I think my father was initially in shock about my mother's suicide. He had never dealt with anything as upsetting before and wanted to get away from all that had happened, literally and figuratively. From my perspective, his decision to remarry three years after my mother died was premature. I was neither emotionally ready nor cognitively prepared for my new life. I felt pulled from one life to another that was so different I could not bridge the gap. The differences went from the superficial to the deep. On the surface, I went from a suburban home on the outskirts of Washington, D.C. to an apartment on the eighth floor of a pre-war building on 93rd St. and Park Avenue in New York City. In Washington I had gone to a small, private Montessori preschool; in New York, I was enrolled in a public school kindergarten class. In Washington, my father and I commuted by car, singing all the way. In New York, I have no memory of how I got to school. I know I felt scared and different—the "new girl" who had entered the class in January.[7] On deeper levels, everything else changed as well. Suddenly I had a step-mother whom I called "mommy"—a tall woman with a large Roman nose—and two older stepsisters.[8] I shared a room with one stepsister, while the older "sister" had her own room. Even my birth order changed: no longer an adored only child, waiting for a younger brother or sister to follow, I was now the youngest of three girls. It took quite a leap to wrap my mind around this change.

I felt as if I had lost all access to my father who now mostly viewed me through the eyes of my stepmother. On occasion, he would solicit my perspective on difficulties I ran into with my stepmother. I appreciated having the opportunity to explain myself yet, ultimately, these conversations were frustrating. After we talked, my father would "check in" with my stepmother and let me know that I misunderstood her—in other words, that my perception was "wrong."

While the connection to my father was not completely lost, I was hanging on by a thread. My overarching experience was of being on my own. He was hard to reach, I had difficulties with my stepmother, and I could hardly find traces of my mother. She was rarely mentioned. There were no pictures or mementoes of her to be found. I did have a relationship with my grandparents, but that wasn't easy either. My grandparents didn't feel comfortable talking about my mother, so it felt as if there was an elephant between us. The situation was further complicated because my father did not remain in touch with my grandparents, leaving my relationship with them outside the domain of everyday life, too intense and somewhat unreal.

One reason reality felt so fleeting was because I had lost my connection to the past, and had no feeling of continuity. Occasionally my father would bring up my mother, but he had an agenda, to discount her significance to me, and discredit her as a person. Our exchanges had a familiar, rote-like patterning. As in a chess game, my father would lead with his opening gambit, "You don't remember your mother, do you?" This question left me with little choice but to nod in agreement. Visibly relieved, he would continue. "That's what I thought. You were too young." He convinced himself that because I could not actively conjure up an image of my mother, the loss was not significant.

On other occasions my father would build a case against my mother. He let me know she had been disturbed, and there was something wrong with him for not having seen it. He told me she was "Manic Depressive," implying such an illness was evidence of her inherent defectiveness. He described her history of emotional instability, evidenced by her promiscuous dating history and ambition. He told me about a paper he had read about her illness and said it was not unusual for people so diagnosed to act impulsively. He told me my mother spent money excessively and had gone through nine jobs in a year before he knew her. She didn't know her place. "When she was a staff writer for Howard McCann, she went into the publishers' office, put her feet on his desk, lit a cigarette and pronounced, 'Let me tell you what's wrong with this magazine.' Naturally, she was let go." My father would look around the room with an air of self-satisfaction, take a deep breath and exhale, "I should have married somebody more like your mother (which meant step-mother). She is content to simply be a mother."

Needless to say, my feelings were complex and difficult to sort. I had the impression my father was building a case against my mother by stretching facts to fit his theory. I felt proud that my mother wrote for a magazine. I wanted to be a writer, too. In addition, I didn't see my stepmother as being content—in fact, I saw her as having very low self-esteem, especially evident in her destructive put-downs of me. I felt protective toward my mother and felt as if by joining my father in his discrediting her, I was being asked to turn against myself. As if it were not enough that my father failed to recognize my need for positive identification with my mother, he just didn't seem able to see me at all. I felt as if my job was to be there for him, to make sense of his deficits, and to reflect what he wanted to hear back to him.

I came to feel like my father's child from a prior life. I was there, but somehow I wasn't part of his new life. My father and stepmother led a full life, crammed with dinner parties, theatre, opera, and travel. From my vantage point it felt empty. In any event, I felt excluded, trapped in a life that felt unreal and had little to do with me, with a past I could not access. I spent way too much time thinking about my mother and trying to understand why I couldn't get her out of my mind whereas she did not seem to be in my father's mind at all. I invented all sorts of theories to explain the difference between my father and me, speculating about the nature of his attachment to his own mother and contrasting it with my experience during my first year of life. I think perhaps that this is the very definition of loneliness—living in a post-apocalyptic world,[9] but one that impacted only me. My father and I had lived through the same experience, yet he was able to "move on," while I was stuck in time.

I spent a lot of time yearning for the life I believed I "should" have had—a life that took place in the suburbs with a mother who loved and understood me. I told myself that if my mother were alive, she would not have made endless jabs about how short I was, how slowly I walked, or how loud my foot thumped when it hit the ground[10]—because she would have looked like me and intuitively understood me. I remember a waitress once commenting that my stepmother and I looked alike. I couldn't understand how anyone could be so blind. Not only did we look very different, but it was also clear we were emotionally disconnected. Yet I could dream and yearn for a real mother who understood me and for a real family who looked alike and cared about one another. While this did sustain me, I also worry that this early pattern of dreaming and yearning set up a lifelong pattern in which I live too much in my head, and too disconnected from people I love.

Living in the shadow

Living in my mother's shadow implies I could not see her as a whole person. She was hidden from plain view, leaving me to imagine what I could not see. Living in her shadow may have made me into the shadow of a person, a shadow of what I could have been. My need to write about my experience can be understood as my need to emerge from the shadows, to shake off cobwebs, to be seen. I will now differentiate between living in the shadows of my mother's life and death, though I suspect this distinction is not so clear-cut, as the shadows blend into one another.

Of life . . .

There are two distinct ways in which I am aware of living in the shadow of my mother's life. They come from my imaginative elaboration—the result of too little information and too much time to think.

I knew certain facts about my mother. She was 25 years old when she married, 29 years old when I was born, and 31 years old when she died.[11] I can also tell you that I was 25 years old when I married, 29 years old when my first daughter was born, and that this "coincidence" was no accident. I was driven to repeat these aspects of my mother's history, yet I am not sure why. Possibly because I had so little access to her, I tried to become her in order to feel her presence inside me (Freud). I suspect I may have also believed that if I could replicate my mother's marriage and the birth of my daughter (who clearly represented me) and not die when my daughter was in her second year, then I could live. It's as if I were trying to take off from where my life with my mother ended, even though I had to juggle the players to make it work.

The other way I am aware of living in the shadow of my mother's life has to do with modeling myself after her as a writer. With the additional assumption that she had been depressed, when I was younger I found myself drawn to a romanticized notion of depression, the Sylvia Plath or Anne Sexton variety. I fear I may have strived to become an exaggerated version of who I thought she was rather than who she actually was. I suspect I spent way too much time alone, content to "perfect" my writing to a degree that now seems obsessive, and difficult to fathom. Each sentence needed to flow into the next. The sound and cadence of language needed to ring perfectly to my ear. I was proud of the accolades I usually received for my writing. Looking back, I think my writing had a driven quality. Sitting by myself for countless hours was a poor substitute for a life filled with the give and take of others.

. . . And death

The main problem with having my mother commit suicide when I was only 26 months old is that her death cast way too large a shadow over the entirety of my life. Her death became too important, and left me in a place where I was more enchanted with death than I should have been. Her death cast a huge shadow of shame over my life, forcing me to hide her absence, leaving me feeling as if by not having a mother, I was defective. I felt as if I had been born at the bottom of the caste system, without the right to needs and desires of my own. This large topic is somewhat outside of the scope of this chapter. For now, I will focus on two central aspects of what it has meant to live in the shadow of her suicide—thoughts about the moment of her death, and intrusive thoughts about her body and bodily integrity.

My father told me my mother tricked the people at Chestnut Lodge. They thought she was okay. I imagined her escape, decked out with red painted lips, pearls, and a glamorous mink coat. She smiled at the guards and they smiled back, imagining she had been discharged or was not a patient, but a visiting relative. After her escape, my mother went to Rock Creek Park. I tried to imagine her route by taxi or bus. Or did she walk, straining her feet in high-heeled pumps? I knew nothing about the geography of the area, the distance or terrain.

Most of my fantasies took place from the apex of the bridge, endlessly replaying the moment between her jumping and landing. What if she regretted this decision, changed her mind?[12] I wondered how much time she had to feel regret and what those final moments felt like. I wondered whether she thought about me, and knew how much I would miss her. I replayed this scenario throughout my development, wondering if when falling, she was thinking about me and how my life would turn out. At different points in my development, I wondered whether she could picture me now.

The second aspect of my mother's death that preoccupied me could be labeled "After the Fall." My main concern was with her body and its intactness. I tried to imagine the place where she fell, but was never sure whether she landed on water or solid ground. If in water, was she fodder for fish and other sea critters?[13] Or did her body splatter into pieces on the ground? Did somebody try to gather the pieces together?[14]

The main reason why thinking about my mother's body was so problematic is because these images were both so pervasive and so intrusive. My anxieties about bodily intactness took many forms and spread in myriad directions. If I was in a biology class learning about vessels in the body such as veins, arteries, and capillaries, I would start to imagine these vessels—my vessels—bursting open, out of control, blood splattered all around.[15] I had to force myself to focus, trick myself into separating these violent images from the cognitive task at hand. Or I might spot an amputee and experience terror, afraid I could not keep my body together.[16]

As if these thoughts weren't difficult enough, my difficulties were compounded by not letting people know what I was thinking. Was I protecting myself because I didn't want people to think I was crazy or was I protecting my mother? Probably both. Even today, more than fifty years after the fact, I find myself feeling apologetic for putting these thoughts on paper, and subjecting you, the reader, to my concerns.

Out of the shadows

Looking back on my journey, I am at a loss to find words to explain how difficult it was for me to tell people that I lost my mother to suicide at 26 months. This is brought home to me when I consider how difficult it was to talk about this with a group I met with for close to five years. I had taught this group in a Continuing Education Course about Working with Adult Patients who had Lost Parents in Childhood, then continued to meet to read everything we could about loss. While the group knew I had lost my mother when I was two, I had not revealed that the loss had been the result of a suicide, and no one suspected. Though shaking inside, I felt it important to come forward with these people who had all shared so much. I needn't have been anxious, for they were supportive and helped me find ways of talking about my experience.

While my secret kept me feeling alienated and alone, I don't think I recognized how much it also kept me feeling safe. I was very adept at keeping my secret, which kept me from exposing myself to others, and risking judgment. When I made the decision to take a public stance, I experienced a feeling of exhilaration that was quickly followed by fears about exposure, and anxiety that I would lose my freedom and independence.

In the past 18 months, I've talked with dozens of people who have lost close friends and family members to suicide. These discussions have shifted and increased my understanding. As I had surmised, a loss by suicide is different from other types of loss, and can be more difficult to mourn. This does not have to be the case, though it frequently is. I have seen there are profound differences between the experience of losing a parent to suicide in toddlerhood, latency, and adolescence, as well as differences between losing a parent in early adulthood and later on. In addition, there are differences between losing a sibling, niece, nephew, lover, spouse, or close friend. Though I never could have imagined anything more painful than losing my mother at age two, my heart goes out to parents who have lost a child. Sadly, I have seen a number of parents who lost their teenage children to suicide in the past year.

Some people want to know what to expect, and I would like to be able to tell them. However, I am of the conviction that everyone's path is different, and this is how it should be. Each loss is unique. Everyone must find their own path. That's where art and creativity lie. I found that group work can be powerful in helping people to grieve by providing a forum in which they feel less alone and ashamed. It is helpful to be with others who understand the language of those bereaved by suicides. These people frequently struggle with such common pitfalls as how to respond when they are asked how their loved one died. There is comfort in knowing that other people have experienced unbearable pain, and have found productive ways to transform that pain. It is good to know that people do recover and go on to experience joy and happiness, and meaning in life. I recommend group work as an adjunctive to individual treatment.

I wonder what people think when I say my areas of expertise include loss, trauma, and suicide bereavement. It may sound incongruous with my usual presentation, which is more lighthearted and fun. I can go to dark places and I can hold a lot of pain. While I have a lifelong preoccupation with death, ironically I think my grasp of loss has increased my appreciation of life and made me strive to embrace it and live it to the fullest extent possible.

While I would not wish my experience of losing my mother to suicide at such a young age on anyone, I am grateful to all who helped give me strength to persevere. Suicide bereavement takes us to depths of pain that are unfathomable. The quest to understand that pain has taken me to places I would never otherwise have known. I have met people who have touched me and enriched my life exponentially. I carry them all inside, forever grateful to those who shared their hearts, expanding and opening me up in ways I could never have imagined.

Notes

1 I am indebted to Freud (1917) for giving me the idea of living in the shadow of suicide, loosely borrowed from his term, "in the shadow of the object." Freud used his term to distinguish between normative and melancholic reactions to loss. He proposed that when a person has had an ambivalent relationship with the object, they are unable to mourn. They internalize an image of the object colored by their aggression.

2 This is particularly true for people who lost parents to suicide in childhood.

3 When I was in my late 30s my father suddenly "found" the home movies he had taken in the first few years of my life. The movies confirmed what I had known in my core—that in my first year of life, my mother had given me the strength of a preliminary sense of self that, though not nearly enough, had sustained me through very trying circumstances. Amazingly, the discovery of the movies coincided with my first year of analytic training at the William Alanson White Institute, and with the beginning of my "training analysis."

4 Shifts in the zeitgeist are contributing to changes in people's perception of suicide, as well as with their grasp of death and trauma. Nevertheless, suicide

was stigmatized in 1956, and was not talked about openly in the 60s and 70s, when I was growing up. I have found that most of the adult survivors I have met had similar experiences of growing up in a shroud of secrecy and shame.

5 In telling this shameful, taboo secret that was integral to my sense of self, I felt as if I was handing over the keys to my soul. From my perspective, this gave the other person way too much power over me. I hoped they would hold the information protectively, but there was always the danger they could use their knowledge to gain power over me, or that they would tell others.

6 Though I did not know it at the time, I now know that this story is not unusual. More people than I ever imagined have suicides "in their closets."

7 Many years later, when my younger daughter was in kindergarten, I had an extreme emotional reaction when a boy from Australia entered her class in January. His mother had a boyfriend in New York and went back to Australia when the school year ended.

8 Naturally, I related to the fairy tale Cinderella and may have taken a masochistic delight in playing out a Cinderella fantasy. I also related to Snow White because of the evil stepmother. I related most to the *The Little Princess*, by Francis Burnett Hodges. Although my father was still alive and present, I felt as if he was gone.

9 Like many people who experienced earlier trauma, I was relieved on 9/11, feeling like I no longer had to hide.

10 In retrospect, I can understand that I walked slowly and deliberately to ensure that the ground underneath me was solid. I imagine I would have had a lighter touch if I knew my mother would be there to catch me.

11 I almost always slip and say she was 31 years old when I died, rather than when she died.

12 In a recent edition of the New York Times Sunday Magazine, there is a piece by a man who jumped off of the Golden Gate Bridge and lived. He was so grateful to be given a second chance that he made it his life's work to go around the country, talking people who are depressed out of taking their lives.

13 How much easier facts are than fantasy. In the spring of 1994, during my first year of analytic training, there was a Div. 39 Conference in Rockville, Maryland. My husband and I walked to the park and stood in front of the infamous bridge. It was very high and daunting. At the same time, it was a relief to see it, as the reality was so much easier than the overriding magnitude of my fantasies.

14 A few years ago, as I was leaving my apartment building with my older daughter, the two of us practically stumbled on top of a man who had just jumped from his seventh floor apartment. While I was shaken up, I cannot begin to describe the level of relief I felt about seeing that this man was intact. Oddly, it was a beautiful fall day in early October, practically the same day that my mother had jumped to her death in 1956.

15 I tried to talk about this in my last analysis when I rang my analyst's bell and was overcome with images of veins and arteries exploding. I told her about this phenomenon, and connected it to my maternal transference. My analyst tried, but she had a hard time wrapping her mind around this. Every time I brought it up she would fuss and fidget, then collect herself and say, "Tell me again, dear. I really do want to hear this."

16 Someone suggested to me that losing a mother at age two would feel like losing a leg or an arm. While I believe this is correct, I feel the violence connected with suicide added the additional dimension of feeling like my body could somehow betray me, just as my mother's body betrayed her and me.

References

Burnett, F. H. (1905). *A Little Princess*. New York: Franklin Watts, 2007.

Epstein, L. (1979). The Therapeutic Use of Countertransference Data with Borderline Patients. *Contemporary Psychoanalysis*, 15:248–274.

Freud, S. (1917). *Mourning and Melancholia*. The Standard Edition of the Complete Psychological Works of Sigmund Freud, Volume 14, 237–258.

—— (1923). *The Ego and the Id*, The Standard Edition of the Complete Psychological Works of Sigmund Freud, 9:1–308.

Klein, M. (1940). Mourning and its Relation to Manic-Depressive States. *International Journal of Psycho-Analysis*, 21:125–153.

Mahler, M. S., Pine, F., & Bergman, A. (1976). *The Psychological Birth of the Human Infant: Symbiosis and Individuation*. New York: Basic Books.

Mitchell, S. A. (2000). *Relationality: From Attachment to Intersubjectivity*. Hillsdale, NJ: The Analytic Press.

Piaget, J. & Inhelder, B. (1973). *Memory and Intelligence*. New York: Basic Books.

Pizer, B. (2006). A Reader's Guide to the Work of Paul Russell. *Contemporary Psychoanalysis*, 42:589–600.

Pizer, S. A. (2006). Repetition, Negotiation, Relationship: An Introduction to the Work of Paul L. Russell, M.D. *Contemporary Psychoanalysis*, 42:579–587.

Stern, D. N. (1985). *The Interpersonal World of the Infant: A View from Psychoanalysis and Developmental Psychology*. New York: Basic Books.

Stolorow, R., Brandchaft, B., and Atwood, G. E. (1987). *Psychoanalytic Treatment: An Intersubjective Approach*. Hillsdale, NJ: The Analytic Press.

Winnicott, D. W. (1969). The Use of the Object and Relating Through Identifications. *International Journal of Psycho-Analysis*, 50:711–716.

Chapter 16

The loneliness of the traumatized analyst and the self-righting function of his private practice[1]

Bruce Herzog

Working in private offices, psychoanalysts risk having little contact with the outside world, and could become very isolated. The nature of our profession includes the possibility of loneliness as an occupational hazard. But just as our practices can isolate us, they can also connect us to the world through our patients. These connections can be gratifying, sometimes providing welcome relief from unforeseen difficulties in our personal lives.

This chapter explores the management of an analytic practice during a life event that rendered the analyst vulnerable and alone, showing how his private practice, far from further isolating him, was instead significantly helpful in keeping him connected to others, functioning as an island of normalcy during a stormy episode.

The traumatized analyst

Very little prepares us for the death of an intimate. Those of us who remain married for life are implicitly charged with carrying the burden of possibly having to bury a spouse; but who talks of this unpleasantness, and where can we learn to equip ourselves to endure it? Many of us know people who have had a partner die, but has anyone explained to us what it is like? Granted, I'm not sure how keen a surviving spouse would be to recount such an intensely painful event. Even in the telling, it would be troublesome to express the most important aspects of the experience that are so difficult to put into words and carry social taboos. And if someone were willing to inform us, would we want to hear? Those of us who don't anticipate this sort of loss anytime soon might not want to dwell on the complications of some distant morbid possibility.

Still, these considerations don't entirely explain why there is so little of this phenomenon detailed in the psychoanalytic literature. Some texts (e.g., Bellak & Faithorn, 1981) have covered many areas of personal crisis in the lives of psychoanalysts. Regarding personal losses, the phenomenon of a lost pregnancy (Dewald & Schwarz, 1993), personal illness (Abend, 1982), or death of a child (Gerson, 1996) have been discussed, but I found surprisingly little that dealt with the loss of a spouse.

Given my own lack of exposure to people who had suffered this kind of loss, I was entirely unprepared when I was confronted with the death of my wife. I'm sure every individual who has lived through the loss of a spouse has certain particularities involving the death that are unique. I'm going to briefly mention a difficulty that contributed to my feeling of disorientation. Within the unfamiliar and often overwhelming pragmatic experiences surrounding a death and funeral, which may include worries about the morgue and autopsy, funeral arrangements, finding a cemetery, selecting a coffin and tombstone, what to write on the tombstone, dealing with relatives, etc., there are also various unmentionables, one of which I will touch on here.

I think the most problematic experience for me regarding the death of my wife involved the sudden discovery of her body. I know not everyone is shocked by the death of a spouse, sometimes it's anticipated, especially when preceded by a severe illness, but in this case the death was unexpected and finding her body induced a squeamish panic in me. You'd think I had never seen a dead body before, which wasn't the case. In my medical training I had on numerous occasions been required to pronounce someone to be deceased, and my wife's body did not look that much different from what I'd seen before.

But it wasn't a stranger; it was her. And not her. When looking at her face—cold, blue, and immobile—I recognized that this was one of the great obscenities that life can hurl at someone.[2] To think of the innumerable times that we were a comfort to each other, using words, gestures, facial expressions, touch . . . This body was exactly the same instrument with the same wiring as before. But it was unplugged. There could be no reasoned words, no calming gestures, no soothing looks, nothing she could offer to help me through the worst event of my life. This time she was the cause, and could offer no solace. Just when I needed her most, she wasn't going to be around anymore.

My focus on her body didn't end there. The suddenness of her death required a medical examination, and my post-traumatic symptoms included not only recurring images of when I found her, but also picturing her being laid out on a cold slab somewhere. I felt desperately helpless at being unable to do anything to bring her home, and was relieved when her body was finally returned to the funeral home to be prepared for burial. This way she would soon be out of the hands of strangers, and safe in her grave. There's little logic behind this kind of thinking, but my need to protect the body that she could no longer defend was quite powerful.

Suffering post-traumatic symptoms, I didn't think I was in the best condition to carry on with my private practice. At the least, my circumstance could distract me from doing effective work. However, work is exactly what I did, for better or worse.

Patient contact post trauma

Following my wife's death it was necessary to announce immediately to individuals in her psychotherapy practice that she had passed away. The timing of this was particularly unfortunate for me because it occurred during a period when I was both stunned by the event and angered by feelings of profound abandonment. It would have been hard enough to re-experience the shock and loss I had already known through telling one of her patients the terrible news. However, phoning upwards of 30 people in succession over 48 hours was almost intolerable. Still, I felt it to be my responsibility. I thought I was best able to empathically handle the situation, and was determined to tough it out.

My halftime practice had been limited to mornings that summer. On the day after her death, I avoided making any decisions about absenting myself by carrying on with working as if nothing had happened. I wasn't exactly ready to manage my practice, but I also wasn't in any shape to announce to yet another group of people that I had just had a family tragedy; and I didn't feel comfortable having someone else do the job. I didn't know what to do, and didn't want to decide impulsively. Going to work seemed the best thing at the time, while trying to make up my mind about what to do eventually. I didn't know how much use I could be for my patients, but I walked into my office as if it was any other workday, still reeling with visual images of her dead body, alternating with dissociative denial of the whole event.

The office felt quite different from my home life, where frantic arrangements for a funeral were being made. Walking around the house with my children and relatives, and handling my wife's belongings triggered not only fond memories of her and expected feelings of loss, but also the traumatic memory of her death, along with current worries about what to do. In my office I was faced with the stories of my patients, and rather than adding to my problems, I was surprised to learn that they functioned to comfort me by drawing me away from my troubled personal life into the details of their lives. This was a welcome distraction, something I wanted to continue doing. At this point it looked like I needed my patients more than they needed me.

Working a few hours a day during this tumultuous time led me to discover that my practice had become an oasis of normalcy for me. Mornings were now a time when I saw patients, then spent time reminiscing with my children. Afternoons at home were when the public aspects of the Shiva[3] came into play, where I gratefully received the pragmatic support of friends and family providing food and cleanup. Their attempts at psychological comfort were less successful, as I heard their condolences through a haze of surreal unreality. While the conveyance of concern was marginally useful, it brought no relief from my posttraumatic symptoms, which I suffered privately. What produced the most benefit for me in my home was the sound of laughter, the voices of children, and other people's stories. Anything that was redolent of life, living, or liveliness. Listening to my patients' stories about their lives was similarly helpful; and I was grateful to know that I was still of some use to them.

I must confess that the decision to continue working was made partly to spare me the necessity of making any announcement, even if only of my own absence, to my patients. I knew it was not an ideal decision, that I was unlikely to be able to hide my upset to the degree that no one would notice anything, but I had learned long ago that most patients can be remarkably forgiving of a temporarily distracted analyst. Maybe I could get through this without having to tell anyone right away. Maybe they wouldn't notice the difference in me enough so that it mattered.

They noticed. It mattered. A few commented that I was distant, far less communicative, and suspiciously quiet. Some asked directly: "What happened?" "What's wrong with you?" Others became silent. A couple of people discussed possibly terminating.

In keeping with my policy of trying to answer a fair, direct question with a fair, direct answer, I began telling those who asked that I had a death in the family. I felt I couldn't do otherwise, as being oblique was very unlike me, and I felt it would carry the risk of leading to a disruption in therapy. So in a sense, my dilemma of when, and whether or not I might report any part of my situation to my patients solved itself. I began letting people know what they asked for, at the time they asked for it.

That allowed for some space between the announcements. In this way, titrating a disclosure to match a patient's inquisitiveness seemed to fit my needs as well. There were a number of patients I told within the first weeks; some were satisfied with simply hearing that there was a family death, others wanted to know who it was, and how the death occurred. My telling them it was my wife who died suddenly seemed to suffice, and they typically respected my discomfort in detailing things further. A few patients didn't seem to notice anything amiss, and weren't told, but one of these did terminate suddenly. Then there were patients for whom the news was delayed up to several months. For these people there were natural entry points that presented themselves much later on, where mentioning the death made sense. The result of this approach created a very tolerable spacing and variable intensity of my broaching the subject, which made my patients' reactions much easier for me to manage. And there was quite a variety of reactions. Some very genuine and helpful communications came from my patients; on the other hand, there were some surprisingly negative responses.

I would like to present two case vignettes from either end of the spectrum. In the first there was a very positive therapeutic relationship, and I told the patient the news quite soon because she made pointed, concerned inquiries about my state of mind. I felt confident the announcement would not be disruptive, and suspect I intuitively knew her reaction might be comforting, although I wouldn't have admitted it to myself at the time. The second vignette involves someone who was experiencing considerable familial upheaval, and in whom the therapy could take dramatic shifts from powerful idealizations to devastating disappointments. Although she knew something was not right with me, I delayed telling her for some months partly because of her difficult current home situation, and partly because I wanted to avoid what I felt was likely to be her dramatic reaction to being told.

Case one

You can learn a lot from someone's immediate reaction to a situation, and the way this person behaved should tell you something about her. Her brief response was spontaneous, genuine, and moving. After a momentary silence, she quietly told me using a few well-chosen words, that she was distraught for me and my children. She had lost her mother in her adolescence, so when she told me how she felt about my family situation, it had deep significance for both of us. Her comment was just what the doctor ordered. I had not expected to have my needs so well met by a handful of simple words, and I am still quite taken with how moving it felt to receive this sincere sentiment from her.

The following day she had a dream. She was in a university setting facing a futuristic machine. She touched it. It turned on and spoke her name, saying, "You have never recovered from the beating you had before you were born." She became upset and confused, running through the university grounds naked. She entered a room with a flooded toilet, where her husband blew on the water in the bowl, starting a fire. Panicking, she ran yelling "Fire," but everyone ignored her. After she recounted the dream, she told me it was connected to how I was reacting to my wife's death. "You're acting as if nothing has happened, that's exactly what I did when my mother died."

A few sessions later, she told me she was feeling "down and alone" and was having difficulty feeling close to me, knowing I was just doing my job. She began to cry. "I'd really like not to want so much from you." She recalled how her mother had abandoned her by acting "crazy all the time." "I can't get close enough to you and I couldn't get close enough to her either." The next day she dreamt of a man in an accident whose head was severed. Looking at the severed head, she could see the man was aware it was "over," and she was filled with despair. She related this dream to her recent reading of "The Idiot" and wondering whether guillotined heads were aware.

It is not unexpected that some patients are very cognizant of the analyst's state of mind. This woman came from a background of intense attachment to a single mother who began acting "crazy" during the patient's adolescence, culminating in the mother's death. Given the patient's history, she was more than capable of perceiving my "craziness," and my potential to abandon her. The session in which she recounted the dream of trying to warn people about a fire in the toilet was concluded by her attempt to caution me about dissociating myself from my grief, as she had done following her mother's death.[4] The dream involving a guillotined head represented her observation of my disconnection between mind and body; how I had severed my head from my grieving heart. As she stared at her therapist, with his detached head, she wondered about his awareness. Does he know it is "over" for him, as it had been for her with her mother; that at some level, the death of such an intimate connection can take something away that can never be retrieved?[5]

Case two

This vignette involves a woman I told four months after the fact, who came from a devastating background. Her parents' continual fighting left them little time and energy to attend to the children. They frequently moved, so she was rarely in the same school for more than a year. Consequently, she felt she never belonged at home or school—there was no place for her in the world. She had great hopes for developing an attachment to me in analysis, but at the same time wasn't expecting much. We'd been together for several years, mostly occupying a positive working alliance, but our connection felt brittle, as if any faux pas by me could create a serious disruption.

After the death, she knew I was distracted, and commented that she sensed there was something wrong with me. When she eventually began to wonder if what she was observing was my disenchantment with her, I felt that continuing to avoid the issue was unfair. Still, I wanted to be careful with how I timed breaking any news of my situation to her, and it continued to get put off. There was always some disaster at work or around her house that we were dealing with, so despite her concerns, it never seemed an appropriate time.

But the time did arrive. Several months after my wife's death this patient began talking directly about our relationship. She felt she was no longer of any interest to me and suspected something had been going on in my life that may have made me not want to be an analyst anymore. She asked what was going on. Well, she couldn't have made a more unequivocal request, and I felt it was an obligatory opening to my mentioning something. I told her she had been perceptive, that I had been distracted during the past few months by the occurrence of someone's death, after which she became quiet and visibly very upset.

The next day she told me she'd felt "disinherited and destroyed" by my not telling her. "I adore you, and what do you do? You do the same thing my parents did." She demanded to know who it was that died, and I told her.

Several sessions later she told me she would have wanted me to tell her about my wife's death right away. She felt the "honesty and integrity (in the therapeutic relationship) died with your wife . . . You're supposed to cross the floor and figure out what it means from this end . . . I was lied to, and I am way over-the-top angry at you."

The following session, she told me my not falling apart following my wife's death revolted her. Further, she found me somewhat impatient and angry since then. She felt she was up against something she couldn't deal with. She was having trouble getting through her day, felt sick eating, was not sleeping well, and was nauseous coming to see me. She recalled a time when she transferred to a new school as a child, and received a welcome invitation to a classmate's house. When she arrived, the girl and her friends were hiding in an apple tree and began pelting her with fruit. The invitation had been a con. She had been totally fooled, and had to walk back home alone in a state of hysteria. That was how unsafe she felt with me. I had acted just as the apple throwers.

Several sessions later, I was told that our work had been jeopardized by my inability to mourn openly. I had become equivalent to her father and husband who remained closed to her in order to deceive her. She'd grown up with a mother who beat and humiliated her, schoolmates who attacked and excluded her, and a father who had cut her off completely. Now she couldn't help thinking that after what I did, I was like all of them.

From a later session: "I don't think you care about your patients anymore. You care about what you used to have and now it's gone and you're mad." From within her catalogue of accusations, this one stood out. It was not far from how I felt; as if she was exposing my darker thoughts. She continued: "You hurt me without explanation and that makes me want to leave." I found myself telling her that her continued admonishments of me felt particularly harsh, and to remind her once more of my explanation: that I did not feel I had been in any condition to tell her of the death shortly after it happened. She responded that in her upbringing, people lied to manipulate her. "No matter how hard it was for you, you can't lie to someone who has this level of connection . . . Still, I have this feeling that you are pushing me away most of the time now, I guess probably for understandable reasons." She was sympathizing with me for my having to weather her considerable anger.

From a letter she wrote me around this time: "I was born to parents who did not want to be parents; I married a man and bore his children who did not want to be a husband or father. And now, I think I'm trying to work with a therapist who doesn't want to be a therapist. So I ask, do you still want to do this work?" Pretty astute, I thought. Transference issues aside, she had picked up on my considerable ambivalence about carrying on with any of my obligations.

My decision to delay telling this patient was experienced as a deception, which led to a loss of trust that took a considerable amount of time and discussion for her to recover from. The feeling of being lied to shifted her into a hostile relational state (Herzog, 2002), which carried memories and the affective experience of being deceived by family and peers. This led to remembrance and working through of her traumatic memories, but not before the therapy was put at considerable risk of her leaving, and risk of me losing my empathic vantage point in the face of her continued attacks. I still believe reporting the death to her at any time would have created disruption, and I would not have been able to manage her reaction as well in the early stages of my grief. Unfortunately I can only speculate as to whether the path I chose was the best decision I could have made for her. She continued to insist it wasn't.

Conclusion

Analysts are not infallible. We have frailties, and because our practices are often, by definition, private, our isolation and resulting loneliness could be seen as inherent occupational hazards. This becomes especially apparent when one of us has experienced a personal upheaval. That fact was brought into sharp focus for me when I needed to make immediate decisions about my practice following my wife's death.

In trying times there is only so much help one can receive from outsiders. During my difficulties, I had felt that the management of my practice would be best handled by me. Whether this was the best option or not, I certainly learned something in the process. I confirmed that patients react to upheavals depending on how they generally assimilate experience. Thus any decision of the analyst can impact either favorably or unfavorably on different patients, depending on what is triggered within them. Some people, when learning of our weakened state, support and help us. Others attack and abandon us. How someone reacts delivers insight into their relational knowledge (Lichtenberg, Lachmann, & Fosshage, 1992; Stern, 1998) and can be a conduit for uncovering related memories of their past experiences of vulnerability.

An analyst cannot entirely separate his practice from his personal life. Intuitive patients will eventually figure out when something serious is going on. The analyst who has been traumatized should consider that his problem may need to be broached with some patients. How this is done should have a lot to do with not only what is best for the patient, but also what will work best for the analyst, especially when he (or she) is feeling vulnerable.

Although taking time off is often recommended for those who have had a loss such as mine, consideration should be given to continuing work. The analytic posture of decentering off our own experience through efforts to empathically immerse (Kohut, 1959) ourselves in someone's story carries benefits that can be found in religion, charitable activity, political causes, or other kinds of altruism. We gain a lot from patients through feeling of use to them. This can be a welcome distraction when situational factors at home are overwhelming.

The analytic relationship is not strictly a one-way arrangement. When a personal crisis requires prioritizing the needs of the analyst, the outcome may be of use to both analyst and patient, providing them with a welcome opportunity for a deepening and expansion of the therapeutic experience.

Notes

1 Dedicated to the fond memory of my wife, Dr. Katy Pastierovic, who encouraged me to write.
2 Sapountzis (2007) has captured the experience of assault that losses can produce in the analyst through his exploration of sudden terminations in his clinical practice and their relation to deaths in his family.
3 See Slochower's (2007) discussion of Jewish mourning rituals from an analyst's perspective, which touches on both its advantages and failings.
4 Dissociation in the analyst as a response to personal loss is rarely mentioned in the literature, but Ryan (2007) effectively described the grief and dissociation resulting from a therapist's loss of a family member.
5 We don't only lose our loved one, but we also lose the naive confidence that life will unfold as we have planned it.

References

Abend, S. M. (1982). Serious illness in the analyst: Countertransference considerations. *Journal of the American Psychoanalytic Association*, 30:365–379.

Bellak, L. & Faithorn, P. (1981). *Crises and Special Problems in Psychoanalysis and Psychotherapy*. New York: Brunner/Mazel.

Dewald, P. A. & Schwartz, H. J. (1993). The life cycle of the analyst: pregnancy, illness, and disability. *Journal of the American Psychoanalytic Association*, 41:191–207.

Gerson, B. (1996). *The Therapist as a Person: Life Crises, Life Choices, Life Experiences, and Their Effects of Treatment*. Hillsdale, NJ: The Analytic Press.

Herzog, B. (2002). *Reconsidering the unconscious: shifting relational states, activators and the variable unconscious*. Presented at the 27th Annual International Conference on The Psychology of The Self, San Diego, Ca.

Kohut, H. (1959). Introspection, empathy and psychoanalysis: an examination of the relationship between mode of observation and theory. In P. H. Ornstein (Ed.), *The Search for the Self*, Vol. 1. New York: International Universities Press, pp.205–232.

Lichtenberg, J., Lachmann, F., & Fosshage, J. (1992). *Self and Motivational Systems: Toward a Theory of Technique*. Hillsdale, NJ: Analytic Press.

Ryan, J. L. (2007). Affects, reconfiguration of the self and self-states in mourning the loss of a son. In B. Willock, L. Bohm, & R. Coleman Curtis (Eds.), *On Deaths and Endings: Psychoanalysts' Reflections of Finality, Transformations and New Beginnings*. London: Routledge, pp.60–67.

Sapountzis, I. (2007). On sudden endings and self-imposed silences. In B. Willock, L. Bohm & R. C. Curtis (Eds.), *On Deaths and Endings: Psychoanalysts' Reflections of Finality, Transformations and New Beginnings*. London: Routledge, pp.303–318.

Slochower, J. (2007). Beyond the consulting room: ritual, mourning and memory. In B. Willock, L. Bohm & R. C. Curtis (Eds.), *On Deaths and Endings: Psychoanalysts' Reflections of Finality, Transformations and New Beginnings*. London: Routledge, pp.84–99.

Stern, D. N. (1998). Non-interpretive mechanisms in psychoanalytic therapy: the "something more" than interpretation. *International Journal of Psycho-Analysis*, 79:903–921.

Chapter 17

The loneliness of the analyst and its alleviation through faith in "O"

John A. Sloane

The ideas in this highly personal analytic narrative have been coming together for some time, finally crystallizing around the notion of loneliness—thanks to those who conceived the theme for the conference on which this book is based.[1] They cluster around the way my faith has evolved through analytic work rooted in the loneliness of the long-distance seeker of something I lost long ago. Part of what I hope to illustrate is the familiar theme of repetition and reparation in both the transference and counter-transference. In doing so, I may disclose more than some are comfortable with. I have always valued the writings of those who were willing to speak personally, allowing the listener to relate not only to their theories, but also to the author's emotional wellsprings. That relatedness is exactly what I had lost—a deep connection with authority and, with it, faith in my father, myself, and any man—as a result of the childhood experiences I outline below.

Despite its historical reductionism, psychoanalysis led me to a deeper faith in a broadly conceived God, immanent in our humanity. Listening to ordinary people, I have come to recognize God in them, in myself, and in what analysts are calling "the Third"—glimmerings arising between analyst and patient (Ogden, 1994; Aron, 2006). In Judaism, there is a tradition of *midrashim*—imaginative stories that elaborate on those in the Bible—retelling them from different points of view, illuminating old truths from new angles. I have come to think of the stories I hear in my office that way, as though I am meeting "Christ" on the road to wherever, even though "He" may be unrecognizable at first. The more I come to know each person, the more the outlines and essence of Biblical narratives re-emerge.

Let me begin with my own story, the death of my father, when I was ten. He was still a god to me; all-knowing, all powerful, intentionally punitive, requiring unquestioning obedience to his Law (Lacan, 1977) and an ability I didn't have to live up to his high standards. He was often absent, but nonetheless ever-present in my eyes. His death was a deeply confusing, disillusioning fact. It shattered my world, affecting every aspect of my life and work.

Ailing with brain cancer that was not diagnosed for several years, he became depressed and strangely disturbed, further straining our difficult relationship. He was small, but hugely authoritative and hot-tempered, as many Irishmen are, having grown up during "the Troubles." When he was a boy and his older brothers were fighting in the First World War, he slept with a gun under his pillow to protect his family. He was a feisty amateur boxer with little time for organized religion, of which he had probably seen more than enough. He became a respected chartered accountant, determined to make a better life for himself and his family in a new land. His illness, however, amplified a dark side of him in ways (spankings, silencings) that were unbearably hurtful, unjust, and senseless to me. Finally, I exploded with all the towering authority I could muster. Standing at the top of the basement stairs looking down at where he stood at the bottom, I let him have it with how I saw things, for a change. My actual words are long since lost in the eruption and confusion that followed. To my utter shock, awe, and lasting guilt, my budding authority was suddenly more powerful and articulate than his! His shoulders slumped. The light went out of his eyes. His fighting spirit was broken. Not long after that, he died.

I'll leave to your imagination "the troubles" such an "oedipal victory" left me with. Suffice it to say it set the stage for my reparative work as a physician (Klein, 1937), drawn to the troubles that were so much a part of every patient in my general practice. It also left a terrible hole in my heart, a loneliness I sought to fill with cigarettes, alcohol, sex, family, friends, ice cream, even Christianity. Each time I went in that latter direction, there was something I couldn't swallow, something that didn't make sense, felt toxic, oppressive, or seemed mere wish-fulfilling fantasy on my part.

That thought, of course, matched one of Freud's—that religion was a neurotic illusion—so my soul-searching led through psychiatry into psychoanalysis. How did such unhealed traumatic experiences, and the longings and fantasies that arise from them, shape our ways of being and believing, for better and for worse? More importantly, how on earth could they be healed? My analyst was a nonreligious Jew who listened empathically and respectfully, responding insightfully as I poured my heart out for several years. When it was time to move on, I missed our ongoing conversations tremendously. I now had no one with whom I could put into words the turmoil that my patients' traumatic outpourings stirred in me, leading me back to my own dark times. Once again, I was alone.

I found myself writing a journal. It became as natural and necessary as a daily bowel movement, a way of processing and disposing of mental "waste materials" that otherwise became toxic—not only to me, but to my growing family who were otherwise a refreshing light in the darkness of my work. Putting my feelings, dreams, and reflections about work and family life into words each morning helped to heal those reactivated wounds and prepare me for my day.

To my surprise, my patients expressed feelings I had just been writing, unaware as I was doing so of emerging unconscious connections. What I thought had to do only with myself, or with a particular patient, turned out to be about others as well. Their "words and music" matched my own in such timely ways that I came to realize that their "unconsciouses" and mine were deeply intertwined. That uncanny "cross-modal matching" of emotional meaning was similar to the attunement Daniel Stern and others have described between mother and child (Stern, 1985; Stolorow & Stolorow, 1987). As I learned to trust that uncanny responsiveness, it allowed me to understand my patients much better than I would have without my morning emotional "toilet." It set the stage for instinctive, wholehearted, relatively clear-headed openness and "optimal responsiveness" (Bacal, 1985) and proved to be deeply reconnecting for both me and my patients. A powerful antidote to loneliness!

At the same time, I began to notice meaningful coincidences, what Jung (1952) called "synchronicity," between my journal entries and events outside my office—in the news, films, poems, and music. Even my children's words as they played near the dining room table on which I worked echoed my thoughts. For some time I had trouble distinguishing these experiences from "ideas of reference," "thought broadcasting," and "loss of boundaries" between myself and others, between reality and fantasy—all hallmarks of schizophrenia! There were even moments as I was listening to patients when I suddenly lost consciousness, lost my *self*, and fell into a black hole or "primal density" (Loewald, 1980; Mitchell, 2000)—a terrifying experience of powerlessness to prevent my own annihilation that, when I "came to," would leave a deep sense of shame in its wake (Dender, 1993; Sloane, 1993b; Eshel, 1998). This psychotic or autistic phenomenon is one that occurs in children who recurrently experience themselves as nonexistent to their parents (Furman & Furman, 1984; Tustin, 1988; Sloane, 1993b; Finnegan, 2007). In "dying" psychically, I paradoxically became the dead or absent parent (Green, 1975, 1986) to whom the child in my patient felt nonexistent, eliciting either an enlivening, self-assertive protest or a deep sense of basic fault (Balint, 1968). This disturbing intersubjective enactment can rupture the analytic process or release a powerful projective-introjective flow for analytic reflection (Sloane, 1993a, 1993b).

At one point I became so perplexed that I high-tailed it back to my own analyst. Although I could not fully convey to him the strange connections and disconnections that I was "discovering," he did help to ground me again and put me back on track. I became able to trust that both the death-like states I was experiencing and the enlivening "correspondence" (my word) I was having with "Someone" out there was "creative" (his word) and potentially useful to me and to my patients, if not to him. Again, there was loneliness in my inability to share such experiences with another person who could actually "go there" with me and see or experience the same things.

My explorations of this inner, yet intersubjective world led me to something I had always thought I "ought" to do but never quite found the
motivation to accomplish—read the Bible, not the way one reads a novel or
studies a medical text, let alone in the way some people approach it as
though it provides authoritative answers, direct from God, that permit no
further questions or critical thought. Instead, I read digestible bites of it in
conjunction with my journal writing, following the Bible-reading guide,
Forward, Day by Day. I found amazingly timely echoes of the intersubjective "music" between and around my patients and my self. In this new
mode of relating to a voice of authority so similar, yet so different from
that of my father, I was free to "talk back."

This "literal" correspondence gave me a remarkable sense of relating to
Someone who was willing and able to recognize, validate, challenge,
stimulate—and accompany me into new territory. Instead of a terrible
absence, there was a loving omnipresence who not only seemed to listen, just
as my analyst had, but responded with surprising relevance to whatever I
was experiencing. My analyst, simply by being who he was, had made it
possible for me to reformulate my "god-representation" into a receptive,
respectful, responsive Presence, part of the developmental phenomenon
Anna Maria Rizzuto (1979) describes in her study of children's images of a
deity. Again, I was no longer alone but had the emotional accompaniment of
other human beings, some of them long dead, who had already "been there."
There were timeless others "out there" who knew what it was like to wrestle
with angels and demons as they tried to make sense of themselves and their
relationships with neighbors, enemies, and loved ones. They, too, were
searching to grasp and be held by the otherwise unconscious "Ground of our
Being" (Tillich, 1948), using their own judgment along the way. What a rich
reservoir the Bible has to offer!—far more than mere doctrines or laws to be
simply received, believed, and obeyed, more than spiritual food to be swallowed whole without tasting, chewing, and spitting out what is indigestible.

The faith I had developed for the analytic process had become one with
what others have known as faith in God, the great "I am" (Exodus 3:14)—
that which: Jews, respectful of the limits of human knowing, refrain from
naming (G-d,); Greeks call the "Unknown God"; Christians call "Christ";
Muslims "Allah"; Christ called "Abba" and offered to us as "our Father."
I believe it is what Freud called the "Ucs" and Jung the "Collective
Unconscious," although each of them conceptualizes and unpacks it quite
differently. Stern (1997) refers to such uncharted territory as "unformulated
experience" which we come to "know" only as we find words for it. Bollas
(1987) refers to the "unthought known," others refer to "the Third"
(Ogden, 1994; Aron, 2006)—that which speaks to us in incidental, dream-
like images that seem to appear of their own accord. All of these notions
are poetic approximations of something in the same vicinity, something
mysterious, beyond our grasp.

No two god-representations (Rizzuto, 1979) are identical, let alone captured for all time or all people by a single word, theory, or doctrine. Each person's image of God emerges from his or her own experience, processed in "transitional space" (Winnicott, 1953) where he or she uses, discards, or reconceptualizes it in his or her own way. In that space, one is not forced to answer the questions: Is this real or imagined? True or false? Created or discovered? Me or not me? Such "castings" can become idolatrous and misleading when they become too concrete or certain (Brothers, 2008). "It is God who has made us, not we ourselves," says an Anglican prayer, but it is we who make our own images of God, whether we believe such a "Being" exists, or not. That co-creative process is captured in Mauritz Escher's image of the "Drawing Hands" emerging from a blank page upon which each is drawing the other.

The way of listening we know as psychoanalysis constitutes an act of faith in "O" (Eigen, 1981). "I shall use the sign O to denote that which is the ultimate reality represented by terms such as . . . absolute truth, the godhead, the infinite, the thing-in-itself" (Bion, 1970). In other words, as analysts we entrust our selves to what we don't yet know or, perhaps, have forgotten. "The doctor should . . . *give himself over completely* [italics mine] to his unconscious (memory)" (Freud, 1912, p.112). What I understand by "O" is the unknown but "ultimate" emotional truth of each session that makes itself known if we can set aside our preconceptions, forgo "memory and desire" (Bion, 1967), and remain open to being surprised (Reik, 1936). It includes the concept of God, just as it does for Bion, who considers analysis, scientific study, and religion as different ways of approaching and being open to "ultimate truth." To paraphrase Jesus, wherever two or three are gathered together in search of truth, in the service of good, willing to face what is bad, and acknowledging the limits of what they know, God is with them (Olthuis, 1994b).

There are many ways of paying meditative attention to the Other-in-relation-to-the-Self, many ways of being in an "I-Thou relationship" (Buber, 1958). Listening in good faith, opening ourselves to the kernel of truth in different points of view, no matter how mad, offensive, or threatening they seem, and speaking from the heart, as best we can, is key. Being open to question, objection, correction, rejection—even risking one's life in the service of what we love—is part of being "good-enough." Such openness is essential to relationships with others in every walk of life, even with mortal enemies. For me, the process of wording what is otherwise preverbal or nonverbal has become one with "the Word" that was there "in the beginning" (John 1:1).

What I encounter again and again as an analyst are experiences of unhealed emotional trauma that have left the person feeling emotionally crucified (Grotstein, 2000). Every child experiences betrayals of basic trust (Erikson, 1950) that leave him or her feeling violated, forsaken, bewildered, and broken, even "dead to the world." Often children are left in that state, feeling deeply unknown and nonexistent to those they count on (Finnegan, 2007) who, for one reason or another, do not have ears to hear, heart to bear, or mind to grasp how unspeakably "bad" the child feels. Then there is an eruption of passions; selfishness, greed, envy, hate, contempt, lust, and mistrust, even pleasure in the power to cause pain or to destroy one's self and others—the last refuge of those who feel ineffective (White, 1963), powerless in the pit of despair.

These universal urges and their repetitive enactment in relationships ranging from intimate to international can give rise to ruthlessly omnipotent invasion, control and exploitation of the vulnerabilities of others. They condense and crystallize in split-off idealizations (or idolizations) of one or another "god-representation," with arrogant assumptions of divine right of sole access to the Truth. (Psychoanalytic institutes are only one example.) It is important, however, lest we too quickly judge such assumptions that override the rights of others, to recognize, in them, the fundamental "birthright" of every child (Atwood, 2000). As such, it must be recognized and understood before it can be authentically integrated and redistributed to other human beings. As the writer of Genesis understood, we *all* incline toward *absolute* knowledge of good and evil (Genesis 3:5), making final judgments and imposing final solutions in the name of whatever we consider pure or supreme. Concrete, narrowly defined images of God, including the Christian God or the "pure gold of psychoanalysis," are used to justify and enforce all manner of evils, large and small.

Such impulses arising from the "heart of darkness" are central to what Freud called "the Id," Jung "the Shadow," and Christians "original sin." They seem to need taming, training, humbling, punishing, or forgiving in order to grow in a civilized way. Many psychoanalysts, especially Winnicott (1969) in his paper on "the use of the object," have shown that when the mother/father/analyst can simply survive such absolute, all-out impulses, bearing his or her own narcissistic injury or elimination, while holding in mind the person's distress without retaliating or crumbling (Bion, 1963; Kohut, 1977; Modell, 1976), the brokenness and all that spills from it can heal.

An essential part of this process is the capacity to recognize the painful, destructive impact of one's own absence or impinging presence. Healing or whole-ing of persons and of the relationships they unconsciously co-create and destroy requires willingness on all sides to recognize and learn from those damaging events in which "we know not what we do" (Luke 23:34). It is the responsibility of those in positions of relative power to do so first, bearing, wearing, and owning the attributions (Lichtenberg et al., 1992) of *both* goodness and badness. "Godness," in other words.

Every infant is born with the capacity to "bring joy to the world," but the child's gifts, passions, and creative energies can be split asunder, exploited, or buried alive under layers of repression and far-reaching defenses until such time as they are recognized and understood as such. That essential recognition can occur naturally in various ways, or in analysis where passions are revived and given voice, time, and space to settle and get back on track. With relatively nonjudgmental understanding, the person can transform a wide variety of passions into wholesome, authentic, and effective ways of being with others (Olthuis, 1994a).

Such "rebirth" (Sloane, 1993b) can happen even years later when conditions such as therapy, a trusting relationship, or a trustworthy community encourage and sustain it. It is possible for people to regressively reopen those highly defended "tombs" where they found it necessary to bury what is most sacred and/or shameful to them. Then there can be a joyful "new beginning" (Balint, 1968), a resurrection of what had seemed lost forever. These are the beautiful moments that "bring light to those who live in darkness" and make such painful work worthwhile. As Margaret Arden (1998) writes in *Midwifery of the Soul*, "The miracle of psychoanalysis— and it is a miracle—is that when a person comes to understand the core of his or her childhood experience, all the anger, all the rejection of life, turns out to have been for one purpose—to preserve at whatever cost, the child who is also capable of love" (p.5). Such moments are vulnerable, exciting, scary, joyful, and profoundly sad, all at the same time, because it's taken so long and cost so much.

A case in point involves a woman I worked with over 30 years ago. She was a child of the Holocaust, haunted by demons neither she nor I could contain. After two years of intensely meaningful, hopeful therapy, there ensued an excruciating disintegration of an idealizing transference, leading to a place of insoluble conflict and utter despair from which she committed suicide by jumping from a tall building.

I felt responsible not only for my failure, but also for an ill-considered impulsive assertion of my needs in the face of her relentless demands and regressive disregard of my boundaries, needs, and limits. There was a deadly transference-countertransference enactment in which I became a Nazi in her eyes and, once again, a "destroyer of worlds" in my own. A recurring nightmare during my youth was of nuclear holocaust in which I experienced boundless dread, not only for the "real" possibility of nuclear war but also, I later learned, for the destructiveness of my own aggressive, self-assertive authority. I could not bear to go to her funeral and face her devastated family, just as I had been kept away (overprotected) from that of my father.

Last year I received a call from her brother (with whose permission I write this) who wanted to meet to find out—and confront—what had happened. Needless to say, that brought back a flood of fear, guilt, shame, and grief, but also deep desire to meet this man who, when he arrived, wanted to talk and enquire more than accuse or conduct an inquisition. He, too, was a small man with a powerful air of authority. Unlike my father, he spoke softly, was more sad than angry, and was deeply grounded in his own experience, in the tragic history of his people, and in Judaism. He was also surprisingly open to the truth as I saw it from a different angle.

We met many times, coming to grips with what had happened to her, to him, and to me as a result of what each of us did and was unable to do. Her "resurrection" in the person of her brother made it necessary and possible for me to revisit the traumatic experiences of her death and that of my father, enabling me to find words for my point of view. Thanks to his honesty and openness, I had the experience of being grappled with, understood, and appreciated for my honesty, rather than condemned. Our conversations were therefore redemptive for both of us. We experienced the forgiveness implicit in mutual understanding and acceptance of our common, fallible humanity. He and I have become friends in a way that has allowed each of us to feel truly known, forgiven, whole, and less alone— enabled to begin again.

My experience as an analyst has parallels to stories in the Bible and makes me keenly aware of the ways in which any belief system, including psychoanalysis and Christianity, can become a means of dominion over others, unconsciously doing to them what was done to us or to those we love. I am currently working with a woman who suffered much damage, deprivation, and degradation as a child, partly because of her mother's slavish obedience to the sexual desires of her husband under patriarchal Church authority. She is filled with rage, hatred, contempt, and distrust for humanity, sexuality, and religion, as well as intense envy (Klein, 1975) for those such as I, who have been "given" what her family's overpopulation so unjustly denied her. When planes destroyed the twin towers on 9/11, she felt deeply pleasurable identification with those who had the power to bring them down so horrifically on the world stage. For many years, she vented those same scorchingly hateful, humiliating, dehumanizing passions at me, complaining I just "didn't get" what her life was like, determined to make me "get it." Her actual words, like mine to my father, are lost in the posttraumatic rubble, impossible to recall or convey. Suffice it to say that she, too, speaks with a tone of absolute authority, demanding immediate, perfect obedience and miraculous salvation, at the same time as she pronounces final judgment and scornful rejection for my failure to be the "savior" she has every right to expect. In speaking this way, she creates an impenetrable wall around her—using the voice her mother used with her, and that my father used with me. Her tone creates an oppressive climate in which there is no air, no room for discussion, no time for thought or analytic reflection, rendering me as shamefully stupid as she sees me to be— ignorant, impotent, and utterly speechless. "You're an analyst, aren't you?" she would mock. "You're supposed to be able to interpret all this!" At the same time, she would sneer at my presumptuousness in even trying to do so, "How *could* you get it, *you* who have everything?"

My failure to be, do, or say what she needs repeats and reverses how outrageously "stupid, and useless" her parents were, as well as how shamefully powerless and lacking in language she still feels herself to be. For me, it repeats how I felt in my father's eyes. Part of that "intergenerational" challenge is to find words to acknowledge the truth of what she is saying and at the same time hold her responsible for the part she plays in its repetition. In part, I do so by conveying something of my countertransference experience of how horrendous it was and continues to be for her, how destructive it is to be unrecognized or scorned as a fellow human being, and how vital it then becomes to be able to destroy the destroyer, the failing, god-like Other.

She now has fleeting, but increasingly frequent and sustained moments of openness in which she feels loving, trusting, joyful, and enjoyable, but also excruciatingly vulnerable to attack or pity, an unbearable sentiment from which she can barely distinguish curiosity or "analytic love" (Shaw, 2003). My spontaneous, nonverbal expressions of interest, compassion, or enjoyment are picked up immediately, evoking shame, rage, and suspicion. She also resents the prospect that I might "get" even more "good stuff" than I already have, mobilizing a scathingly final judgment of my unworthiness, foolishness, and ignorance of how bad things really are, were, and always will be for her. It is that which she repeatedly tries to force me to "get."

When I am able to get it, to follow and stay with her—as well as against her—in these rapidly fluctuating states, an oceanic immensity of grief and sadness emerges between us, connecting us in a way that brings to mind T. S. Eliot's words in his Preludes: "I am moved by fancies that are curled/ Around these images, and cling,/The notion of some infinitely gentle/ Infinitely suffering thing."

Standing up for myself in ways that are firm, without being brutal or banishing, for those parts of her with which I identify more than she knows, and for the value of the relationship she clings to but repeatedly trashes, has enabled me to learn what my father could not force me to "get" with his unforgettable words, "Let that be a lesson to you!" I have become able to use my own authority in the service of the analytic process, in the service of my self and hers, making it possible for her to recognize and contain her own hatred, contempt, shame, and despair with the help of an emerging capacity for concern and loving enjoyment. The lesson I've learned is not one of obedience but, in the words of Kahlil Gibran's (1976) Prophet, that "The deeper that sorrow carves into your being, the more joy you can contain."

Both cases shook the foundations of my being. Each reactivated, differently, a cluster of powerful affects associated with the demise of my father and with my loss of faith in myself and the "voice of Authority," wherever I encounter it. The experience of working through a living hell to a place of mutual understanding has done a great deal to re-establish my faith in myself, in the analytic process, and in humanity. As analysts, we all have areas of emotional crucifixion that make it necessary to do this reparative work. We all rework personal issues as we work through those of our patients and therefore have much for which to be thankful to them. We might all be less alone if we found ways of speaking personally, as well as professionally.

To conclude, I have learned how to speak with authority born of my own experience, while remaining open to that of other wounded, fallible healers, including those we call patients. They unknowingly enable their physicians, therapists, or analysts to heal themselves (Searles, 1959, 1979) by raising and releasing the ghosts (Loewald, 1960; Mitchell, 1998) of their own deeply regressive experience, as well as by entrusting them with what is sacred. They have led me to a place where I am no longer so lonely, but considerably more capable of being alone in the presence or absence of others (Winnicott, 1958). I have found faith that we are not alone, but embedded in Being, becoming more than we can imagine as we keep our eyes and ears open to what we don't yet know (Gargiulo, 2004). This multidimensional analytic process is one in which everyone has no choice but to choose his or her own words. Karen Armstrong (2009) in her most recent book, *The Case for God*, reviews the historical function of faith and the limits of language to define what is meant by "God," whether we "believe" in one, or not. She comes to conclusions similar to mine, similar to those of psychoanalysis, I think, that respect for and openness to that which is sacred to each individual—that which can never be fully conscious or rationalized—is essential to our ongoing, essentially poetic dialogue in search of meaning, and of being wholly human. Similarly, Robert Wright (2009) has written a fascinating, at times funny, and very informative book called *The Evolution of God*, an historical, anthropological, and evolutionary-psychological examination of Man's conceptions of God. For all its dreadfully maladaptive dead-ends, the idea of God survives, he argues, because it serves the purpose of survival, and could yet accomplish that end historically. His well-documented account, focused especially on the Abrahamic religions, parallels and greatly expands what I am trying to describe from a personal, psychoanalytic point of view: the gradual transformation of primitive beliefs in the existence of unseen, supernatural agencies, through a supraordinate, omniscient, omnipotent Agency to whom certain people have exclusive access, toward a more inclusive conception of the Divine, as an underlying, evolving, moral imagination that gives rise to mutual respect, empathy, and co-operation in the interests of the survival of our inescapably shared humanity. Such faith is "the substance of things hoped for, the evidence of things not seen" (Hebrews 11:1). That "substance," I would argue, is personal—possible to relate to, represent, or ignore in ways that are co-determined by the unique experience of each person.

Note

1 I am also grateful to the "men's breakfast" group at St. Clement's Anglican Church and to "The Blank Page" writers group in Toronto for invaluable feedback on earlier versions of this chapter.

References

Arden, M. (1998). *Midwifery of the Soul: A Holistic Perspective on Psychoanalysis.* London: Free Association Books.

Armstrong, K. (2009). *The Case for God.* Toronto: Knopf Canada.

Aron, L. (2006). Analytic impasse and the third: Clinical implications of intersubjectivity theory. *International Journal of Psycho-Analysis*, 87:349–368.

Atwood, G. (2000). Personal communication.

Bacal, H. A. (1985). Optimal responsiveness and the therapeutic process. In A. Goldberg (Ed.), *Progress in Self Psychology* (Vol. 1, pp.202–227). New York: Guilford Press.

Balint, M. (1968). *The Basic Fault.* London: Tavistock.

Bion, W. R. (1963). *Learning from Experience.* New York: Basic Books.

—— (1967). Notes on memory and desire. *The Psychoanalytic Forum*, 2(3):271–280.

—— (1970). *Attention and Interpretation.* London: Tavistock Publications.

Bollas, C. (1987). *The Shadow of the Object. Psychoanalysis of the Unthought Known.* New York: Columbia University Press.

Brothers, D. (2008). *Toward a Psychology of Uncertainty: Trauma-Centered Psychoanalysis.* New York: The Analytic Press.

Buber, M. (1958). *I and Thou* (2nd ed.). New York: Charles Scribner's Sons.

Dender, J. M. (1993). The phenomenon of sleepiness in the analyst. Unpublished presentation at the 16th Annual Conference on the Psychology of the Self, Toronto, October 30.

Eigen, M. (1981). The Area of Faith in Winnicott, Lacan and Bion. *International Journal of Psycho-Analysis*, 62:413–433.

Eliot, T. S. (1917/2004). *Preludes, IV.* In *Complete Poems and Plays of T. S. Eliot.* London: Faber.

Erikson, E. H. (1950). *Childhood and Society.* New York: W. W. Norton & Co.

Eshel, O. (1998). "Black holes", deadness, and existing analytically. *International Journal of Psycho-Analysis*, 79:1115–1130.

Finnegan, P. (2007). *Towards a Fairbairnian understanding of multiple personality.* Master's thesis, University of Sheffield, Sheffield, UK.

Freud, S. (1912). Recommendations to physicians practising psycho-analysis. *Standard Edition*, 12:111–120.

Furman, R. A. & Furman, E. (1984). Intermittent decathexis—a type of parental dysfunction. *The International Journal of Psycho-Analysis*, 65:423–433.

Gargiulo, G. J. (2004). Aloneness in psychoanalysis and spirituality. *International Journal of Applied Psychoanalytic Studies*, 1(1):36–46.

Gibran, K. (1976). *The Prophet.* London: Heinemann.

Green, A. (1975). Analyst, symbolization and absence in the analytic setting. *International Journal of Psycho-Analysis*, 56:1–22.

—— (1986). *On Private Madness.* Madison, CT: International Universities Press.

208   John A. Sloane

Grotstein, J. S. (2000). *Who Is the Dreamer Who Dreams the Dream? A Study of Psychic Presences* (pp.219–279). Hillsdale, NJ: The Analytic Press.

Jung, C. G. (1952). Synchronicity: an acausal connecting principle. *Collected Works* (Vol. 8, pp.520–531).

Klein, M. (1937). *Love, Guilt and Reparation & Other Works 1921–1945* (pp.306–343). New York: Delacort Press/Seymour Lawrence.

—— (1975). *Envy and Gratitude and Other Works 1946–1963*. New York: Delacorte Press/Seymour Lawrence.

Kohut, H. (1977). *The Restoration of the Self*. New York: International Universities Press.

Lacan, J. (1977). *Écrits: A Selection* (A. Sheridan, Trans.). New York: Norton.

Lichtenberg, J., Lachmann, F. & Fossage, J. (1992). *Self and Motivational Systems: Toward a Theory of Technique*. Hillsdale, NJ: Analytic Press.

Loewald, H. W. (1960). The therapeutic action of psychoanalysis. *Papers on Psychoanalysis* (pp.221–256). New Haven, CT: Yale University Press.

—— (1980). Primary process, secondary process, and language. *Papers on Psychoanalysis*. New Haven, CT: Yale University Press.

Mitchell, S. A. (1998). From ghosts to ancestors: The psychoanalytic vision of Hans Loewald. *Psychoanalytic Dialogues*, 8:825–855.

—— (2000). *Relationality: From Attachment to Intersubjectivity*. Hillsdale, NJ: The Analytic Press.

Modell, A. (1976). "The holding environment" and the therapeutic action of psychoanalysis. *Journal of the American Psychoanalytic Assoc.*, 24:285–307.

Ogden, T. H. (1994). The analytic third: working with intersubjective clinical facts. *International Journal of Psycho-Analysis*, 75:3–20.

Olthuis, J. H. (1994a). Being-with: toward a relational psychotherapy. *Journal of Psychology and Christianity*, 13(3):217–231.

—— (1994b). God-with-us: toward a relational psychotherapeutic model. *Journal of Psychology and Christianity*, 13(1):37–49.

Reik, T. (1936). *Surprise and the Psychoanalyst* (M. Green, Trans.). London: Kegan Paul.

Rizzuto, A.-M. (1979). *The Birth of the Living God: A Psychoanalytic Study*. Chicago: The University of Chicago Press.

Searles, H. (1959). The effort to drive the other person crazy—an element in the aetiology and psychotherapy of schizophrenia. *British Journal of Medical Psychology*, 32:1–18.

—— (1979). *Countertransference and Related Subjects: Selected Papers*. New York: International Universities Press.

Shaw, D. (2003). On the therapeutic action of analytic love. *Contemporary Psychoanalysis*, 39(2):251–278.

Sloane, J. A. (1993a). Offenses and defenses against patients: A psychoanalyst's view of the borderline between empathic failure and malpractice. *Canadian Journal of Psychiatry*, 38(May).

—— (1993b). Sleep, death and rebirth: a discussion of Jack Dender's paper, The phenomenon of sleepiness in the analyst, presented at the 16th Annual Conference on the Psychology of the Self, Toronto, October 30.

Stern, D. B. (1997). *Unformulated Experience: From Dissociation to Imagination in Psychoanalysis*. Hillsdale, NJ: The Analytic Press.

Stern, D. N. (1985). *The Interpersonal World of the Infant*. New York: Basic Books.

Stolorow, R. D. & Stolorow, D. S. (1987). Affects and selfobjects. In R. D. Stolorow, B. Brandchaft & G. E. Atwood (Ed.), *Psychoanalytic Treatment; An Intersubjective Approach*. Hillsdale, NJ: The Analytic Press.

Tillich, P. (1948). *The Shaking of the Foundations*. New York: Charles Scribner's Sons.

Tustin, F. (1988). The "black hole": a significant element in autism. *Free Associations*, 1:35–50.

White, R. W. (1963). *Ego and Reality in Psychoanalytic Theory*. New York: International Universities Press.

Winnicott, D. W. (1953). Transitional objects and transitional phenomena. *Playing and Reality* (pp.1–25). London: Tavistock Publications, 1971.

—— (1958). The capacity to be alone. *International Journal of Psycho-Analysis*, 39:416–420.

—— (1969). The use of an object. *International Journal of Psycho-Analysis*, 50:711–716.

Wright, R. (2009). *The Evolution of God*. New York: Little, Brown and Company.

Part VII

Loneliness and yearnings in the sociocultural surround

Chapter 18

Yearning and loss in *No Country for Old Men*

Art Caspary

In 1965, Bob Dylan advised a certain Mr. Jones that he was quite oblivious to great changes that were happening all around him. Despite the wry irony at the expense of the hapless Mr. Jones, Dylan (1965) was predicting that things were going to change for the better.

In 2005, Cormac McCarthy's character, Sheriff Ed Tom Bell, describes his reaction to a man who murdered his 14-year-old girlfriend: In 2005, Cormac McCarthy's character, Sheriff Ed Tom Bell describes his reaction to a man who murdered his 14-year-old girlfriend. He paints a picture of a chillingly amoral young man who killed without passion, but simply because he had been planning to kill someone for as long as he could remember. Bell recalls the man saying that if given the opportunity, he'd do it again and that he fully expected to go to hell. Bell wondered if this boy was something new in the world, something soulless. Then he added that this boy was nothing compared to what was coming.

McCarthy offers us a prediction, too. But the times they have changed. In this story about change and loss, the two central characters, Sheriff Bell and Anton Chigurh, stand in opposition, both in the narrative and as metaphors for different ways of being human. Bell lives by the law of the father. For him morality is a synthesis of fundamental decency and absolute conviction that his moral standards transcend time and culture. They are immutable. He is an essentialist. Chigurh is, put simply, a psychopath.[1] He will subordinate all means to the accomplishment of his ends. But this is qualified. He has one standard that, at least at times, stands in a dynamic tension with more venal goals. He embraces randomness and chaos and thus is linked to mediaeval conceptions of Satan, the destroyer of the certainty of God the Father.

There are two stories here. One is the emergence in our times of a new version of an old character, an efficient psychopath who will do anything to get what he wants. The second story is that of the rest of us: the gradual acknowledgement that we are losing not only a world that privileges honor and decency, but also the conviction that morality is immutable, timeless, and an expression of a just God. This second story is of the loss of the idealized oedipal father who, optimally, serves as an internal beacon, promoting autonomy, a measure of certainty and a discernible course for the regulation of our selves. Bell is everyman and this is his story of the loss of the law of the father and the legacy of yearning that the subsequent yawning emptiness evokes.

The setting is South Texas, a place where the bleak land mirrors the moral landscape in the narrative. The plot is simple. There is a drug war. A man called Llewellyn Moss stumbles on the scene of a massacre and walks away with several million dollars. Anton Chigurh is hired to find him but kills his employers and sets off in pursuit of Moss on his own. The drug cartel orders Chigurh assassinated but, instead, Chigurh kills the hitman. Eventually Moss is killed, though not by Chigurh. Chigurh recovers the money, then kills Moss's wife. As he leaves, he is in an automobile accident. Though injured, he walks away. Sheriff Bell, defeated, retires. The pursuit seems initially motivated by greed and vengeance but as time passes, Chigurh's motives are revealed as something else; perhaps something new in the world but perhaps something ancient.

McCarthy's novel and the subsequent film can be viewed in a number of ways. Certainly it is a bitter, unsentimental lament on the loss of innocence and honor in our times, and McCarthy is unflinching in his vision. He is a moralist, a traditionalist who bemoans the passing of stabilizing ideals and values that express themselves both in everyday civility and in internalized prohibitions that protect us from the horrors of what he assumes is our essential savagery. He shares Freud's vision. He develops the theme of man as hunter. There are references to ancient stone drawings made by hunters. Moss is hunting antelope when he finds the money. Bell is a hunter of men and, in a very different sense, so is Chigurh. Perhaps, McCarthy suggests, the best that we can hope for is an uneasy standoff with our essentially aggressive nature. But then how do we account for the profound differences between Bell and Chigurh?

Bell, a wryly self-deprecating man, loves his wife with humility and gratitude. He is matter-of-fact about his job, acknowledging its dangers without macho bluster. He is stubbornly moral and brooks no disrespect for the dead. He values tradition, authority, and politeness. He believes in absolutes as expressed through Biblical imagery.

He has access to his inner world and reflects on himself and others. He thinks often of change and loss. Again and again he recalls incidents that illustrate the deterioration of values and the escalation of savagery. He is old and he is sad.

Chigurh is, to say the least, different. He's young, with a Prince Valiant haircut and eyes described as moist but opaque, like wet stones. Unlike Bell, he is efficient. Bell wastes moves: wondering about things; bemoaning loss of civility; thinking of his wife; forever squandering time going home for dinner, even enjoying it. Bell often thinks about the past, comparing it with what he sees as a dismal present and terrifying future.

Chigurh does none of these things. He is highly focused for the most part, although occasionally he will indulge in a ritual coin flipping which seems to signify the voiding of agency and implying that things are determined by forces outside human choice. Interestingly, he is not particularly cruel. Only once does he seem motivated by mild sadism and that is when he becomes slightly alarmed that a roadside shopkeeper might be able to identify where he came from. This hint of passion is immediately subordinated to the flip of a coin. Otherwise Chigurh expresses Zen-like calmness.

Bell suggests Chigurh represents something new, something he's never seen, and toward which he experiences unspeakable dread. Chigurh is slouching toward Bethlehem and we might wonder what motivates his character. Who or what does he represent? He is without concern for others' feelings, ruthless in his pursuit of his aims. He seems to be shedding attributes that reduce his effectiveness. He tells Wells, the drug cartel hitman, that killing to prove he can escape the law is an exercise in vanity and he has moved past that. It becomes evident that he is not primarily motivated by the money. Rather, one has the impression he does what he does, not out of purpose or even as an expression of agency, but rather because that is what he has become. He expresses his nature.

In a larger sense I think Chigurh represents an emergent self-state that is a result of complex psychological and socio-economic forces at work in the world today. On a manifest level he is embedded in the drug culture where profits trump everything else. This end permits all means. Lies, betrayal, and murder are simply business as usual. One is reminded of Tessio in a rather better film, *The Godfather*. When Tessio is discovered as complicit in a plot to kill Michael Corleone whom he has known since childhood, he describes his actions as "just business."

I propose Chigurh and drug culture serve as metaphors for a larger, more systemic issue. In developed countries, especially the United States, the processes that characterize the modern corporation have profoundly infiltrated the entire culture, altering the experience of being human. Joel Bakan (2004), a distinguished legal scholar, carefully developed this thesis that the corporation is the most influential entity in contemporary culture and that it is structured both internally and in law to subordinate all means to one end: increasing profits for shareholders. It is illegal for an executive to deploy corporate resources for the greater good of the community unless that can be demonstrated to increase shareholder value. Shareholders are not held legally or morally responsible for the corporations they own. Legal and moral considerations may be seen as constraints by corporate decision makers, but mostly in a pragmatic sense. The corporation, in order to fulfill its mandate and thus survive, will play within the law when necessary and outside the law when it can. Bakan cites numerous examples of the latter.

Bakan further notes that the corporation is recognized in law as a person, with all a person's rights and privileges. He then raises an interesting question: if a corporation is ensconced in law as a person, what kind of a person is it? The answer, according to Bakan, is a person who meets the criteria for antisocial personality disorder, in other words, a psychopath. Bakan presents impressive documentation supporting the assertion that corporations behave in ways characterized by a lack of regard for the moral or legal standards of the community and a marked inability to get along with others or abide by societal rules. They engage in illegal acts, lie and deceive others for profit, always act in self-serving ways, repeatedly assault others, are reckless regarding others' safety, fail to honor financial obligations, and rationalize the pain they inflict on others. In a corporate system, all choices are circumscribed by the superordinate goal of acquisition.

Corporations are enormously influential. They control information through ownership of media and are notorious for acquiring the best politicians money can buy. They shape our work culture (Currie, Dunn, & Fogarty, 1991; Stennett, 1998) and us through the flawed mirror of advertising. They prostitute science through preferential funding and selective publication (Rampton & Stauber, 2002). They undermine democracy by influencing the electoral process through disinformation (Herman & Chomsky, 1988) and subtle reframing of issues in ways that distort (Lakoff, 2008). They are not simply external forces that impinge upon us. They have infected the culture. They are the water we swim in, the air we breathe.

Noam Chomsky (in Bakan, 2004) suggested it serves corporate ends to create a state where individuals are not primarily motivated by concern or sympathy for others:

> The ideal is to have individuals who are totally disassociated from one another, who don't feel concern for anyone else . . . whose conception of themselves, their sense of value, is "just how many created wants can I satisfy? And how deeply can I go into debt and still get away with satisfying created wants?" If you want to create a society in which the smallest unit is a tube, with no connections to people, that would be ideal.
>
> (p.135)

Individual development expresses a dialectic between inherent predispositions and forces that have survival value in a given society at a particular time. There is mounting evidence that we are psychologically and neuro-cognitively predisposed to interact with others (Winnicott, 1945; Kohut,

1977; Stern, 1985; Beebe & Lachmann, 1994; Schore, 1997) and that under optimal conditions we tend to be cooperative, to thrive on mutual regulation (Beebe & Lachmann, 2002), vitalized by intersubjectivity (Benjamin, 1988). To survive in a corporate state we are pulled to become estranged from these fundamental needs and to privilege domination over mutuality, sado-masochism over potential space. It is a recipe for alienation and loneliness.

There are casualties. If what signifies value and defines the self is not simply having things but having more than others and more than one had last year (Wachtel, 1989), then even the illusion of self-cohesion entails constant motion. It is like running up a stairway where each step dissolves as soon as your foot leaves it. Potential selfobjects become competitors. Inherent strivings for mutuality become sources of shame and anxiety. Need becomes weakness. Altruism becomes pejoratively "liberal." Because one continually attempts to satisfy selfobject needs through acquisition, one feels perpetually empty, on the verge of fragmentation. The only available solution is to escalate a vicious cycle of further acquisitiveness and competitiveness (Wachtel, 1989). An analogy to junk food over a nutritious diet is in the right direction but doesn't go far enough. It would be more accurate to say that we eat cardboard and thus are always hungry. Identified with a system that damages people, there is unconscious guilt. Winning is at the expense of others. To maintain the illusion of self-fulfillment, we inflict damage. Sometimes it is up close and personal, more often it is abstract and distant. We see our victims on television and call them the Third World or less developed. They tend to have darker skin and their food smells funny.

The fundamental estrangement from our selves and between ourselves produced by a corporate state is so pervasive that it militates against reparation. It is more adaptive to rely on a very different unconscious strategy, denying the subjectivity of self and other in escalating sequence of projections and projective identificatory processes. The ability to reflect on one's experience is lost and the other is, in imagination, populated by disavowed self-states. Subjectivity of both self and other is lost. When we rely on this defence, we lose our minds. When the capacity for mentalization is impaired, one cannot tacitly know one's experience is constituted by representations. If I think it's true, it is true. If I think you're bad, you are. I have to keep myself busy, continually ridding myself of unacceptable self-states by imagining they exist in others (Altman, 2005). I have to deploy my attention externally and engage in frantic activity to keep my mind off my loneliness, anxiety, and guilt. For many, shopping is just that activity.

In this kind of system, guilt, reaction formation, undoing, and reparation are simply not adaptive. Since corporate processes militate against reparation, the cycle becomes self-perpetuating, escalating (Altman, 2005). It's even worse for corporate executives and those who aspire to be. At this level, personal well-being is defined not solely by the amount and trajectory of acquisitions relative to others, but also by a work environment that is highly competitive and which privileges ruthlessness and expediency. Increasingly, these people determine the terms of reference which dictate our lives.

Like sharks, we must be forever feeding, forever in motion. Chigurh, like the shark, is dedicated, simplified, and highly efficient. It would appear, however, that Chigurh is not one of these causalities. Toward the end of the book, after killing the drug cartel boss who ordered his assassination, he visits a more senior executive in the organization. He returns the money he has recovered and when asked what he wants replies that he is there to establish his value to the organization. He adds that he is both reliable and honest and that he has no enemies because he won't allow that. As the conversation unfolds, the drug lord becomes increasingly uneasy. The reader is left with the impression that this hardened, ruthless criminal is looking into a moral void that terrifies even him.

Chigurh has, I think, valiantly eliminated his humanity in order to become perfectly adapted to the corporate state. He has become *The Prince* (Machiavelli, 1505/1916). There is no illusion of mutuality between the executive and Chigurh and the other man knows it. Chigurh is like a machine; he does not choose but, like the corporation, does whatever he must to advance himself. He is single-minded. There are no conflicts over guilt. He appears to no longer need others to regulate self-cohesiveness or worth. He is increasingly efficient as he systematically pares away those aspects of himself which are not conducive to his sole aim. He leaves the impression that his behavior is not a product of intentionality but, rather, expresses nonsymbolic procedures. It is easy to imagine that when he speaks of himself and especially when he emphasizes the lack of agency behind his actions, he is simply commenting on a process to which he is witness. (His moist, empty eyes may express a vestigial self, helplessly watching and mourning the loss of his humanity.) There is a suggestion that the means of survival have become detached from the ends, for killing Moss' wife does not further his aims. With no sense of agency, Chigurh in that sense is isomorphic with the corporation which also does not choose. All choices are pre-dictated by its mandate to survive and make profit. That is its definition.

But what of Bell? This is really his story, a story of yearning and loss. At the end, two things signify what Bell has lost. He is an essentialist who believes in a moral universe where good prevails and evil is punished. So do we all on some level. One of the most often heard criticisms of the film is that the auto accident after Chigurh leaves his last murder is arbitrary. More disturbing is the fact that he survives. In an indifferent universe, accidents happen and there are no just desserts. Evil walks away.

We last see Bell, retired, defeated by all Chigurh represents. In the book, he sits at the kitchen table and tells his wife that from his point of view he has lived a lie. He believes the medal he was awarded was based on events that did not happen, that he behaved in a self-serving way under fire rather than being a hero. Reflecting on his life and times, he talks of the vast wealth that has migrated to the very few, wealth that surpasses that of nations. He adds he can see no hope in how this wealth will be used, that there is nothing to take heart from.

Finally, Bell talks of two dreams about his father. In the first, his father gave him money but he lost it. In the second, he is riding alone on a dark, winter night. He sees his father: "He rode past me and kept on goin. Never said nothing. He just rode on past . . . I seen he was carrying fire in a horn the way people used to do and I could see the horn from the light inside of it. About the color of the moon. And in the dream I knew that he was goin on ahead and that he was fixin to make a fire somewhere out there in all that dark and all that cold and I knew that when ever I got there he would be there. And then I woke up" (p.309).

This question is left hanging: Did Bell wake up to a recognition that the law of the father (Freud, 1933), with its implications for certainty and moral immutability, are revealed as a myth, frayed to tatters by the sinister shift in the world that has created a culture no longer hospitable to human decency, mutuality, and love?

I haven't believed in Hollywood endings for a long time and I don't believe in either the great patriarch in the sky, the great selfobject in the sky, or pyramid power. I don't believe government will help unless we can recapture it from its current owners. It makes perfect sense to me that evil can and does walk away with the trophy. I know how Bell feels to see the certainty of justice exposed as just one more human creation, corruptible and transient. I agree this is no country for old men because we were taught to believe things couldn't work out this way. We have lost that belief and we are sad for the loss.

On the other hand, if we can face it, we can know that what happens is ultimately up to us. There are no rescuers, parental or celestial. We're on our own. I'm reminded of another Dylan who said: "Do not go gently into that good night. Rage, rage against the dying of the light."

Note

1 There is a nomenclature problem. The Diagnostic and Statistical Manual-IV category that most fits this personality structure is Antisocial Personality Disorder. Defining characteristics include: (1) failure to conform to social norms; (2) deceitfulness; (3) impulsivity; (4) irritability, aggressiveness; (5) reckless disregard for safety of self or others; (6) consistent irresponsibility as in failure to sustain work or financial obligations; (7) lack of remorse. Chigurh meets the

required three of these criteria (aggressiveness, disregard for the safety of others, and lack of remorse). However, in many ways he is highly atypical of those who fall into this category in that he is planful, disciplined, meets his work obligations, and, in a certain sense, acts in a way that does conform to (emerging) social norms. One might consider the word sociopath, defined in the Oxford Dictionary as "a personality disorder manifesting itself in extreme antisocial attitudes and behaviour." One argument in this paper is that Chigurh's behavior is consistent with what is tacitly culturally syntonic in a corporate society. I chose the term psychopath because Bakan (2004) uses it and even though it is antiquated, it connotes the utter ruthlessness that is coming to characterize our times. I use it not as a technical term but rather a literary one.

References

Altman, N. (2005). The manic society: toward the depressive position. *Psychoanalytic Dialogues*, 15(3):321–346.

Bakan, J. (2004). *The Corporation: The Pathological Pursuit of Profit and Power*. New York: Free Press.

Beebe, B. & Lachmann, F. M. (1994). Representation and internalization in infancy: three principles of salience. *Psychoanal. Psychol.*, 11:127–165.

—— (2002). *Infant Research and Adult Treatment: Co-constructiong Interactions*. Hillsdale, NJ: Analytic Press.

Benjamin, J. (1988). *The Bonds of Love*. New York: Pantheon.

Currie, E., Dunn, R. & Fogarty, D. (1991). *The Fading Dream: Economic Crisis and the New Inequality*. In E. Currie & J. Skolnick (Eds.), *Crisis in American Institutions*. New York: Harper Collins.

Dylan, B. (1965). *Ballad of a Thin Man*. Copyright © 1965; renewed 1993. Special Rider Music.

Freud, S. (1933). *New Introductory Lectures on Psycho-Analysis*. In J. Strachey (Ed.), *The Standard Edition of the Complete Psychological Works of Sigmund Freud*. London: Hogarth Press.

Herman, E. S. & Chomsky, N. (1988). *Manufacturing Consent: The Political Economy of the Mass Media*. New York: Pantheon.

Kohut, H. (1977). *The Restoration of the Self*. New York: International Universities Press.

Lakoff, G. (2008). *The Political Mind*. New York: Viking.

Machiavelli, N. (1505/1916). *The Prince*. Marriott, W. K. (Translator). New York: Macmillan.

McCarthy, C. (2005). *No Country for Old Men*. Toronto: Vintage.

Rampton, S. & Stauber, J. (2002). *Trust Us We're Experts: How Industry Manipulates Science and Gambles with Your Future*. New York: Tarcher.

Schore, A. N. (1997). A century after Freud's Project: Is a rapprochement between psychoanalysis and neurobiology at hand? *Journal of the American Psychoanalytic Association*, 45:807–840.

Stennett, R. (1998). *The Corrosion of Character: The Personal Consequences of Work in the New Capitalism*. New York: W.W. Norton.

Stern, D. (1985). *The Interpersonal World of the Infant*. New York: Basic Books.

Wachtel, P. (1989). *The Poverty of Affluence*. Philadelphia: New Society Publishers.

Winnicott, D. W. (1945). Primitive emotional development. *International Journal of Psycho-Analysis*, 26:137–143.

Chapter 19

A dialogue between psychoanalysis and religion regarding loneliness and yearning

Philip Classen

During my 20 plus years of practice as a psychologist and couple and family therapist, I have observed many clients who have an active religious faith. They search for meaning, vitalization, and transformation through powerful relational and transcendent experiences at the heart of their religious teachings, rituals, and shared community life.

I highlight two foundational life-giving characteristics of all major religions. First, faith and faith community life offer nourishing, mystical encounter with the ineffable nature of the ultimate (that is, creative contact with what many people call "God" or engagement with ultimate belonging). Second, faith and faith community life supports a deep social ethic evident in acts of compassion and justice, both received and given.

These mystical and social-ethical religious provisions beg for conversation with psychoanalysis which has so much to say about transformative mental and relational phenomena. I hope to demonstrate that an exploration of, and response to, the universal human experience of loneliness and yearnings can be deepened through a dialogue between psychoanalysis and religion. Human beings are wired for relationship. We seek and need comfort and responsiveness from parents and intimate others throughout our lives so that we are not left with a hopeless, enduring experience of loneliness. As psychoanalysis uncovers the yearning of the lonely person for deep relatedness as well as his/her desire to be a responsible member of a community, religious practice offers readily available forms of these nourishments for the individual and communal human spirit.

I will elaborate on this thesis of belonging and the priority of a social ethic as they relate to faith and faith community life with case studies. I will then expand on parallel notions of belonging and social ethics articulated within the psychoanalytic literature. I begin with my own family's story, followed by examples of clients I have worked with who have found nourishment from faith and faith community life.

My parents had been married for four years when they completed their studies in Christian theology and pastoral ministry. They had a toddler boy (my older brother) and were pregnant with their second child (my older sister). In the fall of 1955, they took a slow freighter from San Francisco bound for war torn Korea. Their religious faith compelled them to pursue missionary service in a land thousands of miles from their home, providing care to children in desperate need. For the next ten years, my mother and father, with help of many others, built and ran an orphanage based on a spirit of compassion and sacrificial service.

I was born in Pusan, Korea in the second year of my parents' 11 years of missionary service. Some of my most vivid memories are of stomping in my bare feet, mixing mud and straw to make adobe bricks that my father and local workers used to build the orphanage. Scores of children who had experienced the horrors of war found love and shelter in these simple but secure buildings.

My parents' work and faith did not protect our family from the universal vulnerabilities of multigenerational patterns of pain and the sometimes blind repetition of problematic behaviors and ways of relating. Our family was, however, fortunate that my mother and father also had enough love and humility to grow as parents and partners, which included seeking help for problems that were beyond them. I have been deeply moved by their capacity to work and grow and by their spiritually informed desire to give to the orphans who came into our lives. They said, "We received so much love from God, and also through encouragement from the friends and churches we were connected to back home. We had enough love provided to us that we could both give to our family and to others including the many orphan children who we helped." My parents also emphasized their faith based enthusiasm about "Jesus's model of sacrificial love, of Christianity's pivotal theology of the incarnation, of God choosing to enter the hazards of being human, of God entering into our suffering," which was directly connected to their choice to enter into the lives of suffering children to live, love, and work with them.

My parents' life and work in Korea was a deeply meaningful expression of their religious faith. This distinctive family history has inspired me when I am unsure of my purpose in life, or when family and work life have weighed me down.

This kind of spiritually informed vision for life guided my parents to meet the relational needs and relational longings of the children and adults they served. Their self-sacrifice sprang from their deep social ethic, which was to share the love of God with their immediate family, and beyond, especially with those who are in desperate need.

The Korean orphan children's predicament of loss of basic relationships as a result of their parents' death in war called for actions of love. My parents experienced much sustenance in and through their religious faith and through faith community life. It was this nourishment that fueled their provision of love to others.

I will demonstrate, from both psychoanalytic and faith perspectives, that having one's needs for belonging and relational sustenance met is not an end in itself. Gaining sustenance is a provision meant to be used for creative work and play. First, as this pertains to religion, I would highlight that the sacred texts and faith practices of all the world's religions condemn the superficiality and joylessness of self-centered living, and exhort the faithful to celebrate life through loving and giving to others in need. When one has been adequately replenished through faith and faith community life, there is a yearning to give to others who are most in need.

In contrast to my family's story of service, there are stories of suffering, rather than comfort, that has been inflicted on people by religious leaders or by fellow religious devotees. These stories are particularly tragic when vulnerable individuals meet with ill treatment, condemnation, and shame. Stories of hurt must be heard so that the injuries are stopped, perpetrators are held accountable, and so that repair, forgiveness, and reconciliation may become available to all parties. South Africa and Rwanda offer excellent examples of the benefits of courageous acts of truth and reconciliation following extreme injury and oppression.

Truth-telling about the actions and impact of religious leaders and religious community life must include celebration of life-giving expressions of religion and not just focus on destructive ones. Religious experience seems to be especially vulnerable to either devaluation or idealization. The history of psychoanalysis, in a notably parallel way, is also vulnerable to the devaluation and idealization of individuals and groups. I wish to take a balanced look at strengths and weaknesses in both psychoanalytic and faith provisions. I will attempt to exemplify what key psychoanalytic thinkers have called "whole object relating" or maintaining of the "depressive position" (Klein, 1952; Grotstein, 1981; Ogden, 1989) in these psychoanalytically informed reflections on religion.

In faith communities I have observed many examples of group support, hospitality, and kindness to suffering people. These generous acts are central to the theology of many faith communities. Because my psychology practice includes a strong referral base from pastors, priests, rabbis, and imams, I have been privy to stories that include both accounts of suffering that has been inflicted by religious leaders and religious communities, as well as stories of alleviation of suffering and healing provided by the same. I will focus on stories of nourishment and of positively transformative teaching, rituals, worship, prayer, and use of the arts.

Antidotes to loneliness and isolation provided by faith communities

Vignette A

A newly separated mother of two young children, whose estranged husband paid no spousal support and minimal child support, was devastated by the loss of her marriage. She was terrified about how to find a job that would adequately provide for herself and her children. In this vulnerable state, she attended a church family function. Several elderly women in the community who had known my client since she was a girl pulled her aside during a community meal and whispered gentle encouragements: "We know you're suffering, and we want you to know that we're thinking of you and your children" and, "If there is anything I can do to be of help, I am available." My client was the recipient of many acts of loving kindness from fellow church members, among them, offers of child-care and meals by these friends and "extended family members" of her long invested-in faith community.

These people and their generous acts were, in my client's words, "emotional life-savers." Their support, along with my client's deep investment in therapy, helped her find the strength to look at herself. She faced her history of denial of fundamental flaws in her marriage and made positive changes to address her and her children's needs.

Vignette B

The focus of a young Muslim couple's therapy was on recovery from the damaging effects of an extramarital affair. They had done sufficient communicating, loving, and forgiving work inspired in part by tenets in the Quran, and were moving beyond the injury to other marriage and family issues. I had the privilege of facilitating a dialogue between husband and wife about their needs regarding daily prayers. They repeatedly got stuck in an argument regarding expectations about how often the family would gather for daily prayers. To summarize several sessions of work, both parties were able to convey to each other what religious rituals meant to each of them. The husband believed that religious rituals should not feel like something that is slavishly enacted. Hearing this, his wife set aside her fears that her husband was rejecting his faith and listened to her husband's concerns "that Allah [God] cares more about the motives of our heart than about a slavish commitment to rigid rituals." She then explained to him that the power and deepest meaning of the daily prayer ritual for her was found in the experience of "regularly physically expressing respect for and dependence on Allah, affirming Allah as the source of all love, grace and creativity in the world." She wanted to model this for their children and to share it with her husband.

Many weeks of psychodynamic exploration of family of origin pain and blocks to creative listening and empathy resulted in helping both of them to soften their attitudes toward the other. It led to a creative compromise in which both parties felt more understood and respected by the other.

Religious music, containment, and comfort

Music, poetry, and stories used in religious practice are also positive resources for the faithful. For example, Negro spirituals help singer and listeners to find mirroring and containment of their pain, as well as hopes for comfort.

As an undergraduate studying liberal arts, I also studied voice and sang two Negro spirituals in a recital. The haunting spiritual, "Motherless Child," beautifully helps listener and singer hold the universal experience of longing and loneliness.[1] The second spiritual, "There is a Balm in Gilead," is deeply moving, with ancient language referring to healing of wounds. It powerfully and poetically expresses a holding and celebration of hope and comfort in the midst of suffering and times of alienation.[2]

Challenges to the potential provisions of religious community life

Religious community life often includes practical support that devotees give one another, varying from help with basic needs and dialogue about beliefs and practices, to the deep relational and emotional supplies that poetry, music, and ritual offer. Community life helps participants hold pain and pleasure, absence as well as fullness, and despair as well as joy.

These transformative experiences occur in churches, synagogues, mosques, and temples all around the world. But how often do these faith communities actually meet the goal of providing vitalizing and transformative experience?

The great Jewish Ethics and Hebrew prophets professor, Rabbi Abraham Joshua Heschel (1955), activist, author, and professor in the 1940s until his death in 1972, commented on the declining interest in religion in North America: "It is customary to blame secular science and anti-religious philosophy for the eclipse of religion in modern society. It would be more honest to blame religion for its own defeats. Religion declined, not because it was refuted, but because it became irrelevant, dull, oppressive, insipid" (p.3).

In contrast to the life-giving examples I have cited, glaring examples of oppressive spirituality have been revealed in distant and recent history in religious extremist terrorism, caste systems that deny basic human rights, priests who prey on young children as sexual objects, and world leaders who claim God's blessings for destructive policies. On a more everyday level, experiences in local religious gatherings are too often irrelevant and insipid.

Heschel also found hope and relevancy in Jewish mystical and prophetic traditions. He embraced the ineffable nature of the ultimate, and emphasized the Hebrew prophets' foundational social ethic. He believed faith is a call to action. That action is to meet the needs of those who are oppressed and marginalized. Arnold Eisen (2008), an expert on Heschel, comments on Heschel's view of the prophets:

The God who created heaven and earth cared about the fate of widows and orphans . . . This is somehow scandalous. This is beyond logic. How could it be that the great God of all the world cares about individuals and therefore about you and about me? Why would this be so?" And the message of the prophets is that God needs us in some way. He's not making a metaphysical statement here. He's not entering into statements about whether God is perfect or in process or any of this; he's just announcing the same message that the biblical prophets did over and over again: that God wants something from us. That God needs us to help God make this world better.

Heschel underscored a vitalized image of religion that the prophets reveal which promotes caring for the marginalized ("widows and orphans"). This is a kind of "incarnational" faith that emphasizes that people are called to be God's hands of comfort and feet of justice. As Heschel said when walking arm in arm with Dr. Martin Luther King Jr. in the 1965 Selma March, "I felt I was praying with my legs" (Eisen, 2008).

There is a rich literature on a dialogue between psychoanalysis and religion pertinent to these key characteristics of faith and faith community life. What does the psychoanalytic literature have to say about religion and its potential to respond to the universal human need for belonging, social responsibility, and connection?

Freud (1962) rejected religion as infantile and pathological. I would argue that the essence of his rejection was driven by his foundational blind spots, namely an over-focus on a psychology of the individual mind, and equating healthy mental life with rational control over instinctual urges. Post-Freud, many creative psychoanalytic thinkers who owe a tremendous debt to his genius, but who moved beyond his views of religion, offered alternative psychoanalytic perspectives affirming the potential life-giving qualities of religion and religious community life. I will focus on a group of mainstream analysts who applied Freud's ideas to religion. These prominent theorists/practitioners were primarily British but I will also highlight a few American psychoanalysts. (Psychoanalytic thinkers from diverse nations and cultures have also written about the positive transformative role that faith and faith practices can play in psychic development, e.g., Rizzutto [1979] and Shafranske [1992].) I am greatly indebted to the excellent work of James Jones (2002) for much of this literature review.

Ego psychologists Heinz Hartmann and Erik Erikson took a step away from Freud to say that religion can provide moral direction and social support, and transmit cultural wisdom to adherents. W. R. Bion (1961, 1970) argued that the rituals and social support available in religious community life may uniquely provide containment of emotions and relational needs and constructively transform primitive states of mind. When individuals and groups believe there is a "primal object" (e.g., a religious figure) who is dependable, to whom they can turn in times of distress, then they are willing to take risks and engage in change and in exploring the unknown (Bion, 1961, p.156 ff). He argued that religious leaders and rituals can inspire values attributed to God, including love, justice, and righteousness. Bion (1970) proposed that religious rituals—such as those connected to birth, death, weddings, and other rites of passage—may be uniquely suited to providing a "containing" function. Ritual can take an inarticulate human process and give it form and consciousness through theological meanings.

Winnicott also affirmed a potentially transformative role for religion and spirituality. A number of analysts built on his ideas about religion, including Bowlby, Kohut, Bollas, Ghent, Loewald, and a lesser known British psychoanalytic writer, Bruce Reed.

Winnicott's (1971) brilliant theorizing brought about a radical reappraisal of Freud's view of the role of religion in psychic development. His ideas about transitional space describe experiences that are neither purely objective nor subjective. Tension between objectivity and subjectivity is temporarily overcome in experiences (including religion) that he describes as transitional—the source of vitality and creativity necessary for the "fully human life" (pp.102–103).

Bowlby affirmed that an internalized image of God can provide attachment security throughout life. Kohut described the universal need to seek comfort from people as a child is lifted up and comforted by mother. He cites experiences which "uplift" us—for example, an inspiring text, the majesty of nature, or the power of art and music. According to Jones (2002), Kohut notes religion's dissemination of an ideal divine reality, and cites "religion's use of sermons, readings, music, art, and liturgy as a major source of that essential experience of feeling "lifted up" or inspired" (pp.22–23).

Jones (2002) also describes Bollas and Ghent's important elaborations on Winnicott's theories about religion and development. Bollas' (1987) notion of "transformational objects" and Ghent's (1990) distinction between "submission" and "surrender" offer powerful critiques of Freud's idea that religion requires masochistic submission to authority. Loewald (1988) wrote that religious experience can open us up to ways of knowing and being rooted in primary process that provide a unitary and timeless sensibility.

Bruce Reed (1978) also built on Winnicott's ideas, but developed his own "oscillation theory of religion."[3] He proposed that religion at its best helps individuals and groups transition into mental states in which they can find holding for their needs for security and comfort.

> The music and words of sacred scripture, creed and sermon are obviously designed to make you think about God . . . There are generous uses of ideas and word-images. The pictures of Father, King, Shepherd, Saviour may evoke feelings of dependence . . . But if you are drawn by them and by the concerted movements of the congregation into the

attitude of worship you may find out that you are being called upon to become respectively child, subject, sheep and sinner.

(p.6)

One can see the influence Winnicott had on Reed in his notion of a creative form of dependence. Reed argues additionally that the relative health of a given religious experience, ritual, or institution can only be determined in examining a final crucial test: Having received sustenance and renewal, does the devotee, or faith community, have a greater capacity to access internalized resources that provide the energy and creativity needed to deal with present and future realities?

According to Reed, healthy religious life is characterized by whether or not it facilitates an oscillation between receiving sustenance and providing sustenance to others. If successful, religion helps individuals move into and do the hard work in life and relationships. This oscillation continues because the work of life and relationships inevitably results in resource depletion and thus the need to once again access creative replenishment.

Reed's model informs the thesis of this chapter which is that if one receives individual and relational sustenance through faith and faith community life—including finding comfort and hope in the midst of loneliness—then another crucial yearning of the human heart is activated and supported, which becomes the fuel and motivation for creative "work" in the world. This work includes expressing compassion toward others and taking action to right wrongs. It means seeking justice and compassion, first in one's most immediate relationships, then extending beyond one's immediate "tribe" to marginalized people within one's sphere of influence.

What I do not mean by this justice seeking social ethic are idealized images or grand ambitious plans for "saving of the world." Loving your neighbor, acts of kindness, forgiveness, and assertively communicating the details of your heart, beginning in your home and expanding beyond is what this is all about. This mindset has guided my desire to do good work. Sometimes the best you can do is plant the seed, attending patiently and reverently to a reality you cannot change quickly or even in your lifetime.

Some have said that religious passions embody infantile wishes to avoid feelings of helplessness. It has become the vogue to rail against religion as the cause of culture's worst divisions and a threat to democracy and civilization. Religion has potential for both terror and transformation. Creative, vitalizing transformation is possible through faith and faith community life. Being part of a church, temple, synagogue, or mosque may provide a sense of belonging and commitment to love and justice.

We all must find ways to acknowledge our need for help from outside ourselves to combat loneliness and meet our yearning for loving engagement. By seeking and finding support, we may then have something to give others. Faith and faith communities can facilitate this ongoing oscillation.

Martin Luther King's (1967) call for accessing a spiritually based uncon-
ditional love is a fitting conclusion to this exploration of faith and
psychoanalysis. At Riverside Church, he said:

> A worldwide fellowship that lifts neighborly concern beyond one's
> tribe, race, class, and nation is in reality a call for an all-embracing and
> unconditional love for all [human] kind. This oft misunderstood, this
> oft misinterpreted concept, so readily dismissed by the Nietzsches of
> the world as a weak and cowardly force, has now become an absolute
> necessity for the survival of [humanity]. When I speak of love I am not
> speaking of some sentimental and weak response. I am not speaking of
> that force which is just emotional bosh. I am speaking of that force
> which all of the great religions have seen as the supreme unifying
> principle of life. Love is somehow the key that unlocks the door which
> leads to ultimate reality.
>
> (p.190)

Notes

1 The text reads: "Sometimes I feel like a motherless child, sometimes I feel like a
  motherless child, sometimes I feel like a motherless child, a long way from home,
  a long way from home . . . Sometimes I feel like I'm almost gone, sometimes I feel
  like I'm almost gone, sometimes I feel like I'm almost gone, a long way from
  home, a long way from home."
2 The text reads: "Sometimes I get discouraged and feel my work's in vain, but then
  the Holy Spirit revives my soul again . . . there is a balm in Gilead to heal the sin
  sick soul."
3 I found Reed's ideas to be so inspiring that I used them as a central thesis for my
  case study based doctoral dissertation (Classen, 1993), so I have been reflecting on
  these themes in the lives of my clients and in my observations and interactions
  with psychoanalysis and religion for many years.

References

Bion, W. (1961). *Experiences in Groups*. London: Tavistock.
Bion, W. (1970). *Attention and Interpretation*. London: Tavistock.
Bollas, C. (1987). *The Shadow of the Object*. New York: Columbia University Press.
Classen, P. (1993). *The Oscillation Theory of Religion*. An unpublished doctoral
   dissertation, Graduate School of Psychology, Fuller Theological Seminary.
Eisen, A. (2008). The Spiritual Audacity of Joshua Abraham Heschel. American
   Public Media radio show, "Speaking of Faith," June 5. Available on the web at:
   http://speakingoffaith.publicradio.org/programs/heschel/.
Freud, S. (1962). *Civilization and its Discontents*. New York: Norton.
Ghent, E. (1990). Masochism, submission, and surrender. *Contemporary Psycho-
   analysis*, 24:108–136.
Grotstein, J. S. (1981). *Splitting and Projective Identification*. New York, NY: Jason
   Aronson.

Heschel, A. J. (1955). *God in Search of Man: A Philosophy of Judaism*. New York, NY: Farrar, Straus & Giroux.

—— (1962). *The Prophets*. New York, NY: Harper & Row.

Jones, J. (2002). *Terror and Transformation, The Ambiguity of Religion in Psychoanalytic Perspective*. New York: Taylor & Francis.

Klein, M. (1952). Some theoretical conclusions regarding the emotional life of the infant. In *Envy and Gratitude and Other Works 1946–1963*. London: Hogarth Press and the Institute of Psycho-Analysis, 1975.

King, M. L. (1967). *Where Do We Go From Here: Chaos or Community?* New York: Harper & Row Publishers

Loewald, H. (1988). *Sublimation*. New Haven: Yale University Press.

Ogden, T. H. (1989). *The Primitive Edge of Experience*. Northvale, NJ: Jason Aronson.

Reed. B. (1978). *The Dynamics of Religion, Process and Movement in Christian Churches*, London: Darton, Longman & Todd

Rizzutto. A. M. (1979). *The Birth of the Living God*. Chicago: University of Chicago Press.

Shafranske, E. (1992). "God Representation as the Transformational Object." In M. Finn and J. Gartner, *Object Relations Theory and Religion*. Westport, CT: Praeger.

Winnicott, D. W. (1971). *Playing and Reality*. New York: Routledge.

Chapter 20

Trauma trails from Ireland's great hunger: A psychoanalytic inquiry

Michael O'Loughlin

Dedication

To the million and more Irish people who perished in the Great Hunger in Ireland and the millions more forced to flee under circumstances of tremendous loss.

They are our ancestors. We are them.

Yes, it felt intensely personal. I had just received pre-publication copies of my book, *The Subject of Childhood*, and eagerly sent copies to my mother and sisters in Ireland, and my brother in Spain. A third of the book is autobiographical. To signal this, I had a photo of my brother, my sister, and me, taken in 1959, on the front cover. The publisher added sepia tone to evoke nostalgia, or perhaps to signal my age. I had dedicated the book to my mother and late father. Completing the book was a daunting task. In it, I explore ways my resistance to writing is grounded in autobiography, noting my desire not to put my poorly educated father in the shadows by claiming prominence for my writing. In an earlier work I (2007) explored how inaugural losses, coinciding with my birth and a lengthy early hospitalization, caused me to develop a sense of loss, a feeling that, in André Green's (1986, 1999) terms, there was a blankness or absence at the center of my being. This book represented my attempt to come to terms with my past, embrace ghosts and spectral memories of my childhood, and finally come to a place of desire. It was time I stopped looking over my shoulder and faced the future.

Such neatly packaged formulations, of course, are fantasies. When I stated that I eagerly mailed the book to family members, I was a little disingenuous. The truth is that I was anxiously seeking their approval for the new space that I chose to claim. I had chosen to take my head out of my books—my favorite refuge—to write a book.

Refrain: *Look at Michael. He always has his head stuck in a book.*

The immediate response to my book's arrival in Ireland was an angry, abusive phone message from one sister, denouncing me for having exposed family secrets and upsetting mother. Having read the discussion of my father's racism, she accused me of putting false words "in your dead father's mouth." My older sister sent me a note reminding me of how many happy things father and mother had done for us as children, so how could I possibly say I was unhappy . . . and why was I so ashamed of my childhood? My brother's note was more cryptic: "Thanks for the book. I read it all." One sister, attempting to calm the brouhaha, proposed: "Why don't we all just forget you ever wrote the book?" My analytic self flew out the window and did not return for some time. I became the sickly, diseased child of my youth. Could I regain my status in the family, and what if doing so meant renouncing the accomplishment that writing *The Subject of Childhood* supposedly represented?

One important contribution of analysis is that in focusing on origins it allows us, in moments like this, to locate our subjective selves historically, ancestrally, socioculturally, familially, and so on. My capacity for thought returned after some weeks. I began trying to ease the gnawing in my stomach by looking for symbolic possibilities. It is surely no coincidence that I almost died of a stomach disorder in infancy.

In *The Subject of Childhood*, I adopt a largely intrapsychic posture. I explore my yearning for my lost—perhaps never claimed—childhood. I explore ways in which my subjectivity, constructed at the nexus of poverty and infant illness, produced a sense of dis-placement, a lack, an absence which has left me with a lifelong yearning for belonging. This longing often takes the form of an impulse to look over my shoulder when something new is offered. I can allow yearning for something new, but this desire is tempered by ambivalence about entitlement and place that leads me back to a more deep-seated longing to revisit the point of dis-placement and lack and render it whole. In like manner, a patient who signed up for an advanced graduate degree that he had long desired sat in my consulting office, emotionally wrenched: "I can't do this degree, Dr. O'Loughlin," he said. "I can't stop thinking back to my father and my childhood."

I frequently encounter stuckness when I try to unravel early knots. Clues are scattered everywhere. When I finally attend to them, the unconscious comes into focus. In this case, I just needed to follow my trail of scholarly interests. I had been reading about the Great Hunger, an event in Irish history I will discuss below, but I had not seen how it connected to the disquieting feelings my family's reaction produced. I wanted to write this chapter about the Great Hunger but I did not quite understand why. During my reading I noticed frequent reference to an article by psychiatrist Garrett O'Connor (1995) but I never bothered to track it down. At an impasse as I tried to find an entry point for this writing, I retrieved a copy of his paper, "Recognising and healing malignant shame."

While I had been reading about the insidious effect of buried trauma and family secrets on contemporary Irish people, the idea had been an intellectual abstraction until I experienced my own family's stifling reaction to my reclaimed childhood voice. O'Connor's paper helped me understand that the yearning and lack I experienced were part of a much larger lacuna in Irish culture that may have left millions of people haunted by ghosts and spectral shadows rooted in the severance of narrative links as a result of historical calamities. What if all of us of Irish descent are emotionally orphaned, fleeing an apparently unmourned past that leaves us with a gaping hole, cut off from the narrative strands that would allow us to stride confidently into the future?

The lesson here is a difficult one for analysts to absorb. I know from my attempts to teach multicultural awareness to doctoral students how difficult it is for them to get beyond the received view that problems are located intrapsychically or familially. There is great resistance in psychoanalysis, too, to thinking expansively about the origins of intrapsychic experience in ways that allow us to acknowledge ancestral, sociohistorical, and spectral origins of current suffering (cf. Derrida, 1998; Guattari, 2009). As one patient, an analyst in training, incredulously put it to me, "You can't believe in ghosts!"

Garrett O'Connor's story

Distinguished psychiatrist Garrett O'Connor emigrated from Ireland in 1968, eleven years prior to my arrival in the U.S. His paper reviews the profoundly damaging consequences of British colonial occupation on the Irish psyche. He draws an analogy between individual pathology and the collective suffering of subcultures or societies.[1] At the individual level, children in abusive families tend to internalize the abuse and develop a personality characterized by "pathological dependency, low self-esteem, and suppressed feelings" (p.1). He refers to the resulting disposition as malignant shame, an internalization that leads to intergenerational trauma transmission of the kind so eloquently documented by Selma Fraiberg and colleagues (1975) in their classic paper, *Ghosts in the Nursery*.[2] A key thesis of his paper is that this process occurred at the cultural level in Ireland, leading to malignant shame in Ireland and its extensive diaspora.

O'Connor argues for a deep sense of cultural inferiority of the kind so ably documented in other colonial contexts.[3] There is considerable support in the literature for the notion that Irish people have particular psychic and character vulnerabilities that emerge from a pervasive sense of inferiority and malignant shame exacerbated by the effects of an Irish Catholic upbringing steeped in puritanical morality and a Jansenist view of the inherent wickedness of people.[4]

The most poignant part of O'Connor's essay is the conclusion in which he discusses his struggles with professional success and personal intimacy and locates his early struggles with alcoholism in the malignant shame internalized from his Irish upbringing. His description of one paper he delivered was eerily familiar, leaving me in no doubt that my feelings reflected a phenomenon larger than my particular experience:

> I have been told in no uncertain terms that my proclivity as a physician to talk publicly about my personal experience with these conflicts is both inappropriate and embarrassing. Instead, I have been advised to confront my cultural demons by disguising them as fictional characters in a novel, or by having them evaluated in the privacy of my psychiatrist's office for a possible trial of medications. After I mentioned, in a public lecture given at Dublin's Peacock Theatre in 1992, that my heroic and marvelous mother was an alcoholic, a member of the family suggested quite seriously that I should cease my cultural researches to pursue other work opportunities. In other words, I should keep quiet.
>
> (p.12)

In 2001, I presented a paper on loss (O'Loughlin, 2007) at Trinity College Dublin. An Irish colleague, addressing what he perceived to be the confessional tone of my paper, blurted out: "Well you'd never get away with writing a paper like that if you lived here." His remark left me as uneasy as my paper clearly left him.

From an analytic perspective, it would appear I have done some of the work we analysts value so much in our patients: I have given up some necessary childhood illusions that had left me with a yearning, a lack that could not be satisfied. With the foundations of my subjectivity upended, I needed to construct a new narrative that would permit me to come to be in a new way. My interest in the historical origins of subjectivity and the mechanisms of intergenerational trauma transmission represent longings for such a narrative. Realistically, my original yearnings and lack will persist, joined by a new narrative to which this writing contributes. The quest is irresistible and healing, yet illusory. Yearning is striving after, a manifestation of desire, never an accomplishment. Symbolization, while helpful, is inherently partial and can never fully repair the tears in the fabric or our subjectivity.

An Gorta Mór: A catastrophic silence

Historian Christine Kinealy's (2006) book, *This Great Calamity: The Irish Famine 1845–52*, is in the vanguard of a movement to reclaim the place of the Famine in Irish life. She notes that the million who died "remained nameless and unrecorded, hard to know or to mourn" (p.xvii). The largest marked Famine grave is in Grosse Isle, Quebec, where up to 7000 Famine victims are buried.[5] Ireland is littered with unmarked graves. During my childhood a mass grave was uncovered within a few hundred yards of my house. The "skeletons," as we ignorantly and dispassionately referred to them, were summarily removed, and excavation proceeded. It is painful for me to think of those "skeletons"—representative of a million or more of my starving forebears—being reburied without memory, without name, without acknowledgment. The barbarity of their abject, anonymous demise from starvation was thereby re-enacted. Restless spirits must surely stalk the land in their wake.

For 150 years there has been a conspiracy of silence between the Irish government and Irish historians to avoid discussing the full scope of the disaster. Revisionist politicians and historians, anxious to escape a binary relation with Britain that placed them constantly in a position of inferiority, sought to develop a nationalist grand narrative for Ireland. This silence precluded whole generations of Irish children from engaging with this catastrophic loss that is embodied in every person of Irish descent.

Cecil Woodham-Smith's *The Great Hunger*, written in England by a woman of Welsh-Irish descent, proved a remarkably readable, empathic account of the suffering of starving Irish people, as well as a carefully documented study of the economics of the Famine. She clearly assigned responsibility to the British for the poor management and callous political use of the catastrophe. Her bestseller has been in print continuously since 1962, yet she was lambasted by Irish academics for her soft-hearted advocacy on behalf of dying peasants. I read it at 16 and found it so evocative that I have not yet steeled—or embraced?—myself enough to reread it. As for its effect on the Irish academic history establishment, they killed it with indifference: "The *Great Hunger* marked an end, rather than a beginning, of Famine research, with little of note being published for the next thirty-two years" (Kinealy, 2006, p.xxi).

Denial of memory appears to represent a collective act of dissociation, a defense against the flood of emotions such painful memories unleash. It would demand of Irish people, as it demanded of O'Connor and me, owning split off parts of experience, parts of our being that we embody and live out every day while apparently unaware of how this historically located suffering structures our being in the world. Despite the upsurge in Famine studies and the construction of a Famine Museum and some national monuments to the Famine in Ireland,[6] there is concern that after this burst of activity, "famine fatigue" is setting in and the dialogue may once again fade out (Valone & Kinealy, 2002).

Refrain: Mind your own business. A closed mouth catches no flies. What you don't know won't trouble you. What's it to you anyway? What do you want to know that for? Sure isn't that all in the past? What are they talking about that for, anyway? Can't you just be happy with the life you have now?

An event without a witness

Psychiatrist Dori Laub (1992) noted that in many respects the Holocaust was an event without a witness in that all those who fully entered the experience of sites like Auschwitz perished. Although there is significant scholarship on Holocaust trauma, the task is complicated by this fact, as well as by the shroud of silence and shame that descended on many survivors (Langer, 1991). Similar and perhaps greater complexity attends inquiry into Famine trauma. Greater than a million people perished of starvation and disease and the colonizing power did not even bother to record the deaths, never mind preserve narratives of suffering. We can never know the struggle they faced.

Much can be learned, however, from folklore, newspaper accounts, and imaginative works. My future research will be directed toward detailed study of this material. Historiographers are indebted to Cathal Póirtéir, a producer with RTE, the Irish national radio and television service, for extensive research into interviews with immediate descendants of Famine survivors done under the auspices of the Irish Folklore Commission in the 1940s.[7] I present samples from this testimony to allow readers to begin imagining the depth of suffering. All quotations come from Póirtéir's (1995a) compilation, *Famine Echoes*:

- *John Doyle, b. 1900.* They boiled shoes in a pan and then fried them and ate them . . . His grandfather told him they killed frogs and fried them and ate them . . . A man went into a house and found the owner dead and a rat eating the corpse. He killed the rat and brought it home and ate it . . . A woman lived in a group of famine houses and she got so hungry that she killed the cat and ate it. She died of fever that the cat contracted from something it had eaten. (p.60)
- *Jim Lawlor, b. 1877.* A cow owned by a farmer in Mullan died with cancer and the poor people, when they heard of it, dug her up and ate her . . . The people mixed cattle blood, mushrooms and cabbage and baked it. They called it relish cakes. (p.61)
- *Liam Ó Floinn.* Years ago, about the time of the Famine of '47 a woman and her husband were journeying along from Anaglen. They were very poor and food was scarce at the time. The man had some bread, scarcely enough to sustain himself. The woman got hungry and asked him for a bit of the bread. He gave it to her. After a time she asked the same request, and he gave her some more, very reluctantly. She asked a third time, so he said to himself, "If this goes on I will starve." They were near the lake by this time and he threw her in. She was drowned. Almost immediately remorse seized him and he then committed suicide by drowning himself also. When the bodies were recovered it was found that the woman was carrying three babies, so

that five drowned altogether. Since then the lake bears the name Loch na gCúigear (The Lake of the Five People). (p.99)

- *Pádraig Mhichíl Ó Suilleabhain, b. 1867*. I heard my grandmother say that the worst sight she saw was, she saw a woman laid out on the street (in Kenmare) and the baby at her breast. She died of the famine fever. Nobody would take the child, and in the evening the child was eating the mother's breast. (p.105)

- *Jim Lawlor, b. 1877*. People who died at Crossbridge were thrown in the river. They had the river dammed and when there would be a lot of bodies collected they let off the water and it would carry the bodies away. (p.196)

- *Daithí Ó Ceanntabhail*. The deaths in my native place were many and horrible. The poor famine-stricken people were found by the wayside, emaciated corpses, partly green from eating docks and nettles and partly blue from cholera and dysentery.

- *Felix Kernan, b. 1859*. The grandmother of the present writer often told me of her experiences when a girl of 17 in those awful days. Her people had a little country shop and those customers who called on any particular day seldom or ever returned to the shop. She said it was usual to see corpses lying by the roadside with pieces of grass or leaves in their mouth and their faces stained with the juices of the plants which they were chewing to try to satisfy their hunger.

- *Ned Buckley*. Michael Matt Dennehy [b.1872] Scrahan, Knocknagree, told me this tale a few days ago. It happened in the townland of Lisheen about two miles from our village in the Kerry side of the Blackwater. A man named Mick Dennehy, Old Mick Dennehy, owned a farm at that time and he was one day in the Spring ploughing in the field near Lisheen Cross in which there was a fine spring well. It was the will of God that he noticed the traveling woman dragging and pulling a strong little girl of about 10 or 12 toward the well. He watched her and the little child was resisting as much as she could. He noticed that when she had the girl near the well she was trying to throw her in and the child was roaring in terror. He ran toward them and found she was trying to put the child into the well. "Woman, what in the name of the devil are you trying to do with that child?" said Old Mick. "Oh sir," said the poor woman, "if the Lord would only call on her I'd be all right. Isn't it better for one to be gone than to have we all gone. She has a wonderful appetite and nothing could give her enough. If she were gone I could get enough for the two more and I must do away with her altogether or she'll starve the rest of us." She had two smaller children with her and they were hungry. "I'm out of my mind," she said, "from her and what can I do with her?" "Stop. Stop." Said Old Mick. "Don't murder your own child. God is good and if you struggle a bit more maybe God will send ye all enough. Come on home now with me and ye all can have a bite to eat, and who knows but God would open up some gap for you and those children." (p.95)

Australian writer Judy Atkinson (2002) speaks of trauma trails—traces of catastrophe in the lives of subsequent generations. As I was compiling information from my mother about the severe privations of her childhood for inclusion in *The Subject of Childhood*, I was struck by the shame and silence surrounding her suffering. It set me to wondering what she might have inherited from her great grandparents that might be embodied in her fatalistic ways of conceptualizing suffering. Likewise, I wondered if the panic attacks my father suffered and the mental disorders and alcoholism in his family of origin might have antecedents in that catastrophe. What can it have been like for people who experienced and witnessed such events and, lacking opportunities to process the pain, could only suffer and move on? What effects did this petrification have on their descendants, including me?

Embracing hungry ghosts

Tom Hayden (1997a) addresses this silence in a book he edited, *Irish Hunger: Personal Reflections on the Legacy of the Famine*. He speaks of the "ocean of silence" that washed over the trauma, characterizing himself as "an orphan from history" because of his parents' failure to share that history with him, though he recognizes they may not have been conscious of this knowledge because of the likely abject silence of their forebears (Hayden, 1997b). The book is premised on the notion that Ireland is a traumatized nation (e.g., Lloyd, 1997; Waters, 1997) and that tremendous damage is being done by a "culture of amnesia," the product of "three generations of horrified silence" (Waters, 1997, p.29). In the context of the workings of malignant shame, the collection is remarkable in its acknowledgment of ghostly echoes of past trauma in our unconscious.

To take just one illustrative story, consider the case of Irish-American journalist, Carolyn Ramsay. She offers a visceral account of the workings of hungry ghosts in her daily life. Having discussed how her grandmother, a child of Famine survivors, developed an obsession for feeding sandwiches to imaginary people in her old age, Ramsay begins to ruminate on her own "need to feed":

> I don't know another working mother who worries about feeding people the way I do . . . It has taken me years, on the other hand, to focus on just feeding my family—not the whole world. On late nights when I've pounded chicken and chopped vegetables alone in my kitchen while my family sleeps, I've wondered precisely what my problem is . . . Part of me passes off the feeding urge as a slightly embarrassing compulsion, although its emotional depth and power

indicate otherwise. After dropping food at a soup kitchen for the first time a decade ago, I had to steer my car to the side of the street because I was sobbing so hard I couldn't see. There's such unremitting sadness at the root of this drive to feed people that I've come to assume that it links me somehow to the dark events in Ireland in the mid 1800s. I can't know this. No famine stories made their way from my migrating great-grandparents to me, or even to my parents. "The Irish aren't real talkers," my mother once said. When I consider how my grandmother's need to feed imagined ghosts has followed me for thirty years though, it seems likely her famine-surviving parents' attitudes towards food made a deep impression on her. How could they not?

(p.138)

Writing in the same collection, Irish poet Nuala Ní Dhomhnaill suggests Ireland is finally waking up from the "zombification" of the colonial era. Her discussion illustrates how difficult it is to gain access to the traumatized unconscious. Reflecting on a recent trip to the very anglicized Irish Famine Museum, she meditates on the inaccessibility of loss that appears lost in translation, to use Eva Hoffman's (1990) felicitous term. Peasants in Ireland in that era spoke Irish. When the British eradicated spoken Irish, they rendered the trauma more inaccessible. She speaks of unconscionable loss:

Unconscionable, because of what has been lost to consciousness, not just the tunes and the songs and the poetry, but because the memory that they were all in Irish—that they are part of a reality which was not English—has been erased so totally from our minds. This seems to be part of the Famine trauma which is still not acknowledged by the post-colonial Irish political reality. This collective memory loss, this convenient amnesia is still one of the most deeply etched results of the Famine.

(1997, p.72)

Skeletons in the closet: The social cost of familial and societal secrets

Jean-Bertrand Pontalis (2002) asks, "Where do you live? 'In the vicinity of the unknown.' What do you do? 'I try to guess the presence of secrets'" (translated and quoted in Garon, 2004, p.2). To be successful, an analyst must have curiosity, and "resonance with pieces of our own history," Garon argues. This is dangerous curiosity because it exhumes secrets buried at the deepest core of the unconscious.

In "Skeletons in the Closet," Garon (2004) speaks of the core of trauma arising not from the traumatic memory per se, but from disavowal of that memory, leaving the experience unsymbolized, hence inaccessible to the psychotherapeutic process Freud referred to as working through. Some analysts refer to such trauma as unspeakable or unsayable (Davoine & Gaudillière, 2004; Rogers, 2006). Drawing on *The Clinical Diary of Sandór Ferenczi* (1932/1995), Garon says that disavowed part of the parent's unconscious becomes an inaccessible *alien transplant* in the psyche of the child (p.2). There is considerable literature on the ways children absorb parental psychic states (such as psychosis and depression) as unanchored, unformalized losses.[8] Traumatic absorption occurs in a climate where a child is forbidden to think. A mother who consistently brushes off a child's persistent plaintive query, "Are you sad mammy?" sets the conditions for such absorption. The situation grows more complicated if the parent has unconsciously inherited trauma from a prior generation. "The ghosting of the mother deranges the psychic economy of the child who has been nominated to carry the spectral prefigurations of the ghost. The one so haunted is spooked by two impossibilities: impossible mourning and impossible longing" (Emery, 2002, p.169).

Garon postulates a mechanism by which trauma changes form across generations. "In the first generation it takes the shape of an object of negation, in the second, denial, and in the third generation family secrets are foreclosed" (p.4). Trauma moves from the unspeakable, to the unnamable, to the unthinkable. In traumatic foreclosure, anything unsymbolized is excluded, engineering its reappearance through symptoms. Somatized illnesses and psychological disorders such as dissociation, depression, psychosis, panic, anxiety, addictions, and eating disorders become disguised manifestations of uncommunicable trauma.[9] The challenge of analysis is to decode the disguised trauma embodied in symptoms. Thinkability requires an act of imagination. For somebody raised with shrouded trauma that is, perhaps, the greatest challenge of all. Garon concludes with a reminder that what is at issue is not discovering the original secrets but, rather, accessing the residual suffering from that ancestral hurt that, as I argued earlier, can manifest in lack and unformulated yearning.

A theory of the phantom: The work of Abraham and Torok

A collection of writings by psychoanalysts Nicolas Abraham and Maria Torok (1994) was published as *The Shell and the Kernel*. Advancing a methodology for understanding the relationship between present symptoms and earlier trauma, they insist on understanding the historicity of experience. As Nicholas Rand notes in the Introduction, Abraham views "the symptom as a telltale memory trace of latent or unavailable promptings and traumas . . . Abraham suggests further that the world and the psyche emerge from catastrophes whose fragmented remnants survive in the phenomena they engender" (p.6). Psychoanalysis of trauma is detective work in which the analyst works with the suffering person "to increase the eloquence and readability of symptoms" (p.7) so that blocked memory traces may give up their secrets. Echoing the notion of implantation advanced by Ferenczi, Abraham and Torok suggest trauma becomes encapsulated in a psychic tomb or crypt where it lives on as unassimilable experience. These become the family secrets Esther Rashkin (1992) discusses. Abraham and Torok's notion of the entombment of trauma as encrypted secrets applies not only to individuals who thereby develop symptoms, but to entire nations or groups who then develop collective symptoms of the kind discussed earlier with respect to post-Famine generations in Ireland and in the Irish diaspora.

A key concept for Abraham and Torok is silence. Through entombment, the trauma is encapsulated so its effects cannot be felt. It becomes an unconscious secret the sufferer must bear. Echoing O'Connor, Rand notes that "unwanted, shameful or untoward realities" (p.102) perceived as unbearable are removed from conscious awareness and the sufferer loses the capacity to grieve: "The words that cannot be uttered, the scenes that cannot be recalled, the tears that cannot be shed, everything will be swallowed along with the trauma that led to the loss. Swallowed and preserved" (Abraham & Torok, 1994, p.130). Entombed and inaccessible to verbalization, the trauma finds opportunities to return in nightmarish forms: "Sometimes in the dead of night, when libidinal fulfillments have their way, the ghost of the crypt comes back to haunt the cemetery guard, giving him strange and incomprehensible signals, making him perform bizarre acts, or subjecting him to unexpected sensations" (p.130). Abraham and Torok emphasize that shame is a key motivator for the entombment of trauma and in a metaphor highly relevant to the million and more skeletons in unmarked mass graves in Ireland, they propose that entombed secrets constitute a memory *"buried without legal burial place"* (p.142).

Turning to mechanisms of intergenerational transmission, Abraham and Torok conceptualize the child as receiving a gap instead of knowledge:

> Should a child have parents "with secrets," parents whose speech is not exactly complementary to their unstated repressions, the child will receive from them a gap in the unconscious, an unknown, unrecognized knowledge—a *nescience*—subjected to a form of "repression" before the fact. The buried speech of the parent will be (a) dead (gap) without a burial place in the child. This unknown phantom returns from the unconscious to haunt its host and may lead to phobias, madness, and obsessions. Its effect can persist through several generations and determine the fate of an entire family line.
>
> (p.140)

Common Irish characterological symptoms such as alcoholism, anger, emotional closedness, cynicism, depression, envy, and psychosis can be viewed as attempts by the unconscious to disguise what Abraham and Torok call a gaping wound that is unspeakable (p.142). While they emphasize the need to seek the entombed phantomic trauma and release it, this may require "psychoanalysis in absentia of several generations" (p.169).

Abraham and Torok note that this notion of haunting and return of the dead exists in all cultures; we have to be prepared for the return of those who suffered shame and took unspeakable secrets to their graves (p.171). This is the true horror of the malignant shame O'Connor discussed: its capacity for regenerative haunting from one generation to the next. The easiest way to detect such entombed phantoms, Abraham and Torok note, is through recognizing surface evidence for them in impediments to living a free life—phobias, neuroses, addictions, relationship difficulties, and so on that drive people to seek therapy or psychiatric care. The symptoms are opaque indicators, disguised signifiers of the entombed secrets. The psychoanalyst's craft is the decoding of these secrets.

The psychic consequences of being born outside genealogy

In exploring spectral aspects of experience, uncanny events, silences, and intrusions, I am suggesting we take seriously aspects of experience beyond the here and now . . . the neat temporal dichotomies of past-to-present-to-future. What if time is not linear, and experience is neither sequential nor cumulative? What if there are dimensions beyond time? What if Derrida (1994), who advocated hauntology as more comprehensive than ontology, is correct that a revenant is simultaneously a jarring new event and a return of spectral memory? What if unformulated yearnings are merely endpoints of trauma trails that reach back into our familial and collective histories?

Engendered mutism and the severed social link

In a paper exploring the relationship between displacements and silences, Erika Apfelbaum (2002) noted that uprootings caused by genocides and wars can sever the link between people and their histories. The results can be catastrophic. "We are inscribed in family and genealogical filiations as well as in world history" (p.79). Drawing on Maurice Halbwachs' (e.g., 1924) writings, she argues that without a framework of intelligibility there is no capacity to break the silence of an event like Shoah. Many Holocaust survivors tried to protect their children from that terrible knowledge. In doing so, they created a vacuum in which spectral presences of trauma continued, without the namable discourse which would allow bearers of such knowledge to render the knowledge thinkable and symbolizable. She summarizes the catastrophic consequences of severing the social link between people and their sociohistorically rooted narratives:

By not assuring the transmission of the family's chronicle, the genealogical continuity is broken, and because of this mutism there is an
increasing rift between family generations . . . Children born outside of
any genealogy . . . can be considered as "cultural orphans". Such a
child faces an eclipse of his/her origins . . . [and becomes] a human
being without "a shadow".

(p.81)

Petrified time and the destruction of autobiographic consciousness

In *History Beyond Trauma*, French psychoanalysts Françoise Davoine and
Jean-Max Gaudillière theorize subjectivity from the case of those who have
lost language and contact with the Other through madness. Such persons
lack capacity for symbolization, at least in the area affected by trauma. They
describe psychosis as destruction of "autobiographic consciousness." Such
patients' silence speaks of their trauma, whether autobiographical or ancestral. Needed is an analyst capable of recognizing the communication, thereby
serving as a new Other for the person suffering from psychosis. Lacking an
Other with the capability to respond truthfully, the suffering person is
destined to experience "an interiority invaded by annihilation, anxiety, and
stress" (p.129). Speaking of children, for whom trauma is almost invariably
embodied rather than cognitively encoded, they describe psychosis in this
haunting manner, raising, again, the problem of illegal burial:

As the child psychiatrist Lionel Bailly puts it, when "children hear the
voices of the dead" they are most often the voices of those who died
without burial, without a rite. This brief hallucination will cease as
soon as it is heard by a therapist in whom the voices of the dead can
resonate instead of remaining in a dead letter. If the voice finds no
echo, he says, "we have the seed of psychosis."

(p.145)

From an analytic perspective, the question the anguish of an individual or
community raises is archeological, pertaining to "where our patients have
been before, and toward which they are, paradoxically, seeking to guide us"
(p.29). In what way might the dead of our ancestral and spectral pasts (cf.
Blackman, 2001; Derrida, 1994; Fraiberg et al., 1975; Gordon, 1997; Venn,
2002) live on within us? Who is equipped and willing to serve as what
Davoine and Gaudillière call a guarantor that from now on those ancestral
experiences will be given voice?

Echoing Apfelbaum, Davoine and Gaudillière argue that dehistoriciza-
tion of experience is particularly traumatic in causing people to lose the link
with their pasts. We must assist them in "regaining a foothold in history"

(p.47). People's bodies can be so numbed by trauma that, as Wittgenstein said, "I turn into stone and my pain goes on" (quoted in Davoine & Gaudillière, p.49). Children are particularly susceptible to noticing the blank affect of petrified adults and are likely to absorb that pain into themselves, becoming "the subject of the other's suffering" (p.49).

Reclaiming famine memory and embracing hungry ghosts

How might we address traumas that cannot be recounted because they were never recorded as past—events that are still "suspended like a present without time"? (p.52). How does one re-vitalize an individual, community, or society weighed down by events that, consciously, they simply do not know they know?

> Perhaps most difficult is the loss of loss itself: somewhere, sometime, something was lost, but no story can be told about it; no memory can retrieve it; a fractured horizon looms in which to make one's way as a spectral agency, one for whom a full "recovery" is impossible, one for whom the irrecoverable becomes, paradoxically, the condition of a new political agency.
>
> (Butler, 2003, p.467)

In those words, written as the Afterword to *Loss* (Eng & Kazanjian, 2003), Judith Butler reminds us of the need to avoid romanticizing recovery of memory through construction of redemptive narratives. It is not that we should aspire to getting over loss, but that we need to learn to live with loss in a new way so that it binds us together in a space in which we can imagine ourselves otherwise. Unformulated yearnings, therefore, should be embraced as important pointers toward these painful unthought knowns.

An important, difficult first step for contemporary residents of Ireland, as well as for the Irish diaspora, is to acknowledge the silencing that occurred and the trauma embodied within us individually and as a people. If we pay loving attention to what our bodies and lifestyles are telling us about who we are, then we can begin listening respectfully to those hungry ghosts who have so much to tell us. Is it not perhaps time we cultivated the art of listening to those spectral messengers seeking reparation? Are they not imploring us to receive love, loss, and community? Is this not a plaintive yearning to which we should pay close attention?

I wish to thank Joe Tobin of Arizona State University for helping me clearly see the link between my own story and the Great Hunger. My colleague at Adelphi, Lahney Preston-Matto, has been generous in advising me on sources. Abby Corrigan in Toronto, Yo Heta-Lensen in Auckland,

and Robbie Lloyd in Alice Springs have helped me receive ancestor wisdom with love. My colleagues in the psychosis project at Austen Riggs Center, Marilyn Charles and Jill Clemence from Austen Riggs, and Gail Newman from Williams College have helped me understand the narrative impasses that lead to the kinds of distress our society calls mental illness.

Notes

1 For discussion of the collective unconscious and psychoanalytic understandings of the effects of immersion in groups and cultures, see Jung, 1981; Alford, 2001; Lear, 2006; O'Loughlin, 2008.
2 For an overview of trauma theory see Van der Kolk, 1987; Herman, 1997. For overview of intergenerational trauma, see Danieli, 1998.
3 For various postcolonial perspectives see, for example, Memmi, 1965/1991; Fanon, 1967; Nandy, 1989; Bhabha, 1994; Hall, 1996a, b; Morley & Chen, 1996.
4 For overview see, e.g., Waters, 1997; O'Faolain, 1999; Dezell, 2000; Eagleton, 2002; Scheper-Hughes, 2001; McGoldrick, 2005. For the relationship between this publicly articulated morality and widespread sexual abuse in Roman Catholic schools in Ireland see, for example, Raftery & O'Sullivan, 1999; Finnegan, 2001; Walsh, 2003; Mullan, 2004; O'Beirne, 2006; Tyrrell, 2006; Commission to Inquire into Child Abuse, Commission Report, 2009.
5 See moytura.com/grosse-ile.htm and pc.gc.ca/lhn-nhs/qc/grossseile/inidex_e.asp for some historical background and images of the Irish graves at Grosse Isle. For critical discussion, see the essays by Gauthier, 2002; Blair, 2002; Garvey, 2002.
6 See strokestownpark.ie/museum for details of the Irish Famine Museum.
7 Cathal Póirtéir (1995b, 1996) also edited two Famine folkore compilations in Gaelic and produced a series of radio lectures for RTE, the Irish broadcasting authority (1995c).
8 See Green (1986, 1999) for detailed discussion of this process. Discussion of Green's work can be found in Kohon (1999) and O'Loughlin (2007).
9 For further discussion and clinical examples see Apollon et al., 2002; Fink, 1995, 1997; Rogers, 2006.

References

Abraham, N. & Torok, M. (1994). *The Shell and the Kernel.* [Edited, translated and with an Introduction by N. Rand.] Chicago: University of Chicago Press.

Alford, F. (2001). *Melanie Klein and Critical Social Theory.* New Haven: Yale University Press.

Apfelbaum, E. (2002). Uprooted communities, silenced cultures and the need for legacy. In V. Walkerdine (Ed.), *Challenging subjects: Critical Psychology for a New Millennium.* New York: Palgrave.

Apollon, W., Bergeron, D. & Cantin, L. (2002). *After Lacan: Clinical Practice and the Subject of the Unconscious.* Albany, NY: SUNY Press.

Atkinson, J. (2002). *Trauma Trails: Recreating Song Lines: The Transgenerational Effects of Trauma in Indigenous Australia.* North Melbourne, Australia: Spinifex Press.

Bhabha, H. (1994). *The Location of Culture.* New York: Routledge.

Blair, L. (2002). (De)Constructing the Irish Famine Memorial in contemporary

Quebec. In D. Valone & C. Kinealy (Eds.), *Ireland's Great Hunger: Silence, Memory, Commemoration*. Lanham, MD: University Press of America.

Blackman, L. (2001). *Hearing Voices: Embodiment and Experience*. London: Free Association Press.

Butler, J. (2003). Afterword: After loss, what then? In D. Eng & D. Kazanjian (Eds.), *Loss: The Politics of Mourning*. Berkeley: University of California Press.

Commission to Inquire Into Child Abuse. (2009). *Commission report*. Dublin: Government Publications Office.

Danieli, Y. (Ed.). (1998). *International Handbook of Intergenerational Trauma Transmission*. New York: Plenum.

Davoine, F. & Gaudillière, J. (2004). *History Beyond Trauma*. New York: Other Press.

Derrida, J. (1994). *Specters of Marx: The State of the Debt, the Work of Mourning, and the New International*. New York: Routledge.

—— (1998). Geopsychoanalysis: ". . . and the rest of the world." In C. Lane (Ed.), *The Psychoanalysis of Race*. New York: Columbia University Press.

Dezell, M. (2000). *Irish America: Coming into Clover: The Evolution of a People and a Culture*. New York: Doubleday.

Eagleton, T. (2002). *The Gatekeeper*. London: Penguin.

Emery, E. (2002). The ghost in the mother: Strange attractors and impossible mourning. *Psychoanalytic Review*, 89(2):169–194.

Eng, D. & Kazanjian, D. (Eds.). (2003). *Loss: The Politics of Mourning*. Berkeley: University of California Press.

Fanon, F. (1967). *Black Skin, White Masks*. New York: Grove Press.

Ferenczi, S. (1932/1995). *The Clinical Diary of Sandór Ferenczi*. [J. Dupont, Ed.]. Cambridge, MA: Harvard University Press.

Fink, B. (1995). *The Lacanian Subject*. Princeton: Princeton University Press.

—— (1997). *A Clinical Introduction to Lacanian Psychoanalysis*. Cambridge: Harvard University Press.

Finnegan, F. (2001). *Do Penance or Perish: Magdalen Asylums in Ireland*. London: Oxford University Press.

Fraiberg, S., Adelson, E. & Shapiro, V. (1975). Ghosts in the nursery. *Journal of the American Academy of Child Psychiatry*, 14:387–421.

Garon, J. (2004). Skeletons in the closet. *International Forum of Psychoanalysis*, 13:84–92.

Garvey, G. (2002). Reflections on the Grosse Ile Memorial in Contemporary Quebec: A response. In D. Valone & C. Kinealy (Eds.), *Ireland's Great Hunger: Silence, Memory, Commemoration*. Lanham, MD: University Press of America.

Gauthier, S. (2002). Le Mémorial: An Irish memorial at Grosse Ile in Quebec. In D. Valone & C. Kinealy (Eds.), *Ireland's Great Hunger: Silence, Memory, Commemoration*. Lanham, MD: University Press of America.

Gordon, A. (1997). *Ghostly Matters: Haunting and the Sociological Imagination*. Minneapolis: University of Minnesota Press.

Green, A. (1986). *On Private Madness*. Madison, CT: International Universities Press.

—— (1999). *The Work of the Negative*. New York: Free Association.

Guattari, F. (2009). *Chaosophy*. Edited by S. Lotringer. Introduction by F. Dosse. Translated by D. Sweet, J. Becker & T. Adkins. Los Angeles: Semiotext(e).

Halbwachs, M. (1924/1952). *Les cadres sociaux de la mémoire*. Paris: PUF.

Hall, S. (1996a). New ethnicities. In D. Morley & K. Chen (Eds.), *Stuart Hall: Selected Dialogues in Cultural Studies*. New York and London: Routledge.

—— (1996b).When was the "post-colonial"? Thinking at the limit. In I. Chambers & L. Curti (Eds.), *The Post-colonial Question*. New York and London: Routledge.

Hayden, T. (Ed.). (1997a). *Irish Hunger: Personal Reflections on the Legacy of the Famine*. Boulder, CO: Roberts Rinehart Publishers.

—— (1997b). The famine of feeling. In T. Hayden (Ed.), *Irish Hunger: Personal Reflections on the Legacy of the Famine*. Boulder, CO: Roberts Rinehart Publishers.

Herman, J. (1997). *Trauma and Recovery*. New York: Basic Books.

Hoffman, E. (1990). *Lost in Translation: A Life in a New Language*. New York: Penguin Books.

Kinealy, C. (2006). *This Great Calamity: The Irish Famine 1845–52*. Dublin: Gill & Macmillan.

Kohon, G. (Ed.). (1999). *The Dead Mother: The Work of André Green*. New York: Routledge.

Langer, L. (1991). *Holocaust Testimonies: The Ruins of Memory*. New Haven: Yale University Press.

Laub, D. (1992). An event without a witness: Truth, testimony and survival. In S. Felman & D. Laub, *Testimony: Crises of Witnessing in Literature, Psychoanalysis, and History*. New York: Routledge.

Lear, J. (2006). *Radical Hope: Ethics in the Face of Cultural Devastation*. Cambridge, MA: Harvard University Press.

Lloyd, D. (1997). The memory of hunger. In T. Hayden (Ed.), *Irish Hunger: Personal Reflections on the Legacy of the Famine*. Boulder, CO: Roberts Rinehart Publishers.

McGoldrick, M. (2005). Irish families. In M. McGoldrick, J. Giordano, & N. Garcia-Preto (Eds.), *Ethnicity and Family Therapy*. New York: Guilford Press.

Memmi, A. (1965/1991). *The Colonizer and the Colonized*. Boston: Beacon Press.

Morley, D. & Chen, K. (Eds). (1996). *Stuart Hall: Selected Dialogues in Cultural Studies*. New York: Routledge.

Mullan, P. (Director). (2004). *Magadelene Sisters*. [DVD]. Miramax Home Entertainment

Nandy, A. (1989). *The intimate enemy: Loss and Recovery of Self Under Colonialism*. Delhi: Oxford University Press.

Ní Dhomhnaill, N. (1997). A ghostly Alhambra. In T. Hayden (Ed.), *Irish Hunger: Personal Reflections on the Legacy of the Famine*. Boulder, CO: Roberts Rinehart.

O'Beirne, K. (2006). *Kathy's Story: The True Story of a Childhood Hell Inside Ireland's Magdalen Laundries*. Dublin: Greystone Books.

O'Connor, G. (1995). Recognising and healing malignant shame. Retrieved from www.aca.si.edu/collections/findingaids/lipplucy.htm on 3/21/09.

O'Faolain, N. (1999). *Are you somebody? The Accidental Memoir of a Dublin Woman*. New York: Henry Holt.

O'Loughlin, M. (2007). On losses that are not easily mourned. In B. Willock, L. Bohm, & R. C. Curtis (Eds.), *On Deaths and Endings: Psychoanalysts' Reflections on Finality, Transformations and New Beginnings*. London: Routledge.

—— (2008). Radical hope or death by a thousand cuts: The future for Indigenous Australians. *Arena Journal*, 29/30:175–201.

—— (2009). *The Subject of Childhood*. New York: Peter Lang Publishing.

Póirtéir, C. (Ed.). (1995a). *Famine echoes*. Dublin: Gill & Macmillan.

—— (Eag.). (1995b). *Gnéithe an Ghorta*. Baile Átha Cliath: Coisceim.

—— (Producer). (1995c). *Famine Echoes: Thomas Davis Radio Lectures*. Dublin: RTE.

—— (Eag.). (1996). *Glórtha an Ghorta: Bealoideas na Gaeilge agus an Gorta Mór*. Baile Átha Cliath: Coisceim.

Pontalis, J.-B. (2002). *En marge des jours* (In the margins of the days). Paris: Gallimard.

Raftery, M. & O'Sullivan, E. (1999). *Suffer the Little Children: The Inside Story of Ireland's Industrial Schools*. Dublin: New Island Books.

Rand, N. (1994). Introduction & Editor's Notes. In N. Abraham & M. Torok, *The Shell and the Kernel*. Chicago: University of Chicago Press.

Rashkin, E. (1992). *Family Secrets and the Psychoanalysis of Narrative*. Princeton: Princeton University Press.

Rogers, A. (2006). *The Unsayable: The Hidden Language of Trauma*. New York: Random House.

Scheper-Hughes, N. (2001). *Saints, Scholars and Schizophrenics: Mental Illness in Rural Ireland*. Berkeley: University of California Press.

Tyrrell, P. (2006). *Founded on Fear*. Dublin: Irish Academic Press.

Valone, D. & Kinealy, C. (2002). *Ireland's Great Hunger: Silence, Memory, Commemoration*. Lanham, MD: University Press of America.

Van der Kolk, B. (1987). *Psychological Trauma*. Arlington, VA, American Psychiatric Publishing.

Venn, C. (2002). Refiguring subjectivity after modernity. In V. Walkerdine (Ed.), *Challenging subjects: Critical Psychology for a New Millennium*. New York: Palgrave.

Walsh, A. (Director). (2003). *Song for a Raggy Boy*. Tva Films.

Waters, J. (1997). Confronting the ghost of our past. In T. Hayden (Ed.), *Irish Hunger: Personal Reflections on the Legacy of the Famine*. Boulder, CO: Roberts Rinehart.

Woodham-Smith, C. (1962). *The Great Hunger*. London: New English Library.

Part VIII

Yearning for nonhuman connections

Chapter 21

Lonely for the other mother: Nature and the relational fourth

Elizabeth Allured

The capacity to be alone with one's self as an adolescent or adult depends upon an adequately internalized attachment relationship to the human caretaker. The ability to enjoy one's aloneness may also depend upon an adequately developed and internalized relationship with the nonhuman world. What we commonly think of as enjoyment of "solitude" is often a turn from human relationships to relations with the nonhuman world of land, flora and fauna, and open space. It is our anthropocentric bias which conceptualizes time spent without relating to other humans as time spent "alone."

As analysts, we have highly privileged the human over the nonhuman world, having practically no literature or institute course offerings about this other domain of life and interrelationship. Emerging from a Freudian tradition, with a Cartesian mind/body split, we have recently broadened our understanding of the essential unitary nature of the bodymind. We have rarely, however, broached the topic of the human/nonhuman split in our focus and in our analytic endeavors.

Jung explored our relationship to the nonhuman world, often living and working in solitude (Sabini, 2005). Thoreau and others, such as ecopsychologist Joanna Macy, have written from a place of immersion in the nonhuman world. Their use of solitude in the development of conscience, purpose, and perspective are worth our study.

Many of us analysts are, I believe, "closet" nature-lovers, though we write papers about love's vicissitudes only in human relations. What may emerge in treatment is not only the longing for human love and tenderness, but also the longing for a closer relationship with our "other" mother, nature, which birthed us all. An exploration of the love and hate in this relationship, as we face environmental anxieties, is very timely and appropriate. Searles (1979) was the first analyst to explore in depth our defensive reactions to our environmental relationship, and his work in this area will be summarized below. The concept of a "relational fourth" which encompasses our relationship with the nonhuman world will be introduced.

A few blocks from my home there is a beach, which no longer resembles a beach. A large transfer station with 18-wheeler trucks operates there 12 hours a day, 6 days a week, with tall industrial cranes that belch black smoke as they crawl over the platform which stretches out into Hempstead Harbor. The cranes scoop up rocks from barges in the water, then dump the stones onto the beds of the 18-wheelers, which will deliver the rocks for road beds, drainage projects, and ornamental uses. Rock dust and black smoke mingle with the high whining vibrations of the cranes' engines and the rumble of trucks. A few hundred feet across the water, on a stretch of littered sand, I sit in meditation facing this scene.

In one of Mitchell's (1999) papers on attachment theory, he described the great shift from seeing the mind as existing within the individual body, to seeing the mind as coexisting among individuals relating with each other, with continual mutual influence in the developing mental capacities. The fallacy of the individual mind was seen as arising out of our view of the physical body: the body in adulthood attains "an almost complete physically functional autonomy" (p.87). If our body is nearly functionally autonomous, the reasoning went, our mind would likewise be. In a conversation with Lew Aron (2008) about this passage, he proposed that if Mitchell were writing today, Mitchell would not write about the functional autonomy of the body, as analysts currently see our embeddedness in many physical systems upon which our physical bodies are totally or partially dependent. But the erroneous metaphor of physical autonomy is, I think, a good thought to keep "in mind," as so many of our current blind spots stem from this fallacy.

Both Freud and Jung were inspired by specific natural settings. Freud (1900) formulated his ideas for his first major work, *The Interpretation of Dreams*, while away in the Semmering Mountains of Austria. Jung built a round stone tower in which to write which bordered on a lake near the woods. He wrote that the goal is not to become natural man. Rather, "What is needed is to call a halt to the fatal dissociation that exists between our so-called higher and lower being; we must unite the conscious aspect with the primitive" (McGuire & Hull, 1977, p.18). The primitive has often been conflated with the sexual, instinct-driven aspects of self. Perhaps this stems from Freud's works. In *Totem and Taboo*, Freud (1913) refers to primitive peoples as "savages" (p.1). He clearly biased the civilized over the primitive in healthy mental functioning, much as the ego stood in relation to the id.

In many cultures, immersion into nature in solitude has been a primary learning methodology. Whether it is called the vision quest by Native peoples in the Americas, the Buddhist's seclusion in a meditation cave, the prophet Jeremiah's time in the wilderness, or Saint Francis' deep communion with animal and plant life near Assisi, *something* is occurring across traditions and times. Perhaps this something includes developing a different kind of object relationship with the nonhuman world. Can we expand our analytic focus to embrace feelings and conflicts experienced with the larger holding environment?

A half dozen white swans venture into this part of the bay, seemingly oblivious to the industrial operation. They swim slowly, keeping together, preening their feathers and occasionally taking a peek under the water. They come here nearly every day that I do—which is nearly every day.

I recently spoke with a woman who is a wilderness counselor on outward-bound-type treatments for troubled adolescents. I asked her if doing therapy out in the wilderness was difficult work. "Not at all," she replied immediately. "The wilderness does the work." The experience of wilderness can calm grandiose fantasies and engender feelings of wholeness and interconnection. It can also provide perspective on time and permanence. Perhaps what the wilderness teaches has to do with unpredictability as well as order, and our need for sensitive perception as well as for aggressive action at times. The wilderness is certainly not a panacea for mental illness. Like Santostefano (2008), I believe our experience of wilderness and outdoor environments is partly determined by our previous relationships with the nonhuman and human environments. Sorting out our feelings and conflicts experienced in specific outdoor environments may clarify how we use or do not use environments in the construction of self and relationships. Who would have guessed, twenty years ago, that analysts would be writing about the practice of meditation (Epstein, 1990; Walsh & Shapiro, 2006) and suggesting their patients meditate, let alone meditating in session with patients, like Wallin (2007) does? Perhaps in the future analysts will be writing about, and suggesting, guided trips to the wilderness and to indigenous communities (few though they may be) to develop a more comprehensive experience of the self/world relationship.

Are we too frightened of the larger environment to discover our own relationship to it, in the absence of others? Are we afraid of finding something that we cannot save from our own destructive actions? What can solitude teach us, about ourselves as well as about the world around us?

A few contemporary analysts have begun to write about the self/environment relationship. In a recent paper Bodnar (2008) discusses her patient's healing from drug addiction through hiking the Appalachian Trail alone for a summer. Santostefano (2008) has attempted to develop a more holistic view of the self/environment paradigm, with an exploration of the "embodied metaphors" that develop as a consequence of interactions with the human and nonhuman world. He suggests we discard a binary view of self/nature and abandon a utopian view of the nonhuman world. He proposes that being in a natural environment would not in and of itself be therapeutic, if the individual had not first met certain critical developmental tasks. These tasks include forming a loving human attachment bond, gaining the ability to assert one's will with another successfully, and developing the ability to regulate one's felt need states in coordination with the needs of another. If these tasks are not successfully met, then individuals cannot experience people or nonhuman environments as safe, enjoyable, or as objects to use in self-development. Santostefano (2004) describes how children and adolescents became increasingly more able to use a garden-like environment during therapy sessions to explore conflicts and limiting self-other configurations, leading ultimately to stronger attachment relationships, more self-reflective functioning, and healthier impulse control. Putting a more inclusive environment at the focus of analytic study and endeavors may lead to productive new dialogues with our patients and with ourselves.

Joanna Macy (1991), an ecopsychologist who is a Buddhist by training, has posited that the pivotal psychological reality of our times concerns the loss of certainty that we as a species will have a future. Although many of us as analysts escape to weekend houses in the countryside, few of us are exploring in our writings our yearnings for a stable, sustaining environment, and our conflicts about its destruction. We explore to the nth degree feelings of conflict about the patient's relationship to the analyst, the patient's relationship to their lover, their child, their mother, but steer clear (as if this were the politically correct thing to do) of conflicts in the patient's relationship to nature and the nonhuman environment. Perhaps this is unexplored territory for most of us, and we do not know how to lead a journey into a wilderness that we have not traversed ourselves, metaphorically or otherwise. Or perhaps we try to leave this love object somehow unspoiled by our analytic struggles and endeavors, afraid to look at our hatred of the biosphere's needs and, instead, acting out our hatred with our environmentally destructive habits and lifestyles. Perhaps if we know and accept our hatred here, as in other relationships, we can begin to act it out less.

Several of my patients have discussed aspects of their movements toward or away from solitude as this relates to the nonhuman environment. One is an Asian-American woman with three young children whose husband has stage 4 stomach cancer. Debra is a very attractive woman in her mid-30s who was shocked 2 years ago to learn that her husband of 10 years had this likely fatal illness. This news was even more tragic in that Debra had lost several relatives to suicide and her relationships with most of her remaining relatives, excepting her husband and children, were shaky at best.

Early in her treatment with me, Debra appeared hopeful, though devastated. She was angry at the surgeon who had matter-of-factly announced to her in the recovery room, at the conclusion of her husband's exploratory surgery, the number of months he expected her husband to survive for. This news had been such a massive assault to Debra's sense of reality that she had fallen to the floor in an emotional and physical collapse. It was clear to me that exploring this potential loss in therapy could not proceed without first finding our way into a trusting therapeutic relationship.

In the early and continuing months of her treatment, Debra did not want to talk about the potential loss of her husband. She wanted specific, concrete help with her problems. For instance, a few months into her treatment, the roadway and bridge between Debra's home and my office underwent major construction, and Debra seemed overwhelmed with how she would manage to get to the office. I brought in an article from the newspaper listing the times the roadway would have lanes of traffic open in each direction so she could decide whether to use it or not. Her face was clearly relieved when I gave her this token of my involvement in her concrete, physical environment. While I do not regularly begin a treatment by working with environmental problems, Debra seemed to need this help in order to trust in me. In retrospect, I think she was testing me to see if I would be incapable of meeting her needs, like both her parents often were. Was I able to bridge the distance between us? She also seemed greatly relieved when I offered specific options to choose from in dealing with interpersonal conflicts, and ways to be assertive with insensitive relatives, which often led to decreased anxiety when she tried them out.

But there was a tentativeness in our bond, which mirrored the unreliability of her parent figures. When she would often arrive late, I frequently wondered if she had decided not to return, or had been in too much distress to attend. In the transference, I became her passive, longsuffering mother who did not think much of my ability to have an impact on others. However, when I asked about my sense that I and the treatment were not important to her, Debra professed great faith in the power of therapy to help with emotional distress, citing her first successful treatment in college. But my sense was that each of us was often alone, together.

Debra told me that she was afraid of being alone. She slept poorly when her husband was away, and had her children sleep on the floor in her room when this occurred. She was able to tolerate separation from others when walking her two dogs in her semi-rural neighborhood. Debra's relationship with her dogs, like that with her children, is a sustaining one. She professes to feel great joy in caring for them as they mature from puppyhood to adult dogs. She especially enjoys taking them for walks by herself in her wooded neighborhood. She sought out the second dog after her husband was diagnosed with cancer. Perhaps finding a companion for the solitary dog was Debra's unconscious belief in her ability to find a loving partner if she were to find herself alone.

Closing my eyes, I slip into more sensory perception—the feel of the wind, temperature, sensation of sand, sun, the cry of seagulls. Most days, thoughts continue to rise and fall like breath, one leading to another. When my eyes open at last, the swans are often swimming around the old pilings of piers from long ago, far across the bay—weaving their way between stumps of rotting logs.

Debra asked me if I had a dog, and I replied that I did. She then asked me for help in finding a place to board her dogs when she and her family went on a much-needed vacation. Rather than interpret this or ask what it would mean to her, I told her about my similar search and eventually finding a well-run facility. In the analytic metaphor, I am helping her find a capable caretaker in our work together.

Debra does profess a trust in nature. She shops organic, has a pond with fish, and enjoys gardening alone in her yard frequently. She recently turned in her SUV for a small sedan after noticing my small hybrid and considering her contribution to global warming. Debra described gaining a sense of stability in her childhood through solitary outdoor play at her home in northern California where she would regularly spend time exploring the woods. In part, this was an escape from the turmoil and strong verbal outbursts in her house which led to her fear there. It appears Debra did not transfer her fears of the aggression in her home onto the nonhuman environment. Her conscious fears have involved the potential loss of her children to environmental toxins, such as radon in homes of friends without radon detectors, or birthday candles at parties with wire wicks containing mercury. Do the deadly candle wicks contain Debra's father's potential for noxious, violent outbursts? Or is there an actual environmental danger with the candles? Or both? Can we as analysts see ourselves working with both types of fears?

For Debra, the natural world has more of an idealized transference, while the man-made world is potentially threatening like her parents' home. The more predictable nonhuman world of animals and plants is helping Debra adjust to the current instability in her most intimate human relationship.

In her early 20s, while away at college, Debra had sought counseling for severe anxiety. She forged a bond with her counselor which had brought relief from her symptoms. Her recollection of this successful therapy, and some positive elements in her relationship with her parents have, I believe, led her to persevere in our work.

I have concerns for Debra, because she has only one close friend. Her enjoyment of solitude with her dogs and in her garden does not protect her from the panic of being alone should her husband die. The nonhuman environmental relationship cannot provide the type of human intimacy and reciprocity that we are born to long for. Debra will need to lean heavily on loving human relationships, in addition to the sustenance and stability she can receive from the nonhuman world. To this end I continue to probe about our relationship, what she expects and what she cannot ask of me. Two months ago, for the first time, Debra called me between sessions. The call was from a hospital a thousand miles away where her husband had just undergone a life threatening experimental surgical treatment. She was in trouble emotionally and trusted that I might help her. As she is now more able to lean on me emotionally and I become a more stable attachment figure, we have ventured into her fear of her husband's death. Am I, in the transference, her first therapist, her passive mother, the forest from her childhood in which she felt safe, or all three? Perhaps our relationship is a configuration of various attachment relationships and objects, both human and nonhuman. In our work as analysts, can we help our patients explore a variety of relationships, including nonhuman, inanimate ones? Can we see these relationships as being as "real" as those we more commonly explore: as being as much a part of the self as the intersubjective, human relationships which are our common parlance?

We as analysts have many terms for our roles and our varying relationships with patients. We are alternately the containing object, the rejecting object, the corrective emotional experience, the provider of a new experience of relationship, the interpreter of defenses, and many others. Likewise, in family therapy there are many terms to describe the couple relationship: distancer/pursuer; egalitarian partnership, one up/one down, and many others. But we have few analytic terms to describe our relationship with the nonhuman world.

Although the ecopsychologists use terms and concepts that are unfamiliar to most analysts, it may be helpful to look at their perspective while we develop a more relational, holistic paradigm of self/environment, and terms to convey this. Macy (1991) has put forth the concept that there are four general types of object relationships with the nonhuman world. She posits an initial position of the individual viewing and experiencing the world as a battlefield, a duel between the forces of good and evil, or light and darkness. She sees this position as being dominant particularly in situations where an imminent threat to life is experienced. This viewpoint can arouse courage, use anger, and strengthen military reserves. It also provides a sense of certainty, with a sense that whatever the outcome, God is on your side and a victory of one sort or another will ultimately result. As analysts, we can see parallels with this viewpoint and the paranoid/schizoid position, and with what are commonly referred to as borderline defenses of idealization/devaluation, denial, and acting out in aggressive and self-destructive ways.

The second way of perceiving the world, according to Macy, involves experiencing the material world as a trap. Many Eastern religions, and some Western ones, espouse aspects of this philosophy, with salvation dependent upon escaping from the material world and the cycle of desires to a spiritual plane while still alive. This detached mode of experience is seen as superior to the confusion and suffering common to daily life. Analytically, this position seems to rely on dissociative and/or intellectualizing defenses, or somatic ones as seen in rituals involving self-flagellation or self-deprivation. Both of these positions involve compromise formations, with intolerance for ambiguity and vulnerability.

The third way of perceiving the world, as Macy describes it, involves experiencing it as a lover, "a most intimate and gratifying partner" (p.8). The Vedantic hymns of Hinduism describe an erotic relationship to the world, with worship of Krishna and the desires of body and soul blending into a sensual appreciation of the natural world of seasons, landscapes, and weather. As analysts, we could see this position as one half of a "real" love object relationship, the other half being hatred of the limitations, unpredictability, and power of the object—in this case, the earth environment, and its needs which are very separate from our desires. In this third type of object relationship with the world, the dissociation appears to be of this other half, with an intact capacity to experience some mutuality, spontaneity, and interdependence. Perhaps there is some reaction formation in denial of the hatred.

The fourth way of perceiving the world involves a shift from a position of separateness, to experiencing the world and the self as essentially the same: where we draw a boundary around the self is arbitrary. Macy refers to Gregory Bateson's notion of self as "the epistemological error of Occidental civilization" (p.183). We know that the skin is not the boundary of self, since minds mutually interpenetrate. How separate are we from the oxygen in our blood vessels? When does oxygen cease to be separate from surrounding air and begin to be part of the blood/self? In the brachiole? In the capillary? In the lung sack? In the windpipe? In the nostril? The self is not able to exist without its environment; it is embedded in a way that makes actual separateness impossible. But this challenges our sensory apparatuses, which developed to make fine discriminations between objects, a skill which was essential to survival. As analysts, we may see this fourth position as using regressive, merging defenses, with an undifferentiated sense of self from other. Yet, in a recent editorial in the New York Times, Thomas Friedman (2008) referred to the earth as "our environmental body" (p.11). This larger physical identification mirrors Macy's "world as self" perspective.

Like the concept of multiple self-states, could it be inevitable that we move between varying types of relational configurations with the larger environment, admixtures of the four above and perhaps others, with mutual influence of self/environment an inevitability? Would it be helpful to explore our feelings of love, dependence, aggression, and fear related to the larger environment?

Searles (1960) believed projections as well as "real" relationships suffuse all relationship domains, including the environmental. He saw us as embedded in the nonhuman world at birth, and not fully achieving separateness from it until about 12 years of age, Piaget's age of formal operational thinking. Searles (1979) saw strong defenses at work which keep us from acknowledging the potentially suicidal path we as a species are on. To acknowledge that we will be outlived by our "mother" is a humbling and perhaps enraging experience. He believed through technology, we achieve an imagined omnipotence. In fantasy, we outlive the "mother" through technological escape to other planets after spoiling this one with our refuse and unresolved rage.

In his comprehensive work on the subject, *The Nonhuman Environment*, Searles (1960) outlined various aspects of relatedness with the nonhuman world, in both nonpsychotic and psychotic functioning. I would like to summarize his thoughts about the beneficial effects of having a "mature attitude" to the nonhuman environment. Searles defines a "mature attitude" as an experience of *relatedness*, specifically a "sense of intimate kinship, a psychological concomitant to the structural kinship, which . . . exists between man and the various ingredients of his nonhuman environment—structural kinship in terms of physiology, anatomy, atomic structure, and so on, as well as kinship with respect to the evolutional history of mankind and the biological fate of the individual human being (the inescapable destiny of our physical body to become a part of the nonhuman environment after our death)" (p.101).

Searles was careful to note that this experience of kinship presupposes a maintenance of a unique sense of self apart from its connection to the nonhuman world, which is often absent in psychotic functioning. He notes that this experience of mature relatedness with the nonhuman environment comes with inevitable conflicts stemming from the fact that we are of nature, yet we are fundamentally separate from other forms of life in our ability to exercise free will and create a unique sense of self through self-actualization. He more fully described some timely aspects of these conflicts in his prescient paper, "Unconscious Processes in Relation to the Environmental Crisis" (Searles, 1979).

Searles (1960) saw four major psychological benefits from moving into a mature relatedness with the nonhuman environment. These were: relief or attenuation of anxiety and other painful affects; self-realization; enhanced sense of one's feeling of reality, as opposed to unreality or psychotic perception; and the development of greater acceptance and valuing of other humans, including a more encompassing sense of the human community as family.

Searles posited that mature relatedness with the nonhuman world compensates in an important way for the anxiety related to the knowledge of our eventual death and our feelings of insignificance, whatever their source. He saw the environmental relationship as a buffer against existential loneliness and as conveying a sense of continuity amidst our own uncertain future and certain death. We may be able to see ourselves as dwarfed by the incredible beauty and sustaining power of the environment. In this way the loss of infantile feelings of omnipotence, which occurs in adolescence and adulthood, can be reckoned with.

At this point early in the twenty-first century, however, the certainties about the nonhuman world have lessened. And one would expect an increase in anxiety as the nonhuman world becomes less predictable and more volatile with storms, earthquakes, and tidal waves. A parallel rise in depressive feelings may occur as species are lost and pristine environments altered irrevocably for resource procurement by people. Nonetheless, most of us, at least some of the time, still manage to gain a sense of peace and reassurance from being in natural environments which will outlive us and which do not require our intervention to be ecologically diverse and sustaining.

The second beneficial result noted by Searles, the development of self-realization, concerned our interactions with the nonhuman environment to foster identity and purpose. We find both our abilities and our limitations in relation to the nonhuman environment, in some ways more clearly than in interactions with other humans. Searles cited Thoreau's description of his time spent in solitude at Walden Pond near Concord, Massachusetts as aptly portraying this process of identity cohesion and creative fruition:

> I did not read books the first summer; I hoed beans. Nay, I often did better than this. There were times when I could not afford to sacrifice the bloom of the present moment to any work, whether of the head or hands. I love a broad margin to my life. Sometimes, in a summer morning, haven taken my accustomed bath, I sat in my sunny doorway from sunrise till noon, rapt in a revery, amidst the pines and hickories and sumachs, in undisturbed solitude and stillness, while the birds sang around or flitted noiseless through the house, until by the sun falling in at my west window, or the noise of some traveller's wagon on the distant highway, I was reminded of the lapse of time. I grew in those seasons like corn in the night, and they were far better than any work of the hands would have been.
>
> (in Searles, 1960, p.127)

I believe most of us can recall productive times spent in solitude with nature in the development of creative aspects of our uniquely individual identities.

Searles' third factor concerns the strengthening of a reality sense by moving into conscious relationship with the nonhuman world. He noted that this factor is closely allied with the second—finding the self in creative interaction with the environment. He chose to differentiate it as a separate factor, however, to emphasize the process of what we would now call "grounding" in the physical world as a means of keeping us from becoming lost in our cognitive ruminations or obsessions. Again, he quotes Thoreau to illustrate:

> Sometimes, after staying in a village parlor till the family had all retired, I have returned to the woods, and, partly with a view to the next day's dinner, spent the hours of midnight fishing from a boat by

moonlight, serenaded by owls and foxes, and hearing, from time to time, the creaking note of some unknown bird close at hand. These experiences were very memorable and valuable to me—anchored in forty feet of water, and twenty or thirty rods from the shore, surrounded sometimes by thousands of small perch and shiners, dimpling the surface with their tails in the moonlight, and communicating by a long flaxen line with mysterious nocturnal fishes which had their dwelling forty feet below, or sometimes dragging sixty feet of line about the pond as I drifted in the gentle night breeze, now and then feeling a slight vibration along it, indicative of some life prowling about its extremity, of dull uncertain blundering purpose there, and slow to make up its mind. At length you slowly raise, pulling hand over hand, some horned pout squeaking and squirming to the upper air. It was very queer, especially in dark nights, when your thoughts had wandered to vast and cosmogonal themes in other spheres, to feel this faint jerk, which came to interrupt your dreams and link you to Nature again. It seemed as if I might next cast my line upward into the air, as well as downward into this element, which was scarcely more dense. Thus I caught two fishes as it were with one hook.

(in Searles, 1960, p.136)

It might be helpful for us to dialogue about ways our patients become more grounded and to explore why individuals are choosing what they come to choose. In my practice, I have had a patient come down from the skyscraper where she works to walk on the sidewalk for a few minutes to decrease anxiety and feel more connected to reality. Another looks out her kitchen window to the cedar deck and the trees beyond. How do each of us strengthen our connection to the environmental ground that sustains us?

The final factor which Searles discusses is rarely referred to in analytic texts. It concerns the ways mature relatedness with the nonhuman environment can enhance feelings of connection with other humans and bring about acceptance of the limitations of others. Searles states that coming to grips with our own humble position in relation to the vast and infinitely more lasting nonhuman environment leads to compassion for the rest of humankind. After all, others share our existential aloneness and our feelings of alienation from that which is otherwise in a type of dynamic synchronicity. As we realize our common plight, Searles posits, acceptance of, and ultimately identification with, others in a compassionate manner results. Searles' writing on this fourth factor was very brief and left many questions in my mind.

Searles noted that the psychoanalytic community of his day treated the nonhuman environment as simply a backdrop for human psychological functioning, rather than as an integral part of it. I believe we have not moved significantly from this position, although we have become more sensitively attuned to cultural factors in the environment.

We as analysts have highly developed the concepts of, initially, the intrapsychic, then the interpersonal and, more recently, the intersubjective third which involves a uniquely co-created mutuality. The larger environmental relationship could be referred to as the relational fourth, implying a more encompassing living relationship whether it is dissociated or not. While numerical terms cannot adequately capture the complexity of mutuality and interdependence, perhaps we should not throw away the language of the baby when defining the bathwater. All four fields contain overlapping conflicts and dissociations that are worthy of exploration. I am not advocating forgoing a thorough exploration of the human relationships in our patients' and our own lives. The recent ground analysts have made in acknowledging ongoing co-created intersubjective experiences in therapy and in life should not be abandoned in favor of an exploration of the relationship with the nonhuman world. These are, I believe, interpenetrating aspects of experience.

But on a few days my thoughts have left like fog lifting, and not returned. With closed eyes, the sensory perceptions of wind, sun, truck cacophony, and birdcall have become a living matrix which is within and without me. Each time this happens, when my eyes open at last, the swans are sitting around me in a semicircle on the sand, grooming themselves and drying their feathers in the sun.

As with my patient Debra, there are many productive and creative ways to explore meaning of self in environment, and self as reflecting the environment. Whether we feel safe, secure, frightened, or lonely in relationship to the nonhuman world reflects multiple internalized and external relationships.

Whether we believe that a discrete intrapsychic entity such as an individual self exists or not, it has been helpful to continue to refer to "intrapsychic experience" and "intrapsychic conflicts" for semantic purposes. We have multiple meanings for the "analytic third" (Benjamin, 2004; Ogden, 2004; Aron, 2006), most of which concern elements of the co-created intersubjectivity of the analytic dyad. Perhaps it is useful to move on to the fourth, to indicate a larger, more encompassing form of relatedness beyond human-to-human intersubjectivity. Or perhaps another term will emerge to more adequately refer to this new field of inquiry.

The experience of solitude can involve an exploration of what we commonly think of as the individual self. It can also be a doorway into multiple and often unexplored feeling states and relational configurations with respect to the larger holding environment. Our experience of self within this holding environment, the nonhuman world, can, and at this time perhaps should, be brought in to the consulting room and, most importantly, into our lives.

I would like to thank Susan Bodnar for her thoughts concerning some of the concepts in this chapter.

References

Aron, L. (2006). Analytic Impasse and the Third: Clinical Implications of Inter-subjectivity Theory. *The International Journal of Psycho-Analysis*, 87:349–368.
—— (2008). Personal communication.
Benjamin, J. (2004). Beyond Doer and Done to: An Intersubjective View of Thirdness. *The Psychoanalytic Quarterly*, 73:5–46.
Bodnar, S. (2008). Wasted and Bombed: Clinical Enactments of a Changing Relationship to the Earth. *Psychoanalytic Dialogues*, 18:484–512.
Epstein, M. (1990). Beyond the Oceanic Feeling: Psychoanalytic Study of Buddhist Meditation. *The International Review of Psycho-Analysis*, 17:159–165.
Freud. S. (1900/2008). *The Interpretation of Dreams*. Oxford: Oxford Paperbacks.
—— (1913). Totem and Taboo: Some Points of Agreement between the Mental Lives of Savages and Neurotics. *The Standard Edition of the Complete Psychological Works of Sigmund Freud*, 13:vii–162.
Friedman, T. (2008). *New York Times*, Week In Review, July 20.
Macy, J. (1991) *World as Lover, World as Self*. Berkeley, CA: Parallax Press.
McGuire, W. & Hull, R. (Eds.) (1977). *C. G. Jung Speaking: Interviews and Encounters*. Princeton, NJ: Princeton University Press.
Mitchell, S. (1999). Attachment Theory and the Psychoanalytic Tradition: Reflections on Human Relationality. *Psychoanalytic Dialogues*, 9:85–107.
Ogden, T. (2004). The Analytic Third: Implications for Psychoanalytic Theory and Technique. *The Psychoanalytic Quarterly*, 73:167–195.
Sabini, M. (2005). *The Earth Has a Soul: The Nature Writings of C. G. Jung*. Berkeley, CA: North Atlantic Books.
Santostefano, S. (2004). *Child Therapy in the Great Outdoors*. New Jersey: The Analytic Press.
—— (2008). The Sense of Self Inside and Environment Outside: How the Two Grow Together and Become One In Healthy Psychological Development. *Psychoanalytic Dialogues*, 18(4):513–535.
Searles, H. (1960). *The Nonhuman Environment*. New York: International Universities Press.
—— (1979). *Countertransference and Related Subjects*. Connecticut: International Universities Press.
Wallin, D. (2007). *Attachment in Psychotherapy*. New York: The Guilford Press.
Walsh, R. & Shapiro, S. (2006). The Meeting of Meditative Disciplines and Western Psychology: A Mutually Enriching Dialogue. *American Psychologist*, 61:227–239.

Chapter 22

On the longing for home[1]

Henry M. Seiden

In a story several thousand years old, the king of a small island is called to war. The exciting cause is domestic—the wife of an allied king has been carried off by the prince of a distant land. An armada is assembled. The boats are primitive, the distance great, the weapons rudimentary. The story involves human travail, sexual and brotherly love, rivalry, jealousy, revenge, slaughter. Reasons, motives, and explanations are primitive, too. The gods want this and that, intervening arbitrarily and for narcissistic reasons. With their help, the king prevails in the war and after. He is heroically strong but, more important, clever, "wily." He relies on distinctly human psychological capacities. For the story's original audience, he is everyman. His motives and struggles are theirs. This is an orienting narrative for a seafaring people, people often far from home.

The war lasts ten years, a kind of mythic forever. The return voyage takes another ten. You know by now I'm referring to Homer's Odysseus and Odysseus's nostos, his endless journey home. There are ill winds and detours, seductions, nymphs with "beautiful braids," demigoddesses who want him, dangers, temptations, monsters, the loss of his ship and many men, cultural and social pitfalls on islands where he washes ashore, along with offers of marriage to a beautiful princess and a descent into hell.

There are desperate physical and psychological trials—encounters with the endlessly mysterious, often terrifying otherness of this world. But always, like a lodestar on the Western horizon, there's home. Odysseus wants only to return there, to be with his family, the son who idealizes him, the loving wife who waits, who herself can never be safely, comfortably at home until he is there. Interestingly—and the ancients understood—homecoming is not simply a matter of landfall. Things have changed. There are enemies waiting. Intimates seem like strangers. There are reconciliations to accomplish.

Altering the usual format for the presentation of psychological papers, I will offer instead a series of narratives in a kind of theme and variations. I will draw on a range of sources: literary, cultural, historical, and clinical. The subject, home and the longing for home, is largely ignored in the psychoanalytic literature. I hope to show that we have much to gain by attending to these matters. Such attention will broaden and make more useful some of our most basic concepts.

When I was a child I loved my mother's stories of her childhood. Her family had a dog, Benjy. Dogs ran free in their suburban town and Benjy, a big, friendly mutt with a lot of Newfoundland in him, liked to follow her and her brother to school. He would then go about his doggy day making his way home by evening, always in time for dinner. One Saturday when she and her brother were going to the city with their father, Benjy followed. After they got on the trolley, they called to him through the windows, ordering him to "go home." He only wagged his tail as if this were a great game and continued to follow. Eventually, he dropped out of sight. That night he didn't show up, nor the next day. Calls to the police were unavailing. My mother remembered how upset she and her brother were. My grandmother insisted it was "good riddance": the dog was a nuisance; he threatened the mailman; chased cars; his barking disturbed neighbors; he was expensive to feed. On the third evening, there was a scratching at the door. I remember my excitement as my mother told me! They opened the door. Benjy! He'd found his way home! He jumped up, big enough to put his front paws on my grandmother's shoulders. He licked her face. She cried.

> Home is an English word virtually impossible to translate into other tongues. No translation catches the associations, the mixture of memory and longing, the sense of security and autonomy and accessibility, the aroma of inclusiveness, of freedom from wariness, that cling to the word home . . . Home is a concept, not a place; it is a state of mind where self-definition starts; it is origins—the mix of time and place and smell and weather wherein one first realizes one is an original, perhaps like others, especially those one loves, but discrete, distinct, not to be copied. Home is where one first learned to be separate and it remains in the mind as the place where reunion, if it were ever to occur, would happen.
> (A. Bartlett Giamatti, classical scholar, former President of Yale and former Commissioner of Major League Baseball, 1998, pp.99–100)

A modern Japanese word seems much like the Ancient Greek *nostos*. A cousin, fluent in Japanese, tells me:

> Japanese has a single verb, *kaeru*, that means return home, and only to your native home . . . The Japanese also use *kaeru* when they talk about returning to their ancestral villages even if they have never lived there. There is a different word for simply coming back to a place that is not your home, *modoru*, and that's the word I had to use to say I was coming back to Japan . . . The return to the ancestral village is another interesting concept in Japan and China. The Japanese "go home" to

their villages once a year in August for the *O-Bon* holiday. The Chinese do the same thing for the Chinese New Year. At those times of year, huge numbers of people are "going home."

(Seiden, 2008)

Because of the territorial behavior of the first modern humans, rigorously maintained as they invaded the world outside Africa, everyone stayed in place in their new home, except for those at the head of the wave of advance . . . For thousands of years thereafter, people lived and died in the place where they were born . . . This conclusion emerges directly from the genealogies of the Y chromosome and the mitochondrial DNA.

(Wade, 2006, p.78)

The loss of home—banishment and exile—is an ancient terror and punishment. Socrates chose poison over banishment. Ovid, banished for expressing anti-imperial sentiments, died in exile, having petitioned repeatedly for permission to return. In 19th century England, undesirables were "transported" to Australia and Georgia, U.S.A. In the 20th century, the Soviet Union sent politically suspect citizens to Siberia.

The history of the Jews has turned on the loss of home and the need to return, establish, and protect a homeland. For believers, this return rises to the level of religious duty, aliyah. The history of the United States has turned on the need of people leaving home to find and make a new one.

Anyone who as a child has gone off to school on a rainy morning—or sent a child off—knows the compelling power of home and its threatened loss. Bowlby, the great theorist of attachment and loss, began those interests at age two when sent to boarding school—a traumatic, life-shaping experience of mourning (Coates, 2004).

Lyrics from popular music and sentimental poetry are replete with themes of home, often intertwined with themes of love of a significant other, the loss of each and both, and longing for return. For example: "Homeward bound, I wish I was homeward bound/Home, where my thoughts escape, at home, where my music's playin'/Home, where my love lies waitin' silently for me" (Paul Simon, 1967). And: "Mid pleasures and palaces though we may roam,/Be it ever so humble, there's no place like home" (John Howard Payne, 1791–1852). And: The Home is Where the Heart is, My Old Kentucky Home, Sweet Home Alabama, Home for the Holidays, Home on the Range, I Feel So Breakup I Want to go Home, Show me the Way to go Home. And: Georgia on my Mind, California Here I Come Right Back Where I Started From, Shennandoah, Swanee River, and Subterranean Homesick Blues. And hundreds more you could list.

I go to my doctor, a woman in her 40s. She has a full life, a busy practice, photographs of husband and children on her desk. She tells me her mother died some months ago and she has made peace with losing her. "But I'm homesick," she says.

A patient in his 50s was recently obliged to find a new job in consequence of "screwing up royally" in a place he had been working for 17 years. Screwing up was the consequence of a manic episode. He has come to terms with and understands what happened. He has settled down in a "good" job. The boss is OK, the work is fine, co-workers are not a problem. But something is still wrong: there's a sadness he can't quite dispel. I say, "I think you've lost a home." "Yes!" he says.

Another patient in her 40s I've been seeing on and off since her early 20s. She came to New York after college out of a need to escape from the stifling rural home where she was born. She married a man she met at work. Among the things she felt to be attractive about him was that he was from a world so different from hers: ethnic, loud, passionate (as well as arguing and complaining)—a welcome, liberating contrast to her tensely quiet, depressive, New England Yankee home. The marital relationship has always been fraught, her in-laws intrusive and difficult. I used to joke with her about being Goldilocks married to baby bear. When she and her husband outgrew their east side apartment, at her insistence they moved to an old farmhouse. She is proud of the fact that her daughters are active in the local 4H club. As for calling her Goldilocks, that story is about finding the chair, food, bed—the place that's "just right"—which for Goldilocks turns out to be the home she started out from.

Another folk tale: a man and woman live like siblings in innocent delight in an extensive park. They are made for each other (quite literally), and happy in their home. In time, in response to impulses beyond their control, they become less innocent with each other. This is against the rules. The lord of the manor, enraged at their disobedience, banishes them to a life of humiliation, hard work, and pain. They and their descendants forevermore long to return. I'm sure you recognize the Judeo-Christian myth of origin. It gives us to believe the longing for a lost home is essential to the human condition—there from the beginning, an inevitable consequence of growing up.

Thus far I have presented a theme and variations. The theme is home and the yearning for it. The variations are expressions of and adaptations to that longing—a longing which persists even in face of the powerful countervailing motive, the need to get away from a home which for one reason or another limits self-development. The need to get away is well studied, an honored narrative in its own right. It is a daily matter for working clinicians who think of it in terms of separation-individuation.

The longing for home is a longing to repair two separations—one in place, one in time. A home lost to time is no longer there. This is true of my childhood Bronx. It's gone—along with my parents, my childhood friends, the neighbors, the smell of my grandmother's soup cooking on the stove of our 4th floor apartment. It was true, even as she told the stories, of my mother's Yonkers and her dogs. Separations in place become separations in time. It's true of the immigrant experience, often in the extreme. The old homeland is transformed, destroyed, or otherwise inaccessible. It exists, perhaps idealized, but on the other side of a temporal horizon.

Alfred Kazin (1951), in his affecting memoir *A Walker in the City*, says of his childhood in Brooklyn:

> Often, those Friday evenings, they spoke of der heym, "Home," and then it was hard for me. Heym was a terrible word. I saw millions of Jews lying dead . . . I was afraid with my mother's fears, thought I should weep when she wept, lived again through every pogrom whose terrors she chanted. I associated with that old European life only pain, mud, and hopelessness, but I was still of it through her . . . In many ways der heym was entirely dim and abstract, nothing to do with me at all, alien as the skullcap and beard and frock coat of my mother's father . . . Yet . . . I often felt odd twinges of jealousy because my parents could talk about that more intense, somehow less experimental life than ours with so many private smiles between themselves.
>
> (pp.58–59)

The need to return, and the need to leave, require rapproachment. The only possible real solution is to find a new home which incorporates vital elements of the old. Sometimes this accommodation is obvious, conscious, and social: think of all the place names in the English-speaking world that begin with "New." Think of all the hyphenated Americans, at home, more or less, in two places.

Giamatti says baseball is "the Romantic Epic of homecoming America sings to itself" (1998, p.104), a game for a nation of immigrants because contestants strive to get home. They score by getting home safely. Still, getting home, each run scored, changes the game. There is no perfect circle: the return is to a new, transformed situation.

The Odyssey is a metaphor for all odysseys. To the extent that separation in place becomes separation in time, these can never be perfect completions. Odysseus returns to Ithaca, a home transformed. He and Penelope test each other elaborately to reassure themselves the transformed other is not an impostor. The ancient myth would have us understand that the place may be the same one, but the home you find is not the same as the one you've left and have ever since been dreaming of, and the one who waits is not identical with the one you've been dreaming of either.

A proper review of Western literature on longing for home would begin at least with Odysseus's nostalgia. It would include Gilgamesh, the Aeneid, as well as Genesis—that is, the major organizing narratives of the Western world. It would also note the fact that our ordinary narratives are replete with the theme of longing for home (and the pain of separation from home). Our folk tales, folks songs, poetry, movies, novels, politics, and economics give expression to the deeply felt need to return and/or the need to make a new home which celebrates and integrates elements of the original. They also express the impossibility of complete return: something is always transformed. Gilgamesh returns home himself transformed. Aeneas must re-establish his home in a new place. Odysseus finds that upon reaching Ithaca his problems have just begun.

Despite the universality of the theme of longing for home and the extensive exploration of its twinned opposite, the separation motive, the psychoanalytic literature has not been particularly attentive to it. Freud (1919) does begin his essay on *The Uncanny*—in German "Das Unheimiliche," literally the "un-homelike"—paying close attention to the word *heimlich* and its affective meanings, including longing for the familiar comforts of home. But Freud's interest is in what is frightening in the familiar (and in the way feelings of uncanniness signal a repression of unconscious motives and feelings toward familiar "objects"). He's not interested in home in and of itself. Nor have psychoanalysts since been particularly interested.

Bettleheim's (1975) classic study of fairy tales, *The Uses of Enchantment*, has no listing for "home" in the index despite the necessary embeddedness of children in homes and despite the message of such tales as Goldilocks, Little Red Riding Hood, Snow White, and Cinderella, which is all about home, whether finding, escaping, or returning to it. Even the supremely, unabashedly oedipal Jack, of Jack and the Beanstalk, who ends up living with his mother lives we are assured, happily ever after—at home.

The term nostalgia (meaning originally the pain of longing for home, from the Ancient Greek *algos*, pain, and *nostos*, the voyage home) was medicalized as early as the 17th century as painful homesickness and a form of depression. But psychoanalysts working in this area since Freud have focused on lost objects, mothers in particular, rather than on the loss of home as such, that is, the larger family, the particular place, the broader experiential and subcultural context that mothers inhabit. Sterba (1934) thought homesickness involved longing for mother's breast. Fenichel (1945) treated nostalgia as a matter of longing for preoedipal mother. Fodor (1950) went back further still, attributing nostalgia to longing for the prenatal state.

Here's a sample psychoanalytic contemplation of nostalgia. You will note that the longing for home has only a kind of fossil presence in it:

> Nostalgia is distinguished from homesickness from which it was originally derived, and from fantasy to which it is related. It is described as an affective-cognitive experience, usually involving memories of places in one's past. These memories are associated with a characteristic affective coloration described as "bittersweet." It is concluded that the

locales remembered are displacements from objects whose representation was repressed. Nostalgia is a ubiquitous human experience that is evoked by particular stimuli under special circumstances, and, while it is generally a normal occurrence, pathological forms occur. Among those . . . are: nostalgia as a substitute for mourning, as an attempted mastery through idealization and displacement of a painful past, as a resistance in analysis, and as a counterphobic mechanism. Nostalgia not only serves as a screen memory, but may also be said to operate as a screen affect.

(Werman, 1977, pp.397–398)

Winnicott (1950) does speak of the "ordinary good home" and seems to be referring to its culture, but he never develops the idea. Kohut in his last book (1983, p.203 and footnote) remarks almost in passing on the alter-ego selfobject function of one's "homeland." (A selfobject in his framework is a presence that completes the experience of self.) While the relatively sparse psychoanalytic literature on immigration (e.g., Grinberg & Grinberg, 1989; Akhtar 1995, 1999; Boulanger, 2004) does deal with the matter of home and losing, it either tends to see the longing clinically as "homesickness" and a form of neurosis or it makes the immigrant struggle largely a matter of accommodating to a new world.

In his effort to shift the focus of psychoanalysis from biological to social, Sandler (1960, 1985, 2003) comes close to acknowledging the importance of home. "Familiar and constant things in the child's environment may . . . carry a special affective value for the child in that they are more easily perceived—colloquially we say that they are known, recognizable, or familiar to the child. The constant presence of familiar things makes it easier for the child to maintain its minimum level of safety feeling" (1960, p.355). From "familiar" to "home" is a small step, but Sandler doesn't take it. He has much to say about "phantasy" objects, but nothing to say about fantasies of home.

"You can't go home again," Thomas Wolfe (1934) insists famously in his semi-autobiographical novel of that title because it is a matter of a dislocation in time, a psychological, developmental matter, not merely a matter of place. Not being able to go home can be painful indeed and the acceptance of one's new home can be reluctant, its rejection disguised. Some examples of such disguise from my practice: A young woman who came for help with depression and marital problems talked about her inability, to the point of "paralysis," to buy a sofa. She just couldn't find the right one. Another couple had similar problems finding a dining room table. They ate on their sofa! A teenager refused get his hair cut. His long hair, because of his baby face, made him look like a girl and he was suffering for it socially. His mother had died. He was living with his aunt. His mother had been the one who cut his hair, in their old kitchen, back home, he wrapped in a towel with a sheet beneath his chair. Typically, psychoanalytic clinicians would look for explanation for each of these puzzling "paralyses" to object relational issues which of course were at play. The matter of home as a time, place, family, and culture tends to stay under the clinical radar, but in each case someone was saying, "This may be where I'm living, but I'm not at home here."

There are moments of reunion when the chronic sense of loss is lifted. A patient, a Jewish New Yorker and frequent traveler, says when his plane lands in Israel something feels different: he is home. When he tells me this, I'm reminded of my father who said with delight upon returning from a first and only trip to Israel: "Even the streets have Jewish names!"

Home is a place, time, family, and culture. Its story has distinguishable elements: an original home supporting an original, authentic sense of identity; a necessary and inevitable leaving in the service of a new self and new authenticity; an accommodation in which the new must honor the old and incorporate elements of it; and finally, because the return is necessarily incomplete, a variety of shifting affective self-states involving longing, idealizing nostalgia, and sometimes a sweet sense of orientation and value.

Perhaps the most interesting of these self-states is the chronic, not-necessarily-neurotic sense of loss we carry into and through adulthood: an affective state which might be thought of as chronic mourning. It is worth recalling Freud's (1917) distinction between mourning and melancholia (i.e., depression): "Mourning," he says, "is regularly the reaction to the loss of a loved person, or to the loss of some abstraction which has taken the place of one, such as one's country, liberty, an ideal, and so on . . . Although mourning involves grave departures from the normal attitude to life, it never occurs to us to regard it as a pathological condition . . . We rely on its being overcome after a certain lapse of time" (p.243). "Normally," he goes on, "respect for reality," that is, the reality of the loss, "gains the day. Nevertheless its orders cannot be obeyed at once. They are carried out bit by bit, at great expense of time and cathectic energy" (1917, p.244). So mourning, Freud thinks, can be protracted without being pathological.

One's original home is a lost, mourned "abstraction," although I argue with the notion that such abstractions are only substitutes for lost objects. That mourning is there as a lifelong longing at some level of consciousness in all of us. Freud himself knew this yearning. In a letter written at the end of his life, after he had to leave Vienna for London, he says: "The feeling of triumph at liberation is mingled too strongly with mourning, for one had still very much loved the prison from which one has been released" (letter to Max Eitingon, June 6, 1938, quoted in Gay, 1988, p.9).

Mourning for a time and place is in our dreams, in songs we sing to ourselves, lullabies we sing to our children, and in the foods we want to eat. If I were to obey my early training as an empiricist and develop a structured interview for assessing the strength of a subject's longing for home, I would include a section on foods of childhood. Do you remember what you loved to eat? Do you find yourself looking for it? When you find it, does it taste the same? Queens, New York, where I live, would be my testing ground for this research. There are innumerable small, authentic, ethnic restaurants each catering to its own seekers. One Polish place has simple wooden tables, food-stained menus, reasonable prices, and windows on the boulevard. It is always decorated simply for the season. Nice place, I've always thought, yet there's a sadness about it. The young waitresses, while efficient, seem depressed, distracted. The clientele are largely older, mittel-Europeans. They order goulash, potato pancakes, blintzes, pirogies, drink hot tea, talk quietly. A kind of mourner's club, a temple of mourning-for-home. I ask the waitress to recommend a Polish beer to go with my goulash. She lights up, smiles, and names one. "It's the best!" she says. The restaurant, in case you want to go there, is called, "Just Like Mother's."

Here's a story of mourning for home about to begin: 17-year-old Maria had been seeing me because she "couldn't get herself to school." This, it quickly became clear, was separation anxiety related to the impending death of her grandmother who had always been "like a mother." Maria broke off treatment—I think because the pressure to grow up and move on, of which therapy had become a part, felt too strong. She spent her time at home caring for, worrying about, her grandmother. I had not seen her for months when her grandmother died. Maria appeared to be doing well but came back to see me at her mother's and aunt's urging. She seemed genuinely to have some perspective on the loss. She acknowledged feeling sad but relieved that the long anxious period of her grandmother's illness was over. She sounded as if she was getting ready to get on with life. I asked what would happen to her grandmother's house which was run-down and in a marginal neighborhood. Maria had lived all her life with her divorced mother in the upstairs apartment. Her grandmother, and grandfather when he was alive, lived below. "Oh!" she said, "they're all talking about selling it. My mother and I would move." She began to cry. "First my grandfather, then my grandmother, then my house!"

Here's a case of what might be called mourning the lost ability to mourn: I've been working with Willy, a man in his 80s and a refugee in his childhood along with his mother, father, and younger brother from Hitler's Europe. Our exchange has focused largely on Willy's fraught relationship with his wife—herself a holocaust survivor—around their difficulties with each other, their children, and grandchildren. A year ago, his oldest daughter died. I had come back from vacation to his numbness and inexpressible grief. Her death had not been unexpected. She had advanced liver disease, the consequence of a life of promiscuity and drug-abuse. Of her death, he would say, with a shrug, "I lost my daughter many years ago." At the same time he would say, "There must be something wrong with me. I can't cry. I can't mourn . . . What's wrong with me?" Over the weeks that followed he would lapse into numb silence, then into repetitive questioning and fruitless self-examination. I sat with him, felt for him, tried to give him a way to think about himself in all the ways psychoanalytic clinicians do: how he might feel; how I might feel, what it all might mean: frustrated anger with his daughter compounding the sense of loss, the disappointment, his self-protective distancing from his own feelings . . . All to no avail. Then some months after the event, Willy was talking about his wife. He was remembering the early sweetness of married life, how much she had wanted a baby girl, a little "meidlele," he said in Yiddish. When the baby was born, "We had our little meidlele." His voice broke and he cried. There was nothing I needed to say. I offered him the box of tissues; I took one myself.

This breakthrough invites commentary from a range of perspectives, among them: the meaning of having long been the helpless, angry parent of a chronic substance abuser; the conflicted mixture of love, rage, and guilt engendered in the lifetime family romance (this was a child that Willy and his wife fought about passionately); the nature of adult onset trauma and its attendant numbness; the immigrant experience generally, sequelae of the holocaust in particular; the interpersonal context of the treatment. But my sense of what is most interesting here is the nature and power of early language. Stern (2003) tells us that words allow us to formulate unformulated experience. Words have resonances, connotations, extended meanings, associations. They connect us to and evoke differing self-states. Old words, like old songs, connect us to old self-states. In what language do we talk to ourselves at our most intimate, unguarded moments? In that session, Willy talked to himself in the language of home.

English, the language of our treatment, Willy learned late as his fourth language. His family came from Europe where as a boy he spoke the language of their country only outside the house. His family spent some years in Latin America where he spoke Spanish outside. Yiddish is his first language. It's the language he spoke with his wife when they met fifty years ago in New York when she was a recent immigrant. It was the language of the home they made together, the language of both his first and second family home.

Meidlele means "little girl," a term of endearment, evoking the fragility of the babe-in-arms, the need to care for her, to hold her, keep her warm, fed, and safe at whatever sacrifice. To say that *heimish* word made Willy into a young father and husband again, a father who lost his infant daughter—a daughter he was helpless to save. Now, in that self-state, it was that infant he could mourn. About that mourning he and I could talk, although (perhaps, alas!) in English.

I began with a story from classical antiquity, I'll end with one familiar and dear to psychoanalysts: Sophocles' version of the Oedipus myth. On the basis of prophecy, infant Oedipus is cast out of his home—a death sentence. He is rescued and given another home but leaves that one in dread of enacting the same prophecy. The story is familiar: his escape takes him through an episode of road rage in which unknowingly he kills his father, and to his apparently successful encounter with the Sphinx. He succeeds in making a new home, becomes its king, marries its queen (unknown to him, his own mother), and thrives. Alas Thebes, his new (old) home, is "polluted" by his unwitting patricide and incest. He doesn't want to see and finally can't bear to see what he has been made to do—by fate and the gods—and blinds himself. Again he is cast out, banished. In part two of Sophocles' trilogy, Oedipus is a blind old man wandering the world, led by his daughter Antigone. He is homeless. Raging against the brother-in-law and son who banished him, he has his revenge, refusing to help them defend Thebes, their home. The king of Athens offers him sanctuary but on "foreign soil," which he cannot accept. He dies and with the help of the gods is interred in a secret tomb in a sacred grove—his final home.

Freud (1900) insists Oedipus' "destiny moves us only because it might have been ours—because the oracle laid the same curse upon us before our birth as upon him. It is the fate of all of us, perhaps, to direct our first sexual impulse towards our mother and our first hatred and our first murderous wish against our father" (p.262). Hidden incestuous traps and murderous provocations are at the heart of the story and I agree Oedipus' struggle with what might be called the unconscious—with at once knowing and not knowing one's fate—is what moves us. I do, however, think Freud's interpretation, because it serves a foregone conclusion, is anachronistic in its emphasis on infantile sexual triangularity. Even an amateur reading of ancient history tells us that in Sophocles's lifetime, home—having, losing, longing for return—was a deep, abiding concern. Herodotus, Sophocles' contemporary, in his *Histories* (Strassler, 2007) makes it plain that in 5th century BCE Greece, Oedipus' treatment as an infant was not unusual: unwanted infants were regularly exposed and abandoned. Furthermore, banishment and exile were frequent outcomes for losers in personal and political struggles. For example, Hippias, the turncoat tyrant and son of the deposed ruling family of Athens, led the Persian army against his ancestral city. The night before the battle at Marathon he had a dream: "He was sleeping with his own mother. He interpreted this to mean that he would return to Athens, recover his rule, die as an old man there in his native land" (p.470). The interpretation falls strangely on post-Freudian ears—the manifest content is incest! The disguised wish is an exiled traitor's longing for home.Reading Herodotus makes it clear that the threat of loss of home was demographic in proportions: mass relocation was a common consequence for the vanquished in endless wars between city-states. Moreover, the Homeric epics, already three centuries old, recording a still more ancient story of nostalgia, were an important part of Sophocles' cultural patrimony.

Not incidentally, these stressed not rivalry but paternal love and filial loyalty, that is, the continuity of home, family, and tribe.

Sophocles' trilogy works on a theme of ever-present dread and archaic anxiety, but this is not of incestuous sexuality. It is of the loss of home. The context for all that happens in the play cycle is home: losing it, finding it, spoiling it, losing it forever, finding it only in death. Incest is a danger because it threatens the order and stability of the home; so too, murderous filial rivalry. For Sophocles, Oedipus' fate is homelessness. His Oedipus, it might be said, struggles with an Odysseus complex.

To conclude, while it is more algebraic to talk about longing for an object than to talk about the smell of our mother's kitchen, her tired smile, and her favorite rocking chair in the corner of our remembered living room, the reduction is seriously narrowing. Objects, that is to say the people there or remembered there, are surely at the center of the longing for home, but there is more to it.

The fantasy of home when we are separated from it—which it turns out that as adults we always are—offers an orienting comfort and expresses a chronic longing. This longing is deeply human and, in evolutionary terms, ancient. The story of Odysseus can be seen as expressive of an ever-present, nonpathological mourning for home—home as embodied in mother, but also father, family, house, place, and time in one's development, a neighborhood, culture, love life, religious sense, and state of mind reflecting belonging, safety, self-definition, comfort, and unquestioned acceptance.

Many of our most important psychoanalytic ideas—separation-individuation, attachment, object relations, applications such as the psychoanalytic understanding of immigration and cultural diversity, indeed the oedipus complex itself—would be deepened by an explicit broadening of our thinking to include the importance of longing for home. I've come to think of Odysseus—not Oedipus—as the figure from antiquity most representative of the universal psychological experience of our species.

Note

1 This paper grew out of much discussion with many colleagues including David Lichtenstein, Robert Prince, Batya Monder, and Nancy McWilliams. I'd particularly like to thank William Zinsser and Victoria Olsen for help in its preparation. First presented at the 2008 Joint International Conference on Loneliness and Yearnings in Vancouver, British Columbia, it was published in *Psychoanalytic Psychology*, 26(2):191–205 (copyright 2009 American Psychological Association, adapted with permission).

References

Akhtar, S. (1995). A third individuation: Immigration, identity, and the psychoanalytic process. *Journal of the American Psychoanalytic Association*, 43:1051–1084.

—— (1999). *Immigration and Identity: Turmoil, Treatment, and Transformation.* Northvale, NJ: Jason Aronson.

Bettleheim, B. (1975). *The Uses of Enchantment.* New York: Random House.

Boulanger, G. (2004). Lot's wife, Cary Grant, and the American Dream: Psychoanalysis with immigrants. *Contemp. Psychoanal.*, 40:353–372.

Coates, S. W. (2004). John Bowlby and Margaret S. Mahler: Their lives and theories. *J. Amer. Psychoanal. Assn.*, 52:571–601.

Fenichel, O. (1945). *The Psychoanalytic Theory of Neurosis.* New York: Norton.

Fodor, N. (1950). Varieties of nostalgia. *Psychoanalytic Review*, 37:25–38.

Freud, S. (1900). The interpretation of dreams. In J. Strachey (Ed. & Trans.), *The Standard Edition of the Complete Psychological Works of Sigmund Freud* (Vol. IV, pp.ix–627). London: Hogarth Press, 1900.

—— (1917). Mourning and melancholia. In J. Strachey (op. cit.), 14:237–258. London: Hogarth Press, 1917.

—— (1919). The uncanny. In J. Strachey (op. cit.), 17:217–256. London: Hogarth Press, 1919.

Gay, P. (1988). *Freud: A Life For Our Time.* New York: Doubleday.

Giamatti, A. B. (1998). *A Great and Glorious Game.* Chapel Hill: Algonquin Books.

Grinberg, L. & Grinberg, R. (1989). *Psychoanalytic Perspectives on Migration and Exile.* New Haven, CT: Yale University Press.

Kazin, A. (1951). *A Walker in the City.* New York: Grove Press.

Kohut, H. (1984). *How Does Analysis Cure?* Chicago: University of Chicago Press.

Sandler, J. (1960). The background of safety. *International Journal of Psycho-Analysis*, 41:352–356.

—— (1985). Towards a reconsideration of the psychoanalytic theory of motivation. *Bulletin of the Anna Freud Centre*, 8:223–244.

—— (2003). On attachment to internal objects. *Psychoanalytic Inquiry*, 23:12–26.

Seiden, M. (2008). Private correspondence.

Sterba, R. (1934). Homesickness and the mother's breast. *Psychiatric Quarterly*, 14:701–707.

Stern, D. (2003). *Unformulated Experience.* Hillsdale, NJ: Analytic Press.

Strassler, R. B. (2007). (Ed). *The Landmark Herodotus: The Histories.* New York: Pantheon.

Wade, N. (2006). *Before the Dawn: Recovering the Lost History of Our Ancestors.* New York: Penguin.

Werman D. S. (1977). Normal and pathological nostalgia. *Journal of the American Psychoanalytic Association*, 25:387–398.

Winnicott D. W. (1950 /1986). *Home Is Where We Start From.* New York: Norton.

Wolfe, T. (1934). *You Can't Go Home Again.* New York: Harper & Row.

Part IX

Expanding our theories to understand and treat loneliness and yearnings

Chapter 23

The threat of exile—and abandonment

Kenneth Eisold

Communities constantly threaten their members with exclusion and exile. Our language has an abundance of terms to suggest the complex variety of ways that the threat can be implemented: banishment, ostracism, shunning, deportation, expatriation, segregation, excommunication, repudiation, disenfranchisement, discharge, expulsion. Moreover, communities can cause individuals or sub-groupings to be disowned, spurned, ignored, disregarded, neglected, marginalized. Targets of such processes become refugees and expatriates, displaced persons and wanderers. At the extreme, they can become outlaws, refugees, nonpersons and pariahs. The final common pathway, the ultimate effect, is that the victims are isolated and alone. The threat to all, at the very least, includes the threat of aloneness and, inevitably, loneliness.

Usually we are oblivious to the subtle, but persistent, powerful pressures groups exert on us to conform. We detect it only in the signs of inner withdrawal when we find ourselves censoring our comments, skipping meetings, avoiding contentious topics, or sticking to issues where agreement is a foregone conclusion. We see the danger of not conforming in the examples of those who speak-up, stand out, and are punished.[1]

The history of psychoanalysis provides a number of striking examples of "deviants" or "dissidents" who have suffered that fate, providing cautionary warnings to those who remain behind. In focusing on such examples drawn from our own institutional history, I am not aiming to foster yet another critical commentary on the checkered legacy of psychoanalysis. Rather I want to bring home, through familiar examples, the pervasiveness and power of this force. My hope is to stimulate greater awareness of how the threats of isolation and alienation continue to affect our membership in all our communities, professional and otherwise, and constrain our ability to adapt by suppressing new and original ideas. Our own history has been dramatic in this respect, but the dynamics of such implicit threats pervade all communities.

The fear of isolation does not have to be explicit or conscious. It is enough that it lurks in the background, that it becomes an unconscious guidepost to the dangers we work constantly to avoid. We all have come to know the unconscious power of our patients' fears—fear of rage, humiliation, failure, etc.—fears that unconsciously direct them to avoid the risk of encountering the experiences that may produce such reactions. In a comparable way, we are all motivated to avoid the threats of isolation in the communities in which we live and work. This is part of the psychopathology of everyday life, the substrate of our social existence that both binds our communities and groups together, enabling them to be familiar, predictable, and known to us, but also, on the other hand, allowing them to constrain us unobtrusively and limit our freedom to think and act.

There is an additional side to this story. When our communities or organizations falter or fail, when they are no longer viable, they cease to provide the security we need or the comfort of belonging. In effect, they abandon us. In that case, we are threatened just as much with aloneness, but not only is the pathway different but the experience of the shrinking band of institutional survivors takes different forms.

If the story of the early years of psychoanalysis focuses so much on its dissidents or deviants, our more recent history is about the collapse of those very institutions that once promised so much support and professional advancement. I will review our early history from the perspective of the threats of exclusion it offered to many of its major figures, and then focus on the relatively little known story of John Bowlby's exile from the British Psychoanalytical Society. The story of Bowlby's relationship with psychoanalysis is particularly interesting as he is now generally thought of as a major figure whose work has done so much to enliven recent psychoanalytic thinking about early development. That success has tended to eclipse his earlier history of persecution by his psychoanalytic colleagues. At the end, I will review briefly what is happening today, how the decline of our institutes and professional organizations affects our professional relationships and haunts us with the specter of a different form of isolation. Both parts of the story tell us much about how institutions and organizations, offering the promise of belonging and meaning, threaten us with alienation and loneliness.

Psychoanalytic tradition

The history of psychoanalysis illustrates how the process of conformity that started out with ruthless expulsions, led by a small cadre of leaders, gradually evolved into a style of management that more subtly proscribed deviance throughout our institutions (Eisold, 1997). The infamous Secret Committee Freud set up at Ernest Jones' suggestion following Jung's "defection," ostensibly to ensure the movement was managed from behind the scenes by a loyal band of brothers, was short lived, but its legacy of scapegoating the sins of ambition and competition was amplified and repeated over the next 50 years. Its implicit pact became an integral part of analytic culture as psychoanalysis concentrated on fidelity to core Freudian concepts. After Freud's death in 1939, his followers continued to monitor and prohibit deviations. Virtually all new, original contributors to psychoanalytic theory were expelled, threatened with expulsion, or forced into public protestations about their fidelity to Freud's ideas. The guardians of his legacy subordinated their originality and aggressively checked that of their peers. They made Freud into a totemic figure.

Perhaps the saddest example of this process was the case of Wilhelm Reich. By all accounts a brilliant, charismatic figure, he made a number of significant contributions while a member, first of the Viennese Society and, after 1930, the Berlin Society, where he found a more congenial group of colleagues for his more radical social views. After the Nazis took power in 1933, fearful about the effect on the movement, the International Psycho-Analytic Association tried to ban political activity, with the effect that Reich was forced to resign. The fear he aroused in his psychoanalytic colleagues, engendered by his radical ideas and activities, led to his expulsion. Moreover, that expulsion had a lasting effect in purging psychoanalysis of virtually any form of political activism (Jacoby, 1983).

In England, Melanie Klein was threatened with expulsion from the British Society when she developed what has come to be known as Object Relations theory. Originally invited to England by Jones, who asked her to analyze his children, she was protected by him during the beginning years of her theoretical originality. When Freud and his daughter Anna settled in London in 1938, along with a number of their Viennese colleagues, she was more exposed to persecution. Only the prolonged and exhaustive series of "controversial discussions," as they have come to be known, eventually forced a compromise. She and her followers were able to maintain their standing in what became, in effect, a partitioned British Institute of Psychoanalysis.

Jacques Lacan, in France, was actually expelled for his deviations from orthodox technique, as a result of an investigation sponsored by the IPA. It was that departure from standard technique, apparently, that provoked his expulsion, but there is no question that the leadership of the IPA, influenced strongly by Anna Freud, acted in a somewhat arbitrary and authoritarian manner in this affair, having made up its mind that he had to go for his far reaching theoretical departures (Turkel, 1992).

In America, Karen Horney was also "expelled" from the New York Psychoanalytic Institute for deviating from Freud's ideas on feminine psychology, though she also provoked the ire of her colleagues by being generally irreverent of established orthodoxies. Actually, she resigned after the New York Institute faculty took the humiliating step of removing her faculty status as the result of her continuing deviations and increasing popularity with candidates. A similar action was taken against Sandor

Rado, who ten years earlier had been recruited from the Berlin Institute to set up the training program in New York. Rado was also incorrigible in straying from orthodox ideas, but he did not resign. Biding his time and gathering allies, he stayed on until, after the war, he was able successfully to set up the rival Columbia Center for Psychoanalysis in New York and gain equal recognition from the American Psychoanalytic Association.

Gathered around Horney was a loosely affiliated group that included Erich Fromm and Harry Stack Sullivan, both of whom emphasized the role of environmental forces in the development of psychological suffering though in quite different ways that led eventually to further schisms among them.

Erik Erikson, originally trained in Vienna, was dogged throughout his career by allegations that he was not sufficiently faithful or rigorous in his adherence to Freudian ideas. Anna Freud and others consistently expressed their misgiving about his work. His brilliant paper on one of Freud's key dreams, "The dream specimen of psychoanalysis," in which he argued for the importance of the manifest content in dreams, was pointedly rejected by *The International Journal of Psycho-Analysis*, but the following year Erikson felt he was offered the opportunity to "rehabilitate" himself by writing a book review. A well-known New York analyst, Abram Kardiner, himself known for his willingness to depart from orthodox theory, characterized him as "an adventurer—reckless, inconsistent, the right hand not knowing what the left is doing" (Friedman, 1999, p.354). The effect on him of these persistent suspicions was to render him circumspect and cautious, obscuring his differences with his mainstream colleagues as well as leading him to conceal the influence of Jung on his thinking about life-long development.

Heinz Kohut was similarly threatened by isolation from his colleagues as his work departed from key Freudian concepts. This is all the more remarkable as he had been an extremely prominent leader of the field, serving as President of the American Psychoanalytic Association and Vice-President of the IPA. His biographer, Charles Strozier, noted: "Not once after 1971 did Anna Freud mention his work, nor was Kohut again to write her about his ideas" (Strozier, 2001, p.269). Privately he became scornful of her, in turn, as well as other colleagues who began to distance themselves. "Kohut had to adjust to what can best be called a kind of psychoanalytic shunning by his orthodox older friends," added Strozier, "and once it was clear that leading figures in the field, especially in the East, had felt Kohut had gone much too far, the rest fell quickly in line" (p.271).

His second book, *The Restoration of the Self*, published six years later, made little attempt to cover over the departure from orthodoxy, with the consequence that he was more openly criticized. His old friend, Martin Stein of the New York Psychoanalytic Institute, reviewing it harshly for *The Journal of the American Psychoanalytic Association*, reached the devastating conclusion: "All that we know as psychoanalysis comes under fire" (Strozier, 2001, p.281).

These are prominent examples of figures who struggled visibly with the threat of exile. We know less about the many others who, seeing these examples, merely fell into line and trod the well-worn paths of their mentors and leaders.

The case of John Bowlby

The troubled history of John Bowlby's relationship with the British Psychoanalytic Society, less widely known, exemplifies these issues of orthodoxy and scapegoating. (I am indebted to Victoria Hamilton for her encouragement in taking on this subject but also for her help in providing many of the documents that recorded these events.) Fifteen years after his death, Bowlby is now beginning to have the impact on psychoanalysis he originally sought, but this is only as a result of having traveled a circuitous route, first exerting a profound influence on the world outside psychoanalysis, in particular on the realm of academic research focused on infant development and on the realm of public policy regarding the care of children and their relationship with their parents. Having established himself in those worlds, he could then be rediscovered by psychoanalysis.

Though his first experiences with the British Society were not promising, he persisted, characteristically self-possessed and determined. Working with a 3-year-old boy whose mother was hospitalized after suffering a mental breakdown, he attributed much of the child's difficulties to the loss of contact with his mother. Klein insisted, however, that such real-life events were irrelevant. All that mattered was the inner life of the child, his relationship with his internalized, fantasized maternal object. Bowlby was shocked by Klein's absolute certainty and intransigence (Holmes, 1993).

Persisting in developing his own line of thought, he gave his first paper before the British Society in 1939 on "The influence of the environment in the development of neuroses and neurotic character," a strong paper that gained his admission to full membership and was subsequently published in the *International Journal of Psycho-Analysis*. The paper, based on his work at the Child Guidance Clinic, engendered significant opposition from Klein's followers and some others as well.

As a forceful and obviously capable personality, it was difficult for opponents to argue against Bowlby's talents. Nonetheless, his determination to assert his convictions about the role of the environment not only elicited strong opposition but also caused apprehension among his supporters. Melitta Schmideberg, Melanie Klein's daughter and an analyst herself, though opposed to her mother's theories, urged Bowlby not to give the paper. She recalled that a few days before she "said to one of the Viennese . . . 'Next Wednesday you are going to get a sidelight on the

London Society. You probably cannot appreciate Bowlby's courage in taking the line he is going to take. You will see how he will be attacked and he must be defended'" (van Dijken, 1998, p.100).

It was not until 1952, when he came upon the ethological studies of Konrad Lorenz and Nikko Tinbergen, that Bowlby's ideas about the essential attachment bond fell into place, and he was able to integrate his observations about childhood separation into a comprehensive theory.

Bowlby's persistence in his convictions, no doubt, stemmed in large part from his personal courage. In the face of opposition, he was not easily intimidated. In addition, according to his son, he was somewhat naïve, never anticipating the antipathy and hostility his ideas aroused. Bowlby himself noted to Melanie Klein's biographer, Phyllis Grosskurth (1986), "I believed my ideas were compatible with theirs. Looking back on the years 1935–1939, I think I was reluctant to recognize the divergence" (p.402).

His persistence was abetted, no doubt, by the fact that, as an extremely capable administrator, he was called upon to play several key roles in the British Society. He had supporters who saw his abilities even though they may have taken issue with many of his convictions. Moreover, he continued to believe his work would only strengthen psychoanalysis, that it was ultimately consistent with Object Relations Theory. As a result, he was able to believe the resistance to his contributions would not last once others saw the opportunity to ground their theory in empirical observation.

A key reason Bowlby was able to maintain his independence and persist in the development of his ideas was his strong ties with institutions outside the British Psychoanalytic Society. Opportunities came, most notably an invitation by the World Health Organization to head a study of the mental health of homeless children. That 1951 report sold 450,000 copies in English alone, making him a world-known figure.

Bowlby's work was taking a distinctive theoretical turn under the influence of ethology. Bowlby (Bowlby, Filglio, & Young, 1986) noted that his papers referring to the work of Tinbergen and Lorenz were "all of them, critical papers for me—and they were not well received at all." He added that he presented a number of papers in America, as well, "in San Francisco, Los Angeles, and at least one East Coast Society, and basically people were 'agin' it" (p.53).

The opposition to Bowlby's work came to a head in 1960 when he was invited to publish a key paper in *The Psychoanalytic Study of the Child*. His paper, "Grief and mourning in infancy and early childhood," was his opportunity to present an overview of his new ideas on attachment and their relevance to psychoanalysis. In an unprecedented and never again duplicated procedure in the history of the journal, it appeared along with three strong critiques by Anna Freud, Max Schur, and Rene Spitz, indicating not only how important a figure he had become but also how dangerous he was seen to be. Bowlby was neither informed of this plan nor offered the opportunity to respond. The critiques made the point, according to Karen (1998), a prominent scholar of Attachment Theory, that "what was valid in his thinking was not new and what was new was not valid" (p.115).

Up until this point, only the opposition of the Kleinians to Bowlby's ideas had been fully predictable and outspoken, but the treatment of his article in *The Psychoanalytic Study of the Child* marked a clear turning point with the Freudians. Up until then his relationship with Anna Freud and her followers had been cordial if cool. He noted: "On all matters at a clinical, practical level, my personal position and Anna Freud's chimed— there was really very little difference between us. But when it came to theory things were different" (Karen, 1998, p.118).

The problem for the Freudians was how to proscribe his thought, warning potential followers away, without fully alienating Bowlby himself. According to one observer, Anna Freud "believed, 'Dr Bowlby is too valuable a person to get lost to psychoanalysis.'" Bowlby, however, did not miss the point of the attack. As he later said: "To say she cold-shouldered it, would be an understatement. She banned it" (Karen, 1998, p.113).

Proscribed by both the Kleinians and Freudians, Bowlby withdrew from the fight. He continued his research and writing, but stopped attending Society meetings. He also felt increasingly marginalized at the Tavistock Institute, as its orientation became increasingly Kleinian and his influence declined. As for his position in psychoanalysis at large, as Karen put it: "Unread, uncited, and unseen, he became the nonperson of psychoanalysis and was lost to his peers for the better part of the next 3 decades" (p.115).

Today some still believe that Bowlby was "against psychoanalysis." But the tide has turned, and there has been a significant convergence of research and clinical practice. "These ideas are absolutely acceptable, if not banal, today," wrote Arietta Slade (2000). "Indeed they seem typical of mainstream psychoanalytic beliefs, particularly those of the relational and self psychological schools" (p.1148).

The age of decline

Many of us would like to believe that the ostracisms and schisms I have described are manifestation of a psychoanalysis that is past, that we are in a new era of pluralism and tolerance. Much of the vicious, open fighting about theoretical issues is behind us, to be sure. Our politics have shifted.

We still do have vestiges of theoretical differences that define different communities. Relationalism has become a new orthodoxy in some quarters, with its own International Organization. Interpersonal theory struggles to distinguish itself and keep up. Modern Freudians and modern Kleinians carve out distinct territories for their members. But the differences and the rivalries, while important within those communities, are either less intense or have gone underground.

The major issue now facing our institutes and professional associations is survival: how is psychoanalysis to stay vital and alive in an era of significantly waning public support? More particularly, will any given institute or professional association find the recruits needed to keep it going? These questions, seldom framed so baldly within the field, can be detected in a host of different issues that reflect specific dilemmas faced within institutes and professional organizations, but the underlying issue is usually the same: survival.

There are essentially two basic positions it is possible to maintain: the "liberalizing" position that the field needs to expand to embrace training in psychotherapy and other forms of applied psychoanalysis, and the "conservative" view that psychoanalysis has to hold firm to its traditional boundaries and standards. The "conservatives" hold to the view that psychoanalysis is likely to continue to decline, but the important aim is to preserve its integrity and tradition as an elite enterprise. The "liberals" are willing to adapt and compromise traditional practices, viewing them as less important than maintaining certain core beliefs while expanding to serve other needs beyond the couch.

Understandably, many senior, established analysts tend to be "conservative." Relatively secure, they have less to lose and hold more entrenched convictions stemming from their lengthy careers. But the lines are not so clearly drawn, as there are other senior analysts who take more liberal positions. Similarly, more junior analysts are divided, often influenced by their ties and identifications with senior analysts with whom they trained— though increasingly many of them simply loosen their connections with their institutes and move into independent careers or form affiliations with other organizations, promising more opportunity.

The ways in which different particular issues surface make it extremely difficult to identify any one person or group as firmly belonging to one camp or the other. If pressed, most would affirm the need both to maintain standards and adapt. They shrink from the harsh, difficult choice, but I think it is not difficult to see that, when forced to face a specific issue, they end up reflecting one or the other underlying positions.

The specific issues are multifaceted and diverse. Torn about the harshness of the choice or unwilling to accept it, anxious about what seems at stake, many will shift positions, not infrequently delaying their choices as much as possible. Those who know where they stand tend to be adamant. The issues easily polarize the institutes or professional organizations in which they arise.

Let me give some examples. A recent new licensing law in New York establishes a license in psychoanalysis, enabling those with two years of graduate training in any field and psychoanalytic training with an "eligible" institute to become a "Licensed Psychoanalyst." Those seeking that license will generally not come from the established mental health disciplines of psychiatry, psychology, and social work, and they are to be distinguished from the psychoanalysts already being certified by established institutes who can continue to call themselves "Psychoanalysts." The law also established a new category of Mental Health Workers for those with a minimum of two years of graduate training. This poses choices for local institutes: are they going to seek to become eligible to train those aiming to become "Licensed Psychoanalysts" alongside the psychoanalysts they are currently certifying? Will they train Mental Health Workers as well (Appel, 2004)?

The underlying issues are complex. Both new licenses are part of an increasing stratification in the field, the creation of psychotherapists with shorter, less costly training, many of whom who will presumably go on to charge lower fees. This is particularly advantageous to insurance companies and clinics that want to provide service at reduced cost. The availability of service from less well-trained psychotherapists poses a threat to the status of traditional psychoanalysts. Originally, the addition of psychologists and social workers to the ranks of psychoanalysts was seen as endangering that status. Now the addition of others with less training is seen as amplifying that danger significantly. On the other hand, the training of a limited number of such candidates at well-established, reputable institutes will not only significantly increase the skills of those candidates, it will boost their status, enabling many of them to open private practices and charge higher fees. And, of course, it would strengthen institutes in search of candidates. Faced with this choice, what should institutes do?

"Liberals" will be more likely to see the opportunity and take the risk of admitting such candidates: here are new constituencies they could train, new recruits to their languishing programs. They will aim to be selective, to be sure, choosing only the most talented, though they may well have to provide additional training to compensate for deficiencies in their graduate preparations. "Conservatives," on the other hand, will be likely to reject the opportunity, continuing to train the more qualified candidates they already train and not bothering to alter or supplement their standard procedures. They will aim to preserve the elite reputation of their institutes, mindful that the institutes that go the other route will run the risk of being less attractive to some of the more qualified applicants who may not want to train with those who are not psychiatrists or psychologists.

Feelings about the issues can run very high because the underlying issue is survival. The problem will rarely be framed so clearly or starkly. For one thing, it is threatening to professional notions of integrity to appear to be compromising standards or making decisions based on economic factors. Professionals are supposed to be above such considerations. Moreover, there are issues of professional identity and personal interests that often preoccupy analysts. But the larger reason, I believe, is that the issue of survival is too threatening to face directly. The result is that only the limited issue at hand will be posed for discussion, and it will seem that everything rests on getting that narrow issue right.

Another specific issue that is grounded in the larger problem of survival is the conflict in the American Psychoanalytic Association between those who favor the "local option" for control of standards for certification as a Training Analyst versus those who favor the maintenance of national standards. That issue now defines different camps that have been battling each other vehemently for several years.

The issue is often posed as autocratic, centralized control versus self-determination and democracy. On the other side, it is cast as a dispute between those determined to maintain standards and those all too willing to compromise the standing of the profession. The underlying issue that animates the dispute, again, is survival. Can institutes expand and adapt or should they hold to their traditional mission?

Years ago, of course, those who submitted to the strict national procedures could anticipate being rewarded by ample referrals from senior colleagues and the prospect of promotion through the ranks. As those referrals have dried up and as service to institutes has become less rewarding or gratifying, fewer want to go that route. Many local institutes have come to feel that their future depends on attracting those candidates who no longer are willing to submit to arduous requirements that, today, have little to do with establishing a successful practice. As a result they are starting to think that the maintenance of strict national standards compromises their ability to recruit candidates.

These are only two of the many proliferating issues that stem from the struggle for survival. There are many others. Should institutes establish training programs for psychotherapy that stand on their own, that are not designed primarily to recruit candidates for their analytic programs? Should they accept Social Workers? Mental Health Workers? What about "lay analysts," those whose previous education and training was entirely outside the field of mental health? What about partnerships with other organizations in the community? What about offering courses or programs in some of the various forms of applied psychoanalysis? Should institutes offer specialized training for specific mental health disorders? Should an institute that occupies an attractive building that has appreciated in value move to a less expensive neighborhood?

Fights over such issues are often highly intense and wounding. Apart from the effect on those who win or lose, such battles do not make institutes more attractive to those who do not care strongly about the presenting issue, one way or the other. Some relish the fight, of course, and enjoy the camaraderie of warfare, but most faculty members drawn into such polarized issues are suffused with tension and anxiety. Many personal relationships among colleagues are irrevocably damaged. The net effect is that many if not most faculty members and students become alienated and that, in turn, further erodes the weakening capacity of institutes to provide a sense of security and support for their members. Ultimately, such disputes, in the service of survival undermine their capacity to carry on (Eisold, 2007).

This alienation is exacerbated because the institutes that trained us usually constitute the boundaries of our professional worlds. They are, by and large, autonomous, separate, and bounded off from each other. Very few of us transcend the limitation of those communities, becoming known outside our local precincts. Bowlby's case is a dramatic exception that proves the rule. So if we do not feel accepted and welcome in our local communities, and if we cannot find that elsewhere, we inevitably suffer a lingering, pervasive aloneness. And, of course, the disaffection of some adds to the loss experienced by others.

Our professional communities, pervaded with conflict and recrimination, fragment into warring camps that distract from the focus on learning and skill development that is the primary work of institutes—and its primary gratification. Perhaps the most damaging effect is to erode the communal bonds that provide the sense of belonging. Faculty members drift away. Meetings are ill attended. It becomes increasingly difficult to fill important positions, to get people to volunteer their time for committees. Graduates find other organizations to join, to devote their spare energies to helping organizations that will provide more recognition and pleasure in return. They join study groups or supervision groups that offer some of the stimulation and camaraderie once to be found in their institutes. Or they preoccupy themselves with their families and private lives.

Meanwhile, classes dwindle in size or cease to meet entirely. The hallways empty. The shrinking communities that once had the power to intimidate by excluding members fail to provide even rudimentary security.

If our institutes and professional associations could more directly face the underlying issue of survival, they would stand a chance not merely to survive but actually to thrive. There is real knowledge and skill in our communities that could be used to craft solutions to the dilemmas posed by dwindling public support. But that would require a frank exchange of ideas and a willingness to express new ideas and to tolerate differences beyond what our institutions have shown the ability to do in the past.

Note

1 The basic theoretical foundation of this way of thinking about groups is provided by Wilfred Bion's (1961) seminal book, *Experiences in Groups*.

References

Appel, P. (2004). The New York State psychoanalytic license: An historical perspective. In: A. Casement (Ed.), *Who Owns Psychoanalysis?* London: Karnac, pp.105–22.

Bion, W. (1961). *Experiences in Groups*. London: Tavistock Publications.

Bowlby, J., Figlio, J., & Young, R. (1986). An interview with John Bowlby on the origins and reception of his work. *Free Associations*, 6:36–64.

Eisold, K. (1997). Freud as leader: the early years of the Viennese Society. *The International Journal of Psycho-Analysis*, 78:87–104.

—— (2007). The erosion of our profession. *Psychoanalytic Psychology*, 24:1–9.

Friedman, L. J. (1999). *Identity's Architect: A Biography of Erik H. Erikson*. New York: Scribners.

Grosskurth, P. (1986). *Melanie Klein: Her Work and Her World*. Random House: New York.

Holmes, J. (1993). *John Bowlby and Attachment Theory*. London: Routledge.

Jacoby, R. (1983). *The Repression of Psychoanalysis*. Chicago: University of Chicago Press.

Karen, R. (1998). *Becoming Attached*. New York: Oxford.

Slade, A. (2000). The development and organization of attachment: implications for psychoanalysis. *Journal of the American Psychoanalytic Association*, 48(4):1147–1174.

Strozier, C. B. (2001). *Heinz Kohut: The Making of a Psychoanalyst*. New York: Farrar, Strauss and Giroux.

Turkel, S. (1992). *Psychoanalytic Politics: Jacques Lacan and Freud's French Revolution*, 2nd edition. London: Free Association Books.

van Dijken, S. (1998). *John Bowlby: His Early Life*. London: Free Association Books.

Chapter 24

Loneliness, longing, and limiting theoretical frameworks

Brent Willock[1]

If it weren't for you, I'd be all alone in my psychic space.
(Patient to analyst)

Being understood may be the most important function performed for us by our selfobjects, Bacal (1998) believed. This gratification is centrally important to the curative process: "No one comes for understanding unless they feel they have not been understood. As analysts, we are constantly confronted with a complex spectrum of varying degrees and kinds of frustrated need for understanding, sometimes of a traumatic order" (p.11).

The schools of thought we do (and do not) belong to have significant bearing on the extent to which our patients can feel understood. If our interpretive framework is not sufficiently comprehensive to encompass certain phenomena well, patients suffering such issues will not feel adequately understood. They may be so used to this state of affairs in life that they are not consciously troubled by its recurrence in treatment. They may, however, be dimly or acutely aware of feeling disconnected, lonely, less alive than they would like. Regardless of their degree of awareness, this matter holds enormous significance for the analysis and the depth of healing that can occur.

Areas of misfit between analyst/theory and analysand are as crucial to therapeutic progress as misunderstandings with parents were to earlier development. Whether based on implicit parental personality theories or more explicit psychoanalytic ones, failures in comprehension, with resultant disconnection, loneliness, and yearning, are central aspects of impasses in both child development and analysis.

Unarticulated loneliness at the heart of our literatures

Loneliness and longing have been underemphasized in psychoanalytic literature. Nonetheless, these twin concepts constitute core components of most of our key constructs. Their importance can be sensed in the relational tradition that began in sectors of Freud's theory, becoming ever clearer as our discipline evolved via such contributions as developmental ego psychology, British Object Relations Theory, Self Psychology, and Relational Psychoanalysis.

Consider the Freudian framework's centerpiece, the Oedipus complex. According to classical theory, traumatic experiences related to the primal scene confront children with a painful sense of exclusion, provoking diverse drive derivatives (sexual and aggressive fantasies, impulses, affects). Loneliness and yearning are undoubtedly prominent among these reactions. These relational states fester at the heart of Freud's universal, varied, infantile neurosis.

In his final instinct theory, Freud (1920) emphasized Eros. This drive works "to establish greater unities among living things" (1940, p.148). "The core of his being, his purpose" is "making one out of more than one" (1930, p.108). In our terms, Eros strives to relieve loneliness and satisfy longings by struggling against separation and alienation. Libido "coincides with the Eros of the poets and philosophers which holds all living things together" (1920, p.50). In contrast, the death drive seeks to "undo connections and so destroy things" (1940, p.148). Dis-integrating relationships, Thanatos produces isolation.

The death instinct arose when the first organism came into being (Freud, 1920). Lacking adequate protection against stimuli, Freud imagined that cell longing for its previous, safe, pain-free, inanimate state. While this speculative hypothesis is not widely accepted, it is interesting to consider in relation to Spitz's (1945, 1946) studies of infants who failed to thrive in institutional care. These babies were cared for physically, but not so well emotionally by busy nurses. Fed from propped up bottles rather than being held warmly and spoken to lovingly, many withered away. Their longing for death, their inability to continue fighting for life, was not so much due to overwhelming external stimulation but rather to lack of appropriate, loving stimuli. They died from loneliness.

Neglected children's painful plight was captured poignantly in *Nobody's Child*. In this song by Coben and Foree (sung by the Beatles and others), an orphan laments that he has no mammy's kisses, no daddy's smile, no arms to hold or soothe him when he cries. Feeling so lonesome, he wishes he could die. In such a *Heartbreak Hotel* (Axton & Durden, sung famously by Elvis): "I get so lonely I could die."

Freud's daughter, Anna (1958) noted that a normal aspect of adolescence, relinquishing parents or their internalized representations as libidinal objects, leads teenagers to feel lonely, unhappy, isolated. This "inner object loss" (Jacobson, 1961), crucial to Anna Freud's view of adolescence, was illustrated in an interview with comedian Sarah Silverman (2010). When her interlocutor mentioned, "You went through pretty severe depression as a teenager," Sarah replied: "I remember when it first happened. I came back from this camping trip, the one where I hid diapers in my sleeping bag, and it just washed over me like a cloud. It was like a cloud covering the sun. I remember the horror story I told myself over and over again: I'm totally alone in my body. Nobody will ever see through my eyes. I'm just completely alone." Asked if that was when she started therapy, Sarah responded: "Yeah. My therapist wrote me a prescription for Xanax and told me whenever I felt sad I should take one. I returned the following week and was in the waiting room. It was . . . the same place I had gone to see a hypnotist for bed-wetting . . . I was waiting and waiting . . . The hypnotist came down, and his eyes were all red and teary. And he was like . . . Dr. Riley hung himself." Sarah seemed to understand her new therapist's suicide in terms of hopeless loneliness and longing: "I remember he had braces. And I was thinking, Wow, he didn't even wait to get his braces off. Braces are a sign of hope . . . Braces mean that someday you're gonna have new teeth. Braces are a symbol that tomorrow will be better" (p.35). It might have helped for Dr. Riley to have had a more psychological grasp of loneliness.

Anna Freud's rival, Melanie Klein, emphasized infants organizing experience via splitting it into good and bad. When a mother does not meet her baby's needs, she is the "bad breast." Infants cannot long for the absent breast as the concept, "not present breast," does not exist. Babies live in the here and now, with either the good or bad breast. When the maturing infant comes to understand that good and bad mother are facets of the same person, s/he has entered Klein's Depressive Position. That label suggests sadness, loneliness, and related emotions.

Klein's framework helps us understand difficulties arising before one has matured sufficiently to tolerate loneliness and longing. Individuals unable to yearn for absent love objects are prone to feeling persecuted by sadistically depriving objects. In defense, they may omnipotently turn the tables, becoming terrifying attackers—a variation on Freud's (1920) notion of turning the death drive outward to survive. Alternatively, they may withdraw, perhaps making mother be the one to carry the feelings of being unloved and lonely.

Just as Freudians focused more on sex and aggression in the Oedipus complex, so Kleinians in their developmentally earlier timetable attended more to managing the death instinct than to the loneliness of the Depressive position. Nonetheless, one can see the importance of lonely yearning in all these core constructs.

Concurring with Klein on the importance of life's earliest months, Fairbairn emphasized exciting and rejecting objects. These tantalizing, needed abandoners stimulate profound anxiety, anger, and hopelessness. Struggling to control this predicament, infants internalize the bad object, replacing unbearable alienation with imaginary, sadomasochistic togetherness. Summarizing Fairbairn's contributions to understanding schizoid phenomena, Spezzano (1993) noted that "The schizoid personality is completely without hope for relief from loneliness . . . The schizoid ego is threatened with a feeling of loneliness that, at its extreme, approaches psychic lifelessness" (p.102).

Fairbairn's student/analysand, Guntrip (1969), discovered that schizoid patients, finding their internalized struggles so stressful, long to exit this supposedly safer domain. Having fractured their internal object (and self) into Fairbairn's exciting, rejecting, and ideal objects (with corresponding libidinal, antilibidinal, and central egos), they perform a further, final split. While parts of self continue trying to cope with external and inner reality, another ego chunk abandons all object relationships, external and internal. This "lost heart of the self" (p.87), buried snugly, or chillingly, in some internal womb, or tomb, contains "the lost capacity to love" (p.90). After this being goes into exile, a lonely, numb shadow of the self remains behind, endeavoring to contend with life's challenges. Rich, rewarding intimacy is not on that agenda.

Guntrip's other analyst, Winnicott (1963), described a strikingly similar state of affairs. His "incommunicado" self is an "isolate" (p.187), forever fearing being found, eternally longing to be located. This "true self" leaves behind a "false self" to carry on daily living.

Another British Middle-Schooler, Michael Balint (1968), emphasized infants' traumatic realization that objects are separate and can abandon them. This frightening fact is memorialized in many, perhaps all person-alities, as a "basic fault," a structural vulnerability to be struggled with, possibly forever. To avoid the terrifying aloneness experienced when dropped from the previous, seemingly secure, "primary harmonious inter-penetrating mixup" (p.66), infants may forge one of two personality styles (or combinations of these "ideal" types). "Ocnophiles" cling to their objects to avoid "horrid empty spaces" (Balint, 1955, p.225) between contacts. "Philobats" opt instead for independence, skillfully navigating the "friendly expanses" (p.225) between interactions with untrustworthy objects. These primal strategies reduce loneliness, yearning, and related anxieties.

The Middle School inspired empirical investigations by Bowlby and his followers. Their key query might be formulated as: In the face of separation and loss (including empathic failure), how do infants with diverse dis-positions form attachment styles enabling them to survive frightening, frustrating loneliness? Answers include dissociation, detachment, denial, narcissistic rage, avoidance, ambivalence, cognitive disorganization, and other maneuvers designed to dispel more profoundly troubling alienation.

Attachment theorists emphasize fear and safety as motivational variables. When too separate in space or time, infants seek security with primary attachment figures. If we are quintessentially social animals, as relational analysts stress, then loneliness must also be considered a powerful moti-vator. Like fear, loneliness prompts affiliative behaviors that have significant survival value.

When primary attachment figures feel unreliable, children develop "insecure" attachment patterns (avoidant, ambivalent, or disorganized). These compromise formations enshrine loneliness and longing as much as insecurity, fear, and anger.

Positing the breast as the template for future loves, Freud (1905) anticipated Klein and British Object Relations theorists' focus on oral origins of oedipal, and all other love. Pondering the possible relationship between the blissful state of the infant at the breast and later adult love, Freud (1905) opined that, "The finding of an object is in fact a refinding of it" (p.222).

Until they refind their object, weaned babies modulate loneliness by nurturing the primal search image they developed during Freud's oral stage. This imago may serve important functions for them well into their adult years. "I looked for you in everyone," Leonard Cohen sang (in *Coming Back to You*), until ultimately he realized he "was only coming back to you."

This brief survey suggests loneliness and yearning have been central concepts, if only implicitly, in most, if not all, schools of psychoanalysis. From Freud until now, no theorist has emphasized the "L word." It is, nonetheless, crucial to the problems concerning them. Their contributions take on added depth, humanity, and credibility when enriched via appreciation of the importance of loneliness in the human condition.

This overview of how various schools of psychoanalytic thought have, and have not, addressed the problem of loneliness points to the value of a comparative-integrative approach encouraging openness to the possibility that segregated psychoanalytic perspectives have more commonalities and complementarities than might sometimes be thought. While no single school sufficiently empowers analysts to comprehend and optimally reduce alienation with all patients, if one draws from a multifaceted framework, one greatly increases one's chances in these regards.

Disavowed emotions

Aligning early object relational ideas with contemporary relational perspectives, Stolorow and Atwood (1992) posited a dynamic unconscious consisting of "disavowed central affect states and repressed developmental longings, defensively walled off because they failed to evoke attuned responsiveness from the early surround" (p.273). Brandchaft (et al., 2010) similarly emphasized the importance of disavowed emotions. Contrasting his relational perspective with classical formulation, he stated that when addressing dissociative systems, analytic understanding "must eschew focus on repressed instinctual drive derivatives in favor of a search for affect states that have been dissociatively sequestered and that thus remain in their archaic form, unavailable for mentalizing and further dialogic processing" (p.228).

In focusing on such affects as depression, guilt, shame, rage, envy, and fear (of separation, annihilation, castration, loss of love, and so forth), psychoanalysis underestimated one frequently "disavowed central affect state," loneliness. This word rarely appears in indexes of psychoanalytic books (e.g., Freud's 23 volumes).

The extremely important concept of disavowed loneliness underlies what Bowlby (1977) referred to as "unexperienced yearning for love and care" (p.207). Unconscious loneliness can be an important part of the "unthought known" (Bollas, 1987), "unformulated experience" (Stern, 1997), and "implicit relational knowing" (Stern et al., 1998).

People talk to clinicians because of disturbing affective experiences, Spezzano (2001) noted. "Regulation of affective states has emerged . . . as a core concern in theorizing and interpreting by analysts of various persuasions" (p.551). In this increasing sensitivity to emotion and the challenges it presents, we must make more space for loneliness. The affect mantle can also help promote comparative-integrative dialogue, enabling "analysts of various persuasions" to learn more from each other than was hitherto possible.

Disowned affect states and repressed developmental longings are banished to some sort of limbo, evocatively defined by Webster's dictionary as "an abode of souls (as of unbaptized infants) barred from heaven through no fault of their own." Freud (1897) believed that myths are based on endopsychic states projected outwards. We might think of this process as one of double dissociation (an initial, internal dissociation or repression, followed by secondary dissociation via external projection). From this point of view, the limbo myth might derive from repressed yearnings for relational qualities insufficiently available in families of origin. Limboic wandering is as poignant a portrayal of loneliness as one could "hope for."

When mothers went sailing

When I attended school in Montreal, nonRoman-Catholics studied under the Protestant School Board. There, young Christians, Agnostics, Jews, and others launched each academic day with a hymn. Compared to the ensuing hours, this exercise felt more like the Village People singing/dancing about the good life at the Y ("Young man, there's no need to feel down . . .").

Whatever one thought of the religion in these morning melodies, many youngsters reveled in belting them out. One by William Hutchings was particularly popular: "When mothers of Salem/Their children brought to Jesus,/The stern disciples drove them back/And bade them to depart:/But Jesus saw them ere they fled,/And sweetly smiled, and kindly said,/'Suffer little children to come unto Me./For I will receive them, and fold them to my bosom.'"

In that hymn, the children trying to get to Him might embody thwarted developmental longings and loneliness. They need acceptance, love, and healing from this omnipotent parental figure because their parents could not provide those qualities sufficiently. In contrast, stern disciples represent unempathic parent figures. Not wanting His children wandering lonely as a crowd, He wishes them to taste heaven on earth. This Messianic encounter reflects longings to "evoke attuned responsiveness" whereupon "there's no need to feel down." Hymns, Village People, and YMCAs dispel loneliness. While youngsters may not know Salem from sailing, they grasp the gist of this hymn.

Jesus' therapeutic function might be likened by self psychologists to a selfobject transference "in which the analyst is established as a secondarily longed-for figure . . . whose availability and receptivity to the patient's experience can alleviate his painful states. A powerful countervailing structure is established to his experience of feeling doomed eternally to be alone or to surrender valuable aspects of himself if he is to avert this fate" (Brandchaft et al., 2010).

Besides its potent theme, an added bonus in Hutchings' hymn was the word "bosom"—in those days taboo. This attractive noun derives from Sanskrit, meaning "abundant—more at big" (Webster's). Kids perked up when this wonderful word-thing gained furlough from limbo. A momentary oasis emerged in the desert of middle childhood education. Regardless of theological persuasion, children embraced Klein's good breast. Refinding this fabulous object was always cause for celebration.

Webster's second definition of limbo, "a place or state of restraint or confinement," captures the dynamic nature of the unconscious where "repressed developmental longings" (aka impulses) yearn to break out, to be received and gratified. They must be restrained by counter-cathexes, incompatible dissociated self-states, unconscious organizing principles, or stern disciples. These orphaned selves long to come in from the cold, to find comfort in the bosom of a good selfobject ("in the arms of an angel," as Sarah McLaughlin phrased it in her popular song).

Webster's third definition of limbo, "a place or state of neglect or oblivion," conveys the abject loneliness associated with failure "to evoke attuned responsiveness from the early surround." The dictionary's fourth definition is "an intermediate or transitional place or state." This lonely locale lies between other, more familiar zones, such as earth, heaven, and hell. In limbo, things are never so bad they couldn't get worse. That's what Hades is for. In lonely limbo, one yearns for amelioration. That's what heaven is for.

Longings for better days embody the constant pressure for "the return of the repressed" (Freud, 1896, p.224). "Unconscious wishes are always active," Freud wrote. They are "indestructible. In the unconscious nothing can be brought to an end, nothing is past or forgotten" (1900, p.577). Disowned impulses are owned unconsciously. They long for relational realization.

"This defensive sequestering of central emotional states and developmental yearnings, which attempts to protect against retraumatization, is the principal source of resistance . . . and also of the necessity for disguise when such states and yearnings are represented in dreams" (Stolorow & Atwood, 1992, p.273). Whether disavowed and disguised or painfully endured, lonely longings constitute an underemphasized constellation of "central emotional states and developmental yearnings" underlying virtually all phenomena important to psychoanalysis (e.g., the dynamic unconscious, resistance, emotional trauma, empathic failure, compromise formation, and dream disguise).

Alienation

Once upon a time, mental health professionals (psychiatrists) were known as alienists. While that term strikes contemporary ears oddly, it has merit. The term derives from French, *aliéneé* (insane), from Latin *alienare* (to estrange). Our Gallic colleagues understood the close connection between estrangement (loneliness) and mental illness.

Citizens suffer from alienation in their histories, current lives, and, sometimes, their mental health treatments. Consequently, humanity readily resonates to the Messianic message, "Suffer little children to come unto me." The corollary that we are all God's children appealingly implies no one will be excluded from His loving embrace. Dismissive disciples shall be disarmed. The demon of loneliness will be vanquished. Alienation will be overcome. Perhaps someday, someone will once again dare hang a shingle bearing the evocative professional designation, Alienist.

If doctors of the soul belong to a profession composed of alienated schools of thought, our collective state may parallel our patients' predicament. The old cry, "Physician heal thyself," may be apposite. "Heal thine discipline," one might add. To optimally "minister to a mind diseased," as Shakespeare phrased it, we must fix fractures in our professional mindbody. If we can repair these cracks (chasms), we will have greater success reaching patients plagued by alienation from others past and present, from internal objects, and from themselves.

The rest of this chapter investigates our fragmented field, proposes a different way of organizing our enlightening, limiting frameworks, then presents a famous case illustrating these concerns.

The state of our disunion

At the level of abstract theorizing, there are many psychoanalyses whereas in clinical theory and practice, there is common ground (Wallerstein, 1988). "Adherents of whatever theoretical position within psychoanalysis all seem to do reasonably comparable clinical work and bring about reasonably comparable clinical change" (p.13). Is Wallerstein's reassuring message true? Many believe so. "Although different schools . . . are very different

... in their general theories, they all center on transference, resistance, and conflict in practice, and are therefore clinically equivalent" (Furer, Nersessian, & Perri, 1998, p.31). Whereas common ground implies overlap, clinical equivalence takes that idea much further, asserting there are no practical differences between clinical theories.

Others challenge this position. Rangell (1988) and Gedo (1984) feel differences exist as much in clinical as in general theory. Green (2000) bemoaned that, "We are practicing psychoanalysis with the use of maps that give . . . contrary directions" (p.447). Cooper (1985) proposed taking "the opportunity of this competition of theories to emphasize the differences in clinical work . . . Only by understanding our differences can we begin to test different treatment methods" (p.19). Underscoring diversity in technique and extolling integrative efforts, Pine (1998) felt this should only be attempted at the level of clinical theory. I believe this project should be pursued in both domains.

Those concerned with our field's fragmentation generally recommend comparative psychoanalysis. Going beyond that desideratum, I advocate a comparative-integrative approach. Partial perspectives can leave patients feeling disconnected, stranded, lonely, and frustrated, consciously or unconsciously, yearning for authentic engagement, empathy, and assistance.

Clinicians locked into models resemble the gentleman whose sole implement was a hammer. To this hapless soul, most conundra resembled nails and were treated accordingly. "A model is a tool, and one tool is no better than another, although in performing a specific task certain tools are more useful than others" (Gedo & Goldberg, 1973, p.9). Practitioners need a variety of implements to engage disavowed self-states longing to leave limbo. In the absence of more diverse armamentaria, analysts of all our alienated schools have some mix of successes and failures. They succeed or fail with different patients and anxiously resist research in this area (Balint, 1968).

"All models of the mind are of equal importance" (Gedo & Goldberg, 1973, p.9). However, being "applicable to different levels of hierarchy, they are not comparably useful in organizing the understanding of a given problem." Each framework influences what can be seen. If some sensibilities are not well represented in our model, then our patients may have no better chance of evoking our attuned responsiveness than they had in the past with parents and others. "What we focus on will have enormous influence on the unfolding of the psychoanalytic process" (Modell, 1987, p.233). Narrow models constrict focus. In contrast, a multifaceted, comparative-integrative framework expands one's perceptual/conceptual field, augmenting therapeutic possibilities.

Discussing contemporary London Kleinians, Schafer (1997a) strove to reopen clinicians' eyes and ears to the primitive world of object relational phantasy that "so many of our patients seem to require us to attend to and that doctrinaire ego psychological work so often encourages us to ignore" (p.429). Merely increasing from one- to two-dimensional theory significantly augments understanding and efficacy.

Latin American analysts attribute burgeoning analytic interest on their continent to receptivity to the "confrontation and clash of every psychoanalytic perspective" (Wallerstein, 1990, p.7). That enthusiastic discourse troubled Wallerstein. Debating theoretical perspectives may be "irresolvable, i.e., ultimately sterile" (p.7), he warned.

After debate, an adjudicative body may declare a winner. Wallerstein, like Schafer (1983), believed we are not sufficiently advanced to judge between the merits of different systems. From that point of view, debate is premature and pointless. From the comparative-integrative perspective, however, debate is the legitimate first phase in dialectical discourse. It must be followed by a stage in which Eros, the drive for unification, ascends, maximizing likelihood of creative outcome. Whatever synthesis is born from such dialogue constitutes a new thesis, evoking a fresh antithesis, and so on, in evolving progression.

Limitations of single-model thinking emerge in case presentations when favored frameworks may strike listeners as inadequate for elucidating complex material. Wallerstein and Weinshel (1989) believed each perspective is a "legitimate framework within which respected colleagues can organize the clinical encounters . . . and interact therapeutically" (p.358). Their stance has some validity, but excessively accepts fragmentation that is not ideal for patients. In contrast, Gedo (1991) asserted that, "The single most important factor impeding full exploration of the psyche is the rigid application of any preconceived conceptual schema" (p.100). In such treatments, patient and analyst talk "past each other" (Modell, 1987, p.234). Gedo, Modell, and other such investigators challenge the assumption that theoretical frameworks are relatively unimportant, that everyone does comparable work, with similar outcomes. Their stance questions whether all is well in our consulting rooms. Each perspective may not be as comprehensive, legitimate, and adequate as might be comforting to believe. The time when it was acceptable to restrict oneself to one paradigm may have passed.[2]

If we ignore insights from models other than the one we trained in, or prefer for other idiosyncratic reasons, we provide patients with an impoverished experience. Without a flexible, questioning, comparative-integrative attitude, the likelihood of engaging the full range of lonely, disaffected self-states and longings decreases. "Doctrinaire misapplication of any of the perfectly serviceable clinical theories at our disposal will bring actual exploration of the analysand's individuality to a halt" (Gedo, 1991, p.100). No perspective provides "a complete clinical and theoretical approach" (Schafer, 1997b, p.12). With a comparative-integrative outlook, one's free-floating attention can resonate with insights from diverse contributors, locales, and epochs.

Schools polemicize limited features of analytic life (Bollas, 1989). Consequently, "Each Freudian should also be a potential Kohutian, Kleinian, Winnicottian, Lacanian, and Bionian" (p.99). Each approach provides a different analytic object, facilitating a particular use of the analyst, Bollas believed. The true self's unfolding depends on provision of these objects. Pine (1998) echoed Bollas' ecumenicism: "I have not come across a patient to whom the full panoply of psychic mechanisms and technical approaches was not relevant. There is no patient who needs, for example, a unitary 'self-psychological' approach, or a unitary any other approach" (p.54).

Eclecticism sometimes receives poor press. Eissler (1965) condemned "the poison of eclecticism" (p.84). In contrast, Pulver (1993) noted that the eclectics comprised a respectable school of Greek philosophers. The comparative-integrative attitude welcomes that spirit and encourages discussions and even confrontations between schools, with an eye toward creating a more complex, multifaceted, useful, psychoanalytic object.

If a limited model impedes an analyst's capacity to tailor formulations and interventions to optimally fit a patient, the analysand may still gain something, but the particular gains that could be acquired through more accurate analytic comprehension and intervention do not seem possible. Consequently, the comparative-integrative perspective supports and challenges Wallerstein's idea that we all do comparable clinical work producing comparable changes.

Shortcomings in analytic comprehension may indicate countertransferential difficulties (Goldberg, 1987). Certain countertransferences may be common in particular orientations (Modell, 1987). It is well known, other than to adherents of a theory, Shane (1987) quipped, that: all Kleinians are crazy, full of rage; self psychologists cover fear of aggression with syrupy empathy; classical analysts mask fear of the primitive with rigid insistence on mature responsibility; developmentalists dignify the banalities of the nursery out of timid need to avoid oedipal passions. Lively derision between schools notwithstanding, antagonists agree on one thing, Shane noted. Their common ground is that mixed-model theorists are obsessively, phobicly, or stupidly incapable of commitment.

In contrast to this fear of embracing diversity, Bollas (1987) believed some theoretical differences occur because different groups address themselves to different transference dispositions, with corresponding countertransferences. "Most analysands live through all the transference positions" (p.241). A comparative-integrative model enables us to address them all.

A senior analyst's work was characterized by Modell as constricted by classical education. That learning could be nonexpansionary might sound surprising. This disquieting position is not just held by one disgruntled analyst. According to philosopher of science, Thomas Kuhn (1970), professionalization leads "to an immense restriction of the scientist's vision and to a considerable resistance to paradigm change" (p.64). Uniparadigmatic training promotes selective inattention, assimilating data to framework, rather than welcoming discrepancies to challenge, alter, or expand one's paradigm.

One would have little trouble finding work compromised by any model. Mistaking part of the truth for the whole is a problem to which partisans are prone. It can be unsettling for them to hear that, "No single theory is fully sufficient to order even one set of clinical observations" (Gedo & Goldberg, 1973, p.172).

In trying to understand the resistance some analysts have toward comparative-integrative, or even comparative psychoanalysis, it is worth considering that many analysts feel overwhelmed by the ever expanding professional discourse, and perhaps particularly by the challenges of pluralism. Publicly we may applaud it. Privately we may clap with one hand.

Protection against stimuli may be more important than reception, Freud (1920) stated. He postulated an inborn shield designed to preserve organismic integrity in the face of external impingement. A similar barrier may be necessary throughout life, insulating us from too many books, blogs, journals, conferences, and internet discussion groups. Paradigms function like shields, encircling us with familiar ideas and like-minded colleagues who agree on the irritating wrongness of others.

A little knowledge is dangerous. Single model training constitutes treacherously little knowledge. "We should not settle into any single, comfortable view . . . There is no room for orthodoxy" (Pine, 1998, p.7). Regrettably, many organizations have little space for heterodoxy.

Some analysts' familiarity with early development appears sketchy. While they may try to comprehend such phenomena in terms of regression from oedipal conflict, they demonstrate relatively little understanding of the domain of fixation in which their patients are caught. They may rely on nonanalytic, even anti-analytic models to explain the etiology, nature, and necessary treatment for disorders exceeding the narrow scope of their model.

Other analysts have a different problem: insufficient knowledge of phallic-oedipal complexities. Feeling Fairbairn focused excessively on dependency, Greenberg (1991) charged that he "collapsed the richness of the oedipal period . . . into a replay of . . . earliest infancy . . . an excellent example of what happens when an analyst is seduced by his theory" (p.70).

Reflecting on his oedipal-centered training, Schafer (1999) "realized how little room was left for . . . the study of the continuing force of early developmental stages in later life" (p.342). Since this lack seemed at odds with what his patients needed, he read Winnicott and the "taboo publications of the early Kleinians" (p.342). This alienist's analysands surely benefited from his violating training taboos.

All patients require the full range of analytically informed interventions, from pacification of primitive overexcitement to interpretation of oedipal conflicts (Gedo, 1981). Verbal interpretations work well at the oedipal level, but relationship is more important when working at the level of the basic fault (Balint, 1968). "It appalls me to think how much deep change I have prevented or delayed in patients *in a certain classification category* by my personal need to interpret" (Winnicott, 1971, p.86). The comparative-integrative sensibility increases our ability to understand and respond to the many conundra with which patients struggle, stumble, stagnate, and from which they may eventually emerge enlightened, less burdened, lonely, and alienated from themselves, internal objects, and others.

Exemplar

Considering Pine's opinion that no patient needs any unitary approach, what happens to analysands who receive them? Some quit. Others continue to an ungrand finale, often giving mixed or negative reviews of analysis. Some seek more analyses or alternative treatments. Many live with whatever they gained, knowledgeable, or oblivious of the shortcomings.

Jeffrey Rubin (1998) believed Winnicott's lifelong concerns with authenticity and relatedness arose from troubling experiences with a depressed mother and an absent, puritanical father, capped by lengthy experiences with analysts who, likewise, "failed to make contact with him at a deep psychological level" (p.82). Winnicott (1969) described ten years of analysis "at the hand of Strachey" (p.129) who "adhered to a classical technique in a cold-blooded way for which I have always been grateful" (Rodman, 1987, p.33). Given that startling language, it is not surprising to learn Winnicott also believed this treatment "did not help him as much as it should have done" (in Grolnick, 1990, p.54).

Seeking to remedy the shortcomings of that analysis, Winnicott asked Klein for treatment. She declined. In a five-year analysis with her follower, Joan Riviere, limitations of his first analysis were not absent. "Patients that go to 'Kleinian enthusiasts' for analysis are not really allowed to grow or to create in the analysis and I am not basing this on loose fantasy" (in Rodman, 1987, p.37), he complained. Riviere's "analysis failed me" (p.34).

Overly identified with a perspective, one tends to regard alternatives as lacking and dangerous. Far from holding theory lightly, a rigid, sometimes paranoid-schizoid flavor characterizes such tenacity. Klein believed Winnicott rejected her work because he resented her not analyzing him (Segal, 2001). She felt "his activities were quite a threat to analytic development in England" (p.404). Comparative-integrative analysis encourages a more productive attitude toward those holding different theories.

Winnicott felt his analysts failed to meet his spontaneous gestures in a way he needed to facilitate authenticity and aliveness. Instead, they participated in a reenactment of the False Self mode that characterized his childhood. In such treatments, the lonely, true self languishes in limbo.

Winnicott's analysts seemed stuck in countertransference. In letters to his wife, Strachey (Meisel & Kendrick, 1985) discussed irritations with Winnicott, including longings to terminate him mid-analysis. He shared details of Winnicott's sexual life in derogatory terms. Riviere told the British Psychological Society that Winnicott "just makes theory of his own sickness" (Kahr, 1996, p.62). She seemed to be a stern disciple.

Riviere's acerbic comment recalls *The Sickness Unto Death*, Kierkegaard's (1941) powerful portrayal of common, often unconscious malaise. Thoreau (1880) felt similarly that "A stereotyped but unconscious despair is concealed even under what are called the games and amusements of mankind" (p.4). Kierkegaard and Thoreau's thinking relates to loneliness and yearning. From a Christian existentialist perspective, Kierkegaard focused on estrangement from self and God, or God's plan for the self. He described ways we flee from our authentic selves. Apart from their religious colouring, his ideas mesh well with Winnicott's true versus false selves, contemporary Relational views on dissociation and multiplicity of self, and with Kohut's concept of the nuclear plan of the self. If Winnicott managed to generate theory out of "sickness" (despair), that feat may have provided a superbly creative antidote to loneliness and yearning unto death.

How does a theorist's private life become realized in theory (Spence, 2002)? "A specific moment of disorder and early sorrow, viewed from the inside, may so sensitize the theorist to certain aspects of the human condition that he or she sees connections that the rest of us never discover" (p.389). In Riviere's terms, this process would be just making theory out of one's own sickness. If we eliminated the word "just," we would have a more appreciative, admiring perspective of such sublimation.

A poem by Winnicott (Rodman, 2003, p.290) shows how deeply he participated in his mother's abject loneliness: "Mother below is weeping/ weeping/weeping/Thus I knew her/Once, stretched out on her lap/as now on a dead tree/I learned to make her smile/to stem her tears/to undo her guilt/ to cure her inward death/to enliven her was my living." Early in life, he acquired the basic materials to pursue a path of lonely despair or creativity unto death.

While one would hope that Winnicott (and anyone else) would have found the antidote to toxic elements in his upbringing in his analyses, the poignancy of those encounters suggests they were sometimes like ships passing, rather than minds meeting. Phillips' (1995) remark that "The risk of psychoanalytic theories, of psychoanalytic expertise, is that it won't even meet the patient half-way" (p.45) seems painfully apposite. Limited theory impedes alienists from becoming transformative objects.

Researching serial analyses, Stein (1991) noted that failed treatments were sometimes not due to deficiencies in the analyst's empathic/affective processes or personal dynamics but "resided in the theory, which soaked through cognitive, perceptual, and affective processes in the analyst" (p.329).

Areas of failure in Winnicott's analyses led him to make them his research focus. The need to discover and express the True Self (Stolorow & Atwood's repressed developmental longings) was at the heart of his oeuvre. Like an existentialist, he proclaimed "each individual is an isolate, permanently non-communicating, permanently unknown" (1963, p.187). Far from lamenting this limboic state, he believed it important that this "incommunicado element" not be found, declaring it would be catastrophic if communication seeped through defenses, violating the self's core. At other times, he claimed it would be disastrous if the hidden self were not located. Rubin's research rooted this conflict pertaining to aloneness/ loneliness in nonfacilitating aspects of Winnicott's childhood and analyses.

"Psycho-analytic research is perhaps always to some extent an attempt on the part of an analyst to carry the work of his own analysis further than the point to which his own analyst could get him" (Winnicott, 1949, p.70). Following a scientific meeting, Winnicott wrote to Klein: "What I was wanting on Friday undoubtedly was that there should be some move from your direction towards the gesture that I make in this paper. It is a creative gesture and I cannot make any relationship through the gesture except if someone came to meet it. I think that I was wanting something which I have no right to expect from your group, and it is really of the nature of a therapeutic act" (Rodman, 1987, p.34). What could not be provided on the Kleinian couch could not be obtained in the scientific forum either. These unrequited longings would have to be pursued elsewhere.

Visiting New York, Winnicott presented his work in the temple of ego psychologists. If he had been hoping for a less alienating, New World reception, that yearning was not gratified. Many believe that failure to "evoke attuned responsiveness" was a factor precipitating his heart attack.

Arguably, Winnicott's most important contribution was his theory of transitional phenomena that help us tolerate separation from mother. Blankies and teddy bears relieve many children's lonely days and nights. Another important Winnicottian (1958) idea concerned the capacity to be alone in the presence of another. This ability may be facilitated by transitional phenomena (for example, a child playing happily "by herself" with toys while mother is busy elsewhere in the room). When not buoying his lonely mother's spirits, Winnicott may have had many opportunities to be alone in her presence.

Kohut's research was similarly driven by a need to obtain what he could not find in his analysis. His *Two Analyses of Mr Z* (1979) is generally regarded as autobiographical, the second treatment being self-analysis. Longing to be understood, Kohut became his own selfobject, reaching out to a lonely self that had remained sequestered in prior allo-analysis.

Winnicott, Kohut, and many other major contributors to psychoanalysis exemplify Storr's (1988) contention that the creative individual constantly seeks to discover himself, to remodel his own identity, to find meaning. This endeavor constitutes "a valuable integrating process which, like meditation or prayer, has little to do with other people. His most significant moments are those in which he attains some new insight, or makes some new discovery, and those moments are chiefly, if not invariably, those in which he is alone" (xiv).

Forging a finer future

Serial analyses try to transcend limitations of unitary approaches, providing sequential lifelines to part-selves languishing in limbo. This strategy does not always succeed. Longings will more likely be met if shortcomings of "cold-blooded" classicists, "Kleinian enthusiasts," and other unitary practitioners are replaced by a more encompassing, comparative-integrative sensibility. Understanding that there are multiple perspectives, some more useful than others in particular circumstances, some not yet formulated, helps one avoid becoming, or remaining ensorcelled by one viewpoint, sure that those who disagree simply manufacture ideas out of malaise.

With multiple theoretical gloves, one has a better chance of catching spontaneous gestures. Wearing a comparative-integrative mitt, less of our patients' efforts to communicate and relate (or avoid these activities) whiz past our ears. The comparative-integrative framework promotes acquiring the range of hermeneutic and technical expertise needed to make more authentic, transmuting connections.

Working with four psychologies (drive, ego, object, and self), Pine (1990) transcended his ego psychological base and felt he worked much more effectively. Similarly, Gedo concluded (1979, 1984, 1991) that his outcomes exceeded those reported by others, not because he had superior clinical acumen, but due to his ecumenical model.

Valuable ideas and interventional modes are currently split off from what could be a more cohesive analytic core. Lodged in separate schools, these fragments need to be drawn together. While this prospect might seem daunting and unwieldy, it is parsimonious compared to the current, excessively fractured, embarrassing state of our discipline. The desideratum of authentic cohesion applies not only to the self, but also to the field. When alienated frameworks find a secure home in a transformed, comparative-integrative discipline, analysts will better comprehend patients' frustrated yearnings. Where loneliness and disconnection were, there understanding and assistance shall be.

Notes

1 Readers desiring more detailed exploration of these ideas can consult *Comparative-Integrative Psychoanalysis* (Willock, 2007). Connections between that volume's concepts and loneliness are discussed here for the first time.

2 In the psychoanalytic literature, the term "paradigm" is often used to refer to one of our models of the mind. Some believe that usage is inappropriate. They believe psychoanalysis has only one paradigm. Spezzano (1998) published an article attempting to clarify this matter. He noted that when Kuhn (1970) returned to the topic of paradigms in the postscript to the second edition of his classic text, he acknowledged that with regard to the issue of "what they can possibly be," his "original text leaves no more obscure or important question" (p.181). Kuhn then discussed three levels of paradigm. Spezzano concluded that psychoanalysis lacks a paradigm (or even competing paradigms) at the level of technique, where clinical problems are solved, though he felt a "soft" use of the term *paradigm* is applicable in discussions of models of mind or theories of development and in discussions of general principles for the conduct of analyses.

References

Bacal, H. A. (1998). Optimal responsiveness and the therapeutic process. In H. Bacal (Ed.), *Optimal Responsiveness: How Therapists Heal Their Patients*. Northvale, NJ: Jason Aronson.

Balint, M. (1955). Friendly expanses—horrid empty spaces. *International Journal of Psycho-Analysis*, 36:225–241.

—— (1968). *The Basic Fault: Therapeutic Aspects of Regression*. London: Tavistock.

Bollas, C. (1987). *The Shadow of the Object: Psychoanalysis of the Unthought Known*. New York: Columbia University Press.

—— (1989). *Forces of Destiny: Psychoanalysis and the Human Idiom*. London: Free Association Books.

Bowlby, J. (1977). The making and breaking of affectional bonds: aetiology and psychopathology in the light of attachment theory. *British Journal of Psychiatry*, 130:201–210.

Brandchaft, B., Doctors, S., & Sorter, D. (2010). *Toward an Emancipatory Psychoanalysis: Brandchaft's Intersubjective Vision*. New York: Routledge.

Cooper, A. (1985). A historical review of psychoanalytic paradigms. In A. Rothstein (Ed.), *Models of the Mind: Their Relationships to Clinical Work*, pp.5–20. New York: International Universities Press.

Eissler, K. R. (1965). *Medical Orthodoxy and the Future of Psychoanalysis*. New York: International Universities Press.

Freud, A. (1958). Adolescence. *Psychoanalytic Study of the Child*, XIII:255–278.

Freud, S. (1896). Extracts from the Fleiss papers. *S.E.*, 1:175–280.

—— (1897). Letter to Fliess (December 12). In *The Origins of Psychoanalysis*. New York: Basic Books, 1954, p.237.

—— (1900). The interpretation of dreams. *S.E.*, 4/5.

—— (1905). Three essays on the theory of sexuality. *S.E.*, 7:125–248. London: Hogarth, 1953.

—— (1920). Beyond the pleasure principle. *S.E.*, 18:1–66. London: Hogarth, 1955.

—— (1930). Civilization and its discontents. *S.E.*, 21:57–157. London: Hogarth Press, 1961.

—— (1940). An outline of psycho-analysis. *S.E.*, 23:139–207. London: Hogarth, 1964.

Furer, M., Nersessian, E. & Perri, C. (1998). *Controversies in Contemporary Psychoanalysis*. Madison, CT: International Universities Press.

Gedo, J. (1979). A psychoanalyst reports at mid-career. *American Journal of Psychiatry*, 136:646–649.

—— (1981). *Advances in Clinical Psychoanalysis*. New York: International Universities Press.

—— (1984). *Psychoanalysis and its Discontents*. New York: Guilford.

—— (1991). *The Biology of Clinical Encounters*. Hillsdale, NJ: Analytic Press.

—— & Goldberg, A. (1973). *Models of the Mind: A Psychoanalytic Theory*. Chicago & London: University of Chicago Press.

Goldberg, A. (1987). A self psychological perspective. *Psychoanalytic Inquiry*, 7:181–188.

Green, A. (2000). The central phobic position: a new formulation of the free association method. *International Journal of Psycho-Analysis*, 81:419–451.

Greenberg, J. (1991). *Oedipus and Beyond: A Clinical Theory*. Cambridge, MA: Harvard University Press.

Grolnick, S. (1990). *The Work and Play of Winnicott*. Northvale, NJ: Jason Aronson.

Guntrip, H. (1969). *Schizoid Phenomena, Object Relations and the Self*. New York: International Universities Press.

Jacobson, E. (1961). Adolescent moods and the remodeling of psychic structures in adolescence. *Psychoanal. St. Child*, 16:164–183.

Kahr, B. (1996). *D. W. Winnicott: A Biographical Portrait*. Madison, CT: International Universities Press.

Kierkegaard, S. (1941). *The Sickness Unto Death*. Translated with an introduction by Walter Lowrie. Princeton: Princeton University Press.

Kohut, H. (1979). The two analyses of Mr Z. *International Journal of Psycho-Analysis*, 60:3–27.

Kuhn, T. S. (1970). *The Structure of Scientific Revolutions*, 2nd Edition. Chicago: University of Chicago Press.

Meisel, P. & Kendrick, W. (1985). *Bloomsbury/Freud: The Letters of James and Alix Strachey, 1924–1925*. New York: Basic Books.

Modell, A. H. (1987). How theory shapes technique: An object relations perspective. *Psychoanalytic Inquiry*, 7:233–240.

Phillips, A. (1995). *Terrors and Experts*. London: Faber & Faber.

Pine, F. (1990). *Drive, Ego, Object, and Self: A Synthesis for Clinical Work*. New York: Basic Books.

—— (1998). *Diversity and Direction in Psychoanalytic Technique*. New Haven & London: Yale University Press.

Pulver, S. (1993). The eclectic analyst. *Journal of the American Psychoanalytic Association*, 41:339–358.

Rangell, L. (1988). The future of psychoanalysis: The scientific crossroads. *Psychoanalytic Quarterly*, 57:313–340.

Rodman, F. R. (Ed.) (1987). *The Spontaneous Gesture. Selected Letters of D. W. Winnicott*. Cambridge, MA: Harvard U. Press.

—— (2003). *Winnicott: Life and Work*. Cambridge, MA: Perseus Publishing.

Rubin, J. B. (1998). *A Psychoanalysis for Our Time*. New York: New York University Press.

Schafer, R. (1983). *The Analytic Attitude*. London: Hogarth.
—— (1997a). *The Contemporary Kleinians of London*. Madison, CT: International Universities Press.
—— (1997b). *Tradition and Change in Psychoanalysis*. Madison, CT: International Universities Press.
—— (1999). Recentering psychoanalysis: from Heinz Hartmann to British Kleinians. *Psychoanalytic Psychology*, 16:339–354.
Segal, H. (2001). Review of Kristeva, "La Genie Feminine," v. ii. *International Journal of Psycho-Analysis*, 82:401–405.
Shane, E. (1987). Varieties of psychoanalytic experience. *Psychoanalytic Inquiry*, 7:277–288.
Silverman, S. (2010). Interview with Eric Spitznagel. *Playboy*, v.57, #3, pp.33–38, 104.
Spence, D. P. (2002). Freud: Darkness in the Midst of Vision: Louis Breger, New York: Wiley. *Psychoanal. Psychol.*, 19:389–392.
Spezzano, C. (1998). The triangle of clinical judgment. *Journal of the American Psychoanalytic Association*, 46:365–388.
—— (1993). *Affect in Psychoanalysis: A Clinical Synthesis*. Hillsdale, NJ: The Analytic Press.
Spitz, R. (1945). Hospitalism. *The Psychoanalytic Study of the Child*, pp.53–74.
—— (1946). Hospitalism: A follow-up report. *The Psychoanalytic Study of the Child*, pp.113–117.
Stein, S. (1991). The influence of theory on psychoanalyst's countertransference. *International Journal of Psycho-Analysis*, 72:325–334.
Stern, D. B. (1997). *Unformulated Experience: From Dissociation to Imagination in Psychoanalysis*. Hillsdale, NJ: Analytic Press.
Stern, D. N., Sander, L. N., Nakum, J. P., Harrison, A. M., Lyons-Ruth, K., & Morgan, A. C. (1998). Non-interpretive mechanisms in psychoanalytic psychotherapy. *International Journal of Psycho-Analysis*, 79:903–922.
Stolorow, R. D. & Atwood, G. E. (1992). Dreams and the subjective world. In M. R. Lansky, *Essential Papers on Dreams*. New York: New York University Press.
Storr, A. (1988). *Solitude: A Return to the Self*. New York: Basic Books.
Thoreau, H. D. (1880). *Walden*. Boston: Houghton, Osgood.
Wallerstein, R. S. (1988). One psychoanalysis or many? *International Journal of Psycho-Analysis*, 69:5–21.
—— (1990). Psychoanalysis: The common ground. *International Journal of Psycho-Analysis*, 71:3–20.
—— & Weinshel, E. M. (1989). The future of psychoanalysis. *The Psychoanalytic Quarterly*, 58:341–373.
Willock, B. (2007). *Comparative-Integrative Psychoanalysis*. New York: The Analytic Press.
Winnicott, D. W. (1949). Hate in the counter-transference. *International Journal of Psycho-Analysis*, 30:69–74.
—— (1958). The capacity to be alone. *International Journal of Psycho-Analysis*, 39:416–420.
—— (1963). Communicating and not communicating leading to a study of certain opposites. In *The Maturational Process and the Facilitating Environment*. London: Hogarth, 1972, pp.179–192.

—— (1969). The use of an object. *International Journal of Psycho-Analysis*, 50:11–716.
—— (1971). *Playing and Reality*. London: Tavistock.

Part X

Reflections

Chapter 25

Looking back on loneliness and longing

Rebecca Coleman Curtis

It is not surprising that relational, and in particular, interpersonal, psycho-analysts have focused on the problem of loneliness. Whereas depression has long been a central problem recognized by many analysts, loneliness is, by definition, an interpersonal problem. Classical psychoanalysis and Kleinian object relations theory were intrapsychic in nature and failed to address adequately this topic. In Freud's culture, people were embedded in families and communities to a greater extent than people today are in North America, and increasingly, in many parts of the world. It is not so surprising that they neglected the obvious impact of loneliness when their patients presented with other problems, although, as Frie noted, existential philosophers themselves, in Europe at that time, were acutely aware of the experience of loneliness.

The mobility away from communities of origin, along with competitive, individualist values, has led depression from emotional isolation to be the primary presenting problem of patients in North America while problems of embeddedness are often still the problems in Asian cultures (Roland, 1988). One in four people in the U.S. say they have no one at all with whom to talk openly and intimately (McPherson et al., 2006). Relationships, along with experiences, are what contribute most to happiness (Gilbert, 2006). Social isolation has an impact on physical health comparable to that of lack of exercise, obesity, smoking, or high blood pressure (House et al., 1988). Fromm-Reichmann (1959), following Sullivan's (1953) focus on the inter-personal, was aware of how crucial the issue of loneliness was and pointed out its importance for understanding mental disorders, as Buechler commented in her chapter.

The treatment of loneliness overlaps considerably with the treatment of depression. With higher functioning individuals, suggestions of ways to increase social contacts and intimacy may suffice, as might be done in cognitive behavioral therapies. Psychoanalysts view real relationships as the solution, not just telephone or internet relationships, as can be seen in the chapters by Barbara Eisold and Lombardi. My own experience has shown that with patients who have a good history of relationships, the suggestion of increasing them is taken seriously and acted on. For example, a divorced woman over 65, who has been in psychoanalysis for many years, repeats frequently how helpful it was that I suggested increasing social contacts as her closest friend was dying, thus avoiding some of the loneliness discussed by Lavender and Cresci. Even a more severely disturbed patient who had been in psychoanalysis for 11 years and cognitive therapy for many years prior to coming to treatment with me stated that the most helpful thing anyone ever said to him was to make friends. When he made a friend, however, he thought that his taking time to go to the friend's house for dinner was equivalent to the friend shopping, paying for, and preparing the dinner. He did not understand when the friend eventually expected him to reciprocate. Nor did he understand why his sister was upset when he arrived at her home the night before Thanksgiving and left dirty dishes in the sink late at night, brought nothing for the meal, and failed to help in preparations or clean-up. In this case, a personality disorder made the loneliness more difficult to treat—a topic I'll return to shortly.

Interpersonal Psychotherapy for Depression (Klerman et al., 1984), derived from the ideas of Sullivan, focuses on increasing social relations in a 15-session treatment. It has been found to be effective with depressed patients who do not also have personality disorders. Unfortunately, for many people, like my difficult patient described above, being told to increase social relationships is not sufficient. Nor is the solace sufficient that can be found in literature as discussed in the chapter by Weisser, creativity in the chapter by Richards and Spira, God or religion in the chapters by Sloane and Classen, nor nature as described by Allured. The people considered in these chapters all had intimate relations with others. With patients who have ingrained problems of avoidance and intimacy, such as those described by Simha-Alpern, Hartman, Taylor, and Sapountzis, a longer treatment is required—one that involves a basic change in views of self and others and in behaviors as well. This is where psychoanalysis becomes the treatment of choice. In a long-term intimate relationship with an analyst, a person will gain confidence that he or she is likable and lovable and that others will not be hurtful or abandoning. Although other long-term therapies may be helpful, research evidence shows that psychodynamic treatment changes views of self and others and changes insecure styles of attachment toward greater feelings of security (Blatt et al., 2008; Fonagy, 2001; Levy et al., 2006).

The greatest difficulty in overcoming loneliness comes with people who suffer from what I'll call pathological narcissism. I'm not just referring to narcissists but to all very disturbed people, regardless of diagnosis. I'll mention three such patients, all depressed. Grandiosity in all of them prevented relationships—they did not want to be with anyone who might want to be with them. One was quite attractive and worked in the arts. She and her sisters had referred to each other by movie-stars' names. Her standards for being thin and dressing fashionably (on her low income) prevented her from going to social occasions to which she might be invited. She wanted to be a painter, but had nothing to paint and no interest in painting in her free time. Another, overweight at age 50, but considering herself to be pretty, was only interested in good-looking men under 40. Not having graduated from high school herself, she wanted to date a doctor or lawyer. Yet another patient never found men to be as humorous as her sister and father. She told me that I did not understand. She did not want to be around other people. She wanted to be happy alone pursuing a creative activity.

The pathological narcissism that presents serious problems for interpersonal relations is characterized by a sense of entitlement, grandiose fantasies, and a vulnerability reflected in a sense of self-esteem contingent on success, hiding the self, and devaluing others. Often, controllingness is also present. For example, the woman who insisted on a good-looking younger man or none at all joined an online dating service. When someone possibly meeting her criteria expressed interest, she told him the day, hour, and place where she could meet him for coffee, without saying that she could consider alternatives if this did not work for him. Frequently, such disturbed persons show up late for social engagements, leaving others waiting for them. They may even fail to show up without phoning first. Answering machines are left on and phone calls often not returned. The shame underneath and the sense of helplessness is so great that the person fails to make an effort, expecting the relationship not to work out. Such people feel criticized by comments that others do not take offense at and may make angry comments themselves, leaving others avoiding them forever. A longer case history of such a patient is provided by Hirsch (Curtis & Hirsch, 2011). If such grandiose patients do not devalue the therapist too much and can be kept in treatment, they can be helped. The psychoanalysts in this volume are engaged in this difficult enterprise.

Several of the analysts have described their own struggles dealing with loneliness. Kaufmann experienced not only loneliness after the suicide of her mother, but within the analytic community out of fear of discussing a taboo subject. Sloane and Buechler experienced loneliness after their patients' death and felt some solace in either speaking to a relative or attending the funeral. Herzog was devastated by the loss of his wife and felt some relief in telling his patients. Kenneth Eisold has demonstrated how analytic communities oust members who do not conform, often to unspoken norms, suggesting that analysts themselves may feel lonely within their own institutes, if their ideas are too different. Norman Cousins (1981) stated, "The eternal quest of the individual human being is to shatter his loneliness" (p.72). This sentence sums up why most people come to psychotherapy and why these authors have addressed this topic.

References

Blatt, S. J., Auerbach, J. S. & Behrends, R. S. (2008). Change in the representations of self and significant others in the treatment process: Links between representation, internalization, and mentalization. In E. L. Jurist, A. Slade, & S. Bergner (Eds.), *Mind to Mind: Infant Research, Neuroscience, and Psychoanalysis* (pp.225–263). New York: Other Press.

Cousins, N. (1981). *The Human Option: An Autobiographical Notebook*. New York: Norton.

Curtis, R. C. & Hirsch, I. (2011). Relational psychoanalytic approaches to psychotherapy. In S. B. Messer & A. S. Gurman (Eds.), *Essential Psychotherapies*, 3rd edn. (pp.72–104). New York: Guilford.

Fonagy, P. (2001). *Attachment Theory and Psychoanalysis*. New York: Other Press.

Fromm-Reichmann, F. (1959). Loneliness. *Psychiatry*, 22:1–15.

House, J. S., Landis, K. R. & Umberson, D. (1988). Social relationship and health. *Science*, 241:540–545.

Klerman, G. L., Weissman, M. M., Rounsaville, B. J. & Chevron, E. S. (1984). *Interpersonal Psychotherapy for Depression*. New York: Basic Books.

Levy, K. N., Meehan, K. B., Kelly, K. M., Reynoso, J. S., Weber, M., Clarkin, J. F. & Kernberg, O. F. (2006). Change in attachment patterns and reflective function in a randomized control trial of transference-focused psychotherapy for borderline personality disorder. *Journal of Consulting and Clinical Psychology*, 74:1027–1040.

McPherson, M., Smith-Lovin, L. & Bashears, M. T. (2006). Social isolation in America: Changes in core discussion networks over two decades. *American Sociological Review*, 71:353–375.

Roland, A. (1988). *In Search of Self in India and Japan*. Princeton: Princeton University Press.

Sullivan, H. S. (1953). *The Interpersonal Theory of Psychiatry*. New York: Norton.

Chapter 26

Loneliness and longing: Crucial aspects of the human experience

Brent Willock

> There is one word—let me impress upon you—which you must inscribe upon your banner, and that word is *loneliness*.
>
> (Henry James, cited in Swan, 1952)

The groundbreaking recording, *Sergeant Pepper's Lonely Hearts Club Band*, can be heard as an ode to loneliness. McCartney and Lennon presented their bleak vision of Eleanor Rigby gathering rice in a church after a wedding. She "lives in a dream" that shelters her from the agony of isolation. Waiting at her window, "wearing the face that she keeps in a jar by the door," no one arrives. (Her plight is reminiscent of Freud's patient who, stood up at the altar, lived thereafter altered.) Even at Eleanor's funeral, "Nobody came." Her life reflected Thoreau's (1886) belief that, "The mass of men lead lives of quiet desperation" (p.6).

Contemplating all the lonely people, the Beatles asked plaintively, "Where do they all come from?" Thanks to our authors, we now know the answer. They come from us, from the human condition. The band's other question was: "Where do they all belong?" Now we know that answer, too. They, which is to say we, belong in compassionate, meaningful (external and internal) relationships.

Eleanor's pastor penned a sermon that no one would hear for "no one comes near." At night, he darned his socks when nobody was around. "What does he care?" the Beatles queried. We can now answer that question, too. No doubt he cared so much, was so lonely, that he had to bury those aches under a noncaring facade, the way he dismissed dirt from his hands when leaving Eleanor's lonely gravesite.

After Ms. Rigby's interment, we learn, "No one was saved." That is, everyone suffers from isolation. If the Lonely Hearts Club band were to reunite, they could sing, "We are the world" (Jackson & Ritchie, 1985).

In another track from the same album, *She's Leaving Home*, separation occurs after living "alone" for so many years. One can be painfully lonely living with others, e.g., parents. ("Even between the closest human beings infinite distances continue to exist" [Rilke, 1969, p.57].) The Beatles say this young woman sought fun. Also, or perhaps more so, she may have been endeavoring to escape loneliness. Our authors suggest it is best to do so by knowing this beast better, working through, rather than around, this difficult affect and the relational configurations pertaining to it.

Far from turning people off with its dysphoria, this idiosyncratic album enlivened multitudes—a wish rendered explicit in Lennon's crooning, no doubt from a place of loneliness, "I'd love to turn you on." Like the Beatles, our authors help us understand that loneliness can be a stimulating, rewarding topic.

Bloody lonely

While treating Emma, Freud associated with Fliess, a physician whose odd theories linked hysteria and the nose. Freud had Fliess remove Emma's turbinate bone. She did not heal well, experiencing persistent swelling, pain, purulent secretion, and, finally, massive hemorrhage. Fliess had accidentally left a half-meter of gauze in Emma's nasal cavity. The following month, she suffered three more hemorrhages.

A year later, Freud offered a psychological explanation for Emma's persistent bleeding. It was hysterical, "occasioned by *longing*" for Freud (1985, pp.116). Emma had always been a bleeder. As a child, she suffered severe nosebleeds. At 15, she suddenly bled from her nose when, Freud says, she wished to be treated by a young doctor who was present. Deeply troubled by Emma's post-surgical problems, Freud thought she experienced his concern as fulfilling her wish to be loved through illness, leading her to feel extremely happy despite her condition. Regardless of the validity of Freud's belief that Emma "bled out of *longing*" (p.183), that he could formulate such a hypothesis suggests he knew the power of loneliness.

Freud's biographer, Schur (1972), interpreted this episode in terms of Freud's unhealthy relationship with Fliess. The incident revealed Freud's neurotic dependency, and consequent need to go to extreme lengths to exonerate his friend. Be that as it may, their relationship was, itself, a manifestation of the universal proclivity for loneliness, and longing for companionship. Freud's revolutionary thoughts alienated him from many. Like Emma and all of us, he needed an intimate with whom he could discuss important matters.

Congruent with Freud's speculation, researchers at the University of Chicago found the lonelier one is, the higher is one's systolic blood pressure. While absence may make the heart grow fonder, loneliness can damage it, markedly increasing risk of cardiovascular disease (e.g., heart attack, stroke). The loneliness people reported at the start of that study predicted how much their blood pressure increased over five years. While loneliness is related to depression, stress, hostility, and lack of social support, those factors could not account for the observed rise. "It seems to be that there is something unique about loneliness," lead author Louise Hawkley (McGinn, 2010) remarked. Unlike other causes of high blood pressure, such as smoking and alcohol consumption, loneliness is far more difficult to treat, she observed. "Unfortunately, there aren't a lot of people yet who have done loneliness interventions to any great success. So even if we know that we should be doing something about it, to find somebody who's effective at helping may be a challenge." Our book may make it increasingly easy to find such practitioners.

One of my patients did not want to attend a work meeting. The perfect excuse, she imagined, would be if an enormous menstrual period made it impossible to leave home. The problem was, being in her late 50s, she had not had a period in years. To her astonishment, on the day of the meeting, she experienced menstrual flow the likes of which she had never seen. One must be careful what one longs for.

This unexpected event reminded my patient that her mother suffered a nonstop period for several years when she was middle-aged. It was so uncontrollable that her physicians scheduled a hysterectomy. As the surgical date approached, this woman suspected her problem might be more psychological. She consulted a psychologist who practiced psychoanalysis. Within three months, her bleeding stopped. I imagine much of the analysis' efficacy with respect to bleeding pertained to its meeting needs concerning loneliness and longing to be understood. She shared with her daughter that prior to analysis, she had not known she had genitals.

In her autobiographical novel, Marie Cardinal (1975) described years in which she had been quite mad. She experienced continuous vaginal (and perhaps anal) hemorrahaging, hallucinated, and had other debilitating symptoms. Like my patient's mother, Marie was scheduled for hysterectomy in an attempt to stop the bleeding. Having read some psychoanalytic texts in university, Marie fled from her physician and, subsequently, from the locked psychiatric ward where she was scheduled to have chemical shock therapy. In psychoanalysis, her bleeding and other symptoms stopped as she explored her life, particularly dissociated and unconscious aspects. Marie discovered her talent for writing, repaired her severely stressed marriage, and became a successful novelist.

Shortly after beginning analysis, Marie recalled her father dying during her adolescence in a noteworthy memory of loneliness and longing.

> That is where the solitude began. This man I didn't know, of whom I had seen so little. He was, without my wishing it, however, my only ally. I had never counted on him and now I had to go on without him, which made a great, inexplicable void. Something tenuous and disturbing had disappeared forever. Today I know where the emptiness came from: I no longer had the certainty of pleasing someone no

matter what I did, as well as having been deprived of tenderness. Even when he had me do homework, his voice, his eyes ready to criticize, there was a kiss which I refused, but which was nonetheless a kiss for me.

(pp.59–60)

As her analysis proceeded, it became evident that Marie's father figured prominently, though highly disguised, in a persistent hallucination. That troubling symptom could be understood as a pathological way of keeping her father with her in order to undo unbearable loss, loneliness, and longing.

Much of Ms. Cardinal's autobiographical novel focused on her mother, whom Marie believed she could never please. She felt unable to have her mother love her for who she was. She had either to become the girl her mother wanted her to be, or else resist that perceived demand. This relationship had significant loneliness and longing that contributed to Marie's severe illness.

Like my patient's hemorrhaging mother, Marie shared toward the end of her analysis, "Now I had discovered my vagina, and I knew that henceforth, as with my anus, we were going to live together, in the same way as I lived with . . . all the parts of my body" (p.261). These and other aspects of her being had been rescued from limbo.

The award winning cover for *Sergeant Pepper's Lonely Hearts Club Band* depicted the fictitious ensemble posing in front of famous individuals including Jung, Einstein, Freud, Marx, and Marilyn Monroe. We might photoshop in Emma, Fliess, Marie Cardinal, and all the other lonely people referred to in our book.

Losing one's mind from loneliness

"Twenty years ago today" I had the privilege of hearing Professor Bertram Karon delivering his Presidential Address to the American Psychological Association's Division of Psychoanalysis. After his talk on *The Fear of Understanding Schizophrenia*, the audience thanked him with the warmest standing ovation imaginable.

Psychoanalytic psychotherapies for schizophrenia are not currently fashionable, not because they are unhelpful, but because they make therapists, as well as the public, uncomfortable (Karon, 1992). It is usually assumed this discomfort is because schizophrenic people are extremely different from the rest of us. (All the crazy people—where do they all come from?) The truth is just the opposite, Karon insisted. What makes us uneasy is not so much their difference from us, but their similarity. They may remind us of painful facts we once knew, but repressed. We do not want to know what they have to teach us about the human condition (Deikman, 1971).

Schizophrenia's characteristic emotion is fear (terror), Karon observed. This affect can mask other emotions. Schizophrenics also frequently experience anger, hopelessness, loneliness, and humiliation, he remarked. In an early examination of masked emotions, Freud (1911) concluded that feared homosexual impulses were projected by paranoid patients, resulting in persecutory delusions about others' homosexual intentions. Karon shared that it is helpful to let schizophrenics with symptoms based on fear of homosexuality know their fear is unfounded (if, as is usually the case, it is), that they are simply lonely, that their loneliness is normal, and that we all need friends of both sexes. Unless they have had a meaningful, benign homosexual relationship, schizophrenics are not helped by reassurances concerning the increased acceptability of homosexuality, but they always feel understood when their therapist talks of loneliness, he reported.

The most memorable moment in Karon's speech concerned a patient who spent his days bowing. Concerned hospital staff consulted Karon. When he asked this man why he bowed, he replied: "I don't bow. (Yes, you do.) No, I don't bow. (Wait a minute. You do this. This is bowing; you bow.) No, I don't bow. (But you do this.) That's not bowing. (What is it?) It's balancing. (What are you balancing?) Emotions. (What emotions?) Fear and loneliness."

When lonely, this gentleman longed to get close to people, so he leaned forward. When he got close, he became scared, so he straightened up, then felt lonely again. "Balancing between fear and loneliness is the best description of what it feels like to be schizophrenic" (p.208), Karon averred. After eight weeks of psychotherapy (without medication), this patient, whose loneliness and yearning were now understood, was well enough to leave the hospital and return to work.

Karon's patient reminds me of a homeless man who joined a hiking group. "If you're alone too much, you think wrong and you become too paranoid or eccentric or something," he confided to a journalist (Small, 2010). When one finds someone willing and able to be with one, listening and trying to help, one's psychopathology may lessen significantly. Clearly one may also become very insightful in the process.

Insights from treating schizophrenics illuminate the human condition. Reciprocally, whatever psychology or psychoanalysis learns about human experience elucidates schizophrenia, Karon averred. Consider the major issue of young adulthood, Intimacy versus Isolation (Erikson, 1950). Those of us with basic faults (Balint, 1968) in our foundation may crack under the stress of desired/feared intimacy/isolation. Major mental disorders often erupt in early adulthood. They may be precipitated (and alleviated) by the issues pertaining to loneliness emphasized by Erikson, Karon, and our authors.

Re-viewing and expanding psychoanalytic theory

Psychoanalysis can be usefully regarded as being primarily a theory of affects (Spezzano, 1993). Psychopathology is designed to make us feel better, or to prevent feeling worse; it is always an attempt at affect regulation, Spezzano noted. Psychoanalytic affect theory's most crucial proposition is that we do not always know how we feel. With conviction, a person can claim to be feeling one thing while actually feeling one or more other affects in addition to, or instead of, the claimed one, he stated.

Not just anxiety, but a whole range of difficult affects can serve internal signal functions (Greenspan, 2007): "Affects become true architects of the mind and operate as the mind's 'orchestra leader'" (p.203), Greenspan noted. Loneliness might be regarded as a major maestro. Mere hints of it can trigger a symphony of complex defensive reactions designed to silence this affect, sequestering it behind less threatening emotions, numbness, symptoms, behaviors, and so forth.

The evolution of psychoanalytic theory can be reconsidered as an increasingly coherent, comprehensive account of affective life. A key question is which emotions are central in the development and maintenance of psychopathology, Spezzano stated. I believe lonely longings deserve a prominent place in that account. Other emotions can often be understood as secondary to this underemphasized affective constellation.

Children sometimes refuse to do homework because it is "boring." Unconsciously, they may feel it is too lonely. If they can do it at the kitchen table with family, or elsewhere with friends or cool music, "boredom" (aka loneliness) may vanish.

Similarly, the much talked about obesity epidemic might be re-visioned as rampant loneliness. The admonition to just say no to drugs (or food) might be rephrased as: say no to (harmful solutions to) loneliness. One patient stopped abusing alcohol when he realized he befriended that drug because he felt so lonely when his wife was at work. No doubt his wife's absences derived much of their power from his early developmental history. Our culture's hypersexuality and penchant for cosmetic surgery might also be regarded, from the perspective of loneliness and longing, as yet another manifestation of yearning for a quick fix to distressing affect.

When psychoanalysts discuss sexualization, what is sexualized, to what end? Sexualization can often be seen as a defense against loneliness. Completing a consultation, Spezzano (1993, p.46) asked if the patient wanted to return. She could not imagine otherwise. It was, she explained, as if after undressing her by listening carefully to what she said, now she was sitting on his bed and he was asking if she wanted to proceed.

Spezzano considered whether his patient and/or he was feeling aroused, consciously or unconsciously, whether he had done something sexually provocative or responsive, and whether any of this should be discussed.

This patient, like many, felt unusually connected by being listened to. Anticipating returning to her bleaker world, her erotic statement might be viewed as metaphoric communication concerning loneliness, connection, loss, and longing.

This perspective on sexualization has commonalities with Karon's statement that schizophrenics do not benefit from reassurances concerning the increased acceptability of sexual diversity, but always feel understood when their therapist talks of loneliness. Spezzano's patient was not psychotic but may have been similarly inclined to interpret situations in an eroticized manner, and act accordingly. She may have been more fundamentally lonely than horny.

Ah, L and H (borrowing Bion's love of abbreviations). Loneliness and Horniness frequently hook up. As merged motives, they have precipitated many a premature union and countless enduring relationships. Understanding their association may even facilitate rapprochement between relational theory (loneliness) and drive theory (horniness). These two perspectives seemed to have needed a period of separation, allowing time for reflection, debate, dialogue, and possible reunification. The comparative-integrative perspective (Willock, 2007) suggests a new marriage between these frameworks is feasible.

Many cases could be usefully viewed, or re-viewed from the loneliness vantage point. In *Relational Child Psychotherapy*, Altman, Briggs, Frankel, Gensler, and Pantone (2002) discussed 7-year-old Ellen. She masturbated in class, standing near the corner of her desk, moving against it, looking distracted. The teacher gave Ellen stickers for every hour without masturbation, but Ellen persisted.

Ellen's home featured considerable nudity and sexual tension. Her father showered with his 12-year-old daughter. Ellen was interested in this sister's changing body and played doctor with a 6-year-old sister. Mother nursed a 4-month-old. The parents were not aware of Ellen having ever experienced sexual molestation. They had a stormy marriage. Nine months before seeking psychological assistance, they informed the children they would be divorcing. Since then, Ellen's masturbation increased.

In individual assessment, Ellen was quiet, but the Squiggle game helped her discuss jealousy of her older sister and anger at other girls. She entered sessions inhibited, but left gleefully. Over the course of assessment, masturbation diminished dramatically and Ellen became more expressive at home. The assessor believed these improvements had to do with Ellen now having her own "special man."

The assessor formulated Ellen's masturbation as a sign of unspeakable anger, sexual tension, overstimulation, guilt, jealousy, and resentment. He explained her feelings about some classmates in light of these family feelings. I would add that a 7-year-old masturbating against a desk is a striking image of loneliness. It is not hard to imagine why Ellen might be feeling lonesome, given parental preoccupations. Father seemed more interested in his pubertal daughter; mother was busy with baby. (Although Ellen usually could not say what was on her mind while masturbating, she once told her mother she was thinking about babies.) To distract herself from troubling loneliness, Ellen may have arranged playdates between the reliable friend between her legs and her desk. The rubbing sensations she generated illustrate what Atwood and Stolorow (1984) described as concrete, sensorimotor symbolization—a mode of managing dilemmas that emerge in specific intersubjective fields. For Ellen, masturbation was not a problem to be eliminated. It was a solution.

Ellen's predicament recalls Otis Redding sitting on the dock of the bay "wasting time." Like her, Otis had experienced loss. More articulate than Ellen, he could lament that "This loneliness won't leave me alone." He had, as Fairbairn would say, internalized the bad object. Before leaving Georgia, Otis felt he "had nothing to live for" and "nothing's gonna come my way." Like Ellen, he couldn't "do what ten people tell me to." Desperately seeking a solution, he roamed two thousand miles "just to make this dock my home." Ellen pursued a similarly lonely odyssey just to make the corner of her desk her home away from home. Fortunately, she finally met a "doc" who provided "live company" (Alvarez, 1992), making sexualization superfluous.

Many other cases in which loneliness is not mentioned can be usefully understood in relation to this affect. This perspective can help clinicians (and patients) better comprehend and work with diverse presenting problems, character styles, and conditions. For example, a recent, extreme case puzzled and perturbed mental health professionals and the public. The commander of Canada's largest military base was accused of sexually assaulting, stealing underwear, and murdering women. He could be considered insane, psychopathic, evil. He might also be usefully regarded as lonely. In his house and garage, he had endless boxes of stolen women's lingerie, each item carefully catalogued. One has to be very lonely to go to such extremes for female contact. One also has to be very angry about one's loneliness to attempt to annihilate it via sexual terrorization and murder.

The distinguished, disgraced Colonel, a tragic figure, floundered on the shoals of loneliness, taking others down with him. His tale is still raw in the public mind. Some readers might be offended by any attempt to understand his horrific crimes as reflecting even a perverted version of deepseated, dissociated loneliness and longing. I understand that reaction. Nonetheless, I believe it is important for us to attempt to comprehend even the worst extremes of human behavior, for many reasons, including the desire, through understanding, to be able to work toward prevention of future horrors. With this higher purpose in mind, I hope most readers will concur that such exploration of highly disturbing material is potentially valuable.

In these criminal cases, loneliness and horniness (L and H) can set up a rather stable ménage à trois with that other drive delineated by Freud, aggression (violence, sadism). A pact with the devil can seem preferable to other alternatives (e.g., a lonely living death in limbo), particularly when major components of the situation are unconscious. In these extreme circumstances, these individuals with compromised consciousness are not operating with a full deck.

The Colonel came from a fractured family. At boarding school, his roommate reports that the Colonel-to-be never talked to him. His wife's work in a different city gave the Commander time to be lonely (and horny and angry), like my patient who had an affair with booze when his wife worked. Needless to say, spousal absence would not have packed enough power to fuel such psychopathology if it did not tap into unconscious reserves of lonely alienation likely dating back to the beginning of the Colonel's life on this planet.

In all these cases, one suspects behind the scenes operation of relational trauma, even though these phenomena can fail to register in observers' eyes for various reasons.

> Trauma introduced into the developmental process has a shattering and enduring impact not just on the victim's subsequent capacity for understanding himself but also on the ability of others in his surround to understand him. Trauma is thus invariably accompanied unconsciously by all but impenetrable feelings of isolation and aloneness, even when these feelings lie stubbornly concealed beneath a façade of sociability or affability or beneath a determination to conform to expectations of the group in which the traumatized person moves. The feeling of aloneness forms the basis of estrangement as a way of life.
> (Brandchaft et al., 2010, p.226)

It takes a worried man to sing a worried song (*Worried Man's Blues*). It takes someone aware of their loneliness to sing a lonesome song. Danger arises when one has repressed or otherwise dissociated lonely longings. In "The Voiceless," Oliver Wendell Holmes (Stedman, 1901) bemoaned, "Those that never sing," that is, those with "hearts that break and give no sign." These tortured souls may yearn for the day when "Death pours out his longed-for wine." Like the policeman who once told me his peers would rather "eat their gun" than see a psychologist, the Colonel could not sing his sad, scary song to anyone, no doubt not even to himself. Instead, he repetitively created an illusion/delusion of having vanquished loneliness. By strangling victims, he made sure these objects of his perverted desire would never sing.

As Khan (1979) noted, perverts strive after intensity of erotic experience in order to avoid the threat of annihilation and catastrophic disillusionment (and, I would add, loneliness, in all its conscious and unconscious manifestations). They carry these horrific expectations and "solutions" everywhere, reflecting unconscious organizing principles forged from infancy onward.

With respect to craved intensity, Khan observed that "This excited state has a distinctly manic quality, and displaces the pervert from his inner space to search for an external area of experience, where, through the instrumentality of another, this excitement can be processed and actualized" (p.136). As is often the case with mania, its intensity can serve to avoid debilitating depression or what we might call the terrifying loneliness that characterizes a particular individual's inner space. What should be a psychic inner sanctum has become, instead, a prison, poisoned with psychopathology, that is, with residues of relational experience that defy digestion. Trapped in their inner matrix of desolate, dangerous, doer/done-to relationships (Benjamin, 1988), these individuals feel they can only escape their lonely, contaminated cells by visiting their most toxic terrors on others.

Incarcerated, the Colonel attempted suicide by shoving toilet paper down his throat. (How else to wipe away the shittiness within?) Attacking himself, he became both doer and done-to. On his cell wall, he scrawled in mustard that his feelings were too much to bear. Without knowing it, he may have been referring not only to his current agony (fear, humiliation, guilt, terror, etc.), but also to a lifelong struggle with intolerable loneliness.

The social pathology of our times

The power of the loneliness hypothesis extends far beyond the consulting room into the realm of social pathology. Consider, for example, recent manifestations of Islamic fundamentalism. At age 18, the Underwear Bomber (who went on to notoriously attempt to blow up an airplane) posted on a chat site, "I feel depressed and lonely. I do not know what to do" (Wente, 2010). At that time, he certainly sounded like a reasonable human being for whom one could feel sympathy. "Maybe what we need is not more high-tech airport scanners. Maybe what we need is more people who can make friends with lonely, disaffected guys on the internet," Wente mused.

"Jihad Jane" traveled to Europe to murder a cartoonist whose work displeased many Muslims (Barrett, 2010). The day she arrived, she married a co-conspirator whom she knew only online. Upon returning to the U.S., she was arrested. Her mother pleaded tearfully that her 31-year-old daughter "is not a monster. These people came into my home through the Internet and they seduced a very lonely, lonely person."

Jihad Jane is not alone in her predicament of loneliness. Over the last two decades, there has been a three-fold increase in the number of Americans who report having no confidante (McPherson, Smith-Lovin, & Brashears, 2006). In 1985, the average (modal) American had three confidantes. By 2004, the average citizen reported having none.

In discussing one patient's experience of an irreversible aloneness in the world, Brandchaft (et al., 2010) wrote, "Such experiences of profound nonunderstanding, I suggest, lie as well at the very center of the cultural phenomenology of alienation that so widely characterizes postmodern experience" (p.227). Despite Facebook having recently recruited its five hundred millionth user, we have not solved the problem of social isolation.

Pondering pervasive loneliness throughout the world, Khan (in Hopkins, 2006) reflected, "How terrible is the abyss of aloneness and how many it has driven crazy" (p.109). How true.

"Karl Marx and Sigmund Freud . . . diagnosed the sickness of the western Judaeo-Christian cultures: Marx in terms of the alienated person in society; Freud, the person alienated from himself" (Khan, 1979, p.9). The messages of those two giants of modern thought, Freud and Marx, that Khan recalled have resonated with multitudes. When we have gained greater understanding and appreciation of those other two giants, loneliness and longing, we will have a less troubled, happier world. Our authors help us find a realistic way to take steps toward this promised land.

Poesy, psyche, and psychoanalysis

Patients like Karon's bower teach powerful lessons about psychopathology and the human condition. His almost poetic performance and words recall Leonard Cohen's (2008) insight that: "When something is said in a certain kind of way it seems to embrace the cosmos. It's not just my heart; every heart is involved. The loneliness dissolves, and you feel you are this aching creature in the midst of an aching cosmos, and that the ache is OK."

Cohen's cosmos contained, calmed, and rendered his loneliness meaningful and bearable. Performing an essential fantasy selfobject function (Bacal & Newman, 1990), it alphabetized his isolation, providing soothing merger, with universal twinship resonance. Everyone experiences loneliness and yearning and it's alright.

Cohen's city mate, Mordecai Richler, characterized his own writerly role as witnessing his times. Witnessing is an important selfobject function (Seiden, 1996). Not only individuals but also cultures have a primal need for someone to be watching, thinking, concerned. So important and scarce is fullfillment of this yearning that it is often delegated to God (or literature). "Nobody knows the trouble I've seen/Nobody knows but Jesus."

Events may need not only witnessing, but also "dreaming," night and day (Bion, 1962). Freud, Kohut, and Jung admired poets' capacity to initiate this reverie process. In "The Loneliness One Dare Not Sound," poet Emily Dickinson (Johnson, 1960) described this dangerous affect. It is frequently buried "Lest itself should see/And perish from before itself/For just a scrutiny." Loneliness anxiety frequently becomes annihilation terror.

Dickinson understood the important fact that loneliness is often rendered unconscious, a "Horror not to be surveyed—/But skirted in the Dark—/ With Consciousness suspended—And Being under Lock." Her description captures key aspects of the Canadian Colonel's situation. He became an expert at bypassing locks to access bedrooms, lingerie, and victims. In contrast, he probably had no clue how to get through the walls and pad-locks designed to prevent him from accessing his unconscious troubles. These greater terrors had to be "skirted in the Dark."

So important is loneliness that Dickinson called it, "The Maker of the soul." Loneliness confronts us with a fundamental choice: "Its Caverns and its Corridors/Illuminate—or seal." Our authors advocate Dickinson's first option, elucidation. The colonel, no doubt, chose seal, thereby losing con-tact with soul (his and others'). Banished to the unconscious, loneliness often wreaks havoc, becoming the twister, constrictor, and breaker of the soul. Our authorial collective argues strenuously against excommunication, and for repatriation, of the lonely self.

Years ago, I worked with a man who endured a lonely childhood related to his mother's depression (loneliness). To escape her debilitating dys-phoria, she struck up an intense relationship with alcohol and Valium. After this patient's marriage ended, he found himself, to his horror, observing, becoming erotically aroused, and sometimes inappropriately touching his daughter when he thought she was asleep. After several months of therapy and jail, he shared poignantly, "I know what loneliness can do." Treatment helped locate and unlock the "Caverns and Corridors," the psychic limbo, where his loneliness long hid. Psychological therapy facilitated finding new ways of coping with ancient and contemporary isolation and yearning.

After several years of analytic treatment, another patient could declare, "I'm lonely and I don't like it." Her disclosure surprised her, striking her as "honest and embarrassing." When asked what made it so shameful, she replied, "It's a dirty secret . . . I don't want to be clingy . . . If I were right inside, I wouldn't be lonely." (The *Sisters of Mercy*, Leonard Cohen's psalm of yearning, echoes my patient's sentiment: "Your loneliness says that you've sinned.") Previously my analysand thought mostly of having an anxiety disorder, depression, or psychosis. She was becoming increasingly able to think of herself in more ordinary human terms, even though that transition was sometimes shocking and shame-ridden.

Collectively our authors' quills counteract the widespread, damaging denial of loneliness, in all its conscious, preconscious, and unconscious aspects. As doctors of the soul, they advocate attending to this pernicious psychic bleeding, removing old scar tissue and gauze from deep cavities of the mind, thereby helping people (and societies) regain health and sanity.

Bearing witness to our times, our investigators shed megawatts of illumination on how immensely important loneliness and longing are in human experience (and nonexperience). Their medium is prose; their message is far from prosaic. May their witnessing and dreaming jumpstart greater awareness and interest in this hitherto neglected, crucial topic.

References

Altman, N., Briggs, R., Frankel, J., Gensler, D. & Pantone, P. (2002). *Relational Child Psychotherapy*. New York: Other Press.

Alvarez, A. (1992). *Live Company: Psychoanalytic Psychotherapy with Autistic, Borderline, Deprived and Abused Children*. London, New York: Routledge.

Atwood, G. E. & Stolorow, R. D. (1984). *Structures of Subjectivity: Explorations in Psychoanalytic Phenomenology*. Hillsdale, NJ: The Analytic Press.

Bacal, H. A. & Newman, K. M. (1990). *Theories of Object Relations: Bridges to Self Psychology*. New York: Columbia University Press.

Balint, M. (1968). *The Basic Fault: Therapeutic Aspects of Regression*. London: Tavistock.

Barrett, D. (2010). Second woman charged in "Jihad Jane" case. *The Globe and Mail*, April 3, p.A12.

Benjamin, J. (1988). *The Bonds of Love: Psychoanalysis, Feminism, and the Problem of Domination*. New York: Pantheon Books.

Bion, W. (1962). Learning from experience. In: *Seven servants*. New York: Aronson, 1977.

Brandchaft, B., Doctors, S. & Sorter, D. (2010). *Toward an Emancipatory Psychoanalysis: Brandchaft's Intersubjective Vision*. New York: Routledge.

Cardinal, M. (1975). *The Words to Say It*. P. Goodheart (Trans.). Preface and Afterword by Bruno Bettelheim. Cambridge, MA: VanVactor & Goodheart, 1983.

Cohen, L. (2008). Quoted in Solvency and rapture. Editorial Page, *The Globe and Mail*, Dec. 27.

Deikman, A. J. (1971). Phenothiazines and the therapist's fear of identification. *Humanistic Psychology*, 11:196–200.

Erikson, E. H. (1950). *Childhood and Society*. New York: Norton.

Freud, S. (1911). Psycho-analytic notes on an autobiographical account of a case of paranoia (dementia paranoids). In *The Standard Edition of the Complete Psychological Works of Sigmund Freud*, 12 (1911–1913).

—— (1985). *The Complete Letters of Sigmund Freud to Wilhelm Fliess, 1887–1904*. Translated and edited by Jeffrey Moussaieff Masson. Cambridge, MA: Harvard University Press.

Greenspan, S. (2007). Levels of infant-caregiver interactions and the DIR model. *Journal of Infant, Child, and Adolescent Psychotherapy*, 6:174–210.

Hopkins, L. (2006). *False Self: The Life of Masud Khan*. New York: Other Press.

Johnson, T. H. (1960). *The Complete Poems of Emily Dickinson*. Boston: Little Brown.

Karon, B. P. (1992). The fear of understanding schizophrenia. *Psychoanalytic Psychology*, 9:191–211.

Khan, M. (1979). *Alienation in Perversions*. London: Hogarth Press.

McGinn, D. (2010). Could loneliness really break your heart? *The Globe and Mail*, March 19.

McPherson, M., Smith-Lovin, L., & Brashears, M. E. (2006). Social isolation in America: Changes in core discussion networks over two decades. *American Sociological Review*, 71:353–375.

Rilke, R. M. (1969). *Letters of Rainer Maria Rilke*. Translated by J. B. Greene & M. D. Hester. New York: Norton.

Schur, M. (1972). *Freud: Living and Dying*. New York: International Universities Press.

Seiden, H. M. (1996). The healing presence: Part I: The witness as self-object function. *The Psychoanalytic Review*, 83:685–693.

Small, P. (2010). Out and about beats down and out. *Toronto Star*, January 3, p.A4.

Spezzano, C. (1993). *Affect in Psychoanalysis: A Clinical Synthesis*. Hillsdale, NJ: The Analytic Press.

Stedman, E. C. (1901). *An American Anthology, 1787–1900*. Boston: Houghton, Mifflin.

Swan, M. (1952). *Henry James*. London: Arthur Barker.

Thoreau, H. D. (1886). *Walden*. London: Walter Scott.

Wente, M. (2010). The global internet jihad: spinning a web of terror. *The Globe and Mail*, Jan. 9, p.A17.

Willock, B. (2007) *Comparative-Integrative Psychoanalysis*. New York/London: The Analytic Press.

Index